Education and the Family

Edited by
LEONARD KAPLAN

*under sponsorship of the
Association of Teacher Educators*

ALLYN AND BACON
Boston London Toronto Sydney Tokyo Singapore

Library of Congress Cataloging-in-Publication Data

Education and the family / edited by Leonard Kaplan under sponsorship
   of the Association of Teacher Educators.
      p.   cm.
   Includes bibliographical references (p.   ) and index.
   ISBN 0-205-13389-4
   1. Home and school—United States.   2. Teachers—Training of—
United States.   I. Kaplan, Leonard, 1935-   .   II. Association of
Teacher Educators.
LC225.3.E36   1992
370.19′3′0973—dc20   91-20401
                                                             CIP

Printed in the United States of America
10 9 8 7 6 5 4 3 2 1   96 95 94 93 92

Contents

Letter to the Association of Teacher Educators　　vii
　by Barbara Bush

Greetings from the Association of Teacher Educators　　viii
　by Dora Scott Nichols

Preface　ix

Acknowledgments　xii

Contributing Authors　xiii

Prologue　xv

Education and My Family　xv
　by Kimberly Boozer O'Rourke as told to Elizabeth Johnson

Preparing for Successful Children　xix
　by Beth Clawson

SECTION ONE
Views of Contemporary Society　　*1*

Chapter 1 • *The American Family*　*3*
　by Alice R. McCarthy

Chapter 2 • *Creating Community Contexts That Educate:
An Agenda for Improving Education in Inner Cities*　*27*
　by Martin Haberman

Chapter 3 • *Helping Families with Developmentally Delayed
Children*　*41*
　by Malcolm Garber

Chapter 4 • *The School–Family Link: A Key to Dropout
Prevention*　*54*
　by John V. Hamby

Chapter 5 • *Families, Schools, Literacy, and Diversity*　*69*
　by Terrence Wiley and John Sikula

Chapter 6 • *Schools as Socializing Agents in Children's Lives   86*
   by Irene B. Ecksel

Chapter 7 • *Parents, Power, and the Public Schools   100*
   by Wilhelmina Perry and Margaret D. Tannenbaum

SECTION TWO
Education, the Schools, and the Family   117

Chapter 8 • *Hierarchy of Parental Involvement in Schools   119*
   by Donna Wissbrun and Joyce A. Eckart

Chapter 9 • *Parent–School Interactions   132*
   by Patrice LeBlanc

Chapter 10 • *Parent–Teacher Conferences and Teachable Moments   141*
   by Donald E. Orlosky

Chapter 11 • *Parent–Teacher Conferences: A Parent's Perspective   158*
   by Irene Meers as told to Sandra Pettapiece

Chapter 12 • *"At-Risk" Youngsters in Public Education   163*
   by Asa J. Brown

Chapter 13 • *The Education of New Parents   178*
   by Bess Kypros

Chapter 14 • *Fostering Early Development   188*
   by Eli Saltz

SECTION THREE
The University and Teacher Education   203

Chapter 15 • *The University as a Change Agent   205*
   by Bettye M. Caldwell and James H. Young

Chapter 16 • *The University and Its Family   219*
   by Peggy Gordon Elliott

Chapter 17 • *The Curriculum of Aspiring Teachers: Not a Question of Either/Or   230*
   by Donna Evans and David Nelson

Chapter 18 • *Parental Involvement Teacher Preparation: Challenges to Teacher Education   243*
   by David L. Williams, Jr.

Chapter 19 · *Needed: A New Knowledge Base in Teacher Education*   255
    by W. Robert Houston and Elizabeth Houston

Chapter 20 · *Teacher Education: Linking Universities, Schools, and Families for the Twenty-First Century*   266
    by Francis Kochan and Barbara K. Mullins

Chapter 21 · *Parent Education in Home, School, and Society: A Course Description*   273
    by Leonard Kaplan

PART FOUR
Response to the Prologue   279

Chapter 22 · *MegaSkills and New Partnerships for Student Achievement*   281
    by Dorothy Rich in collaboration with James Van Dien

Chapter 23 · *Labor and the Schools: Forging a Working Relationship*   293
    by Owen F. Bieber

Chapter 24 · *The Importance of Parental Involvement*   304
    by Ann Lynch

Chapter 25 · *Health, Education, Welfare: America's Families and America's Priorities*   307
    by Keith Geiger

Epilogue   315

Bibliography   316

Index   343

December 10, 1990

To the Association of Teacher Educators:

I am delighted to send greetings to you all through the publication of <u>Education and the Family</u>. You could not have chosen a more important or timely topic -- the home and school are such natural allies, and their active partnership is essential to the well-being of our children.

Our schools play a pivotal role in helping our children learn and grow, but families are the first and most important teachers. If we really are to do our very best to prepare young people for the future, parents and teachers must work together toward common goals, and teacher educators can be so influential in encouraging this special relationship. The more home and school cooperate in the education of our children, the more likely we are to see them become literate, productive citizens.

This book promises to do so much to foster greater understanding among home, school, and community for the sake of better child development, and the President and I are so very grateful. To parents and educators both, we offer our sincerest hope that you will help one another play increasingly more meaningful roles in helping our children to good lives through good education.

Great good luck in this critical effort.

Warmly,

Barbara Bush

Greetings from the Association of Teacher Educators

As president of A.T.E., an organization of broad-based constituencies committed to the education of kids, I hold a great concern for children and their families and how these families function in their relationships between home and school. This is of the highest priority to me, an educator in the public schools in Texas for 40 years.

Unfortunately, home and school have not always been real partners. We have asked for "yes" votes on all bond issues and taxes pertaining to schools, but have been slow to make parents partners in the education of their youngsters. Teacher education institutions throughout this nation have been slow to prepare educators who are more sensitive to how schools can directly be involved in helping parents better fulfill their educational responsibilities as the most important role models for children. As we ask for participation, we must train parents and educators on how to actively participate in this "new" partnership.

The 1992 convention of A.T.E. is devoted specifically to the topic of education and the family as an indicator of our interest to do more for parents and for our communities in the interest of children. Since children cannot be their own advocates we must assume this role. America, now more than ever, must have a literate society so that future decisions for its citizenry will be made intelligently as well as humanely. The Persian Gulf situation brings this home most profoundly.

Public education continues to face some of the most provocative and controversial issues in our history. A call for the restructuring of school educational reform will affect all parents, teachers, and students in all levels of society. Reform can only take place if we joint together as a community committed to the change process.

I believe that A.T.E. stands on the threshold of a new, exciting era in its long and proud history. Members of our Association have demonstrated that they can successfully control and direct A.T.E. The need for our own unity, our dedication to our common purpose, has never been greater.

Dora Scott-Nicols
President, A.T.E.
1991–1992

Preface

It is virtually impossible to pick up a newspaper or see any responsible news program without being reminded of the conflicts and anguish that our children go through on a daily basis. The problems associated with drugs, alcohol, violence, and crime are literally cancers of our society. As much as all of us are aware of success stories, the problems that engulf our youth today seem to be so gigantic in proportion that the successes that go on every day in both home and school pale in comparison.

Scholars and laypeople have voiced the opinion that the family unit is disintegrating. We refer to the "good old days" in the belief that families were warm, compassionate, and a safe harbor from the evils outside. In general, however, historical reviews of families suggest that even in those days the family may not have been all that we recall. In fact, the memory may far exceed the reality. Child-rearing problems, observed Lillian Katz, are often attributed to change, which has always been with us and ideally always will be.

Most educators do not need research to know that parents strongly influence their children's behavior and learning in school. Educators report that it is relatively easy to identify children whose home life is one of support, affection, and stability. It is a bit more difficult but not all that hard to spot the kids whose home life is uneasy, problematic, and unstable. Troubled children tend not to learn to the degree expected of them. How can they? The demographics, which will not be discussed here but are well documented throughout this book, clearly testify to the degree of uncertainty that exists in our homes and communities. The divorce rate continues to be high; single parenting is typical; latch-key children increase in number; abuse of all varieties exists; school lockers are checked for weapons. And we expect kids to memorize their multiplication tables as if the school were an oasis unaffected by what transpires outside of its halls.

The responsibility of the school in this scenario takes on increased importance. Educational report after report describes inadequacies and calls for reform. We hear about teachers who are insensitive and lack content knowledge. "Teachers need more academic preparation, knowledge of child growth and development, better methodology, more preservice experience and improved communication skills. They must be aware and trained in the 'new' techniques." It seems clear, according to some, that educators are not in tune with the needs of society and what it desires for its youth. To the casual observer, the problem is clear. Everyone is incompetent!

The preparation of teachers is not without its critis. Goodlad's fairly recent report describes many problems inherent in teacher education, from lack of financial support, unclear objectives, and inadequate acceptance on campus as a respected discipline to a discussion about whether teacher education is a viable topic for discussion in the university. Does it belong in the schools or in some other arena more in tune with meeting the needs of the workplace? The role of government in setting educational policy is under review. The entire process of teacher and administrator certification is being reexamined. Clearly this is an interesting time to be in the teacher education business. Or is it teacher training?

At the 1987 Convention of the Association of Teacher Educators, a resolution was introduced asking the organization to affirm its commitment to the family as the unit most important in the life of a child. After some debate, the resolution failed to reach the floor of the Convention. It was concluded that: "This issue may not be appropriate for inclusion into a teacher education agenda." To the credit of the leadership of the organization, this view did not prevail, and the Family Ties Commission was established by executive order. The Commission's charge was to study and consider what an appropriate relationship between home and school should look like and to make recommendations to the Association regarding what teacher education should and could be doing in response to an apparent need. The charge called for a plan of action. The group convened and ideas were generated. Open forums were held to give those interested in this work an opportunity for input. This book is the report of the Commission.

Book Objectives

It is our hope that those reading this manuscript will:

1. Develop a better understanding of the relationships that exist between society's needs and the general principles of schools and schooling
2. Gain familiarity with family issues including, but not limited to, demographics, economics, race, ethnicity, politics, and future trends
3. Better understand the dynamics of how family relationships impact the school climate and the general behavior of those who attend. Further, readers will recognize that behavior generated in school affects family cohesion
4. Understand the knowledge base underlying the nature of the American family
5. Have their consciousness raised so they may begin to internalize that what goes on in the home, school, and community must be the backbone of what goes on in teacher preparational programs

The Text

This book represents the work of many people. Contributing authors were contracted because of their expertise and continued efforts in this area of inquiry. While it is true that many outstanding people are not represented, those that are have proven credentials in this field. They also meet deadlines.

Literally scores of people volunteered to read and critique manuscripts.

Many articles were not used even though they were acceptable. Chapter sections were identified by the need to communicate our concerns. Simplistically put, they are:

1. What is the nature of the home, the community, and society?
2. What is happening in education in response to the need? How do professional educators respond?
3. Is the university a proper setting for community action? Are teacher education programs established to meet societal needs?
4. Is there a response from "the establishment" to the call for educational reform?

Acknowledgments

The editor is indebted to so many whose ideas and efforts contributed to the text. It is impossible to identify them all, but they will recognize their thoughts. However, special thanks are given to Mary Crowley, Irene Ecksel, Sandra Pettapiece, Janet Pont, and Feleta Wilson. Their efforts and dedication as members of the Advisory Council are reflected throughout this volume.

Members of the Editorial Board reviewed manuscripts for clarity of thought as well as for getting commas and periods in the correct places—a vital yet not always easy task. They are: Barbara Brown-Allen, Janet E. Haffner, David Makinson, Heather Macheese Pendell, Cheryl A. Plettenberg, Gail A. Rachor, and Michael Rucks.

I am indebted to the members of the Family Ties Commission of A.T.E., whose time, energies, and vision contributed heavily to this work. Good colleagues all. They are: George A. Antonelli, Cheryl Ghristensen, Peggy Gordon Elliott, Martin Haberman, Alice McCarthy, Consuelo Nieto, Janet L. Towslee, and David L. Williams, Jr.

Special recognition is given to Janet Towslee, President of A.T.E. 1987–1988, who had the courage to do what needed to be done to establish the Family Ties Commission. Also to Robert Stevenson, past Executive Secretary of the Association, who was most helpful, particularly in working closely with Allyn and Bacon in working out contractual details. Robert Roth, past President of A.T.E., has been a strong supporter of this effort and has helped move an idea through the bureaucratic process.

Mary Irwin and Ruthannah McCaugney handled the bulk of the typing. A monumental job—always cheerfully done.

And finally to the memories of Ira Gordon and William Blevogel. Two dear friends who started my juices flowing many years ago. They understood the power of the family to change the world.

Leonard Kaplan
Editor

The problem with today's schools is not that they are no longer as good as they once were. The problem with today's schools is that they are precisely what they always were . . . while the world around them has changed so significantly. —ADAM USBANSKI

Contributing Authors

Asa Brown—Professor of Special Education, Wayne State University, Detroit, Michigan

Owen F. Bieber—President of the International Union, United Automobile, Aerospace and Agriculture Implement Workers of America—UAW

Bettye M. Caldwell—Donaghey Distinguished Professor of Education, University of Arkansas at Little Rock

Beth Clawson—Michigan Mother of the Year 1989—mother of six children; elementary school teacher, major emphases physical education, health, and science

Joyce Ekart—Faculty, School of Human and Educational Services, Oakland University, Rochester, Michigan

Irene B. Ecksel—Clinical Project Coordinator, Department of Psychology and Human Development, Vanderbilt University, Nashville, Tennessee.

Peggy Gordon Elliott—Chancellor, Indiana University, Northwest—Gary Indiana; President of A.T.E. 1984–1985

Donna B. Evans—Dean, School of Education—University of North Florida, Jacksonville, Florida

Malcolm Garber—Associate Professor of Special Education, The Ontario Institute for Studies in Education, Toronto, Canada

Keith Geiger—President, National Education Association

Martin Haberman—Professor of Education, School of Education, University of Wisconsin, Milwaukee

John V. Hamby—Assistant Director, National Dropout Prevention Center, Clemson University, Clemson, South Carolina

Elizabeth Houston—Counselor, Valley Oaks Elementary School, Spring Branch, Texas; works largely with at-risk children and parents

W. Robert Houston—Associate Dean for Academic Affairs, College of Education, University of Houston; President of A.T.E. 1985–1986

Elizabeth Johnson—Doctoral student in curriculum, Wayne State University; mother of four boys (three are triplets)

Leonard Kaplan—Professor of Curriculum and Instruction, College of Education, Wayne State University, Detroit, Michigan

Frances Kochan—Elementary Principal, Florida State University—School, and Assistant Professor, College of Education, Florida State University, Tallahassee, Florida.

Bess Kypros—Director of Child Development and Early Childhood Education, Madonna College, Livonia, Michigan

Patrice LeBlanc—Director of Educational Leadership, Barry University, Miami, Florida

Ann Lynch—National Parent-Teacher Association President, 1989–1991

Alice R. McCarthy—President of the Center for the Advancement of the Family, Grosse Pointe Woods, Michigan; editor of the column "Advisory Board," which appears in the *Detroit Free Press*

Irene Meers—Working mother of three children, Villa Park, Illinois

Barbara K. Mullins—College of Education, Florida State University, Tallahassee, Florida

David Nelson—Dean of the School of Education, Saginaw Valley State University, Saginaw, Michigan

Donald E. Orlosky—Chairman, Department of Educational Leadership, University of South Florida, Tampa, Florida

Kimberly Boozer O'Rourke—Single parent of two elementary-age children; presently working toward a high school equivalency diploma

Wilhelmina Perry—Associate Professor of Education, Glassboro State College, Glassboro, New Jersey

Sandra Pettapiece—Elementary teacher, Detroit Public Schools; Finalist, 1987 Michigan Teacher of the Year

Dorothy Rich—Founder and President of the Home and School Institute, Washington, DC; author of *MegaSkills: How Families Can Help Children Succeed in School and Beyond*

Eli Saltz—Director, Merrill-Palmer Institute, Wayne State University, Detroit, Michigan

John Sikula—Dean, Graduate School of Education, California State University, Long Beach; President of A.T.E. 1989–1990

Margaret D. Tannenbaum—Professor of Sociology, Glassboro State College, Glassboro, New Jersey

James Van Dien—Associate Professor of Education, Trinity College, Washington, DC; consultant to the Home and School Institute

Terrance Wiley—Assistant Professor of Education, Graduate School of Education, California State University, Long Beach

David L. Williams—Vice-President, Resources for School Improvement, Southwest Regional Educational Development Laboratory, Austin, Texas

Prologue

Many of us believe that schools were invented to serve society rather than the reverse being true. Accepting this assumption, it is incumbent upon the educator to work closely with members of the community, ensuring that their goals and aspirations correspond to those of the education establishment.

Families represent the backbone of our society. Many of us who attempt to raise our children in ways appropriate to societal goals do so under great hardship, sometimes without appropriate means but usually with good intention. We can document cases of child abuse in the home, but such situations, as ugly as they may be, do not represent the vast majority of parental behavior. Most parents care about their kids, as do most communities. However, it is never easy.

The parents whose words appear in this Prologue represent a cross-section of our population. They do not represent any sort of majority view or for that matter any specific group, except possibly people who want to share their feelings about life and raising children in today's world. Their perspectives are worth our attention.

Education and My Family

KIMBERLY BOOZER O'ROURKE
as told to Elizabeth Johnson

Editor's Note: Once upon a time the Cleaver family lived in a lovely home, drove a station wagon, drank milk, and ate oatmeal cookies as an after-school snack. Ward went off to the office and June stayed at home. Wally and Beaver walked to school with the knowledge that on their return home all would be just as they left it. Was this ever reality? Is this the American dream, or is this the Land of Oz? On the assumption that the Cleavers existed, it is obvious that this is no longer how it is. The demographics discussed in this book indicate that what is happening in the family is a far cry from peace and tranquility.

If home and school are to work closely together in the best interest of kids, it is incumbent upon the schools to better understand our children and how they live. The story contained in this chapter may not be typical. However, it is real, honest, and indicative of many "families." It should gain our notice.

Sometimes when it's quiet, I think back about my school days. I still remember kids slamming lockers and causing trouble in the halls. A lot of kids, including me, would run into the john to sneak a smoke and puff our brains out between classes. Then a teacher would come in, and we'd rush to flush our smokes down the toilet. The stupidest thing was that the teachers who came into the johns trying to catch us were the same ones who smoked in the teachers' lounge. We could never understand that.

Meet Kimberly Boozer O'Rourke, a 32-year-old kid. I use the name O'Rourke because it's my kids' father's name. I don't like using his name, but I feel like I should for the kids' sake. Boozer is my real maiden name, and please don't laugh. I've been teased all my life about it.

I was born in Erie, Pennsylvania, and we moved to Las Vegas when I was 10. Dad, Mom, Sis, Brother, and I lived in a real small house. I was the oldest child, and Dad always put me in charge. Many times I felt like the mom.

Dad was a real proud man and wasn't dumb. He had done well in regular school. He was going to school to learn to be a paramedic, but he dropped out because he couldn't pass the tests. He told us that tests were a waste of time and that the teacher didn't like him because he was a smart aleck. Looking back, I think paramedic training was just too stressful for him.

But what I remember most about my Dad was his drinking. I remember being really embarrassed when the beer truck would deliver cases of brew to our house every week. The driver would stack the cases on a dolly and set them on our back porch. I just passed it off though, because I thought that probably a lot of other people had their beer delivered to them that way too.

When Dad wasn't too drunk, he worked at the Village Department Store as a janitor. When he was working, he carried a .22 pistol in a holster he had made out of an old cowboy boot. He said he carried it because people sometimes stole stuff from the store, and he felt safer carrying a gun. I know it made Mom really nervous.

Speaking of my Mom, I love her so much. We all loved her. Even though Dad cared for Mom, he kept seeing other women. He even divorced her, but they remarried three years later. That was hard on all of us, especially us kids.

Mom kind of minded her own business. She needed to work, but wasn't able. When she got really sick and had to go into the hospital, she almost died. Even though Mom loved Dad very much, she put up with an awful lot from him. We all knew who was in charge—Dad was top dog. As time passed, Mom became more and more depressed, and she started drinking a lot also. The more she drank, the more she tried to spank us. When she did, she would use a large switch from the tree. Thank goodness we could run faster than she, and she usually didn't catch us. I think Mom's biggest mistake, though, was not telling us kids that Dad was mentally sick. He had been called "schizophrenic" when he was a teenager, but he was never treated for it. I guess alcohol was his treatment and his doctor.

When I started fifth grade, Dad put me in a Catholic school, even though we weren't Catholic. I begged him to let me stay at my "normal" school with all my friends. But he said, "Now, Kimmie, I want you to be perfect in school. I want you to grow up right and all, and them Catholics know how to run a tight ship," I hated the uniforms and I hated the school.

Overall, my grades were the pits. Dad expected me to bring home all A's. I made C's and D's, and I don't have to tell you the stuff hit the fan when Dad saw my report card. Besides getting spanked really bad, I got grounded for two months.

What I remember most about junior high is being high. All my friends and I smoked pot to get through those boring classes. A couple of hits and we could sit through the most boring math class. The bad news was that some kids bought marijuana with angel dust hidden in it, and they almost died. That scared me.

I'm a follower, not a leader. My friends could influence me to do anything. In high school the most important thing to me was being accepted by them, but I loved high school the most when I wasn't there. My friends and I "skipped" school every chance we got. We'd gather in the morning by the dead oak tree to smoke. We called it the "smoking section." We'd hang out to see who was skipping school that day. Some kids skipped all the time.

I hated going to classes. My friends and drugs were my whole life. I lived and would have died for my friends. I could do all and be all with a pill or a couple of hits, because then I was fearless.

One afternoon, while Mom and I watched our soap, Dad came over to us, put his arms around us both and grinned, "I love my pretty girls," he said. He turned away, went into the bathroom, and shot himself in the head with his .22 pistol. The ambulance arrived almost immediately, but he was pronounced D.O.A. at the hospital. We had lost our Daddy. We all left the emergency room in shock.

All that changed one day when I met a guy named John. I loved his pretty blue eyes. He asked me to move in with him, and I didn't know what to do. I was torn between John and my mom; I chose John. We lived together for a year before we tied the knot.

John and I had fist fights all the time, and he always won. I always cried. We met up with a group of people who were really heavily into the drug scene, using cocaine, L.S.D., and crystal. We used drugs every night for almost two years, partying down in our trailer and staying high all the time. We then got a divorce. The only good thing from our marriage was our two children, Brandy and Ryan.

Being a mom is extremely difficult, but being a single mom, unemployed, with no high school diploma is close to impossible. But I'm a survivor, and most importantly, I'm the mother of two beautiful children. I know now that I can and must beat the odds. I have no alternative. I must overcome poverty—not only my financial poverty, but an educational one also.

Right now, I am being helped by the state. I am on ADC (Aid to Dependent Children), and contrary to popular belief, I'm not sitting home making babies. I am enrolled in adult education classes, and my goal is to get a high school diploma. My mother and my kids will really be proud of their old "Ma" when I walk across the stage wearing my cap and gown. God, I hope it all happens. I might even decorate my old rusted-out car. Just think, I and the other graduates can go "cruising."

Each morning I go to school just like my kids. The neigbors laugh at me. They think it's a joke. All I hear is "Kim, don't you know no better? There ain't no one gonna hire you without a college education. Why don't you wise up and get a full-time job at McDonalds? It pays five bucks an hour with benefits. You don't need no high school diploma for a minimum-wage job. If you do get a really good job, you'll lose your ADC money." So, I don't even discuss my business with my neighbors anymore. I just go to school with my lunch, books, and cigarettes. I've made up my mind, and nobody's going to change it.

Something strange is happening. I am different. I used to feel like my nickname, "Boozer the Loser." Now, I'm feeling pretty good about myself. Mom says that I have confidence and a twinkle in my eyes. I laugh and say, "Ma, the twinkle in my eyes is not from drugs, it's from school."

My adult education classes have helped me to achieve. They expect me to do well. I am taking classes in math, reading, communications, and writing, and I made an A+, A, and two B's! Now I'm known as "Kimmer the Winner!" I dropped out of high school and into adult education. My classes are hard and demand a lot of time with homework. It's hard on me because I've been out of school for a long time.

One real difference in adult classes is that the teachers pull up a chair and share in our learning. They don't pretend to be know-it-alls and aren't strict. They respect and treat us like we are people and not dumbskulls. How I wish my earlier teachers would have taught this way. Maybe things would have been different.

Through all of this, I have learned a valuable lesson as a parent—make sure that what happened to you doesn't happen to your kids. This is on my mind constantly. I think about all the stuff that I have been through. You better believe that my kids won't hurt like me. I will make sure that I teach them about staying off drugs and alcohol. I have and will talk about my past drug problems with my kids, so they will know why they must not get hooked on that junk. It's too bad I had to be an example of what not to do.

My little girl Brandy is in the third grade, and she is doing great. She makes good grades. That's a relief. I have worried the most about her because she saw me take drugs and act crazy. Brandy's teacher is strict and makes the kids mind. She is also organized. One thing that her teacher does that helps the kids is what she calls her "clearing the head" trick. When kids get hyper or loud, she turns off the lights and asks them to put their heads down. She then talks to them and tells them why they have to act right. This helps them get it together. I am doing better. I do this at home now, and it works.

My little fella Ryan is 6 years old, and he is in kindergarten. He is a typical little boy who moves real fast, but I think he is too nervous. His teacher tells me he is okay. He just needs a lot of activity. I think he needs more attention than Brandy. He wears me out, and I know he must wear out his teacher. She is older and is real kind and loving. She really believes that all kids are good and can make good in school. Ryan is showing more signs that he is having learning problems. Each day he brings home a note from school pinned on his shirt that tells me if he is improving or needs more help. His teacher tells me not to worry but she is thinking that another year in kindergarten might help. I am open to anything that she tells me to do. I really trust her and feel lucky to have her working with my boy.

I have tried to remember back to my elementary school days, but I can't remember a whole lot. I wonder if my teachers were like my kids' teachers? It seems to me that elementary teachers are kinder and care more. It may sound like I am bitter about my earlier teachers, but I'm not, really. I think I am jealous that I didn't have the teachers my kids have had. Maybe we all expect teachers and schools to do too much. They can't do it all. We parents have to do a lot too. And my parents really didn't do a whole lot to help me.

I need only 16 credits to graduate and get my diploma. My counselor tells me that I might graduate with honors. Wow, that will be a miracle if I ever saw one! The best thing of all is that I'm finally able to say, "Kimmer's a Winner!" I used to be a real failure. How could I not have been? I came from two alcoholic parents. My Dad abused me and expected me to be perfect. He was also mentally ill and committed suicide.

More importantly, though, I am the proud mom of two great kids who need me very much. I am their everything. I hope I can be a good mom and prove to them that their Mom is a good person. I love them so much. Most of all I want my kids to be proud of their Mom.

I thank God that I have been given another chance to live and make something good of myself. I know my mom will be proud of me, and if Dad were alive, he'd be proud of me too.

Hooray for Kim! I'm finally "Kimmer the Winner!"

No one can make you feel inferior without your permission.
                                                —*ELEANOR ROOSEVELT*

Preparing for Successful Children

BETH CLAWSON

Editor's Note: The 1989 Michigan Mother of the Year offers practical advice to both parents and teachers. Effective families establish goals that are fair, consistent, and positive. Children must feel as though they are contributing members of the family unit. Parents must be willing to permit their children input into decisions that affect their lives. Most of all, effective parenting means time, commitment, and a realization that quality parenting takes work. Parents who demand the respect of their children must be prepared to offer respect in return.

A Design for the Home

Recently, I was sitting with ten 9-year-old girls in a Sunday School class. Our topic for the day was the story of Ruth from the Old Testament. I began by asking the class, "What do you want to be when you grow up?" Each girl in turn either stated some glamorous profession or shrugged her shoulders. Not one girl said she wanted to be a mother. When I was 9, my future plans all centered around being a mother. The world has changed.

Every future leader for good or ill starts life with a mother, with a family. This primary experience leaves an imprint that sends ripples into the future of everyone who touches that life. What factors are present in homes where children grow up to be productive citizens? What are the goals that encourage individual success? What standards can individual families set for themselves that will help keep the family from being torn apart? What plan can be set up to help children gain confidence and skills that encourage success?

Surveying the comments of mothers throughout the country at a national mother's conference, a common thread of family experience emerged. The experiences seemed constant, though family circumstances varied widely. Those constants included:

1. Children are a priority. There is a place in the day and a plan of nurture and love that assures the child of his or her importance.
2. Children are taught morality, service to others, respect, and honesty by precept and example.
3. Children do not become pawns in confrontation, nor are they pushed to the side to fend for themselves. When there is a crisis (divorce, illness, financial need), the family continues to nurture the children.
4. Children are treated with consistent and fair consideration.
5. Children are given experiences that can build learning. These experiences are different in every family. They include field trips, music lessons, dance lessons, sports, scouting, etcetera. Parents encourage the interests and talents of their children.
6. Children are included in the lives of their parents. Where possible, parents include their children in real-life work activities.
7. Children are surrounded by examples of consistent values that speak louder than the shifting whims of popular society.
8. Children are given an educational focus. Parents are involved in life-long learning. Their example develops educational excitement. This habit of learning lays a foundation that is vital in our information-society.

9. The parents have a support system of relatives, friends, and associates to whom they can turn for advice and support.
10. Family members are guarded against disinterest, neglect, and abuse.

The principles outlined above function well in a democratic atmosphere. Choice and accountability become the underlying thread in every activity. My experiences and observations lead me to believe that family success is predicated on tough-minded parents who have actively chosen to put the welfare of their children ahead of other concerns and interests. The family is a support system to answer the questions and assist in the crises that arise in parenting.

Like a successful company leader, the leader of the home must devise ways to motivate family members. There is a clear "mission statement" around which short- and long-term goals are framed. Family members esteem each other. The power and influence of the parents are maintained without hypocrisy, by persuasion, patience, kindness, faithfulness to family members, and genuine love.

When our children were teens, we did not ever set absolute curfews. The activity was discussed, and a mutually agreed time was set. The children observed the limits because they had helped set them. This dialogue helped develop mutual respect. Through discussions, our children learned the process for making successful decisions.

The nomination papers for Mother of the Year ask for a philosophy of parenting. Mine stated:

> *I married a man who displayed loyalty and devotion to family. We have committed ourselves to staying married. This has developed trust, stability, and security for us and our children.*
>
> *Our family life is based on democratic principles of choice and accountability. We have set goals for our children. We have attempted to instill the values of morality and charity through example and activity.*
>
> *I have been directly involved with the children's activities. The children have been included in my activities. A lesson is learned when you can teach others. I believe the home is the plae to internalize learning.*

In any parenting situation, goals are vital to success. When a goal is set, even small decisions can direct the progress of children. A child is a great imitator. If the parent can set an example of moral behavior, desire for learning, and interaction in the welfare of the family, the child will follow.

Long ago I put a list on my kitchen bulletin board written by Dr. Paul Popenear. As the paper yellowed, I copied it. It was a reminder to me of some elements that would be valuable in helping children. The list was titled, "A Cultured Home."

1. Not overcrowded
2. Planned recreation
3. Books, magazines, newspapers
4. Music
5. Typewriter
6. Phone
7. Parents belong to civic organizations
8. Collections of music, pictures, genealogy
9. Lessons in music, dance, sports
10. A second language

Considering the list merely as a personal reminder, one day I took it down. Before the day had ended, my children wanted to know why it was taken down. I had not realized that the list was a goal statement to them.

The goals of our family were not just a list of items on the kitchen bulletin board. Our family was fully aware of activity goals that we set. They included:

1. Opportunities to read good books, including a large home library
2. Learning to swim, life saving, first aid, and CPR
3. Learning to play the piano and other musical experiences
4. Learning to use the typewriter, and later the computer
5. The Campcrafter certification for our girls and the Eagle Scout award for our boys
6. Learning vocational skills through work in a family business
7. Service to others, freely given
8. Encouragement of individual talents and interest
9. Home support of educational success

The fulfillment of these goals gave each child self-esteem. The activities were wholesome and left little time for children to become bored. Other families need not set the same goals. However, specific, positive goals set by the family and reaffirmed to each member develop individuals with self-esteem and positive attitudes.

Another way to cement the family is to develop rituals and tradition. These rhythms of life tend to anchor the child, giving reassurance and stability. Some family rituals might be reading bedtime stories, chores, special meals on the weekend, 15-minute sit-down talks every day, "status" interviews weekly or monthly, and weekly family home evenings. Parents have found that school grades improve if there is a quiet study hour every evening with all family members studying something, even a crossword puzzle. My husband sang a lullaby to each child every night for many years, until the older teens loudly protested. Years later, a daughter phoned from college one night and asked for a lullaby after a tough day at school.

The Relationship of the Home and the School

After a child's first four years, a second sphere of influence begins to encompass the child. Although the parents are with the child in the evening, the most productive hours of the day are spent in school with adults and children who are not part of the child's family. This experience can build a child's personal self-esteem or destroy it. Parents must balance advocacy for the child with support for the teacher. Both my husband and I are teachers. However, in our relationship with the school, we acted as an advocate for each child. We made time to become acquainted with every teacher of our five children. We introduced ourselves early in the year and followed the schoolwork closely. We questioned parents and administrators so that when choices were available, our children were with teachers suited to their personalities.

It is important that parents take an interest in classroom events. We questioned our children about classroom activities. We participated in celebrations and seminars. We attended every parent-teacher meeting. (At times that was a stretch when we had children in three different schools.) We listened to the goals of the teachers so that we could support the work of the classroom at home. We made our home goals known to the teachers so that they could build on our family foundation in school. Occasionally, we felt it necessary to stand between the child and the teacher if the teacher advocated positions that were contrary to our home ideals.

Teacher Education for a Successful Home–School Connection

I have taken teacher education courses in three states and have taught in several school districts. My experience has shown that many educators believe that a child should be left at the schoolhouse door and the school will take over setting goals and educating the child, unless there is a behavior problem. That kind of responsibility is too great for the school and impossible to implement given the unique values and experiences of each family.

Some schools are trying to bridge the gap between the home and school by drawing the community into the planning process of the school. The danger is tht the process is too narrow and the dialogue needed is restrained by the adversarial climate usually present.

Our schools are trying to prepare children to participate in a complex society. The school and the home must unite to present coherent, understandable, and reachable goals for our children. In a few years, our children will help determine the kind of society in which we live.

> . . . *Thou holdest not the venture of thy self alone—Not of the western continent alone: Earth's resume entire floats on thy keel* . . .
>
> —*WALT WHITMAN*

SECTION ONE

Views of Contemporary Society

Editor's Note: It is the purpose of this section to identify some views of what our society looks like and, to some degree, establish the linkage that should exist between community and family aspirations and professional education—in a sense, to paint a picture. The picture is not always a happy or encouraging one, but it is real.

The chapters present a composite of ideas circling a central theme. The theme is that schools do not operate in a vacuum but rather as a response to a series of complex issues in complex times. The Chapter authors delineate demographics that are essential to consider if we are to understand whom we are attempting to educate. They identify problems all too apparent to most of us engaged in the educational process. Optimally, they also provide some direction to all of us as we attempt to change for the better the linkage between our society and our schools.

CHAPTER ONE

The American Family

ALICE R. McCARTHY

Editor's Note: Most research on schools and families has examined these two worlds as if they were independent entities largely unrelated to each other. There has been little systematic study of the ways in which schools and families influence one another and the child who daily shuttles between them. Even the many national school reform reports released over the past few years have almost totally ignored the family's role in student achievement and school improvement.

Although there is broad consensus on the importance of the family's role in education, the studies are scarce. Researchers have tended to concentrate on schools (what teachers do and what resources they have) to the neglect of families (what parents do to teach their children and to encourage and support their school progress).

The assumption here is that the efforts of schools and families are linked. They can either support and reinforce each other or they can compete and undermine each other. We accept the former option and reject all others. Therefore, we begin by examining the family demographics that outline the realities to which we are inexorably linked, for better or worse.

> *The American Family does not exist. Rather, we are creating many American families of diverse styles and shapes. In unprecedented numbers, our families are unalike: we have fathers working while mothers keep house; fathers and mothers both working away from home; single parents; second marriages bringing children together from unrelated backgrounds; childless couples; unmarried couples, with and without children; gay and lesbian parents. We are living through a period of historic change in American family life.*
> —*J. K. FOOTLICK*

No other Western nation has given as much lip service to the importance of family as the United States. In the early twentieth century, President Theodore Roosevelt opined that the nation's future rested on the "right kind of home life." Lyndon Johnson declared that the goal of the Great Society was to "strengthen the family." Richard Nixon vetoed a child care bill on grounds it would weaken the family. As Ronald Reagan put it: "Strong families are the foundation of society" (Coontz 1989a). In 1980 the White House Conference on Families declared that "the restoration of family life is vital to our society's future."

Historical Perspectives

Historians point to a prevailing nostalgia for the "traditional family," which is assumed once had sheltered its members from the worst effects of economic competition and untrammeled individualism. Coontz notes that such nostalgia is understandable but misplaced. She reports that American family life has historically been very diverse. For each tight-knit colonial family that worked together, another was split up to provide room for apprentices, servants, and slaves. For every nineteenth-century middle-class family, there "was an Irish or Polish girl scrubbing floors in that home, a Black or Italian mother picking clothes or beans, and a Jewish daughter making 'ladies' dresses in a sweat shop" (Coontz 1989b).

As Demos (1986) observes, it is hard to say when the colonial pattern of American family life began to break down, but by the early decades of the nineteenth century, at least some urban middle-class families were launched on a new course, as evidenced by the appearance around 1850 of exhortations against divorce, separation, permissive child rearing, and restless homemakers. But from this period came the image, the myth of the family's "golden past."

The nineteenth-century family, far from joining and complementing other social networks, seemed to stand wholly apart. Home was pictured as a bastion of peace, orderliness, and unwavering devotion to people and principles beyond self. Here the mother and children passed their hours safe from the world, and here was the father's retreat. Perhaps the strongest image of this American family is that of the family as a refuge.

At this time the functions in families were carefully delineated; the family system appeared as one "highly calibrated (with) interlocking parts" (Demos 1986, 53) The father represented the family in the larger world. His success or failure reflected on him and on other family members, a burden too hard to bear for some men. The mother, in trying to meet the standards of the perfect home—the selfless woman—often could not express her own needs. If the nineteenth-century family did not perform in expected ways, there were no institutions to back it up.

In the twentieth century, says Demos (1986), we feel we are not masters of our fate. We have moved from the threatening "jungle" of the nineteenth century to the numbing "rat race" of the twentieth.

As the threat is tempered, the wish for protection wanes. The home becomes the provider of interest and excitement, the stimuli missing from other sectors. The roles and responsibilities within the home are beginning to diffuse. *Egalitarianism* is the new buzz word for husband-and-wife relationships. Parents believe in listening to their children, even believe they can learn from them, an idea that would have been considered preposterous two generations ago (Footlick 1990).

If all goes well, home becomes a bubbling kettle of mutually enhancing activity. Alas, all does not invariably go well, and for the first time we have a negative—"anti-image"—of the family. Monogamous marriage is seen as boring and stultifying, and responsibility for children compounds the problem.

For over a century, Stannard (1979) observes, the American family has been unburdening itself of its responsibility to care for and nurture the weak. Family members are free to pursue an unprecedented range of self-gratifying endeavors.

Stannard says we have clung to the romantic fiction surrounding the family begun in the 1800s. He reports that we have failed to scrutinize, control, or adequately support the institutions who have become the family's surrogate care givers and protectors. Educators of youth understand his statements.

By definition,

the experience in the family, the first and deepest a human being knows, shapes the individual more profoundly than any other set of social-cultural forces. In one sense the family is only an idea . . . nothing more than image, since we cannot know it impartially, and it is never completely separated from our fantasies . . . and unconscious responses. (Tufte and Myerhoff 1979, 15)

The American Family: Graphic Overviews

He looks up to two older brothers who are in jail on murder charges. He's strong-armed safety patrol boys for lunch money and been expelled from school for throwing snowballs at teachers and pulling knives on students.

He allegedly forced an 8-year-old boy to commit an oral sex act and he almost set himself on fire while burning down a garage. School officials call him a "holy terror."

He's just 9 years old, and only 4 feet 9 and 50 pounds.

Sammy, this troubled youngster described in a 1990 article in the *Detroit Free Press* (Kresnak 1990), mirrors a state of distress. Distress originating in the family and the family's living arrangements. Distress projected onto society and the institutions interacting with the youngster and his family— the schools, the courts, the Michigan Department of Welfare.

Much of the increased interest in family-related issues during the past two decades is the direct result of changes that have taken place in patterns of living arrangements. Investigation into these changes brings the realization that lifestyles are dynamic rather than static, shifting as individuals and groups pass through their life courses. Many factors—political, economic, social, cultural, technological, and demographic variables—interrelate to influence behavior reflected in the various forms of living arrangements.

Trends that indicate a movement away from "traditional" family living include the currently high rates of marital disruption, the delay in marriage among young adults, and the increasing tendency for individuals to form households consisting of only themselves or of two or more people not conventionally related to one another. To some analysts these changing lifestyles are considered a momentary product of readjusting to new roles that must be played by more and more adults as they maintain a family in modern society.

According to an August, 1990 report in the *New York Times,* even the most jaded observers seemed to take notice this spring with a report by a panel, including Dr. C. Everett Koop, the former Surgeon General, and Albert Shanker, president of the American Federation of Teachers, came to the disturbing conclusion that teenagers are less healthy today than their parents were when they were the same age. Because of drinking, drugs, unplanned pregnancies, violence, suicide, venereal disease and emotional problems, many of today's teenagers "are unlikely to attain the high levels of education achievement required for success in the 21st century," according to the commission, which was formed by the National Association of State Boards of Education and the American Medical Association. The implication was that America was raising a lost generation, an army of aging Bart Simpsons, possibly armed and dangerous.

Is there anything to this implication, beyond the ritual anxiety each generation feels about its successors? Have a significant number of post-boom babies really inherited serious handicaps, perhaps from the social revolutions of the 1960s and 70s? Given all the choices they have, why do young people seem so confused?

These questions are being asked by social scientists who are doggedly tracking the lives and times of nearly 37 million people between the ages of 15 and 25. The answers, as far as they exist, are inconsistent enough to make demographers wonder if there is a "they" out there after all.

A few facts are clear (*New York Times* August 19, 1990). The people born in the late 1960s and early 70s have sex earlier than their parents did, and they marry later. They buy more condoms than their older brothers and sisters did, but the youngest of them, the 15- to 19-year-olds, have more babies. In surveys, they say they care about poverty and the environment, but they vote less often than their predecessors did and they pay less attention to the news. They spend more time in school but they learn less. Overall, they take fewer drugs than their older brothers and sisters did, yet more of them kill themselves, and each other, than was true for previous generations.

A graphic overview of selected recent trends reflecting changes in the lifestyles of many Americans provides a picture of the American family in the past two decades. Limited commentary is presented on population growth, family formation, family dissolution, and other important social and economic characteristics of families.

Population Composition and Growth

The population pyramids in Figure 1-1 show dramatically the U.S. population has aged since 1960 and will continue to age in the future. The effect of the "Baby Boom" can be seen in the wide bottom bars of the 1960 pyramid—a large proportion of the population is under age 15. In each successive pyramid, one can see that the bulge has moved up in age—and up the pyramid, too. The slight widening at the bottom of the 1987 pyramid is the "echo effect"—these are the children of the original Baby Boomers. This increase in births is not expected to be long-term, however, as can be seen by the pinch in the bar for children under 5 for the year 2000. Shifts in the age structure can be an important influence on the composition and social and economic characteristics of households and families. Racial and ethnic minority populations, most notable blacks and Hispanics, have had and will likely continue to have higher growth rates than the white population (U.S. Bureau of Census 1988a, 3).

Time magazine reports (Henry 1990) that already one American in four defines himself or herself as Hispanic or nonwhite. If current trends in immigration and birth rates continue, the Hispanic population will have further increased an estimated 21 percent, Asians about 22 percent, blacks almost 12 percent, and whites a little more than 2 percent when the twentieth century ends. By 2020, the number of U.S. residents who are Hispanic or nonwhite will have more than doubled, to nearly 115 million, while the white population will not be increasing.

Henry (1990) indicates that political pressure has already brought about sweeping changes in public school textbooks. Troubling, he says, is a revisionist approach to history in which groups that have gained power turn to remaking the past in their preferred images. He reports that professionals

FIGURE 1-1 • *U.S. Population by Age and Sex; 1960 to 2000*

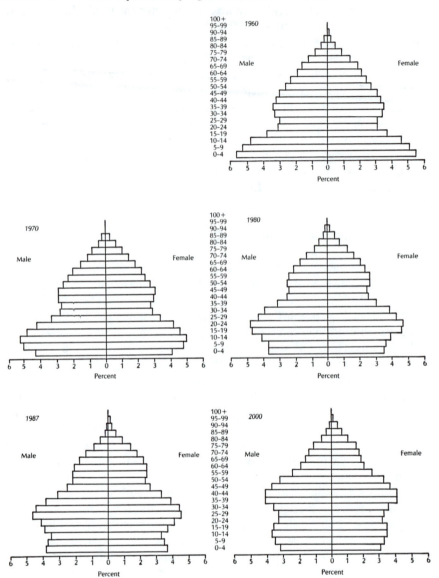

Source: U.S. Bureau of the Census, *Family Summit Chart Book,* (Washington, DC: U.S. Department of Commerce, 1988) p. 4.

have been railed against in New York City, where a task force concluded that "African American, Puerto Ricans and Native Americans have been victims of an intellectual and educational oppression . . . and negative characterizations have had a terribly damaging effect on the psyche of young people" (p. 30). Henry reports that many intellectuals are outraged. Political scientist Andrew Hacker of Queens College says this is not history but a myth intended to bolster the self-esteem of certain children.

Figure 1-2 indicates that the regional pattern of population growth in the 1970s continued through the 1980s. The figure shows that the South and West grew (and continue to grow) disproportionately more than the Northeast and Midwest. Ninety percent of the total U.S. population growth during the 1970–1980 period occurred in the South and West. Since 1980 the growth has been slower than in the 1970s for all regions except the Northeast, which experienced higher growth rates in the 1980s. Half of the growth in the South and West regions was due to immigration, while the Northeast and Midwest experienced a net migration. Differential population growth by region has implications for shifts in political representation and in the revenue bases for individual states (U.S. Bureau of Census 1988a, 5).

Figure 1-3 traces age at first marriage from 1890 to 1989. Since the mid-1950s the estimated median age at first marriage has moved upward gradually, increasing about three years for both men and women. The median age at first marriage for men (26.2 in 1989) now stands at a level close to the

FIGURE 1-2 • *Population Growth by Regions*

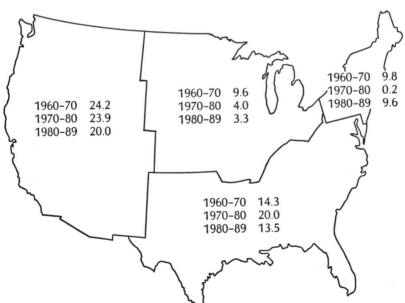

1960–70	24.2
1970–80	23.9
1980–89	20.0

1960–70	9.6
1970–80	4.0
1980–89	3.3

1960–70	9.8
1970–80	0.2
1980–89	9.6

1960–70	14.3
1970–80	20.0
1980–89	13.5

Source: U.S. Bureau of the Census, *Family Summit Chart Book* (Washington, DC: U.S. Department of Commerce, 1988), p. 6.

FIGURE 1-3 • *Age at First Marriage, 1890 to 1989*

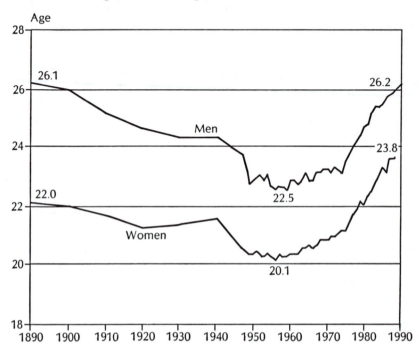

Source: U.S. Bureau of Census, SB-4-89 (Washington, DC: U.S. Department of Commerce, 1989).

figure for men in 1900. The median age at first marriage for women (23.8 in 1989) has been higher during the 1980s than at any previously recorded time.

An increasing age at first marriage is associated with increases in educational attainment (U.S. Bureau of Census, 1988a, 7). In 1975, women received nearly 12 percent of MBA degrees granted; in 1987, they received 33 percent. In 1966, fewer than 7 percent of MDs were granted to women: in 1987, it had reached 32 percent. By 1987, women were earning 40 percent of all law degrees (Naisbitt and Aburdene 1990).

Likewise, increasing age at first marriage is linked to increasing labor force participation for women. In 1990, 79 percent of all women with no children work, but so do 67 percent with children, and over half of women with small children (Naisbitt and Aburdene 1990). As many as 75 percent of mothers with preschool children will be in the work force within the next generation (National Council on Family Relations 1990).

For equality to exist between females and males, a more flexible outlook is needed on the chronology of life experiences. Phyllis Moen (1990), a specialist in women's roles and a faculty member at Cornell University, observes that "the lockstep schedule society demands of professionals—college immediately after high school, graduate school or other advanced training immediately following college, and a continuous career on the heels of advanced study—effectively bars many women from the physical sciences and engineering." Females who plan to have children frequently shy away from high-powered fields in which momentum lost because of child rearing is too often lost forever.

Moen says,

Getting married and becoming mothers constrain women's educational achievements and employment options. Family considerations, in a social and institutional climate that assigns the child-care responsibility to the women and provides few if any supports for students and workers who are parents, constitute barriers that prevent women's uninterrupted educational and career development. (Human Ecology News *1990)*

As Figure 1-4 illustrates, the increasing postponement of marriage is reflected in the substantial rise in the proportion of men and women of historically prime marrying age who have not yet married for the first time. The proportions of men and women who are not yet married grew substantially during the past two decades. Between 1970 and 1989, the proportion of never married at ages 20–24 increased by 75 percent for women and 41 percent for men. The proportion for those in the 25–29 age group tripled for women and more than doubled for men. For those in the 30–34 age group, the never-married proportions tripled for both men and women (U.S. Bureau of Census 1989c).

With reference to Figure 1-5, in 1970, 38 million, or 28 percent of all adults 18 years and older were single (never married, divorced, or widowed); by 1988, this number had grown to 66 million, or 37 percent of adults. Singleness in most instances is a temporary state—about 90 percent of people will eventually marry and, of those who divorce, about 70 percent will remarry (U.S. Bureau of Census 1989c).

Among women who had a child in the year preceding the June 1988 survey, 51 percent were in the labor force in June 1988, as compared with 31 percent in June 1976. Labor force participation rates for women with newborns were substantially higher for women with 4 or more years of college (60 percent) than for women who had completed less than 12 years of school (34 percent).

FIGURE 1-4 • *Percent Never Married, by Age and Sex, 1970, 1989, and 1989*

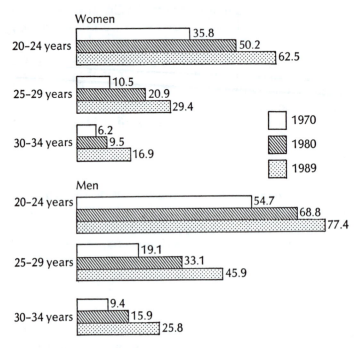

Source: U.S. Bureau of Census, Series P-20, No. 445 (Washington, DC: U.S. Department of Commerce, 1989).

As illustrated in Figure 1-6, the fertility rate for women 30 to 34 years old in 1988 was 81.6 births per 1,000 women, compared with the 1980 rate of 60. The fertility rate for women 35 to 39 years old in 1988 was also significantly above the 1980 rate, and was 50 percent higher in 1988 than in 1976. Fertility among women over 40 still remains relatively low; 2 percent of all births in 1988 were to women over 40.

In 1988, 25 percent of women in their early 30s were childless, still higher than the rate reported in 1980. Hispanic women in 1988 had an estimated fertility rate of 94 births per 1,000 women 18 to 44 years old, significantly higher than the fertility rate for non-Hispanic women (67.5).

Premarital childbearing women under 20 years old has been a national concern since the 1960s. There is evidence that the mothers, the children born out of wedlock, and couples who marry as a result of a premaritally conceived child experience economic disadvantages. Forty percent of first births born between 1985 and 1988 to women 15 to 29 years old were either born out of wedlock or conceived before the woman's first marriage. This proportion

FIGURE 1-5 • *Singleness in America*

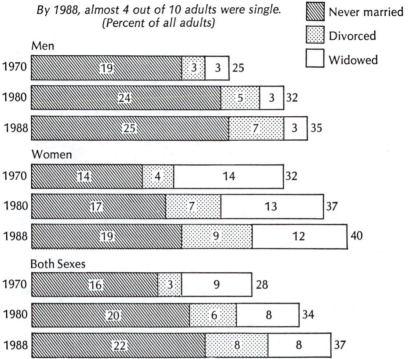

Source: U.S. Bureau of Census, SB-4-89 (Washington, DC: U.S. Department of Commerce, 1989).

ranged from 32.8 percent for white women to 78.8 percent for black women. Among Hispanic women the figure was 42.7 percent. About 87 percent of first births born between 1985 and 1988 to teenage women 15 to 17 years old were either born (72 percent) or conceived (15 percent) before the woman's first marriage, compared to 79 percent for 18- and 19-year-old women, 43 percent for women 20–24 years old, and 15 percent for women 25 to 29 years old (U.S. Bureau of Census, 1989a, 6).

Household Composition

According to Figure 1-7, changes in the composition of households and families as a result of changing marital and fertility patterns have contributed to a decline in the average number of persons in these units. Fewer children

FIGURE 1-6 • *Fertility of American Women: Births per 1,000 Women by Age, 1976 and 1989*

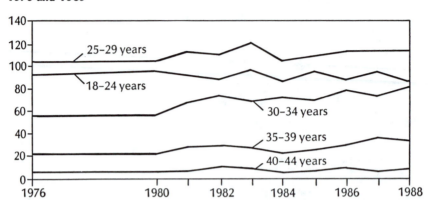

Source: U.S. Bureau of Census, Series P-20, No. 436 (Washington, DC: U.S. Department of Commerce, 1989), p. 2.

per family, more one-parent families, and larger numbers of people living alone are all among the factors contributing to the trend toward smaller households and families that began during the mid-1960s (U.S. Bureau of Census 1988b). In 1989 there were 2.62 persons per household and 3.16 persons per family. These averages have never been lower (U.S. Bureau of Census 1989b).

The U.S. Bureau of the Census identifies two major categories of households: family and nonfamily. A family household consists of the householder and at least one additional person related to the householder through marriage, birth, or adoption. A nonfamily household is composed of a householder who either lives alone or exclusively with persons unrelated to the householder.

As illustrated in Figure 1-8, married-couple households were 70.5 percent of all households in 1970, but only 56 percent in 1989, a decline solely attributable to a drop in the proportion of married-couple households with children present.

Women Maintaining Households

One of the most dramatic changes in the composition of family households during the 1970s was the tremendous increase in the number of families maintained by women (U.S. Bureau of Census 1989b). The data for the 1980s indicate that this type of family household continues its rise. About 17 percent of all family households were maintained by women in 1989, compared with 15 percent in 1980.

FIGURE 1-7 • *Household and Family Size*

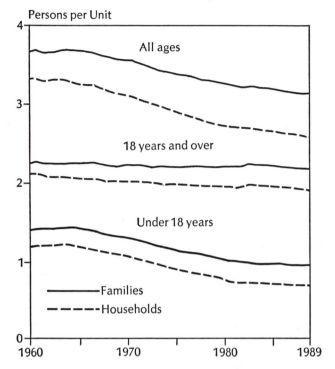

Source: U.S. Bureau of Census, Series P-20, No. 441 (Washington, DC: U.S. Department of Commerce, 1989).

There is substantial difference between blacks and whites in the proportion of families maintained by women. In 1989 about 44 percent of black family households were maintained by women versus 13 percent for whites; these percentages were higher than the corresponding proportions for 1980. Among Hispanics, about 23 percent of families were maintained by women in 1989, about seven percentage points higher than the overall proportion of family households maintained by women (U.S. Bureau of Census 1989b).

There has been a substantial increase since 1970 in one-parent family situations. One-parent families are created either by premarital birth, separation, divorce, widowhood, or adoption. About 9 of every 10 single parents are mothers.

Single parents accounted for 27 percent of all family groups with children under 18 years old in 1987, a proportion more than twice as high as it was in 1970. Among whites, about 22 percent of all family groups that

FIGURE 1-8 • *Household Composition*

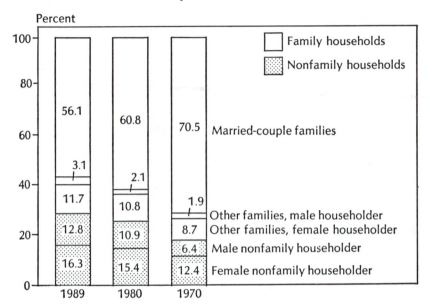

Percent

Source: U.S. Bureau of Census, Series P-20, No. 441 (Washington, DC: U.S. Department of Commerce, 1989).

included children under 18 were maintained by single parents. Among blacks, 59 percent of all family groups with children under 18 were maintained by women, and among Hispanics, 33 percent (U.S. Bureau of Census 1988a).

Figure 1-9 indicates that in 1988, 9.4 million women were living with children under 21 years of age whose fathers were not living in the household. This was a 6.9-percent increase from 1986.

Poverty Rates in Households Maintained by Women
The poverty rate for women with children from an absent father was 33.9 percent in 1987. The poverty rate for never-married women was 57.1 percent in 1987, as compared with a poverty rate of 24.9 percent for married women.

The poverty rate for white women with children from an absent father, 25.7 percent, was about half that of black women (53.3 percent). The poverty rate for Hispanic women was 50.5 percent. Women having less than a high school education who also had children from an absent father had a poverty rate of 59.7 percent in 1987, about twice that of women with at least a high school education.

FIGURE 1-9 • *Marital Status of Women with Own Children under Age 21 from an Absent Father*

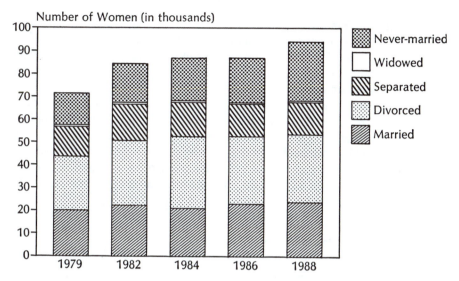

Source: U.S. Bureau of Census, Series P-23, No. 167 (Washington, DC: U.S. Department of Commerce, 1990).

Younger women with children from an absent father were much more likely to have family incomes below the poverty level than their older counterparts. Poverty rates for women ages 18 to 29, 30 to 39, and over 39 with children from an absent father ranged from 49.3 percent to 18.4 percent respectively.

The mean amount of child support received by all women who received payments was $2,710 in 1987. This amount represents a 15.9-percent increase from the comparable 1985 figure after adjusting for inflation. This is a marked change from the 1983 to 1985 period, when the average amount of child support decreased by 12.4 percent in real terms.

Women with four or more years of college received mean payments ($4,310) that were about two-thirds higher than the mean received by women with at least a high school education or some college ($2,595) and about double those received by women with less than a high school education ($1,872) (U.S. Bureau of Census 1990a).

Kalter (1990) conducted research related to single parents and their children and the effects of divorce. The research uncovered disturbing long-term consequences for children. Diamond (1985) provides a handbook for single parents and teachers that can be used to deal with the special needs of children of divorce in school.

Stepfamilies

By 1985, a higher proportion of Americans (23 percent) than ever before had been divorced at some point in their lives. Because most people who divorce eventually remarry, more children and adults experience living as part of a stepfamily.

In 1985, about 4.5 million families contained 6.8 million stepchildren under age 18, 15 percent more than in 1980. Of these families, 2.4 million had stepchildren only and 2.1 million had a mix of at least one child born to or adopted by both parents in the household. The 6.8 million stepchildren accounted for 15 percent of children in all married-couple families in 1985.

As illustrated in Figure 1-10, in black married-couple families, one in

FIGURE 1-10 • *Stepchildren and Their Families*

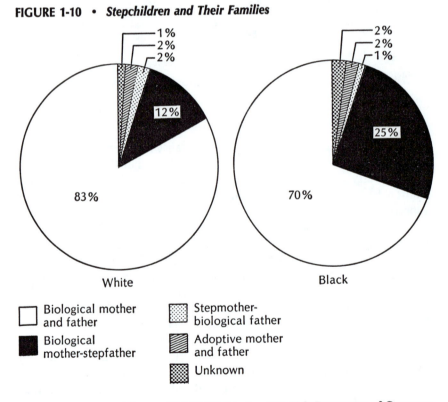

White

Black

☐ Biological mother and father

■ Biological mother-stepfather

▦ Stepmother-biological father

▨ Adoptive mother and father

▦ Unknown

Source: U.S. Bureau of Census, SB-1-89 (Washington, DC: U.S. Department of Commerce, 1989).

four children under 18 in 1985 was a stepchild living with the biological mother and stepfather. One researcher has estimated that about one-quarter of today's children will live with a stepparent by the time they reach the age of 16 (U.S. Bureau of Census 1989e).

Most stepchildren live with their biological mothers and stepfathers. After divorce, mothers are still much more likely than fathers to have custody of their children. Over six million children, or nine of ten stepchildren in married-couple families, lived with their biological mothers and stepfathers. Only 740,000 stepchildren lived with their biological fathers and stepmothers.

Most stepfamilies are at an economic disadvantage as compared with other married-couple families with children. Median income for all married-couple families with children was $28,162 in 1985. Families that contained a biological mother, a stepfather, and stepchildren had a median income of only $25,272. The median income of married-couple families with at least one stepchild and at least one biological child was even lower — $22,932. The striking exception was families with a biological father and stepmother: They had the highest median family income — $34,850.

Parents in stepfamilies were in general less well-educated than parents in married-couple families. Research has shown that 44 percent of fathers and 37 percent of mothers in married-couple families had at least some college education, while only 35 percent of fathers and 29 percent of mothers in families comprising a stepfather, a biological mother, and stepchildren only had at least some college. Biological fathers in stepfamilies, however, were relatively well-educated: 48% had at least some college.

Stepchildren not only have to deal with complex social relationships within their own household, but many also have to deal with complex relationships involving their noncustodial biological parent's family. Data from the National Health Interview Survey in 1981 show that almost half of children living with a stepfather never saw their biological fathers. The recent striking growth in stepfamilies has left little time for individuals, families, and society to develop ways of coping with problems associated with living in families where steprelationships exist (U.S. Bureau of Census 1989e).

Leading researchers John and Emily Visher indicate that no longer is a stepfamily an "alternative" family; it is a normative family with its own challenges and rewards (Visher and Visher 1988). The researchers report:

> *Ordinarily it is not a short journey from stepfamily ambiguity and fragility to solidity and integration. The process can take a minimum of one and a half to two years when the children are young to many more years when the children are older. The relationships in stepfamilies need to shift and develop, going from loyalty patterns that are biologically based to encompassing new and enriching ties growing out of shared experiences and mutual respect. (p. 234)*

Constance Ahrons, a professor at the University of Southern California, therapist, and author (1989), said recently, "If the relationship with the kids doesn't work the marriage isn't going to work" (Nordheimer 1990).

Child Care Arrangements

As children grow from infancy to school age, employed women make considerable changes in child care arrangements in order to meet the needs of their children and the changing demands of their family and their employer. However. problems in finding child care arrangements for young children are often encountered by working adults since organized child care facilities usually deny the admission of infants and very young children. Estimates from a 1987 Current Population Survey show that 51 percent of all women 18 to 44 years old who had a birth in the 12-month period preceding the survey were in the labor force, up from 31 percent in 1976 (U.S. Bureau of Census 1990b).

Data from a Survey of Income and Program Participation (U.S. Bureau of Census 1987) indicate that there were 1.5 million children under 1 year of age in the fall of 1987 whose mothers were employed in the labor force. Seventy percent of the infants were cared for in either the child's home or another home (Figure 1-11). Another 12 percent were cared for in day/group centers, while 2 percent were cared for in nursery/preschools.

Among 1- and 2-year-olds, child care either in the child's home or in another home accounted for 74 percent of all arrangements, while organized child care facilities made up 18 percent of the primary care for these children. For 3- and 4-year-old children, care in either the child's home or in another home accounted for 56 percent of all arrangements, while organized child care facilities made up 34 percent of the primary care.

In fall 1987, 16 percent (1,465,000) of children under 5 years old of employed women were in day/group care centers, while another 8 percent (755,000) were enrolled in nursery/preschool programs. Three- and 4-year-old children constituted the majority (60 percent) of preschoolers using organized child care facilities; 9 percent were under 1 year of age and 31 percent were either 1 or 2 years old.

The economic status of the family is related to the use of organized child care facilities as the primary child care arrangement. Children of employed mothers whose family income exceeded $3,750 per month (over $45,000 per year) were twice as likely to be using organized child care facilities (34 percent) as were children living in families with monthly incomes less than $1,250 per month (less than $15,000 per year). For all of the income groups, day/group care services for preschoolers were used twice as often as nursery/preschool arrangements (U.S. Bureau of Census 1990b).

FIGURE 1-11 • *Child Care Arrangements for Preschoolers, 1987*

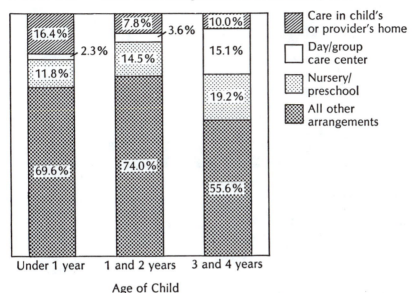

Source: U.S. Bureau of Census, Series P-70, No. 20 (Washington, DC: U.S. Department of Commerce, 1990).

Poverty in Families

Figure 1-12 illustrates that the poverty rate for all families was 10.3 percent in 1989. Married-couple families continued to have the lowest rate, followed by those with a male householder, no wife present, and families with a female householder, no husband present. White families had a lower poverty rate overall, as well as by type of family, than blacks or families with Hispanic origin.

The poverty rate for Hispanic married couples was 16.2 percent in 1989, compared with 11.8 percent for blacks and about 47 percent of both black and Hispanic families with a female householder, no husband present, were below the poverty level. However, female-householder families constituted 73.4 percent of all poor black families, compared with 46.8 percent of poor Hispanic-origin families.

Overall in 1989, 43.2 percent of all poor families were maintained by a married couple, while 51.7 percent were maintained by a female with no husband present.

FIGURE 1-12 • *Poverty Rates for Famiies with Selected Characteristics, 1989*

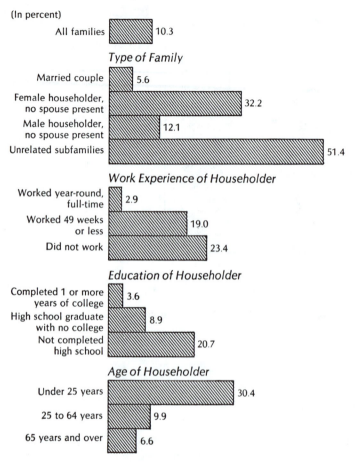

(In percent)

All families 10.3

Type of Family

Married couple 5.6

Female householder, no spouse present 32.2

Male householder, no spouse present 12.1

Unrelated subfamilies 51.4

Work Experience of Householder

Worked year-round, full-time 2.9

Worked 49 weeks or less 19.0

Did not work 23.4

Education of Householder

Completed 1 or more years of college 3.6

High school graduate with no college 8.9

Not completed high school 20.7

Age of Householder

Under 25 years 30.4

25 to 64 years 9.9

65 years and over 6.6

Source: U.S. Bureau of Census, Series P-60, No. 168 (Washington, DC: U.S. Department of Commerce, 1990).

Persons in families represented 76.3 percent of the poor in 1989. The 6.6 million unrelated individuals (persons living alone or with nonrelatives only) who were poor in 1989 accounted for 21.5 percent of the poverty population (U.S. Bureau of Census 1990b)

During the past eight years, America's youth and young families have borne the brunt of economic slumps and have seen their incomes plummet, in constant dollars, during successive economic downturns. After each economic recovery from a series of back-to-back recessions, young male workers' real, inflation-adjusted earnings never returned to 1973 levels. As a result, the earnings of all male subgroups have dropped sharply. While the median, before-tax income of all families has been stagnant for 13 years, major gains were recorded by household heads aged 65 or older (up to 25.9 percent). In sharp contrast, the median income of households headed by persons under age 25 declined 26.3 percent between 1973 and 1986 (in 1986 constant dollars), from $20,229 to $14,000 (U.S. Department of Education 1988). If we recall that the drop in personal income during the Great Depression from 1929 to 1933 was 27 percent, we can better grasp the extent of the "New Depression" being experienced by America's young families today.

While economic analyses differ in many details, there is a growing consensus that this squeeze on family earnings is the composite result of complex factors: (a) the loss of highly-paid manufacturing jobs that has forced young, entry-level workers into the rapidly growing but much lower-paying trade or service positions; (b) slowed productivity and growth attributable to outmoded plants and equipment, reduced capital outlays per worker, poor management, poor worker performance, or a combination of all four; (c) a general reduction of real compensation through cuts in wages and benefits, the reduction of unionized employment, the growing use of part-time employees, and similar measures; (d) a weakened U.S. dollar that raises the cost of most imports; (3) huge foreign trade deficits that have converted the United States into a borrower nation and now require the payment of rents, dividends, and interest on foreign-owned assets in the United States; and (f) the startling rise of female-headed families, especially never-married mothers, whose earning ability is severely restricted and who, without the benefits of a dual-earner household, cannot often attain middle-class status in American society. In this economic environment of intense global competition, the availability of well-paid but relatively low-skill jobs is declining. Jobs at both the low and high ends of the wage scale are increasing: low-pay, low-skill jobs on one end and professional, technical, and managerial jobs at the upper end of the income scale.

Analysis shows that changes in the structure of the urban economy and the decline in the growth of real wages since 1973 have magnified inner-city economic dislocations and increased the incidence and concentration of poverty there. In addition, these changes help to explain the growth in the numbers of poor, single-parent families and the concentrations of impoverished children attending public schools. All these variables profoundly affect the educational attainment and basic skill levels of children who grow up in poverty. Lower basic academic skill and attainment levels, in turn, correlate strikingly with early parenthood and out-of-wedlock birth, dropping out of school, dependence on public assistance, unemployment, criminal arrest, and dire poverty (W.T. Grant Commission, 1988).

Meanwhile, some encouraging progress is explained in a recent *New York Times* editorial:

Youngsters born into poverty aren't truly born equal, but America is now on the way to reducing that tragic inequality. Legislation just enacted by the 101st Congress will give poor children, and their parents, a better, healthier life. . . . By 2003, all poor children through the age of 18 will be covered by Federal Medicaid health insurance. The age limit, now six, will rise by one year annually. The gain to children is obvious, but there's a gain for their mothers and for society. It is an inducement to poor women who have been discouraged from getting a job and off welfare because heretofore that meant losing Medicaid benefits. . . .

In separate, equally dramatic legislation, Congress improved Head Start. This program, now in its 26th year, offers remarkable testament to the effectiveness of early childhood education. But it had been able to admit only about 25 percent of the eligible children. Not anymore. Congress approved a 26 percent expansion in funding, making it possible to enroll 40 percent of eligible children. More dramatic still, the legislation authorizes funds that will make it possible to enroll every eligible child in America by 1994.

Above all, Congress has now enacted child care legislation that is a boon not only for the working poor but a long-overdue response to the new realities of American life. The measure . . . sets up two grant programs to subsidize state child care programs.

The Child Care and Development Block Grant, which spends $2.5 billion over three years, gives states discretion to subsidize child care for working parents regardless of income but with the recommendation that the money go to low-income families. (New York Times, October 31, 1990)

Conclusion: Beyond the Demographics

Roger Bebow was worried Tuesday when his five year old son showed him a message from Wayne-Westland's Albert Schweitzer Elementary School. Two sixth-graders were suspended that day for bringing guns into the school. "I had a gut feeling there was more to it," said Bebow. A day later, Bebow learned that Schweitzer Principal Karen Obsniuk's "Dear Parents" letter had failed to mention one detail: One of the guns, a .25 caliber Raven automatic, was loaded. Westland Police Sgt. Dale Hawkes said an 11-year-old boy broke into his father's gun cabinet and brought a replica gun and the Raven handgun to school along with seven rounds of shotgun ammunition and 14 pistol bullets. "They were playing with the loaded gun in a crowded lunch room" on Monday, said Hawkes. "They were going to take the shotgun ammo apart and make something with the powder." Superintendent Dennis O'Neill said it's the first time a gun was found in a Wayne-Westland District elementary school. (Thurtell 1990).

A review of the demographics related to recent trends in the changing lifestyles of Americans presents a sobering picture. It is estimated that 21 million U.S. children are at risk because of factors such as poverty, child abuse, homelessness, substance abuse, disability, pregnancy, limited English language skills, and low self-esteem. (Kausch Studios and McCarthy 1988).

As many as one-quarter of America's children live below the poverty line; some one million teenagers become pregnant each year, and more than a half million children are migrant and homeless. Such factors are linked directly to at least one million youths dropping out of school each year. For each dropout, four more students consistently rank in the lowest quartile in academic achievement.

Beyond the statistics lies the real human picture. Historically, the public schools have been a steppingstone into the economic mainstream. But now the demands of the workplace and the information revolution require, to an unprecedented extent, that students develop critical thinking skills. Students who are not engaged in learning, who drop out of school, or who fail to acquire the skills they need for the work force more than likely will face economic hardship (National School Boards Association, 1989).

It is possible that during the dawn of the twenty-first century a majority of the U.S. population will consist of racial and ethnic minorities. The largely successful struggles of a previous generation to achieve political freedom for minorities have now given way to the pressing need for affirmative action. A recent study conducted by the Business Higher Education Forum identifies a spectrum of life experiences for black and Hispanic Americans ranging from those who have gained access to the amenities of at least a middle-class income, to those at the margin of economic survival and those very poor and unskilled who constitute an underclass. Beyond the objectives of educational and economic access lies the goal of a truly pluralistic society in which various forms of racial, cultural, political, and personal diversity are positively valued (1990).

Robert Theobald, noted futurist and writer (1986), in an outline for a new book indicates that work and citizenship skills for the twenty-first century will be totally different from those for today. People who live in a learning society and will need to possess communication skills, to work collaboratively, to evaluate activity along multiple scales, to have respect for those who are competent, to shift roles and structures without discomfort, to enjoy change, and, above all, to strive for balance. He writes that in the past, courage has been defined as the willingness to stand for a position against all odds. In the future we shall see that those people who are willing to heal divisions are those who have real courage. They will struggle against oversimplification and violence. They will aim to show conflicting people and groups that their disagreements can be resolved by creativity.

Theobald names the twenty-first century the "Compassionate Era." In this era, he says, we shall create learning systems that develop the potential of human beings. He opines that "it is impossible to guess how much can be achieved as we release people from the fear and power that has brutalized them in the past." Theobald believes that if we encourage citizens to see a broader picture, they will have more faith in themselves and others and will apply the spiritual principles of honesty, responsibility, humility, and love more of the time. He says that the challenges we face are no more daunting than those that confronted our forerunners. They kept going, he added, and so should we. The whole message of the new era is that it is better to travel hopefully than to arrive—he warns that the maps we use will be sketchy (Theobold 1990).

Toffler (1990) concurs, saying that the twenty-first century's path to economic development and power is no longer through the exploitation of raw materials and human muscle but through the application of the human mind. Theobald calls the new era of compassion a revolution that goes as deep as ending slavery. Are families and schools ready for the challenge?

We must learn from the present how to anticipate the future.
—JOHN NAISBITT

Creating Community Contexts That Educate: An Agenda for Improving Education in Inner Cities

MARTIN HABERMAN

Editor's Note: Children who cannot "attend" have difficulty learning. It follows, therefore, that the problems and issues raised in this book must be addressed if the schools are to do any of the tasks required by society. Even though these concerns cut across geographic boundaries, most if not all of them seem to be found within the urban setting. It has been postulated that someone who can successfully teach in the big city can probably teach anywhere. However, the reverse may not be true. Do educators who select to work in "Metropolis" require special knowledge, skills, and attitudes, not required of those in the suburbs or in our rural areas? Do they deserve combat pay?

Attempting to answer these questions mandates some understanding of the inner city, its culture and subcultures. Many have suggested that the cities are in trouble. However, no picture should be painted without trying to understand that the canvas can also portray opportunity, challenge, and a beauty not found elsewhere. The city may be complex, but it is rarely dull.

What we need to do is intervene and do things differently and stop just describing what is.

Educational interventions that will affect the lives of inner-city children and youth in major ways do not occur in vacuum-packed schools. Schools reflect and are affected by a set of specific community contexts, many of which are themselves institutions that educate. While schools should continue to be studied with heightened scrutiny, it is also imperative that we learn more about the range of community institutions that educate, interact with one another, and influence families and the process of formal schooling.

- There is a need to study, in-depth, how community institutions — including informal networks — educate.
- There is a need to derive research questions from the needs perceived in communities.
- There is a need to evaluate initiatives that conceptualize schools as interrelated with other community institutions.
- There is a need to conduct research and disseminate knowledge that cuts across political and bureaucratic lines.
- There is a need to integrate and use the research that already exists.
- There is a need to translate and apply research in order to empower community constituencies.

An Urban Ecological Approach

The classical social science definition of a community is "a social unit which consists of persons who share a common geographic area interacting in terms of a common culture and which incorporates a range of social structures which function to meet relatively broad array of needs of all persons who make up the social unit" (Warren 1978). Another definition of community is that it involves shared life space as people come together over needs, values, and demands.

The basic contention of this chapter is that the most fruitful and least understood level of analysis is the urban community, which directly influences families and individuals through its formal and informal institutions. This is not to ignore the influences of the larger society that provide the context in which communities function, or the direct influences of the larger society on families and individuals that seem to bypass or penetrate the particular community context. Similarly, the emphasis on community as the unit of analysis ignores neither the power of individuals to overcome particular contexts or the range of individual differences that accounts for variations in how individuals develop differently within the same contexts. The essence of my position is that understanding the education of inner-city children and youth transcends understanding them as individuals, or the context provided by their families, or the nature of the schooling provided by the larger society. Stated another way, increased knowledge of variations among individuals and even of how their particular families shape their development is a necessary but insufficient condition for generating the knowledge needed to improve their education in significant ways.

An ecological approach to human development requires understanding and sensitivity to the interaction between individuals and the multiple contexts within which they function: their family, their school, their network of friends, and the community setting. Human development in this sense can be viewed as the "progressive, mutual accommodation between the person and the changing properties of the immediate and broader contexts in which the person lives" (Brofenbrenner and Weiss 1983). The educational research literature has focused on studies of individuals and school attributes and less frequently on families. When the unit of analysis shifts to communities and how they affect schools, families, and patterns of association, the gaps in knowledge become more striking.

It is customary in reports published since 1983 to argue for school change on the basis of demographic indicators that describe low-income and minority children and their families. Less common are attempts to make connections between these indicators and the solutions proposed or undertaken for changing schools. For example, problem statements frequently include indicators such as the following:

- Every day 40 teenagers give birth to their third child (Hodgkinson 1985).
- Every day 1,000 children are abused and 3,300 children run away (Edelman 1987).

The solutions proposed are then likely to include procedures such as raising high school graduation standards or limiting class size in the primary grades. It frequently appears as if the problems and the solutions emanate from different sources rather than from the same report. This kind of irrational thinking might be dismissed out of hand if it did not so frequently result in policy development, state mandates, and additions to urban school bureaucracies.

In more scholarly analyses the demographic indicators are often presented as areas for future study; for example, "Eighty-five percent of the one million dropouts each year possess low level basic skills" (Carnevale, Garner, and Meltzer 1988). We may then seek to explain the problem on several levels. On the individual level we might study behaviors and attributes that describe and predict who will and will not drop out. On the school level we might seek patterns and characteristics of schools that have high and low dropout rates. We might do both. Another possibility is to move the analysis to the level of the family and identify connections between the nature of families and the likelihood of particular children dropping out.

On any of these analytical levels it is necessary to create a *theoretic construct*—a way of explaining direct and indirect causes. Unless this is accomplished, the analysis is based on correlations of conditions with events that leave the reader to assume or create some explanation of causality. In the typical analysis of problems related to inner-city schooling, the analyses have focused on attributes of individual children and youth, the schools they attend, and their families (or all three) and rarely on the community context in which these units operate.

This approach to analysis also characterizes issues stated in societal terms. Consider, for example, the problem of disconnected youth assessed by the "inactivity" rate. This is the number of people age 16 to 19 who are not in school, the military, or employed relative to the number in their age group. From 1978 to 1983 this rate more than doubled. Essentially, about three and a half million American youth were disconnected or inactive in 1983 (Betsey 1985). Estimates are that this rate has continued to increase.

As with dropouts, it is possible to analyze this situation in terms of the inactive youth's attributes, background, family conditions, schooling, or all of the above. The unit of analysis least likely to be pursued and therefore least likely to be understood in terms of its educational influence is the community. Part of the explanation for this condition relates to the difficulty of studying communities.

Beliefs, perceptions, and behaviors that appear to be abnormal or self-defeating may frequently be understood as reasonable when the context in which they are generated becomes known. Seemingly self-destructive behavior may be a perfectly sensible response to a situational press exerted by a family in crisis. And what may seem to be self-generated family crises may be a family making reasonable responses to the immediate but varied demands of a particular community and the conflicting values of the larger society. For the moralist, "To understand all is to forgive all." For social scientists and educators the reason for studying these contexts and their interactions is to be able to explain their influence on the functioning of individuals and families within communities and the larger society. Useful knowledge derived from studying these units of analysis enables us more accurately to predict and more effectively to influence human development.

Schools in Communities

Because schools have a unique and primary role in the development of inner-city children and youth, they are special community institutions and should be the focus of heightened scrutiny. *But the overall focus of future studies should be a better understanding of the education of inner-city children and youth that transcends schooling and includes the influence of all the formal institutions and informal networks by which individuals learn what they know by adulthood. The totality of community influence that directly educates and*

that indirectly affects individuals, families, schools, community organiza-
tions, and personal affiliations will be the primary unit of our analysis. This
is not to assume that community-derived knowledge and belief systems are
necessarily all positive or any more relevant for success in the larger society
than the content of schooling. But to improve the functioning of inner-city
children and youth, it will be necessary to know more about what they know
and believe and under what conditions they learned it before we can develop
realistic guidelines about the most appropriate role for schools vis-a-vis other
community institutions that educate.

Before the education of inner-city children and youth can be improved,
there will have to be changes in the community contexts that educate them
directly as well as in the formal networks and associations that educate them
indirectly. The greatest indirect influence of communities on both education
and schooling may be the influence exerted by community forces on inner-
city families and peer networks.

The need for continued research and theory in systems analysis, particularly their interconnections, is recognized but presents formidable research
difficulties. Dr. David Rogers, president of the Robert Wood Johnson Foundation, in examining the multiple problems faced by low-income families,
states that "human misery is generally the result of, or accompanied by, a
great untidy basketful of intertwined and interconnected circumstances and
happenings" that often all need attention if the problems are to be overcome.
Successful programs recognize that they cannot respond to or overcome these
"untidy basketfuls" of needs without regularly crossing traditional professional and bureaucratic boundaries (Schorr and Schorr 1989).

Recognizing that we already know a great deal about various systems
that are not being utilized, *the first major goal of future research on educa-*
tion in inner cities should be to collect, synthesize in plain English, and utilize
the related research literature dealing with schools, employment, health, and
social institutions.

Employment Systems

Education for people in inner cities has long been more dependent on the
employment system than on the system of formal schooling. Inner cities have
long been populated by poor people. What makes the situation different today? First, we must recognize that urban schools never served the poor immigrant masses nearly so well as did the expanding labor market that provided jobs for "normal" eighth-grade graduates and dropouts (Tyack and
Hansot 1974). For the "involuntary" immigrants the situation was even worse.
"The notion that this nation once had good schools for the masses of African
American students but has since let them deteriorate is inaccurate." (NABSE

1984). "The institutionalization of deprivation and disenfranchisement among schools has permitted race and socio-economic status to function as the chief determinants of access to quality treatment for children. The public schools often represent an integration of society's most crippling diseases— indifference, injustice, and inequity" (NASBE 1974, 37).

Second, some analysts trace the most immediate cause of the current situation to the flight of middle-class blacks and the virtual abandonment of entire black neighborhoods to the poorest of the poor. They contend that this has broken up the black community, draining the ghetto of constructive role models for the young. It is argued that education does not and cannot have a high priority in this setting. A new kind of society has emerged in these communities, one with its own values, which is "utterly different from that of the American mainstream" (Lemann 1986). William Julius Wilson (1987) writes of neighborhoods in which "the chances are overwhelming that children will seldom interact on a sustained basis with people who are employed or with families that have a steady breadwinner . . . [where] the relationship between schooling and post-school employment takes on a different meaning" (p. 61).

Health-Social Service System

More recently, the health and human service systems have received greater attention as potential bases for improving the education of inner-city populations, either as independent systems or in connection with other community institutions and with schools.

Since the creation of Neighborhood Health Centers in the 1960s, we have been experimenting with successful ways to reorganize health care for high-risk families. "No one gets sick in a vacuum," says Dr. Aaron Shirley in explaining the success of The Jackson-Hinds Comprehensive Health Center in Mississippi, which relies upon a dual emphasis of changing high-risk environments and providing high quality services (Schorr and Schorr 1989). The Robert Wood Johnson Foundation coined the word *transmedical* to describe programs that go beyond prenatal care by reducing barriers to access ongoing help with the responsibilities of parenthood.

A second goal of future research on education in inner cities should be an analysis of usable knowledge regarding the synthesis of these major systems at the community level.

Indicators of community health reflect the popular image of the city in crisis. *Urban decline* has several meanings. In the descriptive sense it may refer to the loss of people and jobs. In the functional sense it refers to quality-of-life indicators and to the viability of social institutions (Williams 1989). In 1980, 2.5 million people (labeled the *under class*) lived in our great cities in 880 census-tract neighborhoods where more than half the men worked less than 26 weeks, 35 percent of the 16- to 19-year-olds had dropped out of school, more than a third of the families were on welfare, and 57 percent of the families were headed by women. In these 880 census tracts, 58 percent of the population are black, 11 percent are Hispanic, 28 percent are white; 367 percent are children (Weiss 1988).

In 1985, 77 percent of Americans lived in metropolitan areas; 84 percent of the black population, with 59 percent in the central core. Ninety-one percent of Hispanics lived in metropolitan areas, as did 90 percent of the over 16 million legal immigrants. Like the indicators of family, these and other statistical descriptors are used to support the view that there has been a disintegration of the traditional concepts of community.

This theme that there is, in effect, no viable community to support inner-city schools has now been asserted frequently enough for many to regard it as reliable knowledge. The degree to which this view of dead or dying communities is actually true is an issue in need of further research. It assumes that schools will continue as they now function, and, more importantly, it may underestimate the strengths in neighborhood institutions.

A third goal of future research on education in inner cities should be to learn more about formal and informal community institutions that support families and human development, so that schools might be guided into becoming more relevant and more effective in many inner-city communities now written off by outside analysts.

School Systems

Building a sense of community among inner-city students *in* schools that connect with their lives out of school has now been done frequently enough to support the belief that human capital and viable community institutions do exist. Edmonds's (1982) effective school guidelines are essentially in-school procedures and have helped some inner-city schools improve. But assuming altered forms of schooling *and* connections with formal and informal community institutions, we have yet to learn the potential for improving inner-city education.

There is substantial evidence that changing school climate *and* involving parents on a School Planning and Management Team will substantially raise not only the achievement of low-income, at-risk children but will change their self-concepts and motivation as well. By making teams of school professionals and aides with parents, the "forces of confusion and conflict can be interrupted" (Comer 1984). Deborah Meier's vision of a good school, while different from Comer's, seems equally effective. At Central Park East High School where she is principal, "learning by doing" and "curriculum relevance" are more important themes than school climate. In both the Comer and Meier cases, parental involvement is a critical base for building a new common vision of schooling.

One current approach is that schools must be restructured, but that the schools are, should be, or can become the center of the adolescent's world. If only schooling can become more than a matter of compliance (Elmore 1987). If only students can be made to recognize that teachers can profoundly influence their lives (Elmore 1987). If only educational leaders would "assume the disposition that they can help create a learning community ethos . . ." (Mitchell 1990). These exhortations about schools, teachers, and students all can garner some support from the research literature, but the limit of their usefulness as a conceptual framework seems to have been reached. The problems of inner-city schools not only continue to exist but are worsening. The solution is not to correct the process of blaming the victims by spreading the blame among schools, teachers, families, neighborhoods, and peers. The latter group and its negative influence have been well-documented by researchers who found that many black adolescents are frightened of "acting white." "Peer group pressures against academic striving take many forms, including labeling, exclusion from peer activities or ostracism and physical assault" (Fordham and Ogbu 1986).

Using the school as the unit of analysis, the current change proposals are choice and site-based management: The former empowers parents; the latter empowers teachers. The appeal of these initiatives is not only that they focus on schools, which are assumed to be more amenable to change than are families or communities, but that such changes can theoretically be accomplished within existing budgets.

Because no one is forced to be in a particular school, everyone in a true school of choice has freely self-selected to be there. This ostensibly leads to a shared vision among staff, students, and parents, who can then set out to make *their school an excellent example of their common ideals. Much of the current debate over choice plans relates to differing perceptions of whether true diversity among schools really exists and whether genuine opportunity for entrance into schools of choice can be provided to sufficient numbers of students.*

The concept of site-based management also continues to be widely tested. Using data from 1,000 public and private high schools, one study found that mandates from states and school systems had produced no real improvement in student performance (Chubb and Moe 1988). These researchers concluded that the most crucial element of high-achieving schools was the school's organization, defined as the school's freedom from higher-level administrative control. It is this freedom that permits staff and parents to create a shared vision of education. They concluded that "attendance at an effectively organized high school for four years is worth at least a full year of additional attendance at an ineffectively organized school" (p. 214).

Proposals for Changes

Of the unending proposals for changing individuals, teachers, schools, families, and peer groups, special attention must be given to building schools that transcend traditional distinctions between learning in and out of school, between schooling as a traditional process limited in time and place to the institution of school, and education as a continual life process that occurs in a variety of community contexts.

Inner-city schools are now living out the consequences of the needless rift between learning in school and learning in the community which we were warned against long ago (Dewey 1902). These distinctions need not exist but have unfortunately come to characterize the difference between learning inside and outside of schools.

> *Schooling focuses on the individual's performance, whereas out-of-school mental work is often socially shared. Schooling aims to foster unaided thought, whereas mental work outside school usually involves cognitive tools. School cultivates symbolic thinking whereas mental activity outside school engages directly with objects and situations. Finally, schooling aims to teach general skills and knowledge, whereas situation-specific competencies dominate outside. (Resnick 1987)*

What Dewey asserted with less jargon is that learning is cooperative, experience-based, practical, and not derived from a specific context. Is it the community or the school that meets these criteria?

Views of Schools as the Problem, or the Solution?

In the current debates on the appropriate role of schools and particularly on inner-city schools, there are frequently unspoken understandings that send mixed messages. Schools are sometimes defined as the problem for inner-city children and youth and at other times as the basis of the solution. Considering this range of views regarding urban schools on a continuum, the extreme view of schools as the solution assumes they can exercise an ever-increasing role given sufficient funds and personnel. Without stating this extreme position directly, this is the apparent view of many urban school superintendents who seek a role and funds for expanded vocational training, preschool programs, after-school programs, parent education, literacy training, and anything else that is available. A more "reasonable" position but one that still regards schools as the solution is that schools can broker everything. Consider the following:

Under a new vision the school could become the site or broker of numerous services such as health clinics, child care, alcohol and drug abuse programs, and organized recreation programs. More child care and preschool programs could be located on or near school grounds to provide a better transition with the regular school program. While the school should not financially underwrite these services, it could provide the facilities and welcome city, county, and private agencies to school grounds. Schools would need additional funds to help provide integrated case management of the student with multiple problems and would not be the only place where interagency collaboration might take place. The familiarity of a case manager with all matters of consequence currently affecting the family would improve assistance to parents and youth and help prevent problems before they emerge or become severe. (Kirst and McLaughlin 1990)

This vision recognizes that schools cannot do it all and that health and welfare agencies, churches, the courts, and various programs all affect critical components of children's and youths' lives. But, essentially this view advocates an expanded new way of conceiving the school as bringing together all institutions that affect students' lives. Newly staffed with a cadre of case managers, the schools are now supposed to broker the world for their clients.

More modest views of schools that still regard them as the solution are those in favor of making them more effective given existing structures and existing budgets. This is the position still shared by the majority of taxpayers and supported by a body of research literature (Edmonds 1982).

The New Futures initiative in Lawrence, Massachusetts (one of five cities participating in this project funded by the Annie E. Casey Foundation) is an example of a combined school-community initiative that cuts across multiple programs and institutional changes that must occur within and outside of schools. It is an effort to integrate supportive policies and programs in all relevant youth-serving programs. An Oversight Collaborative was established in each of five New Futures cities to mediate conflicts that might arise among agencies. This model demonstrates greater sophistication than the case manager or school as the broker approach. It is still to be determined whether it can overcome the challenges identified by evaluators (Center for the Study of Social Policy 1989).

Moving across the continuum, the school as solution becomes the school as the problem. On this side are those concerned with increasingly more basic restructuring efforts. Eventually, restructuring is abandoned in favor of plans for parental choice and voucher plans, which argue, in effect, that some schools can only be closed. In some cases, states (e.g., New Jersey) declare a system bankrupt and take over a whole system, as in Jersey City. At the extreme end of the school-as-problem continuum is the advocacy to close and abandon all of them. The proposal to place schools in workplaces would be an example of this view (Hoffer and Coleman 1990).

Solutions within the Community Context

In sum, the various concepts of school as the solution or school as the problem run the gamut of proposals from having schools do it all to having them disappear. However compelling the arguments may be about the need for parental and familial support for their children's schools, the assumption that there must be a tight fit between expectations and realities as a precondition for success in school ignores current social realities. Demographic and cultural indicators show the altered functions that families, community institutions, and schools now play in the total education of children and youth. Today's reform policies are no more likely to "fix" the problems of American youth than did the social policies of the past. Remedies focused on home–school relationships are unlikely to succeed because they ignore the structural realities of today's families, the community resources available to families, and the families' abilities to interact with these community resources and schools. Taken as a whole, indicators of community, school, and family relationships present strong evidence that schools cannot overcome demographic, social, and political realities simply by expanding curriculum, or adopting a parent education program, or testing more, or changing programs for preparing teachers and administrators (Wagstaff and Gallagher 1990). It is my contention that these proposals are not weak simply because they are unrealistic or beyond implementation. They are flawed because they place schools at the center of all children's and youths' learning and assume that schools can build a new social order. My contention is that while schools are clearly the official institution charged with formal schooling, education in the real world occurs in multiple contexts, in combination and in conflict with one another. Education happens.

A fourth goal of future research on education in inner cities should be to learn more about how various community contexts educate (or miseducate) directly and interrelate in their educational impact on children and youth in order to assess and predict the potential of specific educational initiatives in particular communities.

Thus far, I have argued several points: That as the official institution, schools must remain the focus of heightened scrutiny; that education, however, occurs in the community through a variety of institutions and structures; that education in the community also includes powerful informal networks; that education gained from community contexts is not necessarily positive; that the overall community context strongly affects and controls family institutions and schools and may facilitate or prevent changes that may be initiated in schools; that to begin with school change as the basis for changing community structures is antithetic to how people learn, how they live, and the power of communities over their schools; and that the most fruitful model of educational change would be to first create a model of how specific communities educate and then make assessments of particular initiatives.

Each inner-city community creates special tensions for its schools as the schools try to maintain historical functions, adapt to new state mandates, and respond to diverse and frequently conflicting demands of community constituencies. There is no question that local school conflict is shaped by forces outside *and* inside the community. Indeed, there is some question as to whether most inner city schools are *of* their communities at all and not merely institutions almost completely shaped by external forces, staffed by visiting aliens, and effectively walled off from the communities they "serve."

The model of community that should be studied encompasses both the immediately identifiable community institutions that shape and educate people (e.g., local churches, clinics, courts) and the systems of the larger society that also impinge upon and control the lives and expectations of people. The broad contexts with which future research should be concerned include: education systems, including schools; health systems; economic systems, including income maintenance; social service systems; housing systems; political systems; religious and service systems; community organizations and subculture; communication systems, including the media; and transportation systems.

A final goal of future research on education in inner cities should be to provide a framework for considering critical questions: What is the nature of inner-city communities in terms of the education—in addition to schooling—they provide children, youth, and their families? How does this education support or refute the schooling offered to these constituencies? What are the educational expectations of inner-city residents for their children? And the most critical question: What is the nature of the life conditions under which families live that predispose their children to benefit from education delivered by schools as well as other community institutions?

Implications for Teacher Education

Future teachers are needed for inner-city schools who are neither fearful of the inhabitants, nor ignorant of their lives, nor unwilling to interact with community organizations and institutions. Indeed, the teachers needed should be proud of the children they teach, pleased about becoming partners with their parents, and familiar with the neighborhoods in which they work. Further, teachers need to be active students of the resources in their school-communities, learn as much as they can about what their children are learning outside of school, and know how and under what conditions this learning takes place.

Specifically, I would require the following content in all teacher education programs that claim to be preparing teachers for inner-city schools. These are not topics to be included in more required college courses since the typical faculty in schools of education are neither experienced nor expert in these subjects. These topics can be learned best by direct experiences in schools and communities under the guidance of experienced coaches. Such high-level coaches are most likely to be drawn from among the most able, current, inner-city classroom teachers. There may also be some college faculty who have had recent successful experiences in urban schools and neighborhoods who can also coach. These are also needed:

I. Understanding and sensitivity to the cultures of particular neighborhoods. This understanding is manifested, in part, by a familiarity with how children grow and develop in various families and ethnic groups: black, Hispanic, Asian, Arabic, etc.

II. Language facility with "Spanglish," "Black English," and the particular language problems encountered by specific ethnic groups in learning standard forms.

III. Knowledge of neighborhood organizations, agencies, and institutions that educate and, specifically, of how children and youth participate in and interact with such organizations. This includes informal groups such as gangs.

IV. Understanding how various health delivery systems affect the neighborhood. Total health care is basic to children's and youths' school learning.

V. Understanding the economic life of the neighborhood, including the shadow economy. How do the people who take care of children get the money to rear them?

VI. Skills in making home visits, making community studies, taking neighborhood walks. These skills involve issues of safety and the ability to learn from the school environment. People unable to interact with the children, their families, and the people in the neighborhoods cannot teach in the schools of that community. It should be clear, but still is not, that in the effort to achieve this level of knowledge, understanding, and skill with future teachers, traditional college courses will continue to be irrelevant.

VII. Knowledge of how governmental systems, specifically criminal justice, welfare, and health, affect (or ignore) the lives of the families in the community. How are the critical issues of drugs, safety, and abuse currently dealt with?

Schools cannot be foreign legion outposts in a hostile occupied country staffed by foreign mercenaries. To be successful, teachers of the people's children must be of, by, and for the people of the community.

Today in our cities, most learning occurs outside the classroom. The sheer quantity of information conveyed by press, magazines, film, TV, and radio far exceeds the quantity of information conveyed by school instruction and texts. This challenge has destroyed the monopoly of the book as a teaching aid and cracked the very walls of the classroom.
—MARSHALL McLUHAN

CHAPTER THREE

Helping Families with Developmentally Delayed Children: POP as an Model of Parental Involvement

MALCOLM GARBER

Editor's Note: There are many children who, for one reason or another, do not do well in school or in other learning situations. The causes are as numerous as there are cases. It is important to recognize that inappropriate labeling can be most harmful in that it suggests things about children that may be untrue and, particularly, unfair. Not every child who does not sit up straight in class should be classified as a candidate for "special education."

However, there are children who do have special problems that mandate special concern at home and in school. Who are these children? How do families and educators best relate to them? This chapter defines issues, clarifies concerns, and provides insight into some research as well as programs that attempt to deal with this important issue. Special mention is given to the work of Ira Gordon and his colleagues, who developed and pioneered one of the most successful parent-intervention models still in operation.

The Parent Outreach Program (POP) has been helping parents of developmentally delayed children in Toronto since 1975. Paraprofessionals, themselves parents of delayed children, visit other parents, usually once a week, to teach them management strategies, to help coordinate teaching efforts between home and school, and to provide information about available community services. All of the families have a moderately to severely delayed son or daughter who may be mentally retarded, autistic, physically handicapped and/or a combination of all three. The purpose of this chapter, first, is to review some of the important and interesting ideas concerning families with such children. Second, an outline of the procedures employed in the POP will be contrasted with the implementation strategies of the Florida Parent Educator Model developed by Ira Gordon at the Institute for Human Development. Third, a review of evaluation studies of the POP will be provided. Fourth, a description of the POP is provided. Fifth, strategies for program implementation in Third-World countries will be outlined.

Families with Developmentally Delayed Sons or Daughters

Research attentive to families with developmentally delayed children has produced inconsistent, often contradictory findings (Crnic, Friedrich and Greenberg 1983). Experts have claimed that "the effect of the mentally retarded child on his family is most profound and that family life is greatly altered from what it had been previously (Fisher and Roberts 1983, 399).

This idea is predicated on the notion that a type of illness emerges in families upon the birth of a special child. The illness may even be seen to proceed through different phases: "The various stages through which the family goes are: 1) a period of denial, 2) a search for a cure, 3) an attempt to find help for one's own child, and 4) a movement to find help for all retardates" (Fisher and Roberts 1983, 399).

Expert claims about the dysfunctional characteristics of families with exceptional children have been emphatically disputed by Byrne and Cunningham (1985). Referring to the approach as "pathological", they suggest the following:

> This approach assumed that such families are subject to high levels of stress which cause psychological impairment among some, if not all, family members. The assumption that psychological impairment is an inevitable consequence for family members has led in turn to generalization that families of mentally handicapped children form a homogenous group. (p. 847)

A stereotyped perspective of the family with a developmentally delayed member is offered by this deficit model. Professionals and others with such a bias reflect a prejudice that is not based on the actual facts, though this selective perception may have been produced by publications in the field. Crnic, Friedrich, and Greenberg (1983) suggest the following:

> In general, the available literature suggests that the parents and siblings of retarded children individually, as well as the family as a whole,

are at-risk for numerous difficulties in comparison to families with nonretarded children. In spite of these suggestions, inconsistent and contradictory reports are common, due primarily to variations in methodological adequacy, . . . A genuine bias has also existed toward expecting a deleterious or pathological outcome in these families. (p. 132)

In their extensive review of the scientific studies pertaining to families with exceptional children, Bryne and Cunningham (1985) divided the current research literature into three categories: The first seeks to discover which families and which family members are most vulnerable to the presumed stress generated by a mentally retarded family member. Their summary of this first category of research study follows:

The main conclusion of the research which has developed from this first approach is that stress is not an inevitable consequence for families with mentally handicapped children. A combination of factors which as the presence of multiple stresses, the life-cycle stage of the family, the family's interpretation of their situation and the integration of the family prior to the birth of the child appear to predict which families will experience stress and anxiety. (p. 852)

In contrast to the deficit viewpoint that these families are rendered dysfunctional through stress, such stress may not be inevitable. Several of the same factors that would influence stress-producing occurrences in any family have similarly been found to generate stress in families with developmentally delayed children.

Bryne and Cunningham's second approach to research explores the material and practical problems experienced by families and how services might be organized to overcome these difficulties. This approach suggests that it is not the presence of the mentally handicapped child that leads to family stress but, rather the unmet service needs of the family. Because this second category of research tends to be service-oriented, practical, and often lacking adequate scientific controls, conclusions are difficult to summarize. One finding worth reporting is that mothers indicated that they needed additional support with regard to special relief. Such help would be especially welcome during school holidays and weekends. Also, mothers expressed the need for additional baby sitting services and help with transportation. Parents were concerned about their young adult sons and daughters finding jobs, leaving home, and surviving the death of the parents. Too, parents seemed to agree that social services were cumbersome, slow, and insensitive. Finally, marital satisfaction or the security a mother felt in marriage was the best overall predictor of the family's coping behavior.

Bryne and Cunningham's third area of research emphasized the competence of families with developmentally delayed children. It highlighted the differences among such families as well as the similarities to families with nonhandicapped children. The fact that stress is experienced however, "emphasis is placed on the resources which are available to different families to enable them to develop their own coping strategies" (Bryne and Cunningham 1985, 854).

Ways of behaving and special understandings that reduce stress are what is meant by *coping*. Families have certain resources that can be employed to cope more effectively. Coping may be facilitated when the family members are physically healthy, when the family's problem-solving skills are enhanced, when their perceptions and attitudes are adequately framed, and when assistance is available from a support network within as well as outside the family. This third area of research concentrates on the way the family reduces stress through the use of its coping resources.

Inherent in this approach are ideas that come from the science of *ecology*. Ecologists study a field of interactions rather than a single causal relationship. The field is circumscribed by a chain of interdependent causal relationships rather than the impact of a single event on another. An example of this chain of ecological interrelationship is Lovelock's (1984) work on the Gaia hypothesis: "This work resulted in the Gaia hypothesis, which suggests that the entire range of living matter on Earth, from whales to viruses can be regarded as a single entity, capable of manipulating its environment to suit its needs" (p. 100). Lovelock maintains that the world is like one gigantic organism, with the living and dying of every individual life form providing a balance for the rest of the planet's survival.

The family may be regarded as an ecosystem in miniature. The way a child behaves with its mother is dependent on more than just the way the mother stimulates the child (Crnic, Friedrich, and Greenberg 1983). "Family functioning cannot be considered simply as a response to a retarded child; rather, it is more meaningful to consider familial adaptation as a response to the child mediated by the coping resources available and influenced by the family's ecological environments" (p. 136).

For example, how the child feels physically can influence his or her behavior. The way the mother and father are getting along with each other can have a bearing on the interactions between the child and the parent. The child's self-esteem, moderated by physical motivators, may influence the feelings of the child's mother and her interactions with the father. For instance, sensing that a child feels inadequate can be depressing to the extent that a parent curtails expressing warmth and acceptance toward other family members. Lacking ample emotional nurturing at home could diminish a person's flexibility and work performance. The parent's behavior on the job can also alter the child's physical well-being, especially if the parent loses his or her job so that income for healthy nutrition is insufficient.

The ecological field includes the child's physical state changed by nutrition, affected by a parent's job, upset by the relationship between mother and father, swayed by the relationship between mother and child, altered by the child's self-esteem, and influenced by interaction with the mother and father that, in turn, challenges the child's physical condition. And this is only a small part of the field, which also includes the reciprocal impact of institutions such as the school, the housing situation, health care services, social services, income level, social class values, the economy, political predicaments, and cultural variables — all of which influence each other as well as the child.

A multifaceted ecological approach to working with families of developmentally delayed children would be the recommended outcome of this current model of research. As suggested above, coping may be facilitated when family members are physically healthy, when the family's problem-solving skills are enhanced, when perceptions and attitudes are adequately framed, and when the family has adequate assistance from a support network.

Three ecological objectives of POP (Parent Outreach Program) are:

1. To maximize the resources within the families of exceptional children
2. To maximize the family's knowledge and use of existing resources within the community
3. To maximize the development of new, necessary resources not already in place within the community (Garber, Perry, and Stanley 1987).

Though POP resembles the approach to helping parents recommended by Gordon (1977), it also differs in many ways. The program was influenced to a very large extent by the ideas developed by Gordon that produced the Florida Parent Educator Model Follow Through and Planned Variation Headstart early childhood intervention programs (Maccoby and Zellner 1970). What follows is a description of POP comparing it to Gordon's Florida Parent Educator Model.

POP and the Parent Educator Model

Though the POP was organized to help parents and their developmentally delayed children in the Toronto area, it had been pioneered in 11 Florida Parent Educator Model Follow Through communities and 4 Planned Variation Headstart localities throughout the United States.

The POP model originated through collaboration with Ira J. Gordon, whose cognitive approach to working with disadvantaged children in the Florida Planned Variation Follow Through Program was influenced by Piaget's (1963) cognitive developmental theory, the humanistic considerations of Combs (1959), as well as from his own research (1970). Gordon's technique included the use of paraprofessionals who would work in the classroom as teaching assistants and then deliver teaching ideas to parents through regular weekly home visits. The teaching ideas were prescriptions for parents, designed to generate thinking skills in children through the presentation of interesting and challenging professionally developed tasks. From these tasks parents would learn to engage their children in a way that would foster cognitive growth, while children would increase their capacity to learn and problem solve. Recipients were parents and their at-risk children living in both urban and rural setrtings throughout the United States who, because of a culture of poverty, diverged from middle-majority norms. Paraprofessionals worked on a full-time basis and were selected from the same population as the recipients.

The present POP approach differs from Gordon's program in the following ways:

1. Recipients are parents and their children who are developmentally delayed as opposed to culturally divergent. Though there are some parents in POP who differ from the majority on the basis of poverty, most families resemble the middle-majority with respect to income level. The children in the program have intellectual impairments. These may range from moderate through severe to profound, not as a result of poverty but through delays in development due to such factors as genetic abnormalities, infections, gestation problems, traumas, etc.

2. The teaching ideas that POP delivers to homes have parent-selected behavioral objectives. Tasks are developed in conjunction with parents and employ techniques of behavior modification. The emphasis in POP is on helping parents learn to do the following: set behavioral objectives, reduce the objectives into a series of behavioral steps, and select appropriate reinforcers to modify behaviors. This contrasts with the more cognitively oriented approach taken by Gordon in which parents were taught to engage in activities that would develop cognitive skills such as classification, conservation, seriation, etc., thereby enhancing the development of operational thinking ability in the child. Further, Gordon's teaching ideas were developed by professional task writers, often teachers, and did not focus on activities chosen by parents. However, tasks were designed to be interesting and pleasant for both child and parent.

3. POP paraprofessionals teach parents to work with their children in the home, as they did in the Florida program. Also, they provide information concerning services for families that are available within the community. Information regarding services is systematically presented regularly on an updated computer screen. The Florida workers, who labored without benefit of computers, were able to provide similar information.

4. Bi-weekly visits to the school are made to keep the teacher informed

of what is taking place at home so that teaching efforts can be coordinated. Even though POP paraprofessionals teach parents in their home, they do not assist the teacher in the classroom, nor do they take direction from teachers as they did in Gordon's program. In the POP program they work directly on behalf of the parent.

5. Computers are used to focus the home visits, to store and provide information regarding teaching progress, and to collect information for quarterly reports of progress in the POP program. Gordon's program employed paper and pencil techniques for the same purposes.

6. The POP uses computer-based assessment and task-development devices. A 527-item behavioral checklist specifying behaviors in a quasi-hierarchical order has been created for evaluation purposes. Parents are able to select teaching ideas from a library of over 3,000 tasks that are meshed to checklist items. This technology was not available in Gordon's program. In the Florida Parent Educator Programs, assessments of the home environment, teacher practices, classroom interactions, affective development, and the weekly home visit were collected.

7. In both programs, paraprofessionals are selected only if they have children with problems similar to those of their clients. In Gordon's program, paraprofessionals were members of a culturally divergent target group. POP paraprofessionals are parents with developmentally delayed children.

8. The Florida Parent Education Follow Through Model received funding support from the Office of Child Development of the U.S. Department of Education. The POP is funded through yearly grants from the Ontario Ministry of Community and Social Service.

Gordon and his associates (1969) at the Institute for the Development of Human Resources pioneered community-based home visitation programming. By delivering teaching ideas to families in their homes, POP paraprofessionals operate in ways similar to those in Gordon's program. There are similarities between both programs in the way the home visitation process is monitored and the way people with similar problems form a support network for each other.

On the other hand, POP differs from Gordon's programs. Not only are computers used to monitor the teaching that takes place in the home, but the teaching itself is different. Parents decide what they want to teach their children, and they participate in the development of the teaching ideas. Though the paraprofessionals visit schools, they do not work in the classrooms with teachers. Visits are undertaken only to coordinate the home teaching with the teaching taking place in the schools. Instruments have been developed that provide a range of target goals that parents can select to teach their children. The home visit is guided by the computer in the sense that the computer is responded to by both the parent and the paraprofessional. Other computerized evaluation instruments assess teaching outcomes.

Aside from technological differences, POP uses a version of behavioral management that Gordon considered antithetical to his particular philosophy of education. In the POP, parents select behavioral objectives, then reduce them to minimally acceptable steps that can then be rewarded. Rewards are an integral part of the teaching and learning that takes place. Never is a task recommended that uses punishment. Always the positive is accentuated so that the family can smile as teaching and learning occur. While the affective aspect of this approach would, no doubt, have been endorsed by Gordon, he was not interested in teaching parents to modify their children's behaviors. Though this behavioral approach was frowned upon, there is evidence that the POP has been successful.

Evaluation of the POP

Evidence of POP's general effectiveness comes from several sources. Baig (1976) found that 23 children who had participated in the program for 6 months showed significant gains in adaptive behavior, mental age, and goal attainment as compared to 15 children in a no-treatment control group. He also observed that parents in the program had made significant positive changes with respect to their teaching styles. Similarly, Rawson (1977) established that improvements in mental age had occurred in 10 children, as well as improvements in parents' teaching styles. Wadeson (1978) also compared a group of 33 children in the program to a control group and reported statistically significant gains in goal attainment and intelligence test scores for those in the Parent Outreach Program. Two studies (Garber, Pass, and Perry 1985; Garber, Perry, and Stanley 1987) investigated teachers' reactions to working with POP paraprofessionals and found that the program was of value in teaching the child at school and coordinating efforts between the home and the school. Garber, Lindsay, and Perry (1989) reported that parents seemed to find the computer a welcome adjunct to the program. Caruso (1990) also found that parents seemed to appreciate the way the program was delivered by paraprofessionals using the computer. They claimed to be more able to observe progress in their children using the computer; as well, the parents reported finding the computer more interesting to use than paper and pencil instruments. In general, these investigations revealed the program had an impact on the way parents taught their child, that teachers and parents felt the program had improved the children's performance, and that it facilitated communication between parents and teachers.

Program Description

POP operates under a board of directors who represent various community constituencies including parents, agencies serving developmentally delayed people, and the school system. The board of directors has delegated responsibility for program management to the executive director, who is a nonprofessional parent of a developmentally delayed child. The executive director is responsible for operating the entire program, from budget planning to providing services and liaison with other community agencies. Also, the director is responsible for reporting progress quarterly to the board of directors and to the Ontario Ministry of Community and Social Services.

Both the assistant program director and the secretary are also parents of developmentally delayed children. They have worked as paraprofessionals, as has the executive director, and they continue to make at least one weekly home visit to maintain their sensitivity to the issues surrounding the home visiting process. The assistant director reviews and rewrites teaching ideas, which are called *tasks*. Tasks that have proven to be successful are stored in a task library. Task management in the office is only one of the jobs of the assistant director. Speaking at various community agencies, preparing quarterly reports, assisting in training new staff, and organizing and storing information on the computer are work responsibilities with which the assistant director helps the executive director. The secretary contributes to the program by doing the bookkeeping and much of the client intake, answering the phone, and writing checks. Payroll is managed by a paraprofessional who has taken this additional responsibility. No one in the central office, other than the executive director, is employed full-time. All have flexible working schedules that permit them to meet their family commitments.

The bulk of the work of the program is accomplished by paraprofessionals who are also parents of developmentally delayed children. They are trained to make home visits, teach parents more effectively to teach their children using behavior modification techniques, provide information about community services that are available for the child and family, and employ the computer in the process. Paraprofessionals work on a part-time basis so that they can schedule their time around the competing demands of the job and the needs of their own families. A training manual outlining the specifics of preservice training has been developed. Usually, it takes 10 days to generate sufficient skills for working as a paraprofessional. Additionally, inservice training including staff debriefing is undertaken on a regular basis throughout the work year, which starts in September and ends in June.

The program advisor who originated the program assists in staff training as well as trouble shooting and evaluating the program. Some advice regarding the general operation of the program is also provided by the program advisor. However, it must be emphasized that the program currently operates under the direction of its board of directors mainly through the efforts of the executive director and the rest of the staff. This is a self-help program, run by parents for parents.

POP is a program that is located in the metropolitan Toronto community and is run by the people of that community. As such, it meets their needs, their way.

Implementation in Third-World Countries

Very likely, what works well in Toronto will need radical change to be effective in the third world. However, certain program aspects may not need much alteration.

It is assumed that children can be effectively taught by their parents. Techniques that focus on changing behaviors through the process of reinforcing increments of behaviors *(shaping)* should be helpful. Practices that foster cognitive growth other than behavioral management would be welcome, too. Using paraprofessionals who are parents from the program's target area should marshal an involved, sensitive staff.

Even though the assumption is made that these aspects of the program need not be changed, the possibility exists that a few or even many of these program aspects would require changes. However, there is no doubt that two instruments, the Adaptive Behaviors Checklist and the Weekly Evaluation Report Document, will definitely have to be revised.

Adaptive Behaviors Checklist

The Adaptive Behaviors Checklist is modeled after the Adaptive Behaviors Scale (Nihira et al. 1974). No assessment device could be more culturally biased. After all, developmental tasks that deal with personal hygiene, eating, communicating, getting along with others, and similar skills are highly dependent on social norms. For example, though eating with cutlery may be considered an essential aspect of social development in Toronto, Canada, using the fingers to feed oneself may be considered of equal importance in Ajmeer, India. Assessment of culturally relevant aspects of what is deemed important to development necessitates engineering an inventory of a hierarchically ordered set of behaviors that reflect the culture to which the child belongs.

Baine (1988) has recommended that ecological inventories be employed in developing countries for building special education curriculum. Techniques for developing them have been described by Brown and colleagues (1984). The Adaptive Behavior Checklist is an example of an ecological inventory that can be constructed with the assistance of local individuals working in conjunction with POP staff. David and Garber (1989) and Kangethe and Garber (1989) have suggested the possibility that this checklist could be revised for use in India and Kenya.

Weekly Evaluation Report Document

The Weekly Evaluation Report Document plays a dual role in the delivery of service within the POP. First, it focuses the home visit on target behaviors deemed essential to successfully completing a home visit. Second, it provides information regarding the success of the teaching endeavors.

A successful home visit would deal with the following matters:

1. Coding the new teaching task
2. Determining how the new task was delivered to the parent
3. Assessing the child's learning
4. Teaching the parent about setting behavioral objectives
5. Reviewing the issues involved in shaping behaviors
6. Examining the use of reinforcers
7. Developing new teaching ideas
8. Using social services that are available in the community

Since home visits in POP are assisted with portable computers, parents in the POP complete the weekly evaluation form together with the paraprofessional via the computer screen. In third-world countries where computer-delivered teaching ideas may not be feasible either because of lack of funding or cultural restrictions, evaluations of the teaching process can be accomplished with the paper and pencil techniques of the recent past in both Gordon's program and the POP. However, a central office computer would be helpful to connect with Canadian POP staff for assistance.

No great effort is needed to revise the Weekly Evaluation Review Document to accommodate special community requirements. Present POP staff working together with local individuals can design a formative evaluation tool that resembles the present review document but is tailored to the special requirements of a targeted third-world community.

Other Potential Change Areas

POP paraprofessionals reach out into the community by visiting parents in their homes with individualized teaching ideas. Though home visiting is the preferred procedure in Toronto, there may be cutural or monetary reasons for bringing parents to center-based programs in third-world countries.

The possibility of employing professionals in a center-based program may be entertained, though one would miss the special sensitivity of a paraprofessional making a home visit. Year-end evaluations of POP by Garber, Perry, and Stanley (1987) and Garber, Pass, and Perry (1985) indicate strong parental and teacher endorsement of paraprofessional home visits.

Nevertheless, community-based delivery of service in third-world countries remains a viable alternative. The POP delivery system could be modified to accommodate third-world needs. The key is flexibility.

Computer linkages over a system such as Bitnet, using modems and telephones, can connect central offices in third-world countries to a university computer in Toronto. Through such a linkage, tasks can be reviewed and revised for weekly home delivery with the help of POP staff. Also, task libraries, written in culturally significant languages or dialects, could be developed and stored in files rather than computers if desired. Third-world staff can be assisted in developing task-writing skills, in creating an ecological assessment inventory, in focusing the weekly home visit, and in tailoring their own formative evaluation device.

With intensive preservice training courses and computer-assisted inservice instruction, workers in third-world countries could learn the skills necessary to deliver individualized services. The technology for constructing special education programs exists, though different inventories and program evaluation procedures would need to be constructed. With the desire and the funding, service programs similar to POP for families with developmentally delayed children can be put in place.

The Parent Outreach Program is a program through which parents reach out and provide help to other parents. Helping others is self-rewarding. As third-world people master the skills necessary to provide service on their own, we in first-world countries can learn from their experiences. In the process of reaching out to parents of other nations, as they have to other parents in Toronto, the POP staff would benefit, just as any teacher learns from the process of teaching. POP looks forward to the challenge and its rewards.

Summary

In summary, families with developmentally delayed children differ among themselves, but they are not necessarily different than other families. Viewing them as a homogeneous, suffering, dysfunctional group reflects a bias that is not supported by the current literature. An ecological model has been suggested that would help families meet their needs. The Parent Outreach Program was put forth as a program that serves many of the needs of families with developmentally delayed children from an ecological perspective. Comparisons with the Florida Parent Educator Model were made to illustrate how it originated. The POP was described, and studies evaluating it were reviewed. Finally, the possibility of POP parents aiding families in third-world countries was appraised.

Recent events show us that a combination of forces in politics, social change, law, education, and science makes this a time of flux and an optimum moment for seeking new ways for home and school to get together. — *IRA J. GORDON*

CHAPTER FOUR

The School–Family Link: A Key to Dropout Prevention

JOHN V. HAMBY

Editor's Note: In many instances, circumstances have been created that almost mandate unsuccessful school experiences for today's young people. If it were a matter of correcting one facet of the educational experience, it would be accomplished. Why is it that in many of our communities up to 50 percent of our children will drop out of school? Is it poor teaching? Inadequate schools? Lack of parental involvement? Poorly motivated students? Substandard community commitment? Little or no encouragement from government? All of the above? None of the above?

Children who do not or cannot attend to learning will not learn. If what we offer is so unappealing that students do not want to drop in, then surely they will drop out. Just who owns this problem?

Each year nearly a half-million students drop out of public school in the United States (Kaufman and Frase 1990), with an annual economic impact of billions of dollars in lost tax revenues, welfare payments, and crime prevention (Catterall 1986). A more serious effect, however, is the destruction of human potential that slams the door of opportunity in the faces of millions of young people, blocks their path to the American dream, and locks them into a life of disappointment and hardship.

Careful study of the dropout phenomenon reveals it to be a symptom of more serious conditions that have their roots deep in the foundation of our society. Annual estimates of adolescent behavior reveal the following:

- Three-quarters of a million unwed teenage females become pregnant.
- About the same number of children are physically abused, and about 2 percent of boys and 10 percent of girls are sexually abused.
- Almost half a million young people attempt suicide and 7,000 succeed (Capuzzi and Cross 1989).
- Nearly 150,000 youth run away from home (Willis 1986).

Since 1960:

- Arrests for teenage drug abuse have increased sixty-fold.
- Crime rates for youth or young people under age 21 have increased to the point that they now account for more than half the arrests for serious crime.
- Homicide rates for nonwhite teens increased by 16 percent; those for whites increased by 232 percent (Peck, Law, and Mills 1989).

Solutions to these youth problems will be difficult, costly, and long-term because they are complex, involving many segments of society. Nothing short of an ecological, continuum-of-treatment approach to dealing with school dropouts and other youth problems will suffice.

Dropping out of School—Causes versus Correlates

Efforts to reduce the dropout rate are often misdirected because of assumptions about causes. Programs are designed and policies are legislated based on the belief that students' personal characteristics cause them to drop out of school. Thus, efforts are directed toward changing students so they will be more successful and stay in school. Actually, few factors that accurately predict dropping out of school are characteristics of students (Obrzut 1987; Brown 1988; Wells, Bechard, and Hamby 1989; Weber and Klingler 1990; Wells 1990). More often than not, they are factors over which a child has little or no control, such as low socioeconomic level, minority status, parents or siblings who dropped out of school, unstable home environment, physical problems, limited English proficiency, and low intellectual level. Even factors such as frequent school absences and tardies, emotional problems, poor grades and low achievement test scores, grade retention, and discipline problems are not simply characteristics of a student or the student's behavior. Rather, they are products of countless interactions among a variety of individuals and events in the child's life.

Furthermore, some educators and elected officials continue to prescribe single solutions to the dropout problem because they believe in a single cause (Edelman 1987). They fail to realize that "human development is not influenced by one factor but by a whole mosaic of factors. . . . Development has no single cause; development is shaped by multiple factors working together" (Bogenschneider, Small, and Riley 1990). Poverty, limited reading ability, low school grades, or an unstable home environment alone are not more likely to place a child at risk than if none of these factors existed. However, when two of these factors are present in a child's life, the chances of a problem developing are increased four-fold. When four or more of these conditions exist, the risk increases as much as ten- to twenty-fold (Rutter 1979).

The point is not to absolve young people of all the responsibility of dropping out of school. Clearly, as children grow older, they are capable of making choices and must learn to accept control for their lives and the consequences of their behaviors. However, we must recognize that in the final analysis, adults are responsible for children and what they become. If children are at risk, adults — parents and nonparents alike — must accept a large share of the blame. Bogenschneider, Small, and Riley (1990) made this point when they stated, "Children do not grow up in isolation; they grow up in environments. Children are influenced first and foremost by their family, but also by their peers, their school and work setting, and the community in which they live" (p. 1).

An Ecological Approach to Dropout Prevention

Given that the dropout problem is a total community issue, a consolidated community effort is required to effect a solution. Bogenschneider, Small, and Riley (1990) suggest that an ecological perspective that encourages cooperation and collaboration in a comprehensive, multifaceted approach would be most effective. (See Figure 4-1). Such a plan would allow for a two-pronged strategy: (1) identifying and eliminating those "individual or environmental hazards" that increase a child's "vulnerability to negative developmental outcomes," and (2) identifying and supporting or enhancing those "individual or environmental safeguards that enhance [the child's] ability to resist risks and foster adaptation and competence." These factors must be targeted at multiple levels in the community — that is, at individual, family, peer, school, work, and community settings.

Combining the ecological framework with the concept of a continuum-of-treatment (Hamby 1990) produced a blueprint for action that is comprehensive across community situations and time. The continuum-of-treatment approach suggests that efforts must be expended throughout the life span of the person, from the prenatal period through graduation or transition to work (see Figure 4-2). Programs and strategies would differ not only on the basis of the targeted group but also according to the age of the recipients of the programs or strategies.

FIGURE 4-1 • *Influences on Youth Development*

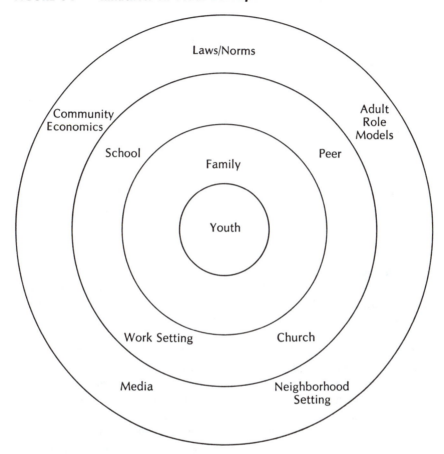

Source: K. Bogenschneider, S. Small, and D. Riley, *An Ecological Risk*-Focused Approach for Addressing Youth-at-Risk Issues (Chevy Chase, MD: National 4-H Center, 1990). Used by permission of Karen Bogenschneider, Stephen Small, and Dave Riley, University of Wisconsin—Madison.

The School–Family Connection

Although other segments of the society such as the business community or social agencies have important roles to play within the ecological or contin-uum-of-treatment framework, families and schools are in the best position to eliminate negative factors and enhance protective factors for children. The family is a system of teaching and learning (Rich 1985), and parents are the child's first teachers (Hausman 1989). The school is the agency whose sole

FIGURE 4-2 • *Continuum of Treatment for At-Risk Youth*

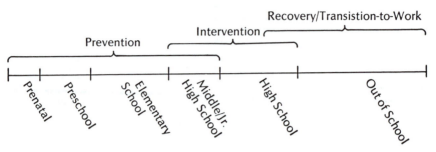

mission is to educate and enculturate all young people in our society. Although they have cooperated with each other on some tasks, the home and school have traditionally gone about their business with no more than a nodding acquaintance of each other's roles. Given the magnitude of youth problems in modern society, however, this situation must change if progress is to be made. Home–school collaboration is the key to unlocking the doors to future success for young people in today's complex world.

In their role as collaborators, parents must become more actively involved in school affairs and take a greater role in their children's education. However, because of the large number of dysfunctional families who will not or cannot take the initiative, the heaviest burden falls upon the school to assume the position of leader. Nicolau and Ramos (1990) described the school's dilemma in relation to Hispanic parents, but the message is clear for the school's role with all parents of at-risk students:

> *The school that is serving large numbers of at-risk families has to function in place of the parents while it goes about the task of seeing to it that the troubled families get the help they require to stabilize their lives and home environment. This has not traditionally been the school's role. Others—churches, social agencies—were charged with these responsibilities. But school may well be the only connection an alienated and isolated . . . family has with any source of help. The schools may have to fill the outreach/referral role and the government and private sectors may have to give the resources to do so. (Nicolau and Ramos 1990, 40)*

Reasons for School Leadership

There are three reasons why schools must assume the leadership role in home–school collaboration: (1) The effects of parental involvement on students' achievement are positive and significant; collaboration with parents would greatly enhance the mission and work of the school; (2) impoverished home conditions of many parents preclude their knowing what to do to help their children or how to do it; schools can provide parents the knowledge and skills they need to be good teachers of their own children; and (3) the school has erected several barriers that inhibit parental participation in school; only the school can tear down those barriers.

Effects of Parent Involvement on Student Achievement

Everyone gains when the school welcomes parents as partners in the educational process, treats them as teachers of their children, and gives them appropriate guidance in how to work with their children. Students have more positive attitudes toward school, better homework habits, higher attendance, lower dropout rates, and improved behavior (Rich 1985; Texas Dropout Prevention Clearinghouse 1989). Achievement increases and is sustained across grade levels for low-income students as well as for middle-income ones (Swap 1990). Teachers come to know and understand parents better. Parents have more confidence in themselves and the schools, demonstrate better attitudes, and participate more often in school activities (Rich 1985). Working together in "connected teaching" (Krasnow 1990) empowers both the family and the school; thus the home and school extend the work of the school in more sustained, systematic ways (Rich 1985).

Conditions in Families

Families of many at-risk children are preoccupied with survival issues such as food, clothing, housing, jobs, illness, and violence. They often have limited coping skills, are deficient in English, are illiterate, have serious marital problems, or are involved with drugs and alcohol (Nicolau and Ramos 1990). One in every four children in this country lives in a family below the poverty level; one in every three children lives in a single-parent home with one in every two being black children. ("Profile," 1990). Sixty-seven percent of married women with children age 6–17 work outside the home. Five to seven million childrend 13 years old and under have parents employed full-time and are without supervision for some part of the day (Rich 1990).

Conditions among young families are particularly critical. About one-third of families headed by a person under age 25 is poor. Nearly three-quarters of the female high school graduates who are heads of households with one or more children are below the poverty level. For female dropouts, over 90 percent are poor. The real earnings of young, non–college-educated males have fallen at least 25 percent since the mid-1970s. The proportion of married 20- to 24-year-old males living with their spouses declined almost 50 percent, and the number of young, single-parent renter households nearly doubled in that same period. It is estimated that young families have to pay about 80 percent of their total income to afford decent rental housing (W.T. Grant Commission 1988).

In many cases, families are so dysfunctional that they need a great deal of outside assistance just to exist. Knowledge and understanding of these circumstances give teachers and other school personnel greater insight into the motivation and behavior of students from these families. Although schools cannot directly meet the financial, housing, and support needs of families, they can perform a referral role for families to social service agencies, as well as being family advocates with policy groups and the business community.

Barriers to Effective Collaboration

One of the major barriers erected by the school derives from the belief of many educators that children from families with some dysfunctional characteristics are unable and unmotivated to learn and cannot succeed in school. These beliefs are particularly strong about single-parent families and those with minority backgrounds. Educators further assume that poor, less-educated, and culturally different parents are neither able nor willing to become involved with their children's education (Krasnow 1990; Quality Education for Minorities Project 1990).

Research findings contradict these assumptions (Rich 1985). Children of working mothers achieve as well as those of nonworking mothers. Working mothers spend almost as much time with their children as do those who do not work. Research has shown that regardless of the socioeconomic status of families, the intelligence of children from one- and two-parent families does not differ significantly. Single parents spend as much time with their children on schoolwork and in talking with the teacher as do two parents. While white mothers participate in school-related activities less when they become single, black mothers do not change their patterns of participation when there is no husband in the home.

Nevertheless, many children in these families receive lower grades, engage in more disruptive behavior, are absent more often, drop out of school more frequently, and, even when they graduate, have lower skill levels than students from two-parent families (Rich 1990; Texas Dropout Prevention

Clearninghouse 1989). Given the research findings in this area, student failure may be as much a function of educators' attitudes as of student characteristics or home factors. Schools must be willing to take some of the blame for student failure. Teachers must understand that learning is not merely a cognitive process dependent on student ability. Rather, learning and motivation develop out of ". . . . a relationship between the teacher and the student, between the school and the community it serves" (Krasnow 1990, 35). Both an inflexible, nonresponsive bureaucratic relationship and an impoverished home life can contribute to a lack of learning and motivation in the student (Krasnow 1990).

Another barrier that separates home from school is the lack of training that teachers have about how to involve parents in their children's education. The teacher is the most important element in the education of the child, but the teacher cannot do it all alone. Parents must be included as partners in education. However, parents, even when they have a desire to help their children, are not likely to become involved without intervention from the school. Therefore, the teacher is the key to parental involvement.

Teachers are more likely to have positive attitudes and involve parents to a greater extent when their colleagues and the principal support the idea (Nicolau and Ramos 1990). A positive attitude alone, however, will not guarantee success. Teachers need training in the areas of structures, family processes, parental roles, cultural diversity, and effective ways to work with parents (Krasnow 1990). This type of training is even more important when we compare the characteristics of the current and future student population described throughout this chapter with the characteristics of new teachers entering the profession. For example, three-fourths of beginning teachers are female and 93 percent are white; only 4 percent are black and 2 percent Hispanic. Three-fourths of new teachers grew up in rural communities or suburbs and want to teach in middle-class schools with traditional rather than experimental programs. Only 20 percent grew up in cities, and only 19 percent want to teach there ("Profile," 1990). The urgency of teacher training for cultural diversity and parental involvement is clear when this latter set of statistics is laid beside those that reveal that the 22 largest school districts in the United States have majority minority enrollments (Quality Education for Minorities Project 1990). Unfortunately, little attention is paid to this subject in preservice and inservice teacher training programs. According to Krasnow (1990), only about 15 percent of the teachers in one survey reported that they had completed a course in parent involvement.

Effective Parent Involvement Practices

Given the desirability of parent–school partnerships to enhance student success and reduce dropouts, and given the need for schools to take the leadership role, what outreach and referral practices have proved effective for recruiting and involving parents in school-related activities?

The success of any plan to involve parents rests upon the ability of the school to effectively recruit families and maintain a harmonious and mutually productive relationship. The following recruitment guidelines have been distilled from successful parental involvement programs.

1. Assess the needs of parents. Ask them what they would be interested in doing. Needs and interests of parents are better starting points for involvement than the school's agenda (Krasnow 1990). According to Nicolau and Ramos (1990), "Schools cannot design rational partnerships programs until they understand who their parents are" (p. 19).

2. Let people who are interested in the school and who know parents and their needs recruit them. Use parent-to-parent personal contacts. Start with a nucleus and radiate from it, building networks of parents. Follow up visits with phone calls. Multiple contacts might be necessary to get some parents involved. Principals and teachers can get to know parents by standing outside the school in the mornings and afternoons to greet parents when they drop off and pick up their children (Nicolau and Ramos 1990).

3. Link parents' involvement directly to their children's learning. The success of one's own child is a powerful motivation for a parent to become involved (Krasnow 1990).

4. When holding events at school, make them as participatory as possible. Parents like to be active and involved (Krasnow 1990). Encourage participation by fathers and other members of the family (Rich 1985). Reward participation by recognizing parent and student achievements (Nicolau and Ramos 1990).

5. Choose many different times to schedule events in consideration of parents' availability, transportation, and child care needs (Krasnow 1990; Rich 1985).

6. Ensure that parents are involved at all levels of schooling. Start programs for kindergarten and continue them throughout the school years. Teenagers need help from parents just as much as younger children do (Rich 1985).

7. Designate school staff members, including teachers, as a liaison team to coordinate and integrate efforts of the school and home (Rich 1985).

8. Use school facilities as the center for school–home partnership activities. The school need not provide and direct all activities. Rather, the school can be the focus of the community and the facilitator of school–home involvement. Activities might include, for example, before- and after-school care for young people, summer programs, and youth organization meetings at school. These activities could be staffed by senior citizens, business people, older students, and members of service clubs under the supervision of specially

trained professionals and parent volunteers. Such activities could be financed through funds raised through home/school/business projects.

The last type of activity listed highlights the referral role the school can play. As has already been stated, schools are not expected to provide services to meet all the needs of students and parents, nor do they have the personnel or facilities to do so. Schools can, however, serve as a clearinghouse and facilitator for services and support to students and parents.

Once parents are recruited as partners, schools can utilize a variety of direct-involvement strategies that include parents as teachers of their own children, parents as partners in other school activities, parents as learners to enhance their own lives, and parents as consumers of information about the school and its activities (Rich 1985).

Parents as Teachers

Probably the most legitimate reason for involving parents in school is to make them teachers of their own children. According to Rich (1985), "If teachers had to choose only one policy to stress . . . the most payoff for the most parents and students will come from teachers involving parents in helping their children in learning activities at home" (p. 19). The "parent as teacher" model is probably the most appropriate for widespread and sustained involvement of families. It is the approach that research links most directly with improvements in academic achievement and is well-suited as a way to involve not only single parents, but also families in which both parents work.

One type of home learning activity, developed by The Home and School Institute, is designed to provide practice in an academic subject and at the same time teach a useful life skill to children. These activities are different from schoolwork but reinforce skills and behaviors needed for success in school. They are inexpensive, take little time, and enhance close parent–child relations. In one such activity, parents and children together watch television news programs with a large map and reference book close by to look up names and locations of countries and cities mentioned in the news. In another activity, parents and children choose a rule that causes family arguments, develop arguments for and against the rule, and explain their reasons to each other. Children then assume the parent's role and the parent assumes the child's role (Rich 1985).

Other types of activities involving parents as teachers include: having parents read to their child (Krasnow 1990); providing "make and take" workshops where parents learn to make educational materials, games, and flash cards to assist their child with basic skills (Nicolau and Ramos 1990); and easy-to-follow activities that help parents express care and concern in adult-to-adult ways with their teenage children (Rich 1985).

Parents as Partners in Other School Activities

In addition to programs designed to help parents teach their own children, parents can be involved in a variety of other school activities as volunteers. For example, parents with children in school can make home visits to other parents to discuss school and family issues, provide materials for home learning activities, and assist other parents in how to work with their children (Krasnow 1990). Parents can also serve on school advisory boards, planning committees, and management teams (Rich 1985; Swap 1990). Some parents can function not only as paid aides in the classroom, but they can also attend parent-teacher association meetings, boosters' club meetings, open houses, and special school events (Swap 1990). Other community-wide projects appropriate for school–parent partnerships include cleaning up lots next to the school, planting shrubbery, building playground equipment, and organizing drives against neighborhood drug dealers. It is important for school personnel to remember that parents must be treated as full partners in these endeavors. They must have responsibility delegated to them and be involved in decision making, planning, and implementing plans (Nicolau and Ramos 1990).

Parents as Learners

With an abundance of educational expertise and access to a multitude of resources, schools are in a perfect position to provide educational programs for parents (Swap 1990). This should include action-oriented projects such as discussing issues or making materials for home learning activities, not just passive listening sessions. For example, parents can attend their children's classes, listen to lessons, and participate along with students in order to understand what their children are learning in school. Parents can attend workshops on various topics such as leadership, English as a second language, or self-esteem, while their children attend tutoring and homework centers at school. Parenting, child development, and self-help instruction are particularly helpful to teen parents (Nicolau and Ramos 1990). Parents appreciate education programs on topics such as children's health and safety, medical and social service resources (Swap 1990), how to apply for food stamps, what to do about child abuse, how to get help for alcohol and drug users, and how to deal with vandalism and violence (Nicolau and Ramos 1990). Peer support groups for teen parents, single parents, and working parents can relieve the stress of daily problems. Parents-without-partners groups can hold meetings at the school and focus on home–school issues (Rich 1985).

Schools need to alternate workshops between topics that parents have identified and those the school thinks are important. Although large-group classes are easy to organize and manage, small-group interaction should be used as well. It is wise to plan several short-term projects with high probability of success, especially at the beginning of the school year (Nicolau and Ramos 1990).

Parents as Consumers of Information about School

Traditionally communication of information (report cards, newsletters, phone calls, or conferences) has been the most frequently used form of parental involvement. Most was initiated by the school, with parents as mere recipients of such information. Techniques such as flyers, handwritten notes from the teacher, notices on bulletin boards, announcements in church bulletins, radio and television public service announcements, newspaper articles, and posters are still legitimate and useful methods for transmitting information (Nicolau and Ramos 1990), but they are the least effective ways to involve parents in a true partnership with the school (Rich 1985).

Parent Involvement Programs

Many of the strategies described in the previous section have been incorporated into programs that involve parents and families in school activities. Nicolau and Ramos (1990) described several programs that were designed especially for Hispanic families.

• *Family Night at McDonald's.* For the first parent–school activity of the year, an elementary school in California held a family night at the neighborhood McDonald's restaurant. The principal and teachers dressed in uniforms, worked behind the counter, and served food to families.

• *Gardening and Sewing Clubs.* As part of a series of ongoing parental involvement projects, another elementary school in California organized clubs to teach parents gardening and sewing skills. In one project, parents prepared props, sewed costumes, built scenery, and helped students practice for a school play.

• *Intensive Training Institute.* The staff of a Texas prekindergarten and kindergarten school held an informal, week-long intensive training institute to help parents learn principles of child growth and development, how to make home learning centers, and ways to enhance their children's motivation and language development.

• *Classroom Activity Centers.* A K-1 elementary school in Boston created classroom-based activity centers for parents. Once a week, parents sat in their children's classes, watched interactions between the teacher and students, and became familiar with the curriculum. Parents were given supplies for use in school and at home with their children. They also attended parenting workshops and counseling sessions.

• *Home Workshops.* The staff of a 3–6 grade elementary school in Texas held parenting workshops in the homes of parent "hosts" who were responsible for recruiting other parents to attend. The school staff conducting meetings were the principal, counselor, nurse, assistant principal, and a teacher. Topics included child care practices, helping with homework, parenting skills, and routines of the school.

The following examples of parental programs were selected from FOCUS, the electronic database of the National Dropout Prevention Center at Clemson University.

• *Parent Cooperative Preschool Laboratories.* To increase the affective and cognitive growth of at-risk preschool children, a preschool staff in Florida invites parents to monthly workshops to teach effective parenting skills. Parents are also involved in classroom activities and participate in community excursions. A "home curriculum" helps parents become partners with the school in their children's learning.

• *Parent-Child Program.* This preschool program in Minnesota is designed to involve parents and their children in activities that stimulate family interaction. Once a week during the school year, parents accompany their children to the neighborhood elementary school. During a two-hour session, parents work and play with their children in special learning stations. They also observe formal model teaching and informal child–teacher interaction and participate in discussion groups facilitated by a parent educator.

• *Parent Outreach Program.* The faculty of an Oregon middle school promotes long-term parental involvement by using a Parent Outreach Specialist to conduct parent meetings and classes and develop resource kits for use with children at home. The staff engages in home visitations to assess needs of parents and to link the home to needed services through a referral system.

• *Parent Involvement Program.* This K–12 program in Alabama seeks to help parents understand their children better, develop skills to help their children at home, and form partnerships with teachers and school officials. School staff, counselors, and community representatives meet with parents three hours each month at locations convenient to parents. Home visits are made for those unable to attend other meetings. In addition to parenting and teaching skills, parents also learn how to obtain help from the school and community agencies.

• *Project Regroup.* This program for mildly handicapped special education students in Washington includes direct intervention for students' families. An individualized program is designed for each family that includes access to community resources, support groups, parent-education classes, summer home visits, and guidebooks for parents.

• Missouri's *Parents as Teachers Program* is probably the most ambitious attempt to involve parents in their children's education. This prevention program operated by the Parents as Teachers National Center uses trained parent-educators to make home visits to provide assistance to parents of children from birth to 3 years of age. Parents receive tips in child development, home safety, constructive play, effective discipline, and other hints about how to encourage their children's development. They also attend group meetings to share experiences and concerns. A referral network helps those parents in need of special assistance such as medical or financial help. Evaluation data from this project indicate that both children and parents have benefited from participation (Hausman 1989).

The Role of Teacher Education in Parental Involvement

In reality, there can be no discussion of public schools isolated from teacher education. Whatever happens in the public schools is directly related to teacher education. What role can teacher education play in parental involvement in the schools? First and foremost, teacher education programs have a responsibility to provide preservice and inservice teachers the training and information they need in order to work with families. Teacher educators are in the best position to analyze, interpret, and translate research and theory into practice and to disseminate it to teachers and principals in usable form. Since public school teachers are not ordinarily trained to work with parents, they need special help in developing and using strategies for dealing with adults (Rich 1985).

In addition to training in methodology, teachers need experiences to increase their awareness of cultural and class differences among their at-risk students and their families. This can be accomplished through examination of personal beliefs, values, and behaviors in a nonthreatening, supportive environment.

An important question arises in connection with teacher education's role in parental involvement in the public schools. While it is clear that public school personnel need the guidance and support of teacher education, how well prepared are teacher educators to give help in this area? Some evidence indicates that teacher education programs are lagging behind public schools in response to the dropout problem (Hamby 1988). Teacher educators will be obliged to restructure their own programs if they are to provide leadership and support for efforts in the public schools. Such a restructuring would include at least four elements:

1. Intensifying minority student recruitment and retention
2. Improving minority faculty recruitment and retention
3. Forming institutional consortia to study at-risk issues and provide support for local school districts in dealing with dropouts and other at-risk youth problems (Quality Education for Minorities Project 1990)
4. Modifying curriculum to include study of at-risk issues and experiences designed to enhance skills for working with at-risk students and their families

Conclusion

Family factors contribute to children's failure in school, which may ultimately lead to their dropping out. While family life is not the only cause of dropping out, what happens in the home is a significant factor. A cycle of failure that begins in the home is often exacerbated and perpetuated by the school. Dropouts become parents, and their lack of education and/or negative values toward education infect their children, thus predisposing them to drop out. Working alone, schools can influence the lives of at-risk students—more than most educators realize. However, without intervention in the home through parental involvement, schools will never break this pernicious cycle. But progress is being made. Some schools are beginning to include parents in their mission. Nevertheless, much work remains to be done if all parents and families are to be embraced as full partners in the academic and social life of the school.

Don't find fault; find a remedy. — HENRY FORD

CHAPTER FIVE

Families, Schools, Literacy, and Diversity

TERRENCY WILEY   JOHN SIKULA

Editor's Note: The ability to be literate may be one of the few objectives that all in society could embrance. Literacy suggests status, social acceptance, possibilities in the workplace, the attainment of civility.

The title of this chapter identifies its message: To be literate cuts across all aspects of our existence. We live with the language of the home, the street, the culture, the subculture. Each may be unique and not quite in harmony with the language text used in school. When the languages agree, it is useful. Lack of agreement may cause confusion and harm. Each of us can document cases that depict a youngster as having difficulty in school due to this incompatibility. Is the school the common denominator, or is it the place that is more the problem than solution?

> If we are to teach, we must first examine our own assumptions
> about families and children, and we must be alert to the negative
> images in the literature ("dropouts come from stressful homes"). In-
> stead of responding to "pathologies" we must recognize that what
> we see may actually be healthy adaptations to an uncertain and
> stressful world. As teachers, researchers, and policy makers, we need
> to think about the children themselves and to try to imagine the
> contextual worlds of their day-to-day lives.
> —DENNY TAYLOR AND CATHERINE DORSEY-GAINS

Broadening the Focus on Literacy

For educators, understanding how children develop literacy is important, both because schools are responsible for initial literacy instruction and because reading and writing are essential for successful academic achievement and progress. But formal education represents only part of the literacy picture. Consequently, a number of researchers have looked beyond the domain of the school to that of the family and to the relationship between family and school (e.g., Clark 1982; Heath 1983, 1988; Leichter 1982; Taylor 1983; Wells 1986). Moreover, for several decades there has been increased public attention on the problem of adult illiteracy (e.g., Hunter and Harman 1979; Kozol 1985). Much of the focus on the problem of adult illiteracy, or, more accurately, adult English illiteracy, has been directed to the knowledge and skills people need to function in society and participate in the economic and political systems (Macías 1988).

Leichter (1982) maintains that most approaches to the ways in which families influence a child's literacy development fall into three broad categories: (1) Research that focuses on the physical environment and on economic and educational resources of the home; (2) studies that address interpersonal interaction among children, parents, and others in the home with respect to literacy; and (3) those that examine emotional and motivational factors within the home.

Within these domains there has been increased focus on such factors as the relationship between parental background characteristics (such as level of education, social class, language background, oral language styles, and culture) and the intergenerational development of literacy. Beyond these issues there are questions related not only to the relationship of home and school to one another, but of each to the broader society at large.

Society's Rising Expectations Regarding Literacy

Expectations regarding literacy are not static. A number of scholars (Clifford 1984; Resnick and Resnick 1977; Scribner 1984) have noted that there has been a tendency for expectations regarding literacy to inflate, especially since the end of the last century. While some indicators of literacy, such as grade-level achievement, point to recent gains among large segments of the population, such gains must be seen relative to the larger sociohistorical context. Universal adult literacy, and even high school completion, have become common expectations. Resnick and Resnick (1977) note that current expectations regarding mass literacy have been held for, at most, three generations. In the past, literacy models aimed at achieving high levels of literacy for elites and low levels for a large number of individuals. Recent calls for high levels of mass literacy can be seen as attempts to take a standard that once applied only to elites and apply it universally. This relatively rapid extension of literacy criteria, once applied only to select populations, raises an issue of the appropriateness of instructional methods and goals, especially since not all segments of the population have come to demand them.

With the increase in expectations regarding literacy, there has come a corresponding increase in the expectations placed upon parents. Literacy (or at least familiarity with print and its functions) is increasingly being seen as a prerequisite for schooling, rather than as a basic initial function of schooling. Illiteracy and low educational achievement have come to be seen as individual failures (or the failures of parents) rather than as the result of inappropriate educational policies, inadequate curriculum models, or unequal and discriminatory practices in the larger society (Auerbach 1989).

Literacy and Acquisition

Definition of Literacy
In modern society it is difficult to understate the significance attributed to literacy given its cognitive, social, economic, and political consequences. Nonetheless, there is little consensus regarding how literacy should be defined. It has been defined narrowly in terms of basic skills used in reading and writing. More broadly, it may be seen as the ability to use print to make meaning and to fulfill various social needs. Literacy may be seen as a marker of social status providing individuals with a sense of legitimacy and cultural attainment. It may also be seen as a tool for personal growth, or for political liberation (Macías 1988; Scribner 1984). In the words of Hunter and Harman (1979), literacy is "simultaneously a statement about reading abilities and an articulation of broader cultural and social content" (p. x).

Literacy Development: Natural or Unnatural?
No one would argue that the development of literacy is inevitable. However, some have maintained that the achievement of literacy is largely an "unnatural act," which requires overt instruction (Gough and Hillinger 1980). An alternate view (Goodman and Goodman 1976) contends that literacy develops "naturally" as an extension of the need to communicate in one's social environment; development is natural as long as one has the opportunity to encounter reading and writing as vehicles for meaningful communication. A growing body of research on the development of literacy within the family supports the notion that children can, and frequently do, learn to read without direct instruction (Clark 1976; Morrow 1983, 1989; Taylor and Dorsey-Gains 1988; Teale 1978) and that home environments can provide a foundation for its natural development (Holdaway 1979; Taylor 1983; Taylor and Dorsey-Gaines 1988; Teale 1982).

Levine (1982) argues that the study of literacy must focus on social practices that reflect prevailing political and structural realities. Street (1984) attacks what he calls the "autonomous model" wherein literacy is studied devoid of social context and functions. Gee (1986) chronicles what might be termed a paradigm shift in the study of literacy, where sociocultural approaches now dominate.

Schools and Social Practices

If the development of literacy can be natural within supportive environments, why does the distribution of literacy abilities remain so varied, and why are solutions difficult to find? While there is much that parents can do to lay a foundation for literacy, the fact is that the promotion of literacy in this country remains largely a function of the schools. Consequently, the persistence of illiteracy and lower academic achievement involves the failure of school practices and programs for many students (Macías 1988). For this reason, researchers have looked beyond school models themselves and recognize them within the broader context of social practices that either help or hinder the promotion of literacy.

Carter and Segura (1979), Leibowitz (1971), and Weinberg (1977) document the negative impact of schooling, particularly on ethnic and language minorities. They argue that for many students the schools become a socially sanctioned mechanism ascribing them a lower status. For example, Weinberg (1977) maintains that, despite persistent efforts to educate themselves, a number of indigenous minority groups historically have been victims of overt segregation and of cultural control through a variety of devices, including language suppression. Prior to the Civil War there were compulsory illiteracy laws for black slaves and penalties for those who would teach them to read and write. Latinos have been denied the use of Spanish, not only as a means of instruction, but also as a means of informal social communication at school. Citing the findings of a 1970 memorandum of the Commission on Civil Rights, Weinberg (1977) characterizes the educational experience of Chicanos into the early 1970s as demonstrating:

> (1) a high degree of segregation, (2) an extremely low academic achievement, (3) a predominance of exclusionary practices by schools, and (4) a discriminatory use of public finance. The pattern is similar to that imposed upon black children, who were regarded by the dominant white society as inferior. Denial of an equal education was a powerful instrument of continued oppression. Those who were not permitted to learn were deemed incapable of learning and could, logically, therefore be confined to a lower status in society. (p. 177)

Given the historical legacy of the minority experience in the United States, educational underachievement by a substantial number of adults is predictable. Consequently, the role of the schools in promoting the general rise of literacy cannot be seen in isolation from sociopolitical ideologies that have sought to promote social control (Illich 1979; Street 1984). Collins (1979) argues that the widespread administration of standardized tests of reading and writing has accentuated social differences between groups.

Schooling does more than promote literacy and academic skills; it also has a status-ascribing function. Erickson (1984) maintains that literacy, defined by school achievement, symbolizes the attainment of culture and civilization. Being "literate" in this sense carries the connotation of being "well educated," and being "illiterate" carries the stigma of being "uneducated."

In a critique of this status-ascribing function of the schools, Erickson (1984) argues that literacy, meaning "being lettered," not only promotes prestige of the literate, but also promotes strategic power for them since it involves mastery of a communication system. He considers the prestige factor as a masking of power that hides the distinctions between schooling and literacy. For example, being "lettered" implies that one not only has skills, but also that one has been to school. Consequently, this elitist view of literacy may also be characterized as a justification for power. Erickson goes on to raise a number of important questions:

> *In current public discourse about literacy, are we talking about knowledge and skill in decoding letters, or are we talking about being "lettered" as a marker of social class status and cultural capital? Do we see the school diploma mainly as evidence of mastery of knowledge and skill in literacy? I don't think so. I think tht the high school diploma functions for low SES students, primarily as a docility certificate. . . . This would especially make good sense if ordinary work in most of the company's jobs does not really require literacy as schools define it. (p. 527)*

Erickson (1984) argues that the notion of "literacy practices" presents a fundamentally different notion of the relations between intellectual capabilities taught in the schools and the social situations in which those capabilities are put to use. For example, despite their similarities, mathematical computations at the grocery store are not the same as those taught and tested in school that *simulate* shopping at a grocery store. Although the computation skills would appear to be the same in both cases, there is a difference in the social context in which the computation tasks are performed. In the workbook-oriented skill-and-drill context of many schools, the learner is not free to negotiate his or her own choices regarding the computation. It is not just that a school computational problem is "out of context" (or, we may add, "in a reduced context"); rather, the problem is that it is used "in a context in which the power relations are such that the subject has no influence on problem formulation" (p. 533).

Erickson (1984) contends that failure in schools is related partly to what he calls a "schismogenesis," that is, development of conflict that is both caused by and results from sociocultural and linguistic differences. Failure in school is "achieved" by a learner's "self-defeating" resistance to being labeled by the school as an individual of less worth than others.

[This] view is at once pessimistic and affirming. It proposes that children failing in school are working at achieving that failure. The view does not wash its hand of the problem at that point. It maintains, however, that intervention to break the cycle of school failure must start by locating the problem jointly in the processes of society at large and in the interactions of specific individuals. (p. 539)

Since the debate over failure in schools often degenerates either into blaming the victim (i.e., the student or the parents), or into blaming the schools, Erickson shows that both "cognitive deficits" (i.e., literacy deficits) and "discriminatory school practices" are insufficient as hypotheses to account for failure.

Erickson points to the work of Scollon and Scollon (1981), who studied the underachievement of Alaska natives in literacy. Scollon and Scollon found that to become literate in the terms of the Western-style school was to lose one's sense of cultural identity. Thus, the Alaska natives resisted school-defined literacy and suffered the consequences of marginal performance.

Similarly, Heath (1980) argues that the extent to which all normal people can become literate depends on (1) the functions that literacy plays, (2) the necessity of having a context or setting in which there is a need to be literate, and (3) the necessity of the presence of literate helpers in the environment. She contends that becoming literate does not necessarily require formal instruction or a sequential hierarchy of skills that must be mastered. Common instructional practices impose a curriculum that slows down opportunities for actual reading experiences. It fragments the process into skills and activities that are alien to the experiences of parents and the community. Literacy instruction as a technical skill is seen to require a level of expertise that leaves parents with a sense of inadequacy, resulting in their seeing little role for themselves in promoting a child's literacy. Heath concludes that effective instruction needs to be presented in a more natural and functional context. She argues that if such changes are made, a truly functional literacy instruction could "alter not only methods and goals of reading instruction, but also assessments of the accountability of schools in meeting society's needs" (p. 131).

Literacy and the New Diversity

In 1970, white (European American) students made up 85 percent of the student population of U.S. schools. By 1980 their majority had declined to 72 percent and by 2000 it is expected to be only 57 percent (Trueba 1988). In California, the nation's most populous state, the white school-age population is now less than 50 percent (Office of Bilingual Education 1989). Consequently, given this recent demographic shift, it is becoming less appropriate to discuss literacy and other educational issues in terms of a majority/minority formula, or to use labels such as "mainstream" versus "nonmainstream," unless by "mainstream" we mean to imply that diversity is the norm. Given this new diversity, it is important to probe the assumptions about cultural norms that underlie both lay and scholarly views.

Illiteracy or Non-English Literacy?

In designing appropriate educational programs for a linguistically and culturally diverse population, there is much to be learned. There is a need for baseline information on the extent of literacy, but this cannot be known without first probing what is included or excluded in the definition of literacy. For example, even in discussions about language minorities in the United States, little distinction has been made between literacy and English literacy. It has been assumed that the immigrant move toward English is inevitable and a prerequisite to literacy. However, such assumptions ignore the fact that (1) there are indigenous (e.g., nonimmigrant) language minority groups in the United States; (2) among immigrants, not all learn English, for a variety of reasons related to such factors as age, cultural identity, opportunity, and motivation to learn the language (Fishman 1966, 1980a; Wiley 1986); and (3) the United States, like most nations of the world, is a multilingual society as evidenced by the fact that it is the fourth-largest Spanish-speaking nation in the world (Simon 1988).

Bhatia (1984) maintains that even in theoretical discussions of literacy, a number of tenuous assumptions are made regarding the linguistic situation in so-called monolingual societies such as the United States. English monolingualism is assumed to have a "feeding relationship" with literacy; multilingualism is viewed as having a "bleeding relationship" (p. 24). In this country, the fact that many people speak languages other than English is assumed to have a negative impact on literacy.

As Vargas (1986) has noted, most measures of literacy used in the United States are inadequate to describe the characteristics among language minorities because no common survey definitions include literacy in languages other than English. Thus, literacy is confused with English literacy, and illiteracy is confounded with non-English literacy. Parents who are literate in languages other than English are perceived by many among the English-speaking majority in the same way as parents who are not literate in any language.

The Extent of Literacy/Illiteracy among Language Minorities

Despite the presence of 35 million linguistic minority persons in the United States in 1980, of whom some 19.5 million were not fluent in English (Trueba 1988), few national surveys of literacy have sampled language minorities (Macías 1988, Vargas 1988; Wiley 1988). The first major survey to do so was the 1975 Adult Performance Level Study (APL). The APL estimated that 56 percent of Hispanics (25 years of age or over) were nonliterate, compared to 34 percent for whites and 39 percent for blacks (Macías 1988; Vargas 1988). In 1982, based upon its English Language Proficiency (ELPS), the U.S. Department of Education estimated that between 17 to 21 million adults (roughly 13 percent of the adult population) were nonliterate. ELPS estimated that the nonliteracy rate for adult Latinos over 20 years of age was between 39 percent and 48 percent (Macías 1988; Vargas 1988).

For the fall semester of 1986, it was estimated that among the children entering school for the first time, one in four was at or below the poverty level, at least 10 percent had parents who were either illiterate or lacked previous formal education, and 15 percent were immigrants of non–English-speaking backgrounds (Bliss 1986). Surveys of immigrant and refugee groups have found low levels of English literacy among various groups. For example, English illiteracy has been estimated at 43 percent for those from El Salvador and Cambodia, 80 percent for Haitians, and as high as 90 percent for those from Afghanistan (Impink-Hernadez 1985).

Confusing Low Second Language Proficiency with Illiteracy

Another area of importance in understanding literacy in language minority families is the relationship between second language literacy and second language proficiency. Vargas (1986) observes that limited language proficiency is commonly confused with illiteracy; it is often assumed that limited proficiency in English "causes" English illiteracy. While one may have oral proficiency in Spanish and be literate in Spanish, these abilities are not recognized as literacy or seen as important because of the dominant language attitudes.

What is not understood (or acknowledged as being important) is that many who read and write in English may not be orally fluent, and that many who are orally fluent in English may not be English literate. Obviously, there are "illiterates" among fluent English-speaking monolinguals as well (Vargas 1986).

The Significance of Biliteracy

Fishman (1980b) has noted: "it may seem rather indelicate . . . to stress . . . that biliteracy—the mastery of reading in particular, and at times also writing, in two (or more) languages—is not at all a rare skill among the portion of mankind that has successfully won the battle for literacy" (p. 49). Especially with reference to language minorities, it is predictable tht biliteracy and non-English literacy (e.g., literacy only in Spanish or Vietnamese) are not uncommon. To the extent that this is true, claims made regarding the prevalence of illiteracy (meaning English illiteracy) among language minorities must be reevaluated (Wiley 1988).

While it is true that English holds the dominant position within the United States, it does not necessarily follow that the English language or English literacy can or should fulfill all of the needs of bilingual families (see Harding and Riley 1986, for interesting cases in point). Nor does it follow that there are no positive benefits to the majority in developing biliteracy among themselves (Simon 1988).

Since literacy in any language provides a foundation for literacy in another (Cummins 1981, 1984a, 1984b, 1985; Cummins and Swan 1986), it is important that educational literacy policies for parents and children view non-English literacy as a resource for the development of English literacy rather than as a detriment.

The Development of Literacy in Home, Community, and School Contexts

Among the growing number of literacy ethnographies, the works of Heath (1983, 1988), Schieffelin and Cochran-Smith (1982), Taylor (1983), and Taylor and Dorsey-Gaines (1988) demonstrate the importance of studying literacy in a variety of ethnocultural and socioeconomic contexts.

Literacy Development in Families of Educated Parents

Sheieffelin and Cochran-Smith (1982) studied literacy development in several contexts, one involving preschool-age children in Philadelphia from highly educated, two-parent families. Literacy acquisition was assumed by the parents and the community. Book reading was valued as a solitary task. Books were treated as valuable artifacts by the community. Here, the print interests of children emerged out of a particular cultural orientation in which children were socialized to be literate, and literacy was an expectation. Literacy occurred in two major contexts—the home and nursery school—and also in church and the general community, which tended to reinforce the authority of print to such an extent that "If you don't read you don't know" (p. 7).

Schieffelin and Cochran-Smith (1982) conclude that the social context itself and the functions of literacy within it were the keys to the foundations of literacy acquisition. Adults played the roles of teachers, helpers, and intermediaries for the children, who were not merely passive observers but who were "consumers of print (who gradually) took over the various roles in literacy events and needed less and less help from adult intermediaries" (p. 8). Importantly, the children learned to control the uses of print before they learned to control the mechanical skills of decoding and encoding.

While story reading was adult-dominated and controlled, it was characterized by cooperative, interactive negotiation between the reader and the listeners. If the children made mistakes, they were allowed to try again.

Schieffelin and Cochran-Smith (1982) note that in environments such as the one described it is assumed that "children will become literate, and so literacy activities often are taken for granted or are background in relation to the social functions and interactions in which they occur" (p. 10). Taylor (1983) has reached similar conclusions.

Literacy Development in a Nonliterate Environment

Schieffelin and Cochran-Smith (1982) compared the proliteracy setting with a largely nonliterate community in New Guinea where literacy was introduced or imposed by missionaries into a culture where oral, face-to-face interactions predominated. In this setting, reading was emphasized more than writing. It was taught by syllabication with emphasis on correct pronunciation. English-based (foreign) words were used for new items, and, as might be expected under such circumstances, there appeared to be no incorporation of literacy into the traditional cultural environment. Children were discouraged from using books since the books were seen as fragile, valuable artifacts that adults did not want handled. Apart from its religious function, book reading had little connection to the broader social life of the community.

Literacy Development among Language-Minority Immigrants

Schieffelin and Cochran-Smith (1982) studied a Chinese-Vietnamese immigrant family in a U.S. urban environment. Several factors regarding this example are important: First, the child's parents were not English literate, but they were literate in Chinese. Second, while the presence of ample books and writing materials within the home environment has often been seen as an important prerequisite for literacy development (Clark 1976; Morrow 1983), there were few in this child's home, and most of these were not in English. Nevertheless, this environment was still a literate one. Third, given the non-English literacy of the children's parents, the child was fulfilling literate tasks as an *access person* for his parents and making links with English-speaking adults in an English literacy network. English literacy was not being transmitted first from his parents to him.

Significantly, while the importance of the need for responsive adults has been stressed (Clark 1976, 1982), this study indicates that is not necessarily mandatory that the adult has to be a parent.

Because he cannot receive assistance in school-related activities from his non–English-speaking parents, his requests for assistance are directed primarily to English-speaking adults who are outside his family network. . . . [Thus] the non–English-speaking child must develop a range of social relationships that are very different from those of the English-speaking child, who may expect to receive assistance from family members. (Schieffelin and Cochran-Smith 1982, 15)

The work of Schieffelin and Cochran-Smith (1982) illustrates that language-minority status itself is not a liability since many such children can get the support they need. However, as Trueba (1988) demonstrates, when appropriate steps are not taken by the schools to consider the language and cultural backgrounds of immigrant and language minority children, "cultural trauma" accentuated by school practices and academic failure is often the result.

Match/Mismatch between Schools and Homes

Olson (1977, 1982) has argued that literate oral language ability and metalinguistic awareness are requisite for the promotion of literacy and academic success generally. Differences in speech styles and varying degrees of linguistic awareness by children from different socioeconomic backgrounds affect the ease by which they become literate and adapt to formal schooling practices.

This view presupposes a kind of "mismatch" between the language of the home and the language of the school. The alleged mismatch between home and school language (and textbook language) implies a qualitative, or even cognitive, limitation in the preparedness of some students from so-called "non-mainstream" environments. However, it is necessary to recognize that non-mainstream children also typically come from literate environments. The abilities and practices of their families also need to be studied to see how these can be recognized and incorporated into the schools, since the failure to do so unfavorably biases school practices in favor of one group over another.

In an ethnographic study of three communities in the rural Piedmont region of the Carolinas, Heath (1983, 1988) studied the development of literacy among a middle-class, largely white community (Maintown), a working-class white community (Roadville), and a working-class black community (Trackton). While all three of the communities were literate and provided opportunities for the young to develop literacy, the literacy practices in the middle-class community were closest to the practices of the schools. For Maintown children, Heath (1988) concludes that bedtime reading provides an early link between ways of talking about books and taking meaning from them, whereby "children learn that written language may represent not only descriptions of real events, but decontextualized logical propositions" (p. 180).

In contrast, Roadville children receive little opportunity prior to school to make analytic statements or assert universal truths, "except those related to their religious faith" (Heath 1988, 180) and it is more important that stories have a moral that fits the experience of people in the community than a strict adherence to logic. Consequently, Heath (1988) recommends that in school, Roadville children need to have distinctions in discourse strategies and structures made explicit for them since narratives of real events involve different discourse strategies than those of imaginary tales and flights of fantasy. According to Heath, the narrative discourse style of these children's community: "is very narrow and demands a passive role" (pp. 180–181).

Literacy development in Trackton is unlike both of the other communities: There are no bedtime stories and few occasions for reading to children. Children's attention is rarely drawn to "labels or names of attributes of items; [however,] . . . they are familiar with group literacy events in which several community members orally negotiate the meaning of a written text" (Heath 1988, 180). Consequently, Heath (1988) argues that Trackton children must learn to distinguish between real-life narratives and fictionalized stories and "recount factual events in a straightforward way and recognize appropriate occasions for reason-explanations and affective expressions" (p. 181). They need to learn mainstream school habits presented to them through familiar activities.

From such descriptions it is easy to conclude that children from lower socioeconomic families come from literacy-deficient environments. In regard to this, Auerbach (1989) observes: "Since authority is vested in those belonging to the mainstream culture, the literacy practices of the mainstream become the norm and have higher status in school contexts. Heath's (1988) analysis suggests that the problem is not one of deficit in the family environment, but one of differential usage and power" (p. 173).

It would appear that rather than concentrating on alleged deficiencies that children bring to school, much more attention should be directed to building upon their strengths. In this regard, Wells's (1986) discussion of his Bristol study, on the relationship between language use at home and in school offers a number of important observations. He contends that too much emphasis is placed on age–grade comparisons of student performance and that too little is given to mapping the individual progress of children. He notes that while it is often assumed that children from lower socioeconomic backgrounds are deficient in their oral language abilities, he found little support for this when a variety of measures were used to evaluate oral language. What he did find was that teachers gave students far less opportunity for exploratory and collaborative talk than parents do (regardless of their social class). They unwittingly reduce children to a passive role and underaccess the language ability of many children.

Wells (1986) found a high correlation between the socioeconomic background of parents and the extent to which they read stories to their children. (Story reading was the most salient literacy experience in predicting success in school). However, he concludes that because schools value literacy at the expense of orality, schools may inadvertently be helping to accentuate the literacy disadvantage of some children by ignoring their strength (i.e., oral language).

To summarize, the work of Heath (1988) and of Wells (1986) is important because these researchers describe family language and literacy practices that predict school success. Their work is also significant because it recommends the incorporation of a variety of ways of learning and talking at school. Failure to do so reduces the role of educational institutions to one of social control facilitated by a so-called mainstreaming process that dictates a restricted way with words.

Bilingual Education and Literacy

Literacy and the Language of Literacy as Instruments of Social Control

Acknowledging that educational policies are always promoted in a sociohistorical context, Castell and Luke (1983) conclude that literacy instruction has been imposed on society rather than derived from it. This distinction is an important one since it is commonly assumed that the product of literacy is somehow distinct from the process of its acquisition.

Illich (1979) has explored the historical imposition of standardized languages of literacy as one means of social control. He provides a provocative critique of the rise of modern schooling practices and their relationship to local varieties of language and literacy. Illich argues that instructional language policies that impose a prescribed "standard" language diminish the value of local common languages.

While Illich's (1979) position is characteristically more radical than most scholars, his view that the school's choice of language and degree of standardization of that language are instruments of social control is difficult to deny. In the promotion of literacy it is difficult to underestimate the importance of the language choice. Macías (1979) has shown its relationship to human rights.

Theoretical Foundations of Bilingual Education

In this country, when the discussion of home/school match/mismatch is extended to language minorities, the controversy intensifies because the focus of difference is no longer only on styles within the same language; rather, the question becomes which language should be used to facilitate literacy and instruction — the student's home language or the language of the school?

Bilingual education has been instituted, at least partly, based upon the assumption that language-minority children are at an inherent disadvantage when they begin instruction in a language other than their home language. Despite its goals of promoting academic achievement and the acquisition of English among language-minority children, bilingual education remains controversial largely because of one of its means — that is, primary-language instruction (see Crawford 1989 and Hakuta 1986 for useful overviews of the evolution of the debate).

There is growing evidence that when adequate resources are provided, bilingual education is effective in promoting literacy and academic achievement among children (Krashen and Bider 1988; Merino and Lyons 1990). While the bulk of the research on bilingual education has been directed at children, there is growing evidence (Burtoff 1985; Malendez 1990; Robson 1982) that it also provides a programmatic alternative to the more typical English literacy and Adult Basic Education (ABE) English as a Second Language (ESL) programs in the literacy education of language-minority adults.

Opponents of bilingual education argue that schools should not waste students' time by developing their primary language. But in practical terms, a student's home language is used as the initial vehicle for instruction because it provides the most accessible medium to promote literacy and academic knowledge. The language-minority child is faced with two tasks: (1) learning English, and (2) maintaining grade-level equivalency in academic knowledge. Despite the importance of language background, several other factors also must be taken into account before one determines what language should be used for initial literacy instruction. The purpose of bilingual education is to promote literacy, academic achievement, and the acquisition of English. Primary-language instruction is one vehicle given the dynamic interaction between home and school factors. However, primary-language instruction is only a means, not an end. To bridge the gap between home and school and to promote long-term academic achievement in English, primary-language instruction (like nonbilingual instruction) must be meaning-based, utilizing the child's social and cultural knowledge as foundations for further learning.

Policy and Program Implications

The low appeal of some adult programs and family literacy programs has been noted by Hunter and Harman (1979). There are alternative explanations for this low appeal: Either the individual parents can be blamed, or the assumptions underlying educational policies can be reevaluated. Levine (1982) observes that reading and writing practices include both activities in which an individual may wish to engage and those in which an individual may be "compelled to engage" (p. 264). Historically, according to this interpretation, many policy makers have viewed literacy as a normative agent. Along these lines, Graff (1979) and Street (1984) argue that mass literacy campaigns can hide a deeper motive, which is to pacify and control those who do not conform to normative middle-class expectations.

To broaden the appeal of family programs, empowerment needs to be foremost among the goals. As Scribner (1984) observes, literacy as power emphasizes the relationship between literacy and the advancement of a group or community, a position that has been most notably pursued by Paulo Freire (1970).

The Need to Reconceptualize Models of Family Literacy

In reconceptualizing literacy from the standpoint of diversity, it is necessary to focus on factors related to ethnicity, culture, language background, and language status. Findings and programmatic prescriptions are presented as if they were universally applicable. In this regard, Heath (1988) cautions: "A unilinear model of development in the acquisition of language structures and uses cannot adequately account for culturally diverse ways of acquiring knowledge or developing cognitive styles" (p. 181).

Heath (1988) has suggested that there is a need for the public schools themselves to become more aware of literacy practices within the communities they serve so that these practices can be incorporated into the school curriculum. This certainly does not preclude teaching additional skills valued by the larger society. It also provides a needed link between the school and the community.

Auerbach (1989) contends further that many of the programmatic prescriptions for promoting family literacy (e.g., Simich-Dudgeon 1986), especially among so-called nonmainstream families (i.e., non–English-speaking and/or lower socioeconomic), are based upon a deficit model. This model implies that failures within the home are the principal cause of low academic achievement and failure in school. Thus, most programs seek "to strengthen ties between the home and the school by transmitting the culture of school literacy through the vehicle of the family" (p. 169).

Recommendations for New Directions

To the extent that family literacy programs are based on a "transmission of school policies" model, they may be alienating and inappropriate. If literacy practices are not to appear imposed from the perspective of the families they are intended to reach, then educational policies and curriculum design must be based upon an assessment of needs that is negotiated with the participants whereby "curriculum development is participatory and is based on a collaborative investigation of critical issues in family or community life" (Auerbach 1989, 177).

There is a need to better develop what Auerbach (1989) has called the "neglected" aspects of family literacy work:

- Parents working independently on reading and writing (to enable them to become less literacy-dependent on their children)
- Using literacy as a means to address both family and community problems
- Parents addressing child-rearing concerns with other parents in family literacy support groups
- Supporting the development of home language and culture to promote academic achievement and positive self-image
- Learning how to interact with the school system

What works well in one situation may or may not work well in another. One important variable is the degree to which local participants are allowed a significant voice in the process of developing policies and procedures to be implemented. While there is no guaranteed recipe for success among alternative approaches to schooling that will allow for programs to be more responsive to family and cultural diversity, alternative approaches have been used with success and can be used as examples to better inform policy makers and program designers. Ranard (1989) notes that successful programs share several features in common. They:

1. Recognize that literacy instruction must be content-based
2. Present content in a culturally relevant and familiar context
3. Take into account what students say they want and need to learn
4. Recognize that the home can be a source of strength and support.

Auerbach (1989) and her colleagues have found success in teaching parents to explore the uses of language and literacy within the home. Parents are assisted in learning how to help their children. They explore cultural issues that can reinforce positive attitudes toward literacy, and they read and write stories and folktales based in their own cultures. Community, workplace, and health care issues are incorporated into the curriculum, and parents are taught how to promote their concerns with the schools.

General directions that may help educational institutions promote literacy amidst the new diversity are trends toward:

- Basic literacy instruction for adults in either English or their native language
- Grass roots empowerment and shared governance that involves opportunities for the exercise of choice and the negotiation of educational goals
- Social support services that provide parents opportunities and assistance to further their own education
- Curricular focus on social needs, problems, and aspirations
- Instruction in, and opportunities to access, technology
- Promotion of lifelong learning through familiarizing parents with educational resources and opportunities
- Higher education/business partnerships that focus their efforts on community needs

Movement in these directions may be helpful not only in professionalizing teaching, but also in sensitizing key agents so that families, communities, and schools may be brought closer together in the effective design and implementation of goals.

If we take from someone his right to decide what he will be curious about, we destroy his freedom of thought. – JOHN HOLT

CHAPTER SIX

Schools as Socializing Agents in Children's Lives

IRENE B. ECKSEL

Editor's Note: Each of us is a product of our environment. If the norm requires sitting up straight, we sit up straight. If it requires an attitude of selfishness, we do what needs to be done. Our family, neighborhood and social systems are defined in terms of what is considered appropriate behavior.

Throughout this book, demographics are cited to illustrate that the world is not as depicted in "Father Knows Best"—certainly not today. What does a youngster do when the messages received conflict with those sent by the school? "Thou shalt not steal," is different from "Thou shalt not get caught."

If the culture of the teacher is to become part of the consciousness of the child, then the culture of child must first be in the consciousness of the teacher.—BERNSTEIN

Introduction

The idea of classrooms having cultures dates back over a half century (see Waller 1932). Socialization enables cultures; it is the process of rendering someone fit for living in a particular society. Michalson and Lewis (1985) suggest that the goal of socialization "is to raise children to behave as do other members of the group," and, in fact, most children do acquire patterns of behavior congruent with the expectations of their culture. But Michalson and Lewis go on to state that "some socialization pressures cause individuals of the group to act not similarly but 'idiosyncratically'" (p. 134).

It has been nearly a quarter of a century since Jencks, et al. (1972) reported on the influence of families in children's school success. Clearly, learners are not only a product of their "formal" education but also of their informal education. The debate (see Averch et al. 1972; Bernstein 1970; Brookover et al. 1979; Coleman et al. 1966; Hauser et al. 1976; Jencks et al. 1972) over whether schools make any difference at all in the lives of learners, in fact, remains a scourge to many educators. Regardless of the position held, it is clear that the parent's role is vital to the growth of the child. It is generally accepted that parents are the primary educators; they are first in the socialization process. Parents

> teach their children by merely living with them in the family group. They are examples which children follow instinctively. They also teach directly by telling and showing, by praising when the children conform and punishing when they fail to measure up to the standards set by the family group. The family is first in time, and in many ways the most important teaching agency in any society. (Frost 1966, 12)

The bulk of socialization literature involves itself with the examination of the interaction between parents and their children, while the bulk of classroom culture literature explores the organization and management of classrooms. Recent research indicates that socialization by teachers is an active process that may demean learning (Ecksel et al. 1991, 1990b, 1990c; Kaplan, Stettner, and Ecksel 1990), clearly antithetical to classroom cultures. The goal of this chapter is to bring together the research on parent/child socialization with that on classroom organization and management and put forth recommendations for *enhancing* learning and building a more productive society through socialization in schools. It will be argued that in the last quarter century, support for building a productive society through socialization has flooded the literature and that despite much information, parents, teachers, and teacher preparation programs have neglected to heed it. The argument will draw on studies primarily in education, psychology, and sociology beginning by describing the social context in which schools operate, going on to address the manner in which children are socialized at home and in school and ending with a discussion and series of recommendations. The opportunity for change faces us now, and a fruitful conversion will result only from a solid foundation of information on where to go, how to get there, how to know if we've arrived, and how to then make it still better.

The reader is referred to Maccoby and Martin (1983) for an in-depth review of the socializing impact parents have on children, Sarason (1971) for an understanding of the culture of schools and its relationship to the society at large, Goodlad (1984) for a comprehensive analysis of schools, and

Bennett and LeCompte (1990) for a review of the social and political contexts of schooling.

The Context

Following an investigation of thousands of teachers, parents, and students, Goodlad (1984) reported that schools serve four functions: (1) *academic,* embracing all intellectual skills and domains of knowledge; (2) *vocational,* geared to developing readiness for productive work and economic responsibility; (3) *social and civic,* related to preparing for socialization into a complex society; and (4) *personal,* emphasizing the development of individual responsibility, talent, and free expression. Given that schools "reflect society," these four purposes must be consistent with the society at large. And the image research reflects of that society is disquieting, to say the least.

Imagine a tornado lifts your house from the ground and sends it spiraling. Outside your bedroom window you see a smiling neighbor in her rocking chair flying through the air; you see farm animals flying, too. Your dog jumps to your bed from your wicked neighbor's basket as she bicycles through the sky. Your house twirls. And suddenly it falls. Frightened and disoriented, you pick up your dog. Together you peer outside and, almost magically, life turns from black and white to color. And this is what you see . . .

"Girl gangs" are on the rise. The majority of children born in the 1980s will, at some time in their lives, live in single-parent homes (Brown 1986). Over 50 percent of mothers of children less than 1 year old are in the work force (Collins 1987). Up to 33 percent of all elementary school children are "latch-key" children (O'Neill and Sepielli 1985). Nearly 40 percent of 17-year-olds cannot draw inferences from written material (National Commission on Excellence in Education 1983). Twenty percent of all children are born to, and raised by, adolescents, described as insensitive to their children's needs, impatient, and inclined to punish (Furstenberg 1976). One in every five or six children in the schools lives with an alcoholic or other drug-addicted parent (Wenger 1985). Forty percent of all minority children live in impoverished homes (O'Neill and Sepielli 1985). Elementary school counselor caseloads average more than 750; the problems they attempt to reconcile involve incest, crack-addicted mothers, and violent homes (Lee 1990). In 1978, student attacks on teachers exceeded 100,000 (National Institute of Education 1978). The National Institute on Drug Abuse estimates that 10 percent of all pregnant women used or are using cocaine, adversely affecting up to 375,000 infants each year (Teltsch 1990). (Others consider this estimate conservative). Twenty-three million American adults are functionally illiterate (National Commission on Excellence in Education 1983). The average teacher is white and female; typically, the principal for whom she works is white and male (National Education Association 1972); about 97 percent of superintendents are white (Marriott 1990); the students they serve, especially in urban areas, are increasingly minority-dominated (Hodgkinson 1985). Dropout rates for Native Americans are reported at 42 percent overall and as high as 90 percent in some areas (Kunisawa 1988). The number of moderately priced rental properties is decreasing as the number of families priced out of the home market is increasing; the threat of homelessness targets especially families with young children (Joint Center for Housing Studies 1988). White high school dropouts from affluent neighborhoods in New York are more likely to be hired into jobs than black graduates from Harlem (Tobier 1984). Nearly two and a half million thefts occur monthly in secondary schools alone (National Institute of Education 1978). Only 30 percent of 17-year-olds can solve a multistep mathematics problem (National Commission on Excellence in Education 1983). All these random pieces of society's image snowball into a formidable challenge to those concerned with the direction of socialization within that picture.

The Process of Socialization

Eisenberg and Mussen (1989), Lewis and Saarni (1985), and other analysts suggest that socialization is associated with two categories of experience: (1) direct, in which conditions are arranged for the child to be socialized in a particular way, for example, instructing or reasoning with a child; and (2) indirect, in which the child is socialized through vicarious observation and subsequently modulates expressions or behavior. These experiences, however, interact with a number of other factors—for example, the quality of the interaction between the child and adult, specifically held beliefs and practices for socialization, the quality of interaction between child and peers, the environment. These factors also interact with one another. The sections that follow will survey the research that lends most knowledge to the issue of children's success in school and the ultimate success of society.

Child–Adult Interaction

It is generally accepted that well-adjusted parents provide more socioemotional stability and security for their children (e.g., Becker et al. 1959; Eron 1982; Sameroff and Seifer 1983). Children who are more secure and more socioemotionally stable are at an advantage for academic success in school (Ecksel 1990a) and competent interaction with peers (Coie 1990). Children who are less secure and less emotionally stable have been circuitously argued as being at increased risk for repeated absence from, and dropping out of, school (Amble 1967; Kupersmidt et al. 1990; Zeller 1966).

Early infant–mother-attachment researchers (e.g., Ainsworth 1967; Ainsworth and Bell 1969) proposed three types of attachment between mothers and infants (i.e., avoidant, secure, and resistant) after observing infants separated and subsequently reunited with their mothers. Based on measures of sensitivity, warmth, supportive and cooperative behavior, etc., mothers of securely attached infants displayed more of these behaviors than mothers of either avoidant or resistant infants (e.g., Ainsworth et al. 1971, 1978; Clarke-Stewart 1973). Secure attachment has been related to more competent interaction with unfamiliar adults (Main and Weston 1981) and peers (Pastor 1981) and is predictive of social competence in school (e.g., Arend, Gove, and Sroufe 1979; Waters, Wippman, and Sroufe 1979).

Research on the manner in which parents parent and its socializing effect has also considered factors such as sensitivity, warmth, support, and cooperation. Parents who are critical and derogatory tend to have children who behave contentiously (e.g., Bandura and Walters 1959; Becker et al. 1959; Eron 1982; Lefkowitz et al. 1977). Punitive discipline by parents tends to be associated with aggression in children (Becker 1964). Ridicule and disappointment expressed by parents are associated with constrained, neurotic (Simonds and Simonds 1981), and attention-seeking behavior in children (Hoffman 1963). Parents who are authoritative—that is, parents who are warm, loving, supportive, and responsive to their children (see Baumrind 1971, 1973, for distinctions between authoritarian, authoritative, and permissive parenting styles) have children who are more socially successful; socially competent children are less likely to be rejected or neglected by classmates (e.g., Ladd and Mize 1983). Baumrind (1988, cited in Eisenberg and Mussen 1990) states that "authoritative childrearing is the only pattern that consistently (and significantly) produced competent children (that is, children high in social competence *and* social responsibility) and failed to produce incompetent children (those low in both social competence and social responsibility) in the preschool years and middle childhood" (p. 81).

Beliefs and Practices for Socialization

People teach according to what they believe. Attitudes shape perceptions of experience. Recent research indicates that role percepts, that is, what individuals believes their function as teachers or parents to be, also affect the manner in which people socialize (Ecksel, Kaplan, and Stettner 1990b). The following narrative, which was told to a researcher by a South Baltimore mother in the company of her 2-year-old daughter, should provide instant clarity:

This guy [who lives] in the back of us, the other night comin' in from work—they said they don't know why he did it—coming home from work he took a lead pipe and beat his wife all in the face and the head with it. Well, busted her eardrums. They had to sew several, the bottom of her chin and all up on top of her head. And he took and drug her from the living room, knocked her unconscious. And he drug her from the living room into the kitchen and finally put her behind the refrigerator. . . . I'm afraid I'd a had picked up somethin', the nearest thing that was to me and slammed him in the head with it before he'd a gotten me real good.

It was this storyteller's position that it was her *responsibility* to prepare her daughter to protect herself in an increasingly angry and violent society. The mother taught her daughter how, when, and with whom to fight through narrative and verbal and physical provocation; this same mother, incidentally, "strongly disapproved of parents who abuse their children and related incidents in which [she was] angered by a parent's mistreatment of his or her child" (Miller and Sperry 1987, 18).

A number of researchers (e.g., Abelson 1979; Bussis, Chittenden, and Amarel 1976; Feinman-Nemser and Buchmann 1985) suggest that teachers' beliefs about teaching, learning, and subject matter affect their classroom conduct, while Brown (1968) suggests otherwise; some suggest that it is only a part of the picture (Ecksel 1990; Ecksel, Kaplan, and Stettner 1991, 1990b, 1990c; Kaplan, Stettner, and Ecksel 1990). While the factors at work have not necessarily been clearly enumerated, it has been documented that affluent children are given more feedback to enhance self-presentation than are poor children (Bernstein 1970; Labov 1972), that teachers of poor urban students respond differentially to emotions than do their suburban, more affluent counterparts (Ecksel et al, 1991; Kaplan, Stettner, and Ecksel 1990), and that teachers interact more positively, and frequently, with high "track" students (Grant and Rothenberg 1986; McDermott, Gospodinoff, and Aron 1978). Sex biases in schools have also been repeatedly documented (e.g., Brophy and Good 1970; Grant 1984; Kelly and Nihlen 1982; LaFrance 1985; Lee and Gropper 1974; Tetrault 1986).

Child–Peer Relations

Positive peer relations have been associated with prosocial and altruistic behavior in children (see Eisenberg and Mussen 1989; Mussen and Eisenberg-Berg 1977). The consequence of poor peer relations is often peer social rejection, the implications of which are vast and multidimensional (see Asher and Coie 1990). Peer rejection has been associated with negative treatment from peers (Dodge 1983), depression (Vosk et al. 1982), changes in children's self-perceptions (Hymel and Franke 1985), personal perceptions of loneliness (Asher and Wheeler 1985), adult psychiatric deviancy (Parker and Asher 1987), and adult criminal behavior (West and Farrington 1973, 1977). The most immediately consequential consideration of peer rejection relative to this discussion is that learning is a socially and emotionally mediated intellectual process (Ecksel 1990); ergo, the rejected child is the child who is at risk for not learning.

The Environment

Organizing safe, productive learning environments is fundamental to all classrooms. Classrooms are, ideally, arranged to minimize disruptive movement by students and encourage supervision of work and behavior — materials, equipment, and displays are made easily accessible (Emmer et al. 1989; Evertson et al. 1989); time for instructional activities is planned and observed (Denham and Lieberman 1980; Stallings 1980); and rules are straightforward and enforceable (Evertson and Emmer 1982). Even the most organized and best-managed classroom is not a guarantee that children will learn, because children live in more cultures than that of the classroom.

Children who are abused often respond to distress calls from peers by withdrawing or aggressing (Main and George 1985). Children who live with "background anger" experience increased stress and assume responsibility for the anger (Cummings 1987; Cummings and Cummings 1988; Cummings, Ianotti, and Zahn-Waxler 1985; Cummings, Zahn-Waxler, and Radke-Yarrow 1981, 1984). Children's stress is not, even in the most cohesive families, exceptional.

Bloom (1976) states that students are judged many times each day in terms of their adequacy relative to others. The student is judged by teachers, family, and peers; more, the student sits in judgment of her- or himself. Regardless of the acceptability of personal accomplishment, if others exceed the accomplishment or the learner does not meet self-set standards, she or he acknowledges the discrepancy. The individual response to being repeatedly judged is a personal one; often it is experienced as stress (Humphrey and Humphrey 1981; Kohn 1986). Exacerbating the effects of personal experiences of stress are external stressors with which individuals must cope. Increasingly there is poverty, abuse (of people and substance), crime, dissolution of the nuclear family, teen pregnancy, teen suicide, unemployment, apathy, and infant mortality.

Problem solving is disturbed when attention becomes focused away from cues relevant to a task (Wine 1971). Negative conditions produce distraction and lead to poor performance (Galassi, Frierson, and Sharer 1981; Hollandsworth et al. 1979; Nottleman and Hill 1977; Zatz and Chassin 1983).

Emotions influence basic cognitive processes even so far as to affect content of perception (Bower 1981; Gilligan and Bower 1984; Hettena and Ballif 1981; Izard, Nagler et al. 1965; Izard, Wehmer et al. 1965). And while a degree of arousal has been repeatedly shown to facilitate learning, intense arousal disturbs the learning process (Izard 1984) and interferes with efforts to glean meaning from content (Kahneman 1973; Mueller 1979; Schwartz 1975).

Discussion

This following discussion is based on an argument that only recently has been put forth (see Ecksel 1990); its components are clearly supported. There is a correlation between resilience, that is, facing extreme stress and soundly recovering, and prosocial behavior (Earls 1986; Rachman 1979). Anti-social actors are often those who are rejected, a status stable over time (e.g., Coie and Dodge 1983; Coie and Kupersmidt 1983). The status of rejection is linked with poor school performance, early withdrawal from school, and psychiatric deviancy and criminality in adulthood.

Children who are quarrelsome and hostile interfere with teachers' abilities to teach; discipline and control are considered the chief problems in schools today (Gallup and Clark 1987; Cruickshank 1981). Coie and Koeppl (1990), citing previous research, state, "negative teacher-student interactions in the classroom may influence a child's social standing among classmates — [T]he tendency of rejected children to be frequently off task in the classroom has been linked to the fact that many rejected children have academic difficulties" (p. 320). Teachers want students who are task-oriented, respectful of materials and the learning process, and who display healthy social interaction. When students have been rejected by their peers, teachers have been noted to consider them as more aggressive even when they are not markedly so (Mize and Ladd 1990). Levine (1983) suggests that social comparisons produce feelings of inferiority, decreased motivation, hostility, competitiveness, and low aspiration in low-achieving students, but schools continue to be based on a model of competition rather than cooperation.

Schools are charged with teaching skills for problem solving. Cognition is aroused by affect (e.g., Kaplan 1978, 1986; Krathwohl, Bloom, and Masia 1964), which is built upon a learner's sensitivity to the existence of certain phenomena, that is, the learner's willingness or ability to "receive" or "attend" to certain stimuli. The ability to attend is curtailed when attention becomes focused away from cues relevant to a task due to stress. Jahoda (1953, 1958) posited that the capacity for problem solving real-life situations is the standard for defining positive mental health. Problem solving involves more than simply applying and testing one's skills and knowledge: an individual's thoughts about his or her abilities, the task, and goal guide one through the problem to solution and accomplishment. People enter problem-solving situations with expectancies for their own capabilities and with anticipations regarding the outcomes of their actions (Bandura 1977); the potential impact of feelings of inferiority and depression upon these expectancies should be apparent.

The emotional climate that the child brings to school is generally regarded as part of the child's makeup: fixed and either advantageous or disruptive to the classroom milieu. Most teacher preparation programs prepare new teachers to teach subject matter and the preparation is based on the notion that the student, while possibly disruptive, is essentially a healthy, "teachable" person. The freshly graduated teacher enters the classroom with this belief set and is often surprised to find that she or he was not adequately prepared to deal with the "reality" of the classroom. It is the reality of the classroom that defines its culture and ultimately advances society.

Recommendations

Learners' needs must be addressed at the outset of all learning tasks. Current educational agendas focus largely on methods by which efficient learning takes place, and little concentration is being placed on the learner as the real receiver of instruction (Bloom 1972; deCharms 1976). Appeals have been made for linking learning theory to educational practice (Beauchamp 1981; Broudy 1966; Bruner 1963; Tyler 1978) and emotional sequelae (Ecksel 1990; Ecksel et al. 1991; Kaplan, Stettner, and Ecksel 1990; Ratner and Stettner 1991), but curricula continue to prescribe to learners as though they were receptacles for cognitive information. Maintaining the current agendas is not only inadequate; but it also fosters a society of individuals unprepared to engage in competent cooperative interaction. It is essential, then, that teachers be adept not only in cognitive methodology but also in affective methodology and understand the mediating effects of emotion.

Children as young as 3 years of age are able to understand what adults consider appropriate emotional responses (Borke 1971, 1973; Gnepp 1983; Shantz 1975) and respond to others' emotional needs (Radke-Yarrow and Zahn-Waxler 1984; Zahn-Waxler and Radke-Yarrow 1982). Eisenberg and Mussen (1989), citing numerous researchers, state: "Among toddlers, preschoolers, and school-age children, expressiveness of feeling—especially of positive rather than sad affects—is associated with spontaneous prosocial actions" (p. 61); later, they submit that, "preschool and elementary school children with strong prosocial predispositions tend to be well-adjusted, good at coping, and self-controlled" (p. 63). Burleson (1985, cited in Dodge and Feldman 1990) suggests that comforting behavior consistently discriminates popular children from unpopular ones. Ecksel and colleagues (1991) and

Kaplan, Stettner, and Ecksel (1990) found that displays of positive affects were generally discouraged by teachers, especially teachers of urban elementary school children. Maintaining decorous behavior in classrooms is a fundamental concern of teachers; what is being exchanged must be fully acknowledged.

The "praise the good stuff and ignore the bad" paradigm is insufficient for keeping classroom order. Adults who are warm, friendly, competent, and responsive have been shown to be more effective models than those who are aloof and distant (Radke-Yarrow, Zahn-Waxler, and Chapman 1983). Judgments of teacher competence by children are often based on the children's perceptions of the teacher's fairness and impartiality relative to their own perceptions (Lee, Statuto, and Vedar-Voivodas 1983). Concise, emotionally-laded explanations have been associated with increased prosocial behavior (Zahn-Waxler, Radkes-Yarrow, and Kilng 1979, cited in Eisenberg and Mussen 1989). "Time-out" obstructs opportunities for teaching prosocial behavior by example. Many teachers make classroom management a primary teaching goal; each is entitled to, at least, this much knowledge.

Generally, students who believe that they have control over outcomes function better on school tasks than those who believe they have little control (Brookover et al. 1979; Stipek and Weisz 1981); likewise, they tend to outperform the others on grades and achievement tests (Chance 1972; Crandall and Lacey 1972; Milgram and Milgram 1975; Norwicki and Walker 1974). These same students are less reactive to very difficult or negative events (Lefcourt et al. 1981) and persist longer in the face of failure (Weiner et al. 1971). They are more effective sources of influence (Baron and Ganz 1972; Baron et al. 1974; Lefcourt et al. 1975; Phares 1976; Rajecki, Ickes, and Tanford 1981) and tend to engage in more goal-directed behavior (Davis and Phares 1967; Gore and Rotter 1963). Sobol and Earn (1985, cited in Dodge and Feldman 1990) suggest that children who are rejected view outcomes as less controllable than do their popular contemporaries. Throughout the day, teachers are engaged in feedback to students; in fact, providing feedback is considered an essential element of good teaching (Brophy and Good 1986). However, the quality and precision of teacher feedback must be considered. The potential impact of a teacher repeatedly telling a student to "try harder" when the student has inadequate knowledge or strategies for success may result in the child's assuming that she or he lacks ability; this assumption authorizes the student's belief of having little control over outcomes.

To assume the implications of a teacher's feeling little control over outcomes is significantly different from that of the students is likely a faulty assumption. Goodlad (1984) said about teachers:

They agreed, generally, on the importance of basic skills and subject matter and of increasing students' store of information about the various fields of knowledge. At the same time, they perceived the necessity for teachers to be in control of classroom circumstances . . . teachers, aware of the rather crowded box in which they and their students live each day, see the need to be in control, to prevent unruly students from dominating, as a necessary condition for student learning. . . . A class out of control and a teacher's giving praise generously for student accomplishment are incompatible. A class out of control is not a class engaged in academic learning . . . when asked to select what they perceived to be their school's one biggest problem, teachers tended to select problems affecting their teaching but appearing to be beyond their control—*lack of student interest, school too large and classes overcrowded, lack of parent interest, administration, inadequate resources, and, at the junior high school level, in particular, students' misbehavior.* (pp. 174–175) (italics added)

A teacher's self-concept has an effect upon the development of student self-concepts (Edeburn and Landry 1976). While it has been stated that there is no causal relationship between general self-image and academic performance (Harter 1983), it is intuitively supportable that someone (student, teacher, or parent) who believes herself or himself incapable of implementing solutions will not attend to those resources available that facilitate problem resolution. Prospective teachers must be prepared for the reality of teaching: There *will* be a lack of student interest, classes *will* be overcrowded, some parents *will* lack interest, the resources *will* be inadequate, and students *will* misbehave; if a teacher is not fully informed and walks into the classroom with a set of false assumptions, these assumptions authorize the belief that she or he has little control over outcomes.

Much of the research on ability grouping and tracking suggests that such practices have a detrimental effect on students (e.g., Allington 1977; Barr 1974; Cazden 1986; Cicourel et al. 1974; Dreeben 1984; Featherstone 1987; Shavelson and Stern 1981). Students, it is suggested, are "tracked" not necessarily according to ability but rather according to the attributes of their parents (e.g., single parent, poor parent) and their cultures. Low-track students receive less attention and instructional time; instructional time is correlated with student achievement (Berliner 1979; Berliner and Rosenshine 1977; Stallings 1980; Walberg, Schiller, and Haertel 1979). The expectation of low-track students being students of "low ability" is, then, strengthened. Schools are still typically organized in this manner. Interdependent cooperative learning teams, in which group rewards are based upon the output of the group rather than of the individual, produce students who are more tolerant of ethnic diversity, are more prosocial, and are academically improved (Kagan 1986; Slavin 1983). Does this support the suggestion of Apple (1982, 1986), Aronowitz and Giroux (1985), Giroux (1988), and other researchers that this prejudice is planned and is what society really *does* want, or, on the other hand, does it suggest that teachers are ill-prepared to construct such environments or even to articulately advocate for such an approach to their schools and districts?

Most theories of instruction (e.g., Landa 1976; Reigeluth and Stein 1983; Scandura 1977, 1980) suggest that content knowledge be organized (and delivered) in a systematic fashion to facilitate higher-order thinking skills; drill-and-practice paradigms are antithetical to this end, but they continue to be the most widely used paradigm in K–12 schooling. Until teachers are adequately versed in instructional theory, they will continue to utilize drill-and-practice paradigms or whatever instructional blueprint is most fashionable. The same argument may be dealt on behalf of curriculum theories. Until teachers are versed in curricular decision making, they are instructional managers; until they are versed in instructional decision making, they are classroom managers; until they are versed in socioemotional and cultural knowledge, they are, at best, safekeepers.

Cultural patterns learned at home that conflict with cultural patterns in school promote withdrawal and indifference in students (Philips 1983). This piece of research is shared in recognition that most teachers are not teaching children who are "like them." Teachers must be literate about the cultures from which their students are coming (see beginning quote).

Conclusion

One need only look at the Jencks et al (1972) report, in which it was reported that "family background explains nearly half of the variation of educational attainment" (p. 143), to understand how critical it is for parents and teachers to unite in the education of children. This chapter has suggested that families are, indeed, vital elements in the production or destruction of society and that teachers nurture the course either through direct processes or ignorance.

Teacher preparation programs are commissioned to prepare teachers to prepare students to function seemly as members of a "civilized" society. A civilized society is one with a pluralism of ideas and values; the skills needed to cultivate this pluralism are *not* acquired through happenstance. Teacher education programs must begin to expect prospective teachers to have criterial information in *at least* learning theory, cultural sociology and anthropology, instructional theory (including adult learners), curriculum theory, negotiation and conflict resolution, life-span human development, observation and measurement, educational foundations (including philosophy, history, and legal aspects), family dynamics, and an array of teaching models. Neglecting to accrue this collection of skills built upon a solid arts and science foundation relegates teachers to paraprofessional status. Teachers' roles demand

quick thinking and intuiting far beyond the subject matter they are required
to teach. Intuitive judgments *necessarily* require a solid knowledge base if
the judgments are to be consistently sound.

Apple (1982, 1986) has explored the extent to which decisions about
instructional matters have been expropriated from teachers; they are "de-
skilled," he suggests, in part because of technological innovation and in part
due to the prescriptive nature of curricula and teaching plans. If teacher
preparation programs were designed to engender in teachers those same beliefs
as are planned for children (e.g., school is a safe environment for taking
intellectual risks, intellectual risks promote learning, learning is fun and
worthwhile, higher-order thinking skills are a valued commodity, prosocial
and cooperative interaction are vital, differences are assets, etc.), there would
exist the inherent belief in the profession of teachers that is essentially empowering and contrary to de-skilling.

Prospective teachers must begin to insist upon adequate knowledge if
they are to fulfill their roles as professional educators and coordinate efforts
with parents. Students whose parents are integrally involved in their education fare better in school. Schools are, for many, the first institution in which
they participate and repeatedly fail. Given human nature, it is not surprising
that many parents would choose to avoid returning to an environment where
they have a history of failure; pressure to do so only makes it worse. Despite
complaints by many teachers of their early educational experiences, for the
most part their experiences were successful; many of their students' parents
were demoralized in their own early educational experiences, and for teachers
to fail to appreciate that is an injustice to both the parent and the student.
Teachers need to know how to reconcile parental concerns, to teach parents
to be educators of their children, and to view parents as allies with a common mission. These are essential social skills with which every teacher should
be endowed. The fact that teachers are social animals does not mean that
they have a natural tendency to successfully work *with* others; were that the
case, the market on self-help books would be drastically reduced. Again, these
are skills that prospective teachers should insist upon from teacher preparation programs.

Parents must understand that their children's successes and failures
belong to the child and not to them. Teachers *are* professional educators and
do have knowledge that parents cannot be expected to have. Parents should
insist that teachers work *with* them for the benefit of the child and the community. They should insist that their questions be sufficiently answered and
should not lose sight of the fact that teachers are there because they really
do want to teach (Goodlad 1984). Parents and teachers, again, should be
allies; they have one mission: the child.

The picture of society these days is a fairly disturbing one, and every
institution is feeding and nurturing it. Supported information exists that

makes continued hope viable, but it will require a great deal of effort. It is time to acknowledge the material and start the reform process, for if we do not we are disregarding the cost to this and future generations. May each with our own expertise, join and believe that we *do* have control over outcomes and begin to move purposively toward an improved society.

Give our students the capacity to look at things as if they could be otherwise. — *JOHN DEWEY*

CHAPTER SEVEN

Parents, Power, and the Public Schools

WILHELMINA PERRY   MARGARET D. TANNENBAUM

Editor's Note: Parental participation in educational decision making is not new—its focus merely changes. Presently, calls for some type of voucher system or school-based management are hotly debated topics proceeding, in some states, all the way to the ballot box.

This chapter calls into question the purpose of gathering public support for schools. It does this by discussing some of the history of parent involvement, tracing its roots and drawing reference to how it can be implemented in today's complex society.

Introduction

This chapter will examine parental involvement with American public schools. The primary aim is to describe and analyze the climate and dynamics of the relations between schools and families, reflect on the historical and social contexts of the dynamics, and evaluate the implications of such analyses for enhancing the relationship between schools and families. Of particular interest are those interactions between schools and parents that are characterized by tension and controversy. A special feature of the chapter will be a section that examines original research data, collected for this book, on the dynamics of parental involvement at the organizational level.

1. A discussion of the underlying assumptions and conceptual orientations
2. A short history of parent-school relationships

3. A delineation and critique of models of parental involvement
4. A research-based discussion of the dynamics of state PTAs and a comparison of PTA views regarding educational issues with the views of teachers' and administrators' associations

Underlying Assumptions and Conceptual Orientations

Underlying Assumptions

Fundamental to the historical and sociological considerations of parental involvement with the public schools are four major premises:

1. *Parent/family involvement can make a difference.* Research generally indicates positive consequences for student achievement, attitudes, and behavior when teachers make parental involvement part of their regular teaching practices. However, current research results may be skewed because involvement occurs primarily on the part of middle-class parents (Ascher 1988; Lareau 1987, 1989; Oyenmade, Washington, and Gullo 1989).

2. *The American family institution has changed dramatically.* Increasingly, people speak of the "breakdown" of the American family; they refer to the dual-career family, the soaring divorce rate, more single-parent homes (especially mother-only families), and more out-of-wedlock births. However, the assessment of these changes need *not* be pessimistic or alarmist, because neither the school nor the institution of the family is necessarily endangered by the changes (Rich 1987).

   a. There is a changing work status of mothers, three-fifths of whom are in the labor market.
   b. Differently structured families are more widely represented in the schools. American family history has been a story of expanding choice, and thus there is extraordinary variation of family arrangements, dynamics, and experiences. What must be noted, in particular, is the increasing number of children of divorced parents and in reconstituted families.
   c. Parental views about acceptable school standards have been changing because many parents have as much formal education as their teachers. As Davies (1976) commented, "In the 1950s and 60s, expectations for what the schools could do shot sky high."

   3. *Currently, home–school relations frequently include parental distrust, distance, and even hostility.* This assertion should not conjure up images of apathetic, uncaring, indifferent

parents or, at best, lukewarm and half-hearted parental supporters. It would seem the problem is not apathy but rather unproductive parent–school relationships. As Oldham and Oldham (1979) declared, there is a love-hate relationship: "Despite all the criticisms, the public wants schools and wants to like them" (p. 1), but not as they presently exist. (Also see Calabrese 1990.) It is "the personal touch" that parents report they want in school relations (Lindle 1989). Thus, according to several writers, the public's confidence in our public schools is weak (e.g., Comer 1986; Psyzkowski 1990; Diner 1990).

   4. *"Differences are endemic to the very nature of families and schools as institutions"* (Lightfoot 1981, 55). These adversarial relationships emerge significantly out of roles defined by the social structure. Moreover, Tyack and Hansot (1981) have expressed the viewpoint that Americans have no ideology that legitimates conflict in public education. Thus, the gap between family and school cannot be easily understood.

Conceptual Orientations

Three directions will stand out in the discussion in this chapter:

1. The focus will be, as much as possible, on parents' involvement (in contrast to general community involvement) with the public school (K–12).
2. Attention will *not* be given to the education that takes place independently of the school, within the family, as in Leichter's works (1979) on the family as educator.
3. Discussion will center on individual and collective parent–school interactions as they relate to parental power and nonpower involvements.

Historical Background

This section examines the interactions between families and schools during the development of the bureaucracy of public school systems, focusing on the tension and conflict that emerged. From the earliest establishment of schools in colonial New England, government steadily increased its control over the form, content, funding, and clients of schools, and that control became increasingly centralized.

Nineteenth Century

Although national leaders made many efforts following the American Revolution to turn public and legislative attention to the establishment of a national public school system, their attempts were unsuccessful. However, during the latter half of the nineteenth century, emerging from the increasingly successful efforts of the Common School reformers, two major developments impacted on the ability of families to exert influence on schooling. First, the state government established the right to dictate the form schooling would take and to tax the public to provide it (*Kalamazoo,* 1874). Second, with the passage of compulsory attendance legislation and child labor laws, the state mandated that if parents were to have access to their tax dollars for schooling, they would have to send their children to schools approved by this same state government. Sectarian schools that had been receiving government funds had to reject their sectarian orientation or lose that funding. Thus, the parents' opportunity to choose what they perceived to be the best school environment for their children was severely limited.

In 1857 the National Education Association was founded. By 1892 a movement within this organization was instrumental in the forming of a committee whose purpose was to standardize the high school curriculum, thus beginning the process of professional control over educational content (Ornstein and Levine).

Twentieth Century

In 1900 the National Congress of Parents and Teachers (PTA) was founded to achieve two primary goals: parent education and the enlisting of parents in improving educational conditions for children. These tasks from the beginning were not easy, as by this time political and social forces were moving together to increasingly drive a wedge between the school and the home as joint participants in the education of children. American education more and more became a situation of "the home *versus* the school and particularly the parent versus the teacher" (Overstreet 1972). PTA efforts to bring parents into the schools and classrooms on a regular basis were not without resistance from teachers, administrators, and board members (Overstreet).

By the time the last state (Mississippi) passed its compulsory attendance laws in 1918, there was a clear hegemony of the state government over the family in educational matters. As school districts consolidated and school boards decreased in both number and size, fewer and fewer people had more and more power. In addition, professionals were consolidating their positions as educational experts through the growing use of testing and the increasing importance of superintendents and middle-level administrators. Reflecting the impact of the National Association of Manufacturers and their charges of "gross inefficiency" in the schools, these early twentieth-century administrators increasingly attempted to organize and run schools as businesses—in which nonprofessionals (parents) were not welcome.

According to M. Williams (1989), there were two basic types of reactions to this increasing bureaucratization of schools. First, the liberal Progressive reform movement (1900–1930s) saw the development of the concept of the school as a community center, loosely derived from the idea of settlement houses. The underlying assumptions of this approach were basically those of *noblesse oblige* in which ordinary citizens were seen as victims of their own ignorance and the school as a place to imbue them with middle-class virtues. Second, the political activist approach, by contrast, was manifest in the wave of boycotts by blacks as they were increasingly pressured to attend segregated schools, many of which offered only industrial training.

The twentieth century also saw the emergence of the first citizens' advisory committees, although they were not very prevalent or active until the post–World War II era, when they were formed to deal with building needs. The majority of these locally initiated committees, however, were without legal status as they were grassroots rather than governmentally sponsored organizations.

Certainly the *Brown* v. *Topeka* (1954) decision was the beginning of a new period in which activism at the local level would make a difference in educational policy and practice. In the 1960s and 70s, most federal legislation that provided money to local school districts required the participation of citizen advisory groups. Included was legislation such as the *Elementary and Secondary Education Act* and the *Education for All Handicapped Children Act* (1975). During the 1970s a number of states also passed legislation that required citizen participation in newly established programs. Further, major cities engaged in districtwide decentralization designed to provide far more citizen control of local schools. It must be remembered, however, that—with the exception of the PTA—none of these trends had its locus of power among parents wanting to have more impact on the education of children.

By the 1980s, schools were experiencing two diverse trends in the struggle. With the publication of *A Nation at Risk* in 1983, there was a call for reform that focused on more demanding requirements for both teachers and students. As this movement gained strength, countermovements emerged among both teachers and parents. The objectives of these countermovements loosely fell under the rubric of school restructuring. This concept presently includes at least two major proposals relevant to the discussion in this chapter: site-based management for schools, which would provide policy-making councils composed of both teachers and parents at the individual school level, and schools of choice, which are seen by many as the means for placing control of schooling in the hands of families in a way they have never experienced in the past.

It can be clearly seen, then, that the government in this country gained early formal control of the education of the nation's children. Some scholars have said educational reformers imposed public education upon unwilling, even resisting working-class parents (Katz 1971). On the other hand, there are scholars who maintain that, while greater literacy in colonial and nineteenth-century America made parents more capable of educating their children at home, most parents were willing, in principle, to expand the schools. This was so even though, in practice, parents often voted against any increases in their taxes for public education and disagreed with some specific educational and disciplinary practices (Vinovskis 1987). There was, according to this second school of thought, "no conspiratorial plot" by educational reformers to "dominate, channel and objectify" schooling, although governmental control became a fact (Hogan 1985).

Perhaps the debate about family tensions in the past is an academic point. It is, however, very timely now. *Tensions are very apparent, and discussions of parents' rights and power are new dynamics in the American public education system.*

Taxonomy of Models of Parent Involvement

This section focuses on recent directions and issues in the increasing hodgepodge of publications concerning parental involvement with the public schools. What is especially striking is the dearth of scholarly interest in the theoretical/conceptual issues and implications. It must be noted that there are limited attempts to even classify the various roles of parents relative to the schools.

One early attempt at classifications came from Petit (1980), who specified levels of increasing involvement, from being aware to active participation in the classroom. Rasinski and Fredericks (1989) found Petit's approach intriguing, but they created an additional level they called empowerment. At such a level there would be mutual trust and work in advising, planning, and administering, as well as implementing programs. In a similar vein, Seeley (1989) has discussed the paradigm shift in education from a delegation model, which limits the primary responsibilities of the citizen to paying taxes and holding offices, to a collaborative model in which parental involvement is a necessity and is empowering.

Most of the involvement typologies have centered on support or nonpower roles (see Fanini as cited in Ornstein 1983; Jenkins 1981; Stallworth and Williams 1981). Perhaps Epstein (Epstein 1987, 1988; Brandt 1989) has established one of the best-known and most elaborate identifications of traditional parental involvement types. She has discussed (1) basic parenting obligations to make children ready for school, (2) school-to-home communication (as in conferences), (3) parental involvement and assistance at the school, (4) parental involvement in home-based learning activities, and (5) parental involvement in governance and advocacy. Jackson and Cooper (1989) would add two less traditional parent roles to Epstein's list: (1) individual decision maker in school choices for offspring, and (2) social network member in self-help and school improvement. The two critics argue that such new efforts would empower families as key decision makers.

The following discussion is an attempt by the present authors to organize and analyze a typology of the dimensions of parental involvement activities. It acknowledges both supportive and adversarial roles. Each of four models articulates the underlying assumptions that both school professionals and parents/families make about the nature of schools and the nature of families. Also, the authors highlight some of the distinctive benefits and limitations of each model, as deduced from the literature. Finally, there are illustrative cases.

Child-Centered Model

Child-centered models directly involve parents in the education of their own children, and are generally supportive of the schools. As Gallup polls for the last several years have noted, parents are somewhat more positive toward the schools than is the general public. Usually the school initiates the formalized aspects of this first mode of involvement, but appeal is to the most basic parental motivation to help one's own child. Thus, some sort of self-interest is at stake.

In this model, parents may become involved in home–school coordinated learning activities for the child at home. This parent-as-tutor approach is cited in the recent literature as most directly linked to improved academic achievement (Epstein 1987). Another relevant and popular activity is the parent-teacher conference. A 1987 Metropolitan Life survey showed that single working mothers as well as dual working parent families value teacher contact and consultation. Moreover, data on direct observations of teacher conferences with parents of learning-disabled children indicated that the additional presence of the school counselor as a parent advocate generated significantly high parental participation in the conference (Goldstein and Turnbull 1982). Also, research results show that among blacks, certain family types (e.g., being a single parent) or socioeconomic conditions (e.g., being an employed mother) are not inherent barriers to parent–teacher communication at the school site (Leitch and Tangri 1988).

Many of those writing about the child-centered type of parental involvement share, either implicitly or explicitly, an organizational model of the public schools based on the building as the primary unit. The parent is part of a network of interrelated positions directly linked to the organizational goal if imparting knowledge and skills to the students at a particular school.

The prime explanatory limitation of this model has been cited by educational sociologist Neal Gross (1958), who argued that the formal organizational goal of public school systems is vague and ambiguous, in comparison with the objectives of other types of organizations. Thus, it is not always clear what specific role expectations schools hold for parents in this model.

Collaboration Model

The second model centers on the collaborating parent. In this model there is more than just a linkage or interconnectedness, as in the first model, but the organizational assumption is still evident, either implicitly or explicitly. The parent is mainly a service-oriented assistant, assuming such roles as accessory or educational volunteer.

The most intense form of collaboration, partnership, is an idealistic claim espoused by school personnel (Seeley 1981, 1984). However, the picture of teacher and parent as partners or at least allies in supporting the school is generally marred by a frequently acted-out teacher belief that a "professional–client relationship" is more productive than a partnership one. Thus, teachers welcome "only particular types of parent involvement in schooling— involvement they defined as supportive" (Lareau 1989, 35). For example, in a study of programs for the hearing-impaired, Twilling and Bock (1989) observed that support groups for parents of such children, led by a team of school personnel and mental health professionals, achieve open discussion between parents and teachers. Moreover, even in the Comer Process (or School Development Program), which is a school-based effort that has had successes particularly with poor, minority children, parent collaborators contribute mainly in the area of school climate, thereby helping to eliminate "harmful stereotypes that staff members may harbor about the community served by their school" (Comer 1986, 446).

Even those school personnel who extol the virtue of involving all parents as partners question whether the current system could stand such commitment and energy. Indeed, the time resources required to involve parents in the school program seem presently stretched. (See Wolf and Stephens 1989).

Decisional Participation Model

In the third involvement type, the decisional participation model, the parent is a participant in planning, policy development, and decision making.

Salisbury (1980) and others have called this "instrumental participation," namely participation intended to influence policy and to obtain access to school governance. Inasmuch as the corporate board and manager constitute the governance model, the focus in this present discussion is on the school board as entry to parent power in education. (Also see Ziegler, Jennings, and Peak 1974; Zerchykov 1984.) Studying parents as board members, not just parents "going to the board," reveals that board memberships are demographically skewed toward males, whites, and high status groups. Kapel and Pink (1978) have commented that "the very people calling for representation and who need to be heard from most are disproportionately underrepresented [on boards] following a standard election procedure" (p. 21). Moreover, Gittell and colleagues (1979) found that even boards that are demographically representative are not thereby any more responsive as collectives. Greene (1990) found contradictory responses from board members with respect to their interactions with parents. but in her exploratory study of the dynamics of school board actions, Tallerico (1989) discerned that individual female board members more often exhibited vigilance than did their male counterparts.

Nonetheless, the increasing presence of parental advisory committees suggests politic parental participation. Beyond ad hoc committees to address a particular need, usually a building program, or ongoing committees to deal with more persistent special concerns such as substance abuse, public relations, or curriculum, many school districts will establish broader, ongoing site or districtwide parent councils. The purposes are to gain input from parents on a routine basis about varied school matters, have a vehicle of communication with parents in individual schools, and in general maintain good public relations. In some cases the PTA will play this role, but frequently both school districts and local parent groups prefer not to be controlled by the rules of a national organization.

Parent Activist Model

The fourth type of parental involvement is the parent activist model. This activist or conflict pattern is likely to be evident where there is urban socioeconomic and ethnic diversity. Interestingly, Meighan (1989) claims that those parents frequently perceived to be the most civil by school personnel "are those who in their actual behind-the-scenes behavior signal a sustained criticism of the school regime" (p. 107). Most frequently, parent activist groups are attempting to bring about more grassroots involvement in schools and greater educational equity. It must be noted that school administrators tend to interpret pressure-group tactics in one of two ways: as a dreaded participation that challenges professional hegemony over significant school areas or as a sign of a working liberal democracy. In some city and suburban areas, ad hoc citizen groups that have formed in response to a perceived specific local crisis will occasionally consolidate into more ongoing citizen watchdog networks and organizations. An example is the Swarthmore, Pennsylvania School Action Committee, which has fought for a decade to retain local control. Some of the groups have such national affiliations as the National Committee for the Support of Public Schools, Citizens for Better Schools, and the National Committee for Citizens in Education.

Lightfoot (1978) believes that home–school relations are inherently in conflict because there are tensions between the particularistic concerns of parents and the universalistic concerns of schooling. However, it must be noted that the goal of most action parent groups is reform, not abolition. For example, in his research on citizenship participation in the public school, Salisbury (1980) reflected that parental participation is mostly a supportive rather than a purposive alteration of the status quo. Also, Parelius and Parelius (1978) observed that "most boards operate much of the time within a generally calm, nonpressured socio-political environment" (p. 257). For instance, Saxe (1975) commented that political scientists usually regard "the PTA to be a 'kept' organization, one that acts on behalf of the schools, rather than as an independent pressure group." He acknowledged, though, that the organization has been moving toward "a more independent, assertive" advocacy posture.

Aspects of the Dynamics of a Selected Parent Involvement Organization

The function of this section is to help the reader learn more about parent–school interaction by discussing the group dynamics of the most well-known parent organization, the PTA. The authors' research efforts uncovered no comparable study. In the early summer of 1990, the authors used a structured questionnaire instrument to tap the observations of the president or executive director of the state Parent-Teacher Association in each of the 50 states. The survey objective was to study how the PTA functions as a voluntary special-interest group on the public school scene. The questionnaire included items about the nature of the PTA organizational goals, aspects of recruiting and mobilizing members, the nature of programs and accomplishments, and organizational perceptions of educational issues. In order to do a comparative analysis of the PTA perceptions of issues, the authors also undertook a questionnaire survey of state leaders of four other groups: two teacher organizations, the National Education Association (NEA) and American Federation of Teachers (AFT), and the National Association of School Administrators and the National School Boards Association. Focus was on organizational perceptions about recent public school issues and concerns, especially those involving parent–school relations. (By "organizational perceptions" is meant the estimated perception of the body of members, not the personal attitudes and opinions of the respondent.) The outcomes of the overall assessment are (1) a profile of the PTAs and (2) a discussion of the comparison of the PTA responses with those of various state education organizations regarding educational issues.

PTA Profile

The data on the state PTAs were supplied typically by state presidents who had been active in their organizations for an average of 11.5 years, or sometimes by executive directors or office managers who had been active for an average of 8.3 years. Data analysis (based on 36 returns out of 50, 72 percent) showed the median membership to be 60,000 with a range of 1,300 to 815,000; 30 percent of the respondents recorded memberships of 100,000 or more. There has been a gradual increase in membership.

An interesting perception of the survey participants revealed that urban areas (defined by the Census Bureau to include suburbs) are the most active locales in their states. Two-fifths (14) of the state PTA officials reported big-city units as dominating in the state organization, and only 3 perceived farm/rural communities as providing the highly active PTAs.

The respondents believe their organizations try to be "inclusive," but this goal is evident more in terms of socioeconomic status than in minority representation. Only 2 state officials (6 percent) disagreed with the statement "The organization's membership of parents occurs at all economic levels and is not concentrated in a particular social class." But 24 respondents (67 percent) disagreed or were uncertain about the increasing membership of minorities in the state organizations.

Although a majority of the respondents saw the state PTA agenda as "a mixed bag of programs and services," the authors easily reduced the list of the major accomplishments of the state PTAs during the last five years to three categories. The most noticeable category centered on *parenting education.* Parent education programs had directed attention to various specific concerns (e.g., child abuse) as well as general parenting awareness. In second place were improvements in *organizational dynamics.* Some respondents pointed to increased visibility, respectability, and credibility as assets of their PTA dynamics during the last five years. Also noticeable as a category were *expanded advocacy/activism* projects. Among the examples of activism were advocacy for children, youth, and education before legislators and state task forces.

The state PTA officials overwhelmingly attributed their recent accomplishments to specific PTA features at the national, state, and local levels:

better trained and informed leadership utilizing more effective and focused strategies, active local units and "grassroots involvements," "committed" members who are well informed about educational issues, increasing resources (including national PTA grants), good public relations, and more field service. Also, two-thirds of the officials were decisive in their view that the state PTAs had disseminated vast amounts of written information to members. A few respondents acknowledged that, in addition to these features, "the timing was right" for the state PTA successes, given, for example, actions by state departments of education. Finally, other factors contributing to success were "the spirit of American volunteerism" in general and the fast-growing awareness of the need for parental involvement with education and for PTA services in particular. One commentary was that "people are feeling frustrated with the educational system and are seeking a positive vehicle for participation."

When they considered interorganizational cooperation and networking, respondents (with one exception) recognized unanimously the significance of working ties with the national PTA. Half of the state PTA officials reported close working ties with teachers' associations (mainly NEA and AFT state groups); almost one-half mentioned state administrators' associations, with some citing individual superintendents and principals. In some instances, respondents also reported networking with state school board associations. One out of every three reported working ties with other state PTAs. State governmental agencies, such as the Department of Education, were also among the contacts frequently noted.

With respect to organizations or populations that had been opponents to state PTA programs, three-fifths of the survey participants disclaimed significant opponents. The others listed varied opposing groups, typically in single-issue situations, such as a school tax referendum.

With respect to relations with school personnel, the state PTA officials expressed less alienation than the general literature had led the researchers to expect. Fifty-five percent of the respondents strongly disagreed and another 22 percent simply disagreed that antagonism of school personnel toward the state PTA has increased. Eighty percent agreed or, at worst, were uncertain, that there had been, in meetings and correspondence with the state group, only rare references by local chapters to a distrust of school personnel. Moreover, there was confidence that the state PTA is "highly respected among school personnel," a description that for 75 percent of the respondents applied well to their organizations.

There is widespread confidence also that the state organizations are making a difference in matters about children and schooling. Three-fourths of the PTA correspondents reported that the influence of their state organizations reached far beyond the actual membership. Only two disagreed with the statement that the state organization had expressed viewpoints rather strongly to the public relative to matters involving children. Moreover, the officials communicated almost unanimously a perception, although not a very strong one, that a major impact of the PTA has been to increase parental participation in school decision making. On the other hand, 60 percent disclaimed that their organizations have been "very important" in mediating between citizens and school personnel in matters relating to teaching. Moreover, two-fifths of the officials were uncertain about whether the state organization was "a significant channel for communication between school personnel and citizens." This perception was consistent with another reported judgment: Only one-fourth agreed or agreed strongly that their state groups exercised "considerable pressure" on the schools. Interestingly, some respondents objected to such wordings of the authors as "pressure" or "mediating." They preferred to evaluate the posture of the state unit as "influencing."

In general, the accounts of the state PTA officials suggested a changing social scene and an optimism about prospects for more PTA significance. Foremost among the social context aspects mentioned as providing the most momentum for state PTA change during the 1980s was the transformation in family structure and life, especially the trend toward working mothers and the increased needs of children. There was also a growing perception of the imperative of parental involvement with education. The second most mentioned social context feature centered on governmental mandates/regulations and political support of educational reform and parental involvement. Thus, respondents saw that powerful agencies have been appropriately legitimating parental participation in the schools. In third place among the listed social forces of the 1980s was the remobilization of PTA leadership. The declining interest in volunteerism in the 1970s had been reflected in the PTA imperative for more effective organization and more leader training "to fill the gap". Three-fourths of the respondents reported that the state organization had responded with a well-defined ideology and opportunities for participation (of males as well as females). Finally, there were comments about increased public dissatisfaction with education and about heightened multicultural awareness.

Those state PTA officials who reported organizational experiences with issues and controversies about parent–school relations during the past five years named two in particular: school funding issues and the generation of more parental involvement. State PTA leaders have sought, in "unenthusiastic" school environments, to achieve "parent-friendly schools," parental involvement in curricular decision making, "less administrative restraint and distrust of parent/community involvement," greater accommodation of working parents, more information about the schools, and so on. The exact nature of funding issues varied. There were parent–school disputes about the adequacy of school/program funding, the method of financing education, the conditions of PTA fund raising, and the use of PTA funds by the schools (e.g., "for gifts that cause inequities").

Perceived Significance of Various Types of Parental Involvement

Of the seven types of parent-school involvements reported by PTA respondents, all but one—court cases initiated by parents—were seen as "significant" sources of controversy by over 50 percent, with volunteer activities and parental activism seen as significant by 91 percent and 89 percent, respectively. *This is in stark contrast with the responses of all the professional organizations.* In fact, the only area of parent-school involvements that more than half of the other respondents reported as a "significant" issue for their groups is parental activism, by 52 percent of AFT respondents. Some areas show dramatic differences between the PTA and the professional organizations. Whereas 80 percent of PTA respondents saw parent-teacher conferences as a significant issue, only 9 percent of administrators and 17 percent of AFT respondents did. Along the same line, 91 percent of PTA respondents saw volunteer activities in the school as a significant issue, but only 20–36 percent of the others did. Further, 77 percent of PTA respondents saw parents in advisory roles as significant, while only 26–43 percent of the others did. Although the differences are not as great, a similar pattern exists for parental activity at school board meetings and parental empowerment strategies.

If the leaders of these state organizations accurately represented the views of their members, it can be speculated that those who run the schools do not see parental involvement in any form as a significant source of organizational controversy or tension.

Educational Concerns

The leaders of state organizations responded to 13 educational concerns, rating each to be "Not Significant," Somewhat Significant," or "Significant." The two areas that were most significant for all five groups are funding and educational legislation, ranging from 87 percent of the AFT respondents to 99 percent of the NEA and administrator respondents. That issue the fewest respondents in all groups saw as "Significant" is extracurricular activities. The widest divergence of opinion concerned personnel negotiations; only 15 percent of the PTA chapters reported this as a significant concern, while 87 percent of the NEA chapters did. Interestingly, at the same time, only 61 percent of the AFT state units did.

Other educational concerns on which the state PTAs differ from all the other organizations are standards of professional performance and health, safety, and security. A substantially smaller percentage of the PTA respondents saw standards of professional performance as a significant organizational concern, and a far higher percentage of PTA respondents saw health, safety, and security as a significant organizational issue than did the other organizations. In fact, only funding and educational legislation exceeded this matter as an educational concern for the PTA organizations.

Other than extracurricular activities, those items least reported by PTA respondents as "Significant" are bureaucratic school practices, transportation, and personnel negotiations; for the NEA and AFT it is transportation; for administrators and board members, discrimination against minorities and transportation are the least significant concerns.

Conclusion

Parental participation in American public schools is not novel. Within the past few decades, however, there has been a resurgence of interest, and also turmoil, relative to parental educational activities. Given a number of educational reforms driven by federal and state mandates, contemporary educators have promoted parental involvement. A great deal has been published about blueprints for taking positive steps to increase parental involvement activities and programs. Also, given the impetus of effective school research that maintains public school children are "eminently educable," school personnel are intervening to improve home–school connections. Shapiro (1989) put it bluntly: "What is the use of our exquisitely elaborated pedagogies if we lack the capability of mobilizing significant public support and affirmation for them" (p. 21). In fact, National PTA leader Ann Lynch (1990) writes that some barriers to involvement are overlooked by school personnel" who unconsciously may be sabotaging their own efforts" (p. 40). Moreover, there have been more vocal parental demands for avenues to significant participation and for opportunities to influence public education. Politicized parent organizations are holding schools to close instructional accountability and to equity in policy making.

In this chapter, focus has been not only on initiative for change coming for professional educators, but also on what parents are doing, especially to empower themselves. These latter efforts have included the attempts of independent parent organizations to provide focused advocacy and to claim decision-making roles in school matters.

There have been mixed results when parents have served as advisors, decision makers, and advocates. Some of these efforts have been "perfunctory" or *"pro-forma"* and "window-dressing" (Henderson, Marburger, and Ooms 1986; McLaughlin and Shields 1987). Other efforts have greatly increased cooperative teacher–parent relations and have called attention to the broad scope of possibilities for school personnel and parents to work effectively with each other. (See, for example, Moles's 1987 analysis of "working" programs and practices in locations across the country, the Williams and Chavkin [1984] description of "promising" programs, or the January 1991 issue of *Phi Delta Kappa* on parental involvement edited by Joyce Epstein.)

It must be pointed out, however, that even if one can demonstrate the efficacy of various strategies of parental involvement, it is the well-planned, comprehensive, and long-range perspective that will make the greatest difference in the reform to achieve excellence. Furthermore, educators must exert themselves consciously and beyond rhetoric to organize and support parental participation. Schools of education must take the responsibility for preparing future teachers in this important area. To do so they must require courses and experiences that provide these future teachers with the insights, understandings, and skills to work effectively with parents and parent organizations. Such courses would focus on school and community relationships and include units on organizational dynamics in general and parent organizations in particular, encouraging student observations of PTA meetings and school board meetings. Prospective teachers should acquire knowledge about legal decisions relative to parent-initiated cases against schools, informational and referral services that parents might find useful, and various kinds of parental involvement activities. Of particular importance is providing them with skills and practice in conducting productive parent-teacher conferences and avoiding problems in parent–teacher relations.

Finally, as Lightfoot (1981, 55) has proposed, some discontinuities between family and school should be treated as reflections of "differences in their structural properties and cultural purposes." Given this reality, "the issue of parental involvement in the school's curriculum is an important, but second-order question." A more important task for further exploration would be to search for ways in which antagonisms "might be resolved or channeled into productive disagreements" and meaningful participations. As Lightfoot (1981, 66) has insisted, we need to operate on the basis of the concept of "creative conflict" rather than that of "negative dissonance" between family and school. The benefits might well be worth the burden. *So the agenda before us is rich in its challenge and wide in its possibilities for social invention relative to parental participation in public education.*

SECTION TWO

Education, the Schools, and the Family

Home, school, and community, working together. . . . After identifying the demographics and key issues, we turn to some theories and proposals for productive cooperation. When there is care enough to want to know the student, there may be resources enough to develop this bond. A key is trying to understand what it is we have in common and sincerely wanting to help all children. We can begin to reduce the numbers of children "at risk" by developing a community which considers children more important than procedure or policy. The purpose of this section is to provoke discussion regarding this coalition.

Chapter 8 postulates a hierarchy of parental involvement in schools, with suggestions for helping all parents (with special attention to parents of at-risk children) move beyond the "Spectator Level" to become supportive, engaged, and, in some cases, even involved to the point of decision making. Chapter 9 discusses the highest levels of parental participation in terms of cultural and political contexts that typically hamper interaction but that can be used to advantage if recognized and adapted to. Parents and community members who are highly engaged in schools to the point of setting policy may find some worthy suggestions to advocate in Chapter 12, which explores family and social factors that put students into the "at risk" category and suggests curriculum improvement strategies—five proven "old warhorses" and one new approach—for improving the chances for such students.

Chapters 10 and 11 both deal with parent-teacher conferences—first from the viewpoint of how teachers can use these meetings as opportunities to improve the school–parent–child relationship, the second from a parent's viewpoint on how to get the most out of such conferences. Parental success is also the focus of the last two chapters of the section. Chapter 13 describes current programs that successfully assist mainstream, nontraditional, and at-risk families to help their children get a good start in education. Chapter 14 offers even more specific suggestions for a "head start" for children, giving "how-to" advice for parents who want to enhance their children's early development.

CHAPTER EIGHT

Hierarchy of Parental Involvement in Schools

DONNA WISSBRUN   JOYCE A. ECKART

Editor's Note: Even though the bias favoring parental involvement in our schools is clearly stated throughout this book, it is also clear that effective intervention does not just happen without dedicated effort on the part of all involved. Not every parent is a joy to work with. The same can be said of educators. Effective involvement of parents in school activities is an educational process. It is one thing to ask parents to bake cookies. It is quite another to have their input into decisions regarding curriculum.

The process of developing reliable and informed parental support continues to be controversial. Mistrust between home and school exists. A question to be answered is: What do the schools want of parents beyond cash?

Parents are the one continuous force in the education of their children from birth to adulthood. —E. H. BERGER

Historically, the home was the center for teaching and learning; parents had primary responsibility for educating their children. Communication skills, values, traditions, and wisdom gained through experience were and still are taught through parental example.

The status and value of children in society have changed with time, but the process of socializing children has always been considered the responsibility of parents. Rules and consequences were clearly defined; obedience was demanded; discipline was enforced. Society held parents responsible for the behavior of their children. As parents have delegated or relinquished responsibility for their children's education to the schools, district parental involvement in the process of education has diminished. Yet, as early as 1897, at the "Congress of Parents and Teachers", parent-teacher groups (PTA) were established to support school activities. Growth in membership of PTA groups and parent eduction groups has increased, but the level of involvement has been limited.

Coping with societal pressures takes an enormous effort. Parents strive to live the "good life" and to secure it for their children. Increasingly, parents are voicing displeasure with the services provided by schools in preparing children who can deal with societal pressures and attain the "good life." Thus, current concerns about the effectiveness of schools are not surprising.

Dissatisfaction with schools' performance causes parents to reassess the degree of responsibility and decision-making power that schools have enjoyed. The desire to have their children be successful in the world of work is a catalyst that causes parents to become increasingly involved in their children's education. The degree of involvement depends on factors unique to the parent, the child, the school, and the community. Still, "study after study has shown that a parent's involvement in education is a powerful predictor of how that child is going to do in school" (Caminiti 1990, 25). Ideally, this involvement reflects a shared responsibility. Both parents and schools share ownership and accountability for the end product. Thus, parents, as well as schools, are accountable for how well each child accepts the responsibilities associated with adult life. Knowing this, it becomes imperative that processes be created to support parental involvement in school decision making.

Hierarchy of Parental Involvement

The degree to which a parent becomes involved with the child's school and/or teachers will depend not only on the parent, but also on the educational system. In most schools, policy decisions are made without parental input. Either parental involvement is not encouraged or when parental involvement is encouraged, parents often appear indifferent or disinterested. Since the needs of the school and the needs of the parents are often different, we see various levels of parental involvement emerging during the child's schooling.

The process of parental involvement can be envisioned as a hierarchy. Visually, this model of parental involvement can be illustrated as follows:

DECISION MAKING
ENGAGEMENT
SUPPORT
SPECTATOR

Four levels emerge: (1) Spectator, (2) Support, (3) Engagement, and (4) Decision Making. A parent's movement from one level to another does not seem to have a predictable pattern and is subject to frequent change. However, it is possible for schools and parents to take actions to promote higher levels of parental involvement.

Level I: Spectator

At the first level of the hierarchy, parents perceive the school and teacher as autonomous authorities who do not want parents to interfere. They view school doors as a barrier. Any activity requiring parental participation, if done, is completed away from the school.

The role of spectator is limited. It might include sending the child to school, but enforcement of an attendance policy is viewed as the school's responsibility. As a spectator, parents receive school-generated communications that are typically ignored. Personal communication, whether written or by telephone, is not welcomed. Much of this communication takes the form of complaints, which parents either resent or ignore. Worse than ignoring, a parent might overreact to information regarding a child's poor performance or behavior at school by openly criticizing the school, punishing the child, or unfortunately, abusing the child.

When examining the reasons for a parent's behavior at the Spectator Level, it becomes clear that people will react to the school according to their life situation. Parents who are living their own stressful lives cannot cope with additional responsibilities. They are caught in forces of unemployment, divorce, inflation, and other social changes and feel unable to respond to their child's school needs and demands. Some parents have had negative experiences in school themselves, so their lack of interest stems from anger and resentment regarding their own education. When their child has difficulty in school, such parents may see a pattern repeating itself and feel helpless to change it, or they may feel ignorant and unable to communicate their feelings appropriately with the school.

The outcomes of this behavior are varied. Schools become dissatisfied with the lack of parental support and blame parents for the child's problems. Parents blame the school for both their own and their child's failures. Sometimes the school reduces efforts to involve parents because there is an assumption that parents will not protest decisions made regarding the child. The child assumes responsibility for learning in an often stressful, if not hostile, environment. Success in school is linked to the persistence of the child. The self-motivated children of spectator parents might be successful in school; however, the child who seeks support is at risk. All too often, this child is forgotten in a system too large to meet individual needs.

Level II: Support

In the second level of the hierarchy, parents do assume some role in the education of the child. Parents at the Support Level still perceive the school as an autonomous authority that might or might not want them in the school. Parents complete specific tasks as requested at specific times, if the tasks can be completed at home with little demand on the parents' time and energy. They can be expected to come to school for brief visits if requested to do so by the school. Commonly these visits take place during parent-teacher conferences.

Other tasks characteristic of this level include: (1) seeing that the child attends school on a regular basis, (2) reinforcing behaviors expected at school, (3) checking that homework is completed, and (4) reading and responding to school communications. In addition, parents at this level contribute to school fundraisers, pay PTA dues, and vote for school bond issues. Some services that parents provide may be unrelated to either academic or financial support. Supporting parents are willing to bake for school parties, sew costumes for plays, and contribute in any way that does not require coming to school.

Parental involvement at this level is based on the belief that education is a way for children to achieve a lifestyle better than the one into which they were born. In spite of personal, past experiences with schools, parents at this level see education as necessary to gain employment and financial security. Therefore, they are willing to invest some minimal time in supporting the child's school experience. These activities are considered a necessary part of parenting.

At the Support Level there is a general sense of satisfaction among all parties and is the level of involvement for most parents. Parents feel in touch with what is happening at school. Parents do not block efforts of the school, so the school has freedom to function and to make decisions with little parental involvement. Schools can rely on voter support of school bond issues, and they feel free to experiment with instructional programs without justifying these decisions to parents. Classroom teachers ask for help from home and expect parents to respond. Sensing a supportive attitude, children are likely to ask their parents for help with homework and for contributions to school activities.

Level III: Engagement

At the Engagement Level, parents perceive a relationship of mutual respect between themselves and the school. Parental participation is based on two general needs: (1) to observe the school and its impact on the child and (2) to be seen by the child as a participant in the child's world of school. The school, however, remains the primary decision maker.

Activities of parents at the Engagement Level are characterized by increased exposure in the schools. At this level, parents can be expected to: (1) assume responsibility for leadership roles to support schools, (2) develop and distribute resource information for the school and local community, (3) participate in PTA-sponsored events in the school and in the neighborhood, and (4) work as volunteers and/or resource persons to share their special interests, talents, and knowledge with students. Teachers feel free to ask these parents to accompany students on field trips and provide transportation to events. In the classroom, these parents tutor students and carry out other academic activities under the supervision of the teacher.

At home, parents reinforce academics by using the guidelines provided by the teacher. They attend workshops to help their children succeed in school, and at home they use the strategies learned. Parents reinforce acceptable school behavior for their child based on plans of action designed cooperatively with the teacher. Through these activities, parents show a commitment to be involved in their child's schooling.

One reason that parents arrive at this level is their desire to have an influence on their child's school experience and perhaps the experiences of other children. Parents see the function of the school to offer not only employment skills but also quality-of-life skills. They value education as a factor in developing the whole child and in preparing children to assume meaningful roles in society.

Given this type of parental involvement, schools become more sensitive to the knowledge and attitudes that parents have when making decisions. At this level, schools relinquish autocratic power and begin to reflect local community values. The decision-making process becomes slower and involves input from more people who share accountability.

The role of administration within the school changes at this level. The principal must be able to nurture the school–home relationship in response to increased parental involvement. The leadership provided should be directed to balance the power of groups for the good of the child. Decisions teachers make are influenced by how parents will react. Conservative decisions to teach a more basic curriculum with traditional instructional approaches might occur because teachers have to justify these choices to parents.

Parents expect schools to be accountable to them and want explanations for school decisions. If schools do not offer this information, parents demand it.

Based on the attitudes and actions of their parents, children feel that school and/or teachers' rules can be questioned. They, too, expect to be given reasons why they must comply with school decisions. Individual behavior reflects how well the school and parent interact and how parents' attitudes are transmitted to the child.

Level IV: Decision Making

At the advanced Decision-Making Level, parents demand an interdependent relationship between the home and the school; school power comes through parent channels. Parents have responsibility for all school children. Consideration is given to local community and/or future generations who will be citizens of a global community. To satisfy these demands, parents: (1) feel confident setting priorities for educational outcomes; (2) are self-motivated, open to feedback, and wiling to learn; and (3) exhibit a sense of self-determination with a willingness to take risks by asserting their rights. No longer willing to rely upon the school as a primary provider and initiator of decisions, parents affirm their right to be at the center of educational decision making. At this level of the hierarchy, the system requires the expertise of individual parents, parent groups, community leaders, business and professional organizations, and institutions of higher education. Decision making becomes a joint effort among those who have a stake in the future of society. Carried further, decision-making power may not be shared with the school because parents are willing to accept complete accountability.

Activities assume a different profile at this level. New dimensions of parental influence are direct results of parents' belief that schools have failed and that parents must intervene if society is going to survive. Therefore, parents will: (1) initiate, join, and lead problem-solving groups focusing on the needs and interests of the local community and/or society at large; (2) become members of independent advocacy groups that work for school improvement by helping to form policies and procedures; and (3) identify resources available at local and district levels to make them available for children.

At the school site or in the district, parents will: (1) be part of policy-making boards and committees to set goals and direction for the school and (2) initiate and direct special activities such as conducting needs assessments and planning and conducting workshops for other parents and teachers. In general, activities of this level are characterized by consistent parental influence in decision making in all educational areas.

Basically, the reasons for the increased parent assertiveness come from anger and frustration with the past performance of schools. Parents are determined to change the power base within schools because they believe that educators are incapable of producing the desired outcome.

Within the Decision-Making Level, schools' power declines more rapidly and accountability increases more rapidly. Principals serve at the will of parents. If carried to an extreme, a focus on pleasing parents could interfere with making decisions for the good of the child. In addition, as the school begins to reflect more of the attitudes, values, and prejudices of the community, there is a danger that the child will be denied the experiences necessary to be tolerant of people who are different from themselves.

Forces of Change

There is every reason to believe that the level of parental involvement in schools can change through the efforts of parents, teachers, and administrators. The question is whether the change is necessary and desirable. Some administrators feel that parents who assist teachers in the classroom or manage special events represent enough parental involvement in the building; some parents support the notion that "education should be left to the educators." If they are asked to become more involved, these parents feel that they are being asked to do the teacher's job, and protest, "What are the teachers being paid for?"

From many administrators' and/or teachers' points of view, increased parental involvement means a restriction of the educators' freedom to make decisions. When schools are autonomous, educators can quickly make and implement decisions based on their professional training and experience. However, when more people are involved in decision making, the process is slower. Furthermore, when some of the decision makers have neither a knowledge base nor experience about the issues, reaching consensus becomes an arduous task. Thus, increased parental involvement can mean increased conflict and confusion.

In general, too much of a good thing can be bad. If all parents decided to become involved at the Decision-Making Level of the hierarchy, the decision-making process would become ineffective and dysfunctional; chaos would prevail. Consequently, the most desirable scenario would be as follows: All parents would function at the Support Level. Having parents who support the teacher and the school increases student achievement (Walberg 1984). From this broad support base, a smaller number of parents would participate at the Engagement level to give assistance to the teacher in the classroom. An even smaller number would function at the Decision-Making Level; these parents would provide a community perspective and contribute unique skills and expertise.

What Parents Can Do

Movement between levels of the hierarchy occurs when parents see a need, which usually involves their own child. Parents weigh these five factors: (1) need/issue and degree of concern, (2) knowledge of the need/issue or a willingness to learn about it, (3) risk involved in becoming active, (4) amount and flexibility of time to devote to school participation, and (5) degree of commitment to make a difference. They then decide what to do. A sample plan-of-action sheet is supplied at the end of this chapter. Part I is a "Parent Profile," to help parents identify their attitudes, needs, interests, and abilities at a given time. Responses to the Parent Profile change depending on parents' satisfaction with their child's day-to-day school experiences and their interest and ability to be involved. Part II is a "Plan of Action," to help parents identify ways to become involved, plan activities, and track their progress.

Usually, parents learn about school problems from assignments, report cards, and communications with teachers. Other information may come from listening to children's comments and observing their behaviors, observing problem situations firsthand, checking out rumors, talking with other parents, and/or listening to neighbors' concerns.

As interests and concerns are expressed, the parent watches for explanations from the school; this is a critical point in the home–school relationship. Parental interest is encouraged if the administrator creates a climate of acceptance, shows respect and appreciation for the parent's ideas, takes action to solve the problem, and reports back to the parent on what action has been taken. If the administrator ignores the parent's concern, or if parents feel they are trespassing on forbidden ground, parental involvement could be removed. On the other hand, parents might become so frustrated by the impersonal attitudes of school personnel that they will push even harder to influence decisions made in the school. These parents usually band together in an "us against them" attitude, by-pass the administrator, move to the district level, and become vocal participants at school board meetings.

What Teachers Can Do

Initially, in all grades, the teacher can cultivate school–home relationships with a planned process for communication. The teacher can: (1) send parent-signature return forms with newsletters, student work folders, and homework schedules; (2) appoint a parent as the classroom representative to provide information regarding special projects and long-term assignments to other parents and to give parental feedback to the teaher; (3) organize informal, neighborhood coffee hours that the teacher attends to share ideas and information with the community; and (4) prepare a daily recorded message on their school or home phone to list and explain homework assignments or to remind parents of special activities.

Many elementary teachers have already discovered the benefits of supportive involvement from parents. They ask parents to send in supplies or party treats, to assist with a special project, or to accompany the class on field trips. At the secondary school level the use of parents has been limited in the Support Level to fund raising, booster/athletic club activities, car pooling, and giving money.

Helping parents become engaged in the classroom requires a time commitment from the teacher. After surveying and interpreting parents' interests, talents, and skills, teachers: (1) see where a match of need and support can be made in light of the curriculum, (2) delegate and explain specific tasks to parents, and (3) work with the parent to increase their effectiveness in the classroom. Since high-schoolers might not welcome the presence of parents as helpers in the actual classroom, the sensitive teacher will use parental talents in more select ways. At this level, teachers would remain content experts, while parents who have been trained by the teacher could assist students and monitor progress in projects and real problem-solving situations, or parents could be invited to describe their jobs.

Parents must be brought to school and given a role where they can be successful and not be exposed to things that make them feel bad (Goldberg 1990). Parents who help in these ways and who are trained by the teacher will understand the challenges of teaching and the reasons why instructional decisions are made. These parents are likely to support the actions of the teacher, to defend these decisions to other parents, and to feel that they are making academic differences in children's lives.

At the Decision-Making Level, teachers in the elementary grades can ask parents for input and support about their child's learning needs. A cooperative approach can be designed to diagnose the child's problems, prescribe solutions, and implement plans of action. Parents could coach their children at home using materials supplied by the teacher. Parent-child activities that focus on the child's learning needs and that give satisfaction to the parent-helper promote parental involvement (Berninger and Rodriguez 1989). At the secondary school level, parents are interested in how well the school prepares the student for employment and/or for further schooling. The question parents ask is, "How do graduates from the school function in society?" Depending on the answer, parents will either become more or less involved in the decision-making process at this level.

What Administrators Can Do

Administrators must recognize that parents are linked to teachers and schools through their children (Melvin 1982) and that parental involvement is also an essential element in effective schools (Epstein 1987a). Since the role of parents in the schooling of their children is shaped by the administration, administrators must make certain that the school projects a friendly climate that welcomes visitors. When parents feel welcomed by secretaries, custodians, teachers, and others, they are more likely to engage in school activities.

"Communicating effectively in an organization requires skills beyond the interpersonal level" (Smith & Andrews 1989, 46). The administrator can:

(1) establish procedures regarding the formats and methods for school communication; (2) provide policy handbooks, bulletins, and monthly parental updates outlining activities, issues, and needs for parental help; (3) furnish financial support for special parent-teacher-administrator lunches to encourage parents to visit the school and to discuss school needs and issues; (4) provide transportation to functions; (5) arrange for child care services during functions; (6) schedule school events with parent work schedules in mind; and (7) reserve weekly time-slots when parents can speak with him or her in private.

While communication is vital in developing home–school relationships, administrators cannot consider the job complete if they do not plan for parental involvement at higher levels of the hierarchy. Parent advisory councils should be organized with the expectation that they will be empowered equally with administrators and teachers in setting goals, designing strategies, implementing plans, and evaluating outcomes. These councils or committees provide a framework for meaningful participation by many people in the school community and bring different perspectives and insights into the decision-making process (Weinstraub 1985).

Administrators must provide training for parents that is thorough and scheduled on a regular basis. The physical arrangement assigned to the advisory council reflects the degree of acceptance the administrator has for the role parents are to play in decision making. Providing a work area for the advisory council near the administrator's office communicates that there is a partnership between the council and the administrator. The advisory council work area would be an appropriate place to house resource materials for all parents. These materials might include: (1) information about school-related subjects and parenting topics; (2) videotapes about parenting skills and other topics relevant to parents' needs; and (3) a VCR, books, and magazines to be checked out. Administrators who provide these materials for parents demonstrate their commitment to share knowledge. "Knowledge is power." Therefore, this provision of materials by the administrator is a deliberate sign of readiness to share the power base with parents who are willing to learn and to become informed decision makers.

What Business Leaders Can Do

Communities have become concerned with the business of education. Among the complaints are that students who graduate from high school and apply for entry-level positions cannot properly complete employment application forms. In response to this concern, businesses can: (1) outline skills that high school graduates need to enter the job market and share them with schools; (2) bring local students, teachers, and parents to the company site and explain the skills their employees need; (3) hire students in work-study programs; and (4) supply equipment, such as computer labs, to schools.

Employees can also become involved in the educational system. They can: (1) become a mentor for at-risk students; (2) promote time off to team teach in schools; (3) trade roles, so teachers could work in business and industry while they teach in schools; (4) find out how their company is involved in remedial training for job applicants; (5) put pressure on statements for school reform; (6) sponsor college days for high school students; and (7) provide money for achievement incentives, special projects, and college funds (*Fortune,* 1990).

At-Risk Students

Special consideration must be given to the parents of "at-risk" students — children of poverty, abuse, or discrimination — because these parents often resist involvement in schools. According to studies done by John Ogbu (Hill 1990), these students and their parents distrust the educational system because it has failed them. Many are fearful of revealing problems at home; some feel helpless over their child's failure; others sense their lack of parenting skills. They believe that they might do something "wrong" and interfere with what the teacher wants. Finally, they do not know how to participate. Yet James Comer, from his work with disadvantaged families, says:

> *Things can be turned around. But enough people need to understand that education really has to be based on what kids are like and what kids need. If we can get bureaucracy and processes in education really designed to address the needs of children, then we can turn education around. (Gursky 1990, 54).*

The approach for building home–school relationships among these groups will require special planning. Parents will need: (1) consistent and continuous communication with the school, (2) training in parenting skills that will incorporate the informal teaching that parents must do at home, (3) reminders of the benefits of education, and (4) specific feedback concerning the value of their support of the child's schooling and their involvement in learning activities at home. If these parents are shown how to tutor and support their children, if they are told what they have to do, if easy-to-use materials are provided, and if they are given positive feedback that they are improving the chances that their children will be successful in school, resistance to being involved might be overcome. Building the self-esteem and hopes of those parents is a vital part of the process for developing a state of interdependence between home and school. It is the responsibility of schools, PTA and other parent groups, and businesses to form collaboratives for nurturing families who are at risk.

Conclusion

This nation is facing a serious problem. The percentage of job applicants who have the basic competencies necessary for entry-level jobs is declining. Many workers cannot meet the needs of industry, even in basic skills. The statistics of illiteracy, especially for at-risk populations, are staggering. Workers are not able to support industry, nor is there a pool of creative thinkers to expand or to begin new industries. Thus, increasing the skills of K–12 students must become a priority issue. Solving this problem calls for solving a host of subproblems: (1) teachers who are burned out, (2) students who are unmotivated, (3) administrators who are autocratic managers, (4) business and community groups who blame schools for all the problems of society, and (5) parents who have disengaged from parenting.

Since parenting includes a responsibility not only to teach children informally at home, but also to aid the school in efforts to educate children formally, there must be a national commitment to include parents in all levels of schooling. "As parents become more knowledgeable about children's learning and the ways in which their children grow and develop, they develop an improved level of competency from which their children benefit." (Roach, Bell, and Salmeri 1989–1990, 15). As parents become competent and confident role models, the focus of formal schooling will be to assist parents in education. It remains the responsibility of all elements of society to guide this change.

> *My grandfather once told me that there are two kinds of people; those who do the work and those who take the credit. He told me to try to be in the first group; there was less competition there.* —INDIRA GANDHI

Parents Profile

Directions: In order to get in touch with your attitude toward parental involvement, complete these statements.

1. My favorite thing as a child in school was _____
   _____.

2. If a teacher asked for my help at school, I would _____
   _____.

3. I feel comfortable helping children _____
   _____.

4. Children age _____ are fun to work with.

5. If I could change one thing at my child's school, it would be
   _____.

Plan of Action

Directions: In order to assess your readiness for increased involvement in schools, read each statement and check as many options as you think are relevant.

1. I have a concern about _____
   _____.

2. I want more information from the (a) teacher, (b) principal, or (c) other parents concerning this problem.

3. I am willing to (a) read information, (b) listen to a speaker, (c) view videotapes to learn more about the problem.

4. I am willing to devote (a) 1–3 hours a week, (b) 1 day a week, or (c) unlimited time to working toward a solution.

5. I will be satisfied if a solution is reached in (1) 1 day, (b) 1 week, (c) 1 month, or (d) this school year.

6. I am willing to share what I learn with (a) other parents, (b) teachers, (c) students, and/or (d) administrators.

7. At this time, I consider myself (a) a spectator, (b) a supporter, (c) an engager, and/or (d) a decision maker in my child's school.

8. Until there is a solution, I will be involved as (a) a spectator, (b) a supporter, (c) an engager, or (d) a decision maker in my child's school.

CHAPTER NINE

Parent–School Interactions

PATRICE LeBLANC

Editor's Note: A distinction is made between involvement and participation. To be involved suggests support, while participation stands for action or potential change.

Citizen interaction with school decision making brings together a coalition of business, labor, quasigovernment, religious, parents, and other interested parties (some with children, some concerned about children). Many pay direct school tax, others indirect. We all participate in one way or another.

This chapter further defines and discusses parent–school interactions. What forms do these interactions take? Who participates in parent–school interactions? How can parents and citizens increase their participation in schools? These questions and others are answered in this chapter with an emphasis on explaining what drives parent–school interactions and how to make these interactions more successful.

Involvement or Participation?

Parent–school interactions fall into two categories: parental involvement and parental participation. Don Davies, president of the Institute for Responsive Education, defines *participation* as occurring when parents influence, or attempt to influence, decision making in areas of substantial impact: personnel, programs, and budget (Davies 1981). In effect, participation implies a share in the decision-making power in schools. *Involvement,* on the other hand, refers to all other types of activities that generally support the school and its programs. The focus of this chapter is participation rather than involvement because the source of power for change lies in participation.

An important addition to parent–school interactions is made here, that of *citizen participation*. Citizen participation is included because citizens (community residents without school-age children) make up 80 percent of the taxpayers in today's communities (Jennings 1989). They have the power to dictate what resources are available in schools, and therefore should be included in the decision-making processes. In addition, citizens can provide linkages to the community that have the potential to enhance the overall growth of education and the family. These linkages can range from small business partnerships with schools to support for school bond issues.

What Are the Forms of Participation?

Participation in schools takes many forms. Four types — individual, voucher, litigious, and collective — are briefly described here.

First, there is *individual participation*. This refers to parents and citizens who participate in educational decision making as individuals. Examples of individual participation range from voting on school issues to parents making choices about special services their children will receive.

Voucher plans are a second form of participation. In this case, students are not preassigned to a particular program or school. Parents receive a voucher that they use to select the program or school of choice for their youngsters. This is considered a form of participation because parents are offered choices for their children, necessitating decision making.

Litigation is a third way that parents and citizens can participate in schools. Litigation has enabled parents and citizens to restructure the education their children receive. For example, judicial decisions have resulted in desegregation, the growth of bilingual and ESL programs and the development of special-needs programs.

The fourth, most popular form of participation, is collective. *Collective participation* usually occurs in school site councils, which range in structure from advisory boards to site-based management cadres. These forms are briefly discussed below.

Collective participation grew from the idea advocated in the late 1960s and early1970s that "those most affected by public institutions should have more of a voice in them" (Foster 1984, 28). Collective participation is sometimes mandated, as in the case of Parent Advisory Councils for federal Chapter I programs, and is sometimes parent- or citizen-initiated, as in the case of a local school playground committee. School site councils have become particularly popular in recent years, with initiatives such as school improvement councils in California and Massachusetts and councils in Illinois and Florida that include parents and citizens in the site-based management of schools. Site-based management is seen as a positive step toward shared decision making because all the participants have a share in making critical decisions for a school. In general, the belief system supporting collective forms of participation is that "dynamic home-school-community partnerships established through site councils can result in improved schools that better serve their communities" (Jennings 1989, 42).

Who Participates in Schools?

It is important to look at what the research on citizen and parent participation says about who actually participates in the decision making in schools. Certain trends in the characteristics of participants have been identified to occur over time. Findings indicate that the participants are of middle-class socioeconomic status (Lightfoot 1978; LeBlanc 1990), are long-term residents in a community (Salisbury 1980; Wilson 1985), and tend to be well educated (Cardoso 1987; LeBlanc 1990). In addition, minority and bilingual representation in school site councils has been found to be minimal, and women have far outnumbered men except in leadership positions (Davies et al. 1977; LeBlanc 1990).

These findings are somewhat disheartening. They do not show true democratic participation in the schools. They do tell us that if you are a white, well educated, middle-class woman, there is a greater chance you are a participant in a nonleadership position. The question is: What factors can influence who participates, and how can the quantity and quality of participation be increased? The answers lie in culture.

What Are the Influences of Culture?

Consider this: Schools as organizations are part of a larger whole, and that whole is the culture of the dominant segment of society. Historically, this dominant segment has been white, middle-class (Burnett 1970). Therefore, middle-class values, beliefs, behaviors, and expectations have been a part of the school culture. According to the National Coalition of Advocates for Students, these values in the school culture have meshed well with the values of the predominantly white teaching staff nationwide (NCAS 1985). These same values have then been communicated in the schools and have functioned as the school's cultural norms (NCAS 1988). However, do these white, middle-class cultural values reflect the varied composition of today's schools? What impact do these values have on parent and citizen participation?

Traditionally, the composition of schools was defined by the geographic neighborhood. Community residents worked, lived, and sought recreation in the same neighborhood locations. However, today's society presents a changing picture. The separation of work and residence has created dramatic shifts in the compositions of neighborhoods (Coleman 1985). Today's suburban communities tend to be homogeneous. Urban centers tend toward cultural and racial diversity. As a result of geographic neighborhood changes, urban schools must maintain cultural and racial balance through desegregation plans. Are the white, middle-class values advanced in school culture appropriate in culturally and racially diverse schools?

Future demographic trends will further influence the nature of schools. These trends demonstrate that by the year 2020, whites in America will account for 70 percent of the total population. By the year 2050, more than one out of three Americans will be nonwhite, with increases in the black population and rapid growth in the Hispanic and Asian populations (NCAS 1988). The dominant segment of society will no longer be white, middle-class. Will the values, beliefs, behaviors, and expectations of schools become modified with the growth in cultural and racial diversity? The answer to that question lies in what happens in schools now. Currently, multicultural curricula (NCAS 1988) and empowered students, parents, and citizens (Cummins 1986) are seen as viable solutions to creating environments that support cultural change. Examining what exists now identifies the basis from which growth must occur (Brandt 1989).

As defined previously, what exists now is the dominance of white, middle-class culture. This culture influences participation in three ways. First, the culture dictates who participates in schools. The research findings support this historical trend. It is white, middle-class parents who tend to have successful participation because they share the same values and norms as the school personnel. Second, parents and citizens who come from a diverse racial or ethnic background may hold differing values and norms than those of the community and school culture. What results is a cultural clash and less productive home–school interactions, if any at all. A third result of the cultural effect on schools is that parent- and citizen-participation initiatives often realize much less than what is originally intended. This gap between intent and practice has also been traced to what is known as local political culture (Huguenin, Zerchykov, and Davies 1979; Wirt and Kirst 1982; Julian 1985), or how politics "play out" at the local level. There is increasing evidence that the political culture of communities, districts, and states influences schools (Timar 1989). Therefore, the most viable tool to increase parent and citizen participation is using the political culture to achieve desired changes.

How Do Politics Influence Participation?

Building on the premise that schools are dependent upon their larger environment, they are not only culturally dependent but they are also dependent on the community in other areas. These includes economics, legal issues, and politics. Because school boards and schools had become embroiled in politics, efforts were made earlier in this century to depoliticize the schools. Centralization was one outgrowth of this movement. In some respects, depoliticization was achieved, but short of operating in a vacuum, a school still is dependent upon the community. Therefore, some local politics still influence the schools. For example, today's politics dictate who sits on school boards and how much money is authorized by the local community for school issues. There are also other, more subtle, ways in which local politics influence the schools, particularly in the area of parent and citizen participation. Examining the types of political culture provides background knowledge on how these influences tie into the schools.

There are three distinct types of political culture in the United States — Individualism, Moralism, and Traditionalism (Elazar 1984). *Individualism's* major goal is economic development. Leaders operate according to what suits the situation. They can be influenced by individuals or pressure groups if there is economic gain attached. "Dirty politics" is often part of Individualism. *Moralism* can be traced to the idea of a commonwealth — for the good of the community, participation for all is desired. Moralists may initiate changes on their own and respond to the perceived needs of the community. *Traditionalism* seeks to maintain traditional patterns. The leaders take on a trustee role where they see themselves as the elite, chosen to make decisions. They are influenced by the ideas of those in the inner circle.

Returning to the three influences of culture upon parent and citizen participation, a parallel can be drawn between these influences and political culture. First, parents and citizens who do participate in schools share the same demographic and economic background and the same cultural values as the school personnel. School personnel are seen as professionals, and they tend to act as trustees. The emphasis of participation is to maintain these existing patterns. This constitutes Traditionalism. Second, cultural clashes are produced when parents and citizens from diverse racial and ethnic backgrounds attempt to interact with the schools. Little real change occurs due to the constant cultural conflict, again reinforcing and maintaining the traditionalistic patterns of the schools. Third, often the intent of parent and citizen participation in school decision making is not realized. Traditionalistic school personnel attempt to control the process and outcomes of decision making, often under the guise of professionalism. On the surface, school personnel often appear Moralistic, inviting collective participation in advisory councils and other committees. However, close examination of the processes and outcomes show the true Traditionalism previously described (LeBlanc 1990).

In general, the white, middle-class culture and the schools that are dependent upon it seek to maintain their existing dominance. However, this phenomenon does not preclude change. Productive parent and citizen participation can be achieved.

What Works to Increase Parent and Citizen Participation?

The key to enhancing parent and citizen interactions with schools is knowledge of the factors that influence it. The following paragraphs suggest three steps to take in assessing these factors in your community and schools and how to move forward with that knowledge.

Step 1. Know the Culture.

1. What are the demographic and economic characteristics of the community and the school? (Look at race, ethnicity, socioeconomic status, etc.)
2. Can the community be characterized as diverse or homogenous?

Step 2. Know the Politics.

1. What are the politics of the community?
2. How much dirty politics is there? (Individualism)
3. Are there open meetings with participation by everyone? (Moralism)
4. Do those in power see themselves as insiders and everyone else as outsiders? (Traditionalism)

Step 3. Apply what You Know.

1. If the community and school are white, middle-class, the two will have shared cultural values. If you share that culture, access is easy. You can then work toward the quantity and quality of participation that you desire by appealing to the established values and norms.

If you do not share the culture of the community and school, your access may be more difficult. Here is where you need to use the politics of the community. If the community is Individualistic, try approaching individual school personnel. Look for links related to economic development. Economic development ranges beyond money—starting a parent and citizen volunteer program is economic enhancement. It also gets your foot in the door. If the community politics are Moralistic, chances are your participation is invited. If the community appears more traditionalistic, you need to use someone on the inside. Make connections and use them to get your point of view heard. Use whatever forms of parent and citizen participation that will work, given the local political culture.

2. If the community and school populations are diverse, look at the school personnel. Do they reflect the diversity? If not, one objective is to increase that diversity. Start with the school board. Again, use your political knowledge. Take an approach that fits with the political culture of the community and you'll have more success. For example, in an individualistic or moralistic community you might organize a group of interested parents and citizens to press for change. Start small but think big. Fernandez (1984), of the Philadelphia Parents Union for Public Schools, reported that the union was able to have positive influences on the schools, ranging from getting new school leaders to influencing the budget process. They accomplished big things.

Suggestions for Success

To make parent and citizen participation more effective, use what you know. Two examples of areas for parent and citizen participation using methods based upon the political culture are: (1) parental participation for increased services for special education youngsters and (2) parent and citizen participation in athletic program development.

Individualistic Culture

In an Individualistic political culture the mode for increasing participation that is most effective combines a group approach and an appeal to economics. First, attempts to influence change should start with the principal and work up. Second, parents should band together to press for the increased services. The individualistic culture is responsive to pressure groups and coalitions if those in power can see some benefit in the change. Therefore, the third step is to approach the economics of the issue.

In the example of special education services, parents need to make clear that increased costs for services may be reimbursable under state and federal laws. In addition, parents might suggest the initiation of home-school study programs in cooperation with the new services, to increase student achievement. By suggesting that parents participate in the child's education at home, they are offering home support for increased services with no additional cost to the school.

In the case of athletic program development, parents and citizens need to know how current budget expenditures and estimated costs affect ongoing programs. Parents and citizens can conduct fundraisers to attract new moneys for the school. Parent and citizen volunteers participating in program development also create increased cost savings. Participating can help add funds and can help save funds. It makes sense.

Moralistic Culture

Since the moralist culture is based on the philosophy of participation for all, parent and citizen participation is encouraged. In order for parents and citizens to increase their voice in participation, they need to appeal to values. This can be done both as individuals and through groups.

In the example of the special education services, parents can appeal to the values embodied in special education legislation and emphasize that increased services are for the good of the children. In addition, home-school study programs developed in cooperation with new services can promote program effectiveness and student development.

Athletic programs address the physical health and social development of youngsters. Such an argument appeals to values. In addition, demonstrating that these programs allow for participation by all students reinforces another value in the moralistic culture. Parent and citizen participation in athletic program development generates increased support for the school, another moralistic goal. Also, athletic achievement on the part of some students may result in their being offered scholarships for advanced schooling.

Traditionalistic Culture

The best approach for increasing parent and citizen influence on decision making in a traditionalistic culture is through individual connections, wherever they lie in the school organization. Identify the power brokers and use them. The selling point should center on how decisions can maintain existing patterns. Be patient, as influencing the traditionalistic political culture is a slow process.

Parents of special education youngsters can appeal to those who have power by emphasizing the history and tradition of the school. For example, a parent might approach the increase of services as a way to maintain the existing program while enhancing it. A straightforward personal appeal to the person in power, capitalizing on past relationships, is often successful.

As in the preceding example, athletic program development can be approached from a historical perspective. The way to increase participation in a traditionalistic culture lies in personal power connections.

Conclusion

The description of the research on parent and citizen participation shows that participation has historically been driven by a closed mindset: white, middle-class values held by the dominant segment of society. Given the changes in today's society and the projected demographic trends, that mind-set needs to be opened up and enriched by participation from parents and community members, particularly those from culturally and racially diverse backgrounds. Using the political culture was identified as a tool for increasing parent and citizen participation. Ways for parents and citizens to use specific knowledge and processes in the political culture were identified based upon the particular political culture of the community. By discovering and using the match between the community's political cultural process and the processes of citizen participation in the schools, parents and citizens can broaden diversity in participation as well as enhance the quantity and the quality of their participation, thereby creating positive school interactions.

> *Closer contact between parents and teachers will give each a more complete picture of the child's abilities and improve consistency in working toward desired goals. Most important, perhaps, the child will identify both the school and the home as places to learn, and the parents and teachers as sources of learning.* — W. UMANSKY

CHAPTER TEN

Parent-Teacher Conferences and Teachable Moments

DONALD E. ORLOSKY

Editor's Note: The parent-teacher conference can be an effective method of bridging the gap between home and school. A respect between parties that each has an imperative role to play in the success of the learner will go a long way to ensure cooperation. Each participant wants the conference to succeed. However, a lack of understanding regarding the purpose of the meeting can play havoc, especially if there are learner problems to discuss.

Conferences should be convenient and helpful. Above all, they should provide direction. Competent teachers recognize those "teachable moments" that can facilitate proper communication. (Please get some comfortable chairs.) This is not the time for anger or remorse; it is the time for mutual goal setting. Easy to say, not always easy to do.

One potential outcome of teacher-parent conferences is to strengthen the relationships among the school, the parents, and the child. Another potential outcome is the flip side—relationships among teacher, parent, and child may become worse. This chapter discusses ways to promote the first of these two possibilities and to decrease the likelihood of the second.

Contexts of Conferences

The changing context in which schools function and today's social conditions call for a reexamination of the historic relationship between schools and homes. Schools have traditionally been institutions whose responsibilities were to reduce ignorance, provide a safe environment, and promote acceptable social behavior. These functions are seldom challenged, but the idea that schools should assume responsibilities beyond these three is often met with resistance. However, circumstances in today's society often place youth in jeopardy because the traditional roles, rules, and relationships have eroded. It is now worthwhile and important to consider reasons why schools should play a larger role in working with youth than they have in the past. Additional areas to consider is the responsibility of schools to help parents. There is a growing belief that "parents and teachers are more in need of each other's support than ever before" (Swap 1987, 1).

Effective parents are the best allies a teacher can have. Those who have studied the role of parents in respect to their impact on the schooling of their children have concluded that "in studies involving children at all levels, from infancy through high school, parent involvement made a difference" (Berger 1987, 20). If teachers assist parents in becoming part of the support system for schools, then time spent with parents will return dividends to schools that may, in the long run, reduce the burden on schools rather than increase it. Those who accept this position will place a high priority on parental education because they know that if the schools abandon parents, they do so at their own peril.

Another reason to enlarge the school's role is that many of today's homes no longer provide the stable, two-parent haven that is needed to nurture youth. There is no other agency to whom students can turn to elevate their home life and for parents to improve their knowledge and skills about parenting. Since schools are the primary institutions outside the family responsible for helping youth enter society, schools cannot abandon one of the most significant influences on their students—the home. In the light of these factors, schools serve their own interests best if they also help parents with the responsibilities they face.

The ideal partnership between teachers and parents is difficult to achieve. The typical relationship between home and school and the priorities of each often detract from the establishment of a productive alliance. Many contemporary parents are the victims of a society in which pressure on them has reached unmanageable levels. One of their hopes is that schools will provide custodial and instructional services and will also help students become socialized. When any of these purposes are not met, the blame is often placed on the parent and/or child. If students misbehave at school or achieve below expectations, parents are usually asked to confer with school personnel. When problems at school are added to those at home, in the workplace, and on the street, parents may see the school as another villain in a hostile world. It is not surprising if this combination of pressure in society and potential threat from school generates a negative mindset for parents when they are asked to meet with teachers. At the very least the parent's schedule is disrupted, but there are often other complications, such as taking leave from a job, hiring babysitters, arranging transportation, and nearly always, feeling threatened. These irritations are not the best ingredients to bring to a parent-teacher conference.

Teachers may also be upset by the inconvenience of parent conferences because these discussions intrude on their busy schedule. They also may feel anger toward parents and blame them for failing to remedy the student's problem at home. A confrontation with misbehaving and underachieving students and combative parents is no treat. Teachers can certainly justify negative attitudes about parental conferences, and attempts to avoid parental conferences or to use them to "preach" to parents are understandable. These pessimistic attitudes can get in the way of the positive results that should be the consequences of teacher-parent conferences.

Positive Results Through Teachable Moments

The discussion in this chapter focuses on the belief that the relationship between parents and teachers can be positive and productive and that the parent-teacher conference provides an excellent opportunity for the promotion of healthy relationships among teachers, students, and parents. Effective parent-teacher conferences depend on a variety of factors. Some of these factors include the topic of the conference, the background of the parent(s), the skill and knowledge of the teacher, the policies of the school, and so forth.

The Concept of Teachable Moments

Though many factors influence the nature of conferences, it is not possible to elaborate on all of them in this chapter. However, many parental conferences will provide an opportunity for teachers to employ a particular behavior that can be crucial to improve parenting skills, and the narrative in this chapter focuses on that particular approach. The central emphasis here is that teachers have a powerful technique at their disposal that is often used in the classroom and can be transferred to interactions with parents. This technique calls for the recognition of *teachable moments* in parent-teacher conferences just as effective teachers use this approach in the classroom. Capitalizing on teachable moments in parental conferences is not a panacea that will solve all the problems involving parents and students. There are serious problems that will call for much more. Many "routine" parent-teacher conferences would be improved by teachers providing a timely comment that provides useful direction to parents.

Teachers are familiar with teachable moments in the classroom in which a special set of circumstances occurs that enables the teacher to capitalize on an event, often unplanned, to teach a lesson. The competent teacher recognizes when a special opportunity arises and capitalizes on it to teach a lesson that might not be as effectively taught under any other circumstances. The same principle can be applied to conferences with parents. The teacher must recognize when a teachable moment occurs and what to do about it.

A basic consideration is for the teacher to remember the multiple goals that may be met in parent-teacher meetings. One common purpose of parent-teacher conferences, and a paramount goal, is to resolve the problem under discussion. However, as mentioned earlier, the pressure and stress of parenting and the importance of helping youth reach their potential through school and parental support require an additional concern. This concern calls for teachers to be aware that when they interact with parents they are in a special position to help parents and, as a consequence, to make the present and future lives of their students better.

Two Scenarios

Two scenarios are provided next that illustrate the potential and the importance of recognizing the role teachers can play in providing parents with appropriate help. These scenarios are based on actual events and are presented to illustrate the difference between actions by one teacher who used a teachable moment productively and one who failed to recognize a similar opportunity. (The comment by the teacher that provides the parents with instructions about parenting is in italics.)

When JoAnn failed to perform according to her ability in mathematics, her 8th-grade teacher, Ms. Grayson, talked to JoAnn about improving her work. JoAnn resented the teacher's comments because even though she had slipped academically, she was still doing better work than almost anyone in the class. She limited her reaction to an angry stare at Ms. Grayson and then told her parents that her math teacher was "picking on her." Her parents were confused, as well, because JoAnn was earning "A" grades. When Ms. Grayson saw the continued negative reaction in school by JoAnn she contacted the parents and asked them to confer with her at the school open house that was scheduled in a week. Both of JoAnn's parents came to the open house and Ms. Grayson arranged time for a private conversation with them. Ms. Grayson explained that JoAnn had probably been praised throughout her schooling and that it was a new experience for her to be criticized, especially when she was earning excellent grades. She then asked the parents to think with her about the consequences of a bright student who did not do her best work and was unable to accept constructive criticism. Ms. Grayson was also quick to emphasize that she had the highest regard for JoAnn and respected the excellent role her parents had played in raising her.

The remarks by Ms. Grayson provided JoAnn's parents with a different perspective about their daughter. They knew she was a good student and that she also had never been in any kind of "trouble" at school. They had not thought too much about how capable JoAnn was or what her long-range plans might include. They were told that they had a very capable daughter whose work habits and standards should not be compared to those of other students. They should be based on the ability of JoAnn. Ms. Grayson then recommended a conference with JoAnn, her parents, and herself. She also urged the parents to express their high regard for their daughter when they returned home that evening and to emphasize the high hopes they and their teacher had for her. She also urged them to avoid any hint of disappointment or anger toward JoAnn. She asked them to view themselves, JoAnn, and herself in a partnership that would provide support to enable JoAnn to build her best possible future.

The parents left the conference with a positive feeling toward Ms. Grayson and an even higher regard for the potential of their daughter. They were able to relate their conversation with Ms. Grayson to JoAnn and told her they were looking forward to a meeting with JoAnn and her teacher. A second conference was arranged that included JoAnn, and some new and positive attitudes began to emerge from JoAnn.

As the term continued, JoAnn obviously understood what Ms. Grayson had said to her. JoAnn's parents were equally supportive without adding unrealistic pressure to her academic efforts. At the end of the semester, JoAnn received an academic award for her work in mathematics and her parents attended the award assembly. As the parents and JoAnn said their farewell to Ms. Grayson for the year, JoAnn said to Ms. Grayson, "You have no idea how angry I was at you when you told me to work harder! But, after our conversations with you and my parents about your reasons, I really feel good about myself and this award has shown me how satisfying it can be to do my best."

If this episode had not actually happened, it would be classified in the "too good to be true" category. The episode included a number of factors that contributed to the happy ending, including some of the tactics employed by Ms. Grayson to focus on the relationship between JoAnn and her parents. Some of these factors will be addressed later. Meanwhile, another scenario that also is based on a true incident illustrates a different result.

Mr. Allen gave a weekly 10-item true-false oral quiz on Thursday that counted on the students' final grade and also served as the basis for a weekly review on Friday. Mr. Allen graded the quizzes on Thursday night, and when he returned the papers on Friday for discussion he also invited students to inform him if any grading errors had been made. Howard sat at the back of his row and seemed to have an unusual number of grading errors on his weekly quiz—and the correction was always to Howard's advantage. Mr. Allen began making copies of Howard's answer sheet and found that Howard was changing his answers after he received his graded quiz on Friday. Since Howard sat in the back of the row, he could hide behind other students and change answers without being seen. One day Mr. Allen collected Howard's answer sheet and asked him to come see him after school. When Howard arrived, Mr. Allen asked Howard if he could explain why his paper frequently had grading errors. Howard feigned ignorance. Mr. Allen then showed him copies of his answer sheet and compared it to the one he had collected from Howard. One of the answers had been changed. Howard still persisted that "someone else" must have made the change as his paper was passed down the row. Mr. Allen then reminded him that only he (Mr. Allen) and Howard actually had the paper long enough to change answers and then asked Howard if he was "accusing me of cheating?" Howard broke down and cried and admitted he had changed his answers. He also said that his parents would not accept anything less than perfection from him at school and he cheated to avoid their criticism.

Mr. Allen thought it would be best for Howard to tell his parents what had happened. He told Howard to tell his parents and to ask his parents to call him to make an appointment for a conference. Several days passed and the parents did not call. Howard said he had not told his parents and Mr. Allen gave him another day. Then Mr. Allen called Howard's home and explained to his mother what had happened and asked her to encourage Howard to talk about his history class and try to lead him into a "confession." After several trial conversations, Howard's mother lost her patience and confronted Howard with the information she had. Howard's parents became extremely angry with him, punished him by removing privileges for an excessive period of time, then called Mr. Allen and said they had taken care of everything at home and no conference was needed.

When Howard came to school the next day he cowered at the sight of Mr. Allen and did not participate in class discussions. Despite efforts of Mr. Allen to reduce the tension among parents, student, and teacher, no one was willing to meet in a conference or to even discuss the event any further.

Howard's parents were never provided constructive and/or supportive advice. Nearly all actions were aimed at forcing Howard to confess and leave him either at the mercy of his parents or the whim of the teacher. The major focus of these interactions was on the cheating that Howard did; almost none of the concern was on Howard, Howard's relationship with his parents, or the consequences for Howard over time. Howard happened also to be a bright student whose academic potential was extremely high. No opportunity arose to supply Howard's parents with this information or to address the question of the pressure they were placing on Howard to achieve.

The results of these two episodes were quite different from one another. In the first instance the parents and their child developed stronger ties and more focused goals. JoAnn became more aware of her potential and how to work with her parents and school to achieve successful results. Howard and his parents increased the conflict and tension in their relationship, and Howard's regard for his parents and trust in school were both diminished. In both cases, these events could be significant turning points in the lives of these students.

Both these episodes include teachable moments in teacher-student-parent relationships. Under what conditions do parents and teachers confer most effectively? What is most helpful to ensure that teacher-parent interactions will be positive, open, and trusting? What are the barriers and facilitators to obtaining parental attention and support? What should teachers know and do to be effective parent educators? What are appropriate topics for teachers to address in providing parent education? The remainder of this chapter provides information that addresses these questions about teacher-parent interactions.

Parent-Teacher Interactions

One of the fundamental considerations for teachers in respect to interactions with parents is to address the question of "what are the intended outcomes of conferring with parents?" The recommendation here is that two of the most important goals of parent-teacher interactions are to (1) strengthen the ties between the parent(s) and their child and (2) provide parents with specific and positive help in their role as parents. The suggestions presented in this chapter do not require additional responsibilities for teachers—they may require a change in attitude. They do not require more investment in time—they may require a different use of time. They do not call for teachers to tell parents how to raise their children—they call for teachers to view themselves as partners with parents. They do not call for teachers to judge parents or students—they call for teachers to respect and empower parents and their children.

The evidence that supports the concept of teachable moments as a useful technique in teacher–parent conferences is sparse. However, the literature in the areas of guidance, counseling, supervision, and communication provides a basis from which it is reasonable to infer that the strategies used in these fields can also be effective in conferences with parents. The discussion that follows draws on these related fields as the basis for the recommendations that are made.

The attitude and priorities teachers bring to parent conferences are critical. Some elements that contribute to these attitudes and priorities include: (1) respect, (2) empathy, (3) knowledge, (4) listening skills, (5) communication skills, and (6) significant topics.

Respect

Parent–teacher conferences will be strengthened to the extent that each person has respect for the other. Among the fundamental ideas expressed by mental hygienists is that "each person is worthy of respect" (Association for Supervision and Curriculum Development 1962, 214). Respect for oneself and respect for others help promote a level of interaction in which high regard for one another is the norm. The concept of respect is a complex abstraction that can be analyzed from diverse philosophical positions. The view proposed in this chapter was articulated by Thomas Hill, who suggested that if respect is thought of as an appreciation of the rights of people that "one should respect oneself as well as every other human being. And, in that sense, absence of self respect tends to undermine respect for others" (Hill 1982, 137). Given this orientation, it seems clear that respect, like charity, begins at home. Teachers whose behavior validates their self-respect are not only respected by others but also are more apt to accept the worth of others. Mutual respect is a powerful force in the creation and maintenance of healthy relationships. If one accepts the premise that respect for self and others contributes to more positive and open interaction, then those attributes that contribute to self-respect will tend to generate respectful reactions from others. The behavior that conveys respectfulness in this sense encompasses such actions as: composure under duress, knowledge of professional and academic responsibilities, pride in personal appearance, and an attitude of caring for and respecting others. The teacher who is sloppy and careless in demeanor and work most of the time cannot suddenly expect to be an effective influence during a critical moment. The ability of a teacher to be influential with and respected by parents begins the first time that teacher meets with others — including other teachers, administrators, pupils, and parents. Professional and competent performance by teachers can pay impressive dividends in the marketplace of interactions between themselves and others. When teachers are in a situation to provide direction for parents, the teacher who has demonstrated respect for parents and him/herself will be more influential than the one who respects neither.

One reasonable way to gain respect from parents is to recognize that the best time to prepare for a parent–teacher conference is long before the conference occurs. Teachers should behave as if every student's parents will, at some future time, confer with the teacher about an academic or personal concern of that pupil. Teachers can set the stage for that future conference by gaining the respect of pupils through their actions from the first day of class. Pupils talk about school at home, and the teacher whose reputation with parents is enhanced by pupil reports has an advantage in future discussions with those parents.

Teachers who are self-respectful and confident have an advantage in parent conferences because there is no need for them to overpower the parent and prove their "superiority." The confident teacher can allow parents to be authentic and accept the views of parents without feeling threatened. They can be open to the experience the parent brings and benefit from it. They can give dignity to the parent and empower the parent by acknowledging their comments as legitimate and worthwhile. Such a tone or climate in parent interviews will help defuse tension and provide a base from which honest and open conversation can follow.

Teachers who treat parents with respect will not necessarily elicit respectful behavior in return. Initial feelings of anger by the parent may persist over time, or the negative image some parents have of schools and teachers may not diminish quickly, or at all. Even in these cases the teacher gains nothing by engaging in disrespectful behavior. There is also the possibility that the parent will eventually recognize the civilized approach represented by the teacher and appreciate, and possibly emulate, a more respectful approach.

Thus, respectful, informed, rational, and positive approaches by teachers represent a professional and potentially productive strategy to employ in parent-teacher conferences.

Empathy

Empathy involves "sharing the perceived emotion of another – 'feeling with' another" (Eisenberg and Strayer 1987, 5), the capacity to understand and identify with another person's view or situation. Teachers may have some difficulty altering their role as a teacher of children to that of being a partner with parents. "It is an occupational hazard – teachers tend to be 'teacherish.' This is a useful attribute for work with children but it can be ruinous in a parent-teacher relationship" (Rich 1987, 23). Empathic behavior calls for more than mere words that convey compassion. It calls for teachers to put themselves in the position of the parent and to think as a parent thinks. It is through this sensitive awareness that the teacher will be able to establish the rapport that will promote the level of open discussion necessary to create the desired partnership.

Though empathy is a useful concept to understand another person, it does not necessarily lead to agreement with another. It is possible to understand how parents may experience severe frustration for such reasons as poor health, economic hard times, and dissatisfying employment. If the parent regards these circumstances to justify irresponsibility, alcoholism, or other misbehavior, the teacher can understand the parent's behavior without agreeing with it.

Teachers must avoid relating to the parent as a client who will be "cured" by the parent–teacher conference. Schools and teachers have their limitations, and providing therapy for parents exceeds those boundaries. Teachers who go beyond their prerogatives and try to solve parent problems that exceed their reach will most likely do more harm than good. In fact, teachers should be careful not to assume ownership of problems that belong to parents. Such forays into parent needs will also consume valuable time that could be spent better in the teacher's area of expertise.

The role of the teacher is to be an advocate for the parent's child. For example, when a parent admits to anger and hostility when frustrated, the teacher is not likely to change the parent's behavior by admonishing and telling the parent to "straighten up." However, the teacher can ask parents to think about the impact of their behavior on their child, especially in respect to a specific school incident. They may even ask the parent if they have sought help for their own problems, but the focus must remain on the relationships among the parent, child, teacher, and school. To do otherwise is to enter areas that are too complex to expect teachers to handle.

Knowledge

Knowledge in any profession includes the ability to diagnose and prescribe. Competent teachers classify student performance and then treat the student according to the assessment of the student's characteristics. When teachers confer with parents, professional knowledge is power and can be shared effectively with parents. A major difference between laypeople and professionals is that professionals know "why" they take certain actions. Parents will be helped when teachers interpret this professional knowledge and present it to them in a useful form.

Before meeting with parents, the responsible teacher will learn as much as possible about the child, the parents, and the situation that has prompted the conference. The following suggestions about preparation for the conference are important to consider:

1. Try not to bring memories of previous conferences into this conference.
2. Be ready to share your concerns, your problems—without trying to assign blame.
3. Make a list of questions to ask and invite the parents to also prepare a list. (Rich 1987, 50–51)

Communication Skills

Communication involves sending and receiving messages. When receiving messages, the active listener makes it clear that the words and feelings of the sender are being heard and understood. They accomplish this with their posture, their mental state, their body language, and their words. Each of these features contributes to the quality of the interaction and the resultant relationship. When sending messages, the effective communicator is open, honest, authentic, and tactful. These sending and receiving behaviors contribute substantially to the kind of relationships people establish.

Relationships can be classified into closed, open, and transitional categories. In the *closed relationship,* both parties are protective, suspicious, mistrusting, and unwilling to be honest or candid. In a closed relationship both parties are left in doubt about the other person, their relationship with that other person is unclear, and each person is unwilling to reveal honest feelings and thoughts to the other. The relationship is superficial and the parties involved are psychologically distant from one another.

An *open relationship* is characterized by authenticity, honesty, and trust, and both parties know and accept the relationship they have with each other. An open relationship is found, for example, among close friends and in good family relationships.

A *transitional relationship* is characterized by one person behaving as he or she would in an open relationship and the other as he or she would in a closed relationship. Over time, the person who behaves as a closed relationship person may change and become more open and the relationship will become more open. Or, alternatively, the person who has been responding openly may become discouraged with the other person's response and either dissolve the relationship or revert to a more closed behavior pattern.

These categories are rarely "pure" and can be distributed along a continuum for discussion purposes as presented in Figure 10-1. As relationships tend toward the 9 or 10 end of the scale, the opportunity for meaningful discussion increases. As relationships move toward the 1 or 2 end of the scale,

FIGURE 10-1 • *Range of Personal Relationships*

Closed Relationship			Transitional Relationship				Open Relationship		
1	2	3	4	5	6	7	8	9	10

the level of discourse tends toward the superficial and is counterproductive and the relationship becomes closed or even hostile.

The relationship that effective teachers can create with parents is at least a transitional relationship (4–6 on the scale). The behavior of only one person is necessary to create the transitional relationship, and the teacher can always be open, honest, candid, and tactful. Even though the parent may not initially respond openly, the possibility an open relationship may develop exists if the teacher continues to be open. However, when teachers avoid the real (and often difficult) concerns with ambiguous, evasive, and judgmental approaches, they promote a closed relationship.

It is unlikely that many teacher–parent relationships can or should reach a 10. There are many personal and private matters that typically are part of a totally open relationship that are inappropriate for a professional relationship. However, when teachers are candid (not combative) and describe their concerns honestly but tactfully, they promote an open relationship that has the potential to reach the higher ranges on the scale. Today's typical teachers have received training in active listening and effective communication skills. If they will remind themselves to use these skills in conferences with parents, they will make more progress than if they ignore the basic principles of effective communication. Much has been written about effective communication skills (Rutherford 1979; Stewart 1986; Knapp and Miller 1985) that teachers can learn about and practice. Space does not permit elaboration on this body of literature, but teachers who have not had the opportunity to study and practice effective communication skills should take advantage of the opportunities to develop these abilities.

In any conference dealing with a problem or conflict, there are four possible outcomes: (1) The problem is resolved and the relationship is strengthened; (2) the problem is solved and the relationship is damaged; (3) the relationship is strengthened but the problem remains unsolved; and (4) the problem is not resolved and the relationship is damaged. Of these outcomes, the first result is preferred. Appropriate listening and sending techniques will promote the resolution of problems and the promotion of positive relationships.

Significant Topics

Parent–teacher conferences have the potential to make an important difference in the lives of all concerned. This opportunity to make an important impact should not be treated lightly. The limited time available for most conferences makes it important to focus on crucial matters and to do so effectively and efficiently. The preliminary comments that help build rapport and establish a conversational atmosphere are important factors in the conference, but the central purpose of the conference should be addressed as soon as possible. This approach will optimize the use of time.

Though a specific issue or problem may be the reason for a conference, the prepared teacher is aware that other topics will often surface. There are valuable sources of information that could prove critical in helping parents. Berger (1987) has prepared a list of resources whose categories reveal some of the topics that may arise in a parent/teacher conference. These categories include: (1) parenting skills, (2) parent–school relationships, (3) childrearing, (4) the working mother, (5) the stepparent, (6) discipline, (7) fathers, (8) divorce and the single parent, (9) parenting for teenagers, (10) health and nutrition, (11) sexual abuse, (12) physical abuse and neglect, (13) learning activities for home and school, (14) child development and parenting, (15) how children learn, (16) parent–child relationships, (17) issues that affect family life, (18) special children, and (19) coping with family change.

Teachers who converse with parents will be better prepared to respond to parent concerns if they are knowledgeable about the topics listed in the preceding paragraph. The challenge for teachers to keep abreast of new developments in curriculum, instruction, and content can be extended to include knowledge about the lives of parents and the issues that evolve in families. Teachers who are armed with knowledge about families and parenting will be more helpful in providing parents with suggestions about how to interact with their children and how to help their children succeed in school, making parents feel good about their parenting in the process.

Views about How People Grow

Teachers should not be surprised to encounter parents whose views about raising children or whose priorities are contradictory to their own. A fundamental consideration in nurturing the young is the view of adults about how children grow. When teachers meet parents whose views about their children differ from their own, it is not always easy to discern who is "right" because there is no magic formula for raising children that will work with everyone. However, there are some fundamental principles about raising children that every teacher should take into consideration when conversing with parents. Some of these fundamental factors are identified by a noted psychologist (Elkind 1981) who has studied children and the circumstances surrounding their maturation. In his popular book, *The Hurried Child*, Elkind provides descriptions that identify contrasting views about children. His descriptions help to classify some of these differences and to anticipate responses to situations encountered with parents.

One view of the child is illustrated by the metaphor that children are like marble to be shaped by the hand of the sculptor. A contrasting metaphor is that of the child as a growing plant that grows appropriately if properly nurtured. Those who work regularly with children often see themselves as "gardeners" who help students grow. It is common to see those in a position of authority, including parents who exert authority over their children, hold the view of themselves as "sculptors" who shape raw material into a preconceived and measurable product. Elkind elaborates on these contrasting views when he describes those who adopt the metaphor of the growing organism envisioning "the school as a farm where living things grow freely" and those who "prefer the view of children as malleable entities awaiting the imposition of form from without" (1981, 24) and see schools where students are products of the assembly line. These metaphors help explain two different views of youth. When parents adopt the role of sculptors, they impose their will on their children and they feel personally accountable for the actions of their children. When they hold this view, they have difficulty trusting the "normal" stages of development, they want to control their offspring, and they have trouble letting go of their children to allow them to learn from their own choices. Some gentle nudging from teachers may help these parents relax their dominating behavior and provide breathing room for children to develop with less pressure.

Another pervasive trend that calls for attention is the impact of changes in family life on parents and their children. Families with both parents working, single-parent families, and parents with threats to their very existence as job markets shift and employment is automated away have little time or emotional energy left to raise children. They are preoccupied with self-preservation. Though the two aforementioned metaphors characterize divergent but viable views about children, neither metaphor may fit with some parents because child raising is put aside and is a low priority in the lives of adults who are preoccupied with taking care of themselves. More and more parents are raising children in their spare time. These parents place a low priority on child raising and often resent the demands and responsibilities imposed by children on them.

Teachers should expect to encounter parents who perceive children as: (1) raw material to be shaped by adult sculpturing, (2) growing organisms to be nurtured and supported, and (3) intruders on adult lives.

Parental Views of School

Teachers will learn about parents' perceptions of schools during the parent-teacher conference. They will find out if the parent is angry or docile. They will discover if the parent has faith in schools or distrusts them. They will learn about the value placed on education by the parent, and they will discover how the parent relates to his or her child. They may also see changes in parents as the conference proceeds. Anger can become cooperation, and distrust can change to trust. The conference can be a powerful event in the life of the parent and in the future of the student. For these reasons it is important to be alert to the possible reactions of parents but to suspend judgment until the conference occurs. Prejudging and stereotyping parents will probably interfere with the development of a cooperative partnership.

Another element in the dynamics of the parent-teacher conference is that the conference is held on the teacher's turf but also on turf where the parent previously trod, but in an entirely different role. One writer on parent–teacher relationships has described the consequences of this background as follows:

> *Underneath most parents is a student—Someone who went to school, sometimes happily, sometimes unhappily. What often happens when the parent-as-adult returns to school, or has dealings with teachers, is that the parent as child/student returns. Many parents still enter school buildings flooded with old memories, angers, and disappointments. Their stomachs churn and flutter with butterflies, not because of what is happening today with their own children, but because of outdated memories and past behaviors.*
>
> *Consequently, teachers may have trouble getting these parents to act like the mature adults they are. Just as it is vital that teachers treat parents as adults, parents need help to recognize their own pitfalls that may prevent them from acting like adults in schools. One way for teachers to address these ghosts is to spend a few minutes talking with parents about their own school experiences. This helps to separate earlier reactions from what is happening with their own child in the present. (Rich 1987, 24–25)*

Teachers are in a special position to provide parents with information that will help them acquire accurate information about schools. The perception parents have about school may be based on their personal school experiences, the stories their children bring home, the information they receive through the media, or the opinions of their friends. Their perceptions may be accurate or inaccurate, positive or negative. The teacher who establishes a cooperative partnership with parents and provides specific information about their child can give parents the most viable basis for them to judge schools. The teacher who is able to solicit parental support and provide a solid basis for parental behavior can convert parents into supportive allies and enlist parental power to be a positive force for schools. Parental perception of schools should be considered as important for the teacher to address as the objectives of a lesson in a classroom. Conferences provide teachable moments for parents to improve their parenting skills, and they also provide teachable moments for parents to learn about the realities of schools. Teachers have an obligation to capitalize on this opportunity.

Summary

Schools should view interactions with parents as an opportunity to provide parents and students with support that goes beyond the academic or behavioral concerns of today's students. Schools can give attention to the broader outcomes of helping parents without violating the legitimate territory of parents or the limitations of schools. These broader outcomes include attention to such matters as parent–student relationships, parental responsibilities, student responsibilities, support for parents and students, and the promotion of socially acceptable and productive behavior.

Educators who believe that schools and the family form a symbiotic relationship will subscribe to the principles that:

- Schools do have some responsibility to assist parents to work with their children.
- Schools are particularly suited to assist parents.
- Parents, teachers, and pupils can form a partnership that will strengthen all three.
- The effort by educators to provide parental education yields a positive return that makes the investment worthwhile.

The strategy proposed in this chapter for teachers to use is the concept of teachable moments. Teachable moments arise spontaneously and within a context that is usually unplanned. The alert and prepared teacher recognizes when such an opportunity arises and knows how to capitalize on it. The application of the teachable-moment strategy calls for the recognition that important outcomes of a parent conference are to provide help to parents that will (1) assist them in their parenting behavior and (2) strengthen the relationships among parents, students, and schools. A few well-chosen comments at a critical time, delivered effectively, can make all the difference in how parents respond to their children. And the way parents respond to their children can make a critical difference in the lives of those children and the ability of schools to provide the instruction and socializing influence that will help the next generation become productive adults.

> *Helping the parent to feel more adequate for this task is fully as important from the point of view of public education and the welfare of society as is the education of the children themselves. Moreover, an educated parenthood facilitates the task of the schools and insures the success of its educational program with the child.*
> —*PENNSYLVANIA DEPT. OF PUBLIC INSTRUCTION*

CHAPTER ELEVEN

Parent-Teacher Conferences: A Parent's Perspective

*Summary of an Interview with Irene Meers
as told to*

SANDRA PETTAPIECE

Editor's Note: Parent-teacher conferences have been going on for a long time. The side of the desk you're on presents a unique set of problems and opportunities.

Teachers must prepare for these meetings carefully, putting together information, both written and anecdotal, that identifies the learner's strengths as well as growth areas. Teachers do not just "wing" their way through these important meetings.

However, it is not always clear that parents are the equal partners in this dialogue. They possess insights as well as data crucial to the educator as he or she plans educational experiences for their youngster. Parents have not always been adequately prepared to understand their role in this session and how vital they are in this process. In other words, parents cannot "wing it" either.

Even though this is written by and for parents, I hope that teachers will read it and pay attention too. This is about working together. I will try to identify, from a parent's point of view, four issues: the purpose and nature of parent-teacher conferences; getting ready for a conference; the conference itself; and, finally, what happens after the conference. Some of the ideas, strategies, concerns, frustrations, and fears that parents bring when they return to school for parent-teacher conferences will be discussed.

Purpose and Nature of Parent Teacher Conferences

As a parent, it seems to me that parent-teacher conferences are a chance for the adults at school and the adults at home to work together toward common goals. Both sets of adults want the child to get as much as possible out of the school experience and to be successful and happy.

As important as working together is, it's not always easy for a parent to get ready for the conference. Childhood memories of teachers as the authority as well as old feelings about school in general can return and make a parent feel uncomfortable. It's hard to put away those feelings and return to the place where teachers were in charge. A couple of thoughts can help a parent get past those intimidating feelings. First, it helps to remember that you are an adult who has the right to speak and to listen. You don't have to control or be controlled by the teacher. The other thing to remember is that both adults have important contributions to make. Parents can and do share insights into the child's strengths, weaknesses, interests, fears, worries, and attitudes. For example, one of my children who has a learning disability was motivated by art books. I believe that this was useful in helping him complete high school and continue his education after high school. Teachers may not know that a child is interested in art books. It is important to share the information, because the teacher can also use it to help the child. Another of my children was in a gifted program. After watching her, listening to her, and thinking about her, I decided the pull-out gifted program was not in my child's best interest. I shared that information with the teacher and have since removed her from the program.

On the other hand, teachers have information about the child that parents need. They can and do share information about the child's school achievement and about his or her skills in academic and social areas. It is helpful to remember that sometimes children are different people at home and at school. For example, I learned that another of my children was the class clown and as a result was having behavior problems. I received information about his program, his behavior, and his academic strengths and weaknesses. In addition to information about the child, teachers also can and do share information about their educational beliefs, programs, and plans. By attending conferences, parents learn not only about the teacher's goals and attitudes, but also how those goals, beliefs, plans, and program "fit" their child.

Finally, two-way communication can clear up misunderstandings. A teacher was not responding to information in meeting one of my children's needs. It appeared that she was ignoring these needs, as though she were not concerned. It turned out that the information that I had sent to the school through the school office was not given to the teacher. After discovering the misunderstanding, we both felt better and my child's needs were addressed.

Concerns arising from misunderstandings like the one above can lead to unscheduled conferences. Problems that arise at home or at school can also create the need for unscheduled conferences, which can optimally alleviate misunderstandings and solve problems. Occasionally these conferences called specifically to solve a problem or clear up a misunderstanding may create tension for the parent, the teacher, and the child.

Regularly scheduled conferences can help lessen the tension when unscheduled conferences become necessary. Unscheduled conferences thus become less negative. The parent and the teacher have already become a team with common goals. Both scheduled and unscheduled conferences can be used to set goals, plan strategies, and evaluate what progress is being made toward achieving the goals.

Regularly scheduled conferences are an expectation in the K–6 program in our school district. Two days are set aside for the "every parent" conferences. Parents of elementary school children are invited to share in the education of their children. When children begin their secondary education, however, parents are no longer invited to attend regularly scheduled conferences. Beginning with the seventh grade, progress reports are sent to parents, instead of invitations to parent-teacher conferences. Of course, parents and teachers can initiate "special" conferences to solve problems by requesting an unscheduled conference. Although special conferences can result from progress reports in the secondary schools, regularly scheduled conferences in middle schools and high schools would be beneficial.

Getting Ready for the Conference

Whether the conference is routine or initiated by the parent or teacher, planning is important. Several issues need to be considered. First, there are logistical issues. Prior to the conference, parents and teachers need to set a time, place, and a list of things to be shared and considered. Efficient and effective meetings require agenda. By making a plan for the parent-teacher meeting, everyone can be prepared. A focus for the meeting is most likely to facilitate the child's progress and solve problems. Knowing what will be discussed can reduce anxiety for both the parent and the teacher.

Anxiety in the child can also be reduced through using an agenda. When the parent and the teacher both know the agenda, they can reassure the child about the purpose of the meeting. Both adults can share what they anticipate will happen. This sharing of expectations helps the child understand that the home and the school are working together on his or her behalf, rather than plotting against him or her. Children need to know that the home–school team is working for them.

The child will also provide information, feelings, and insights that are useful to the adults. In addition, it may also be helpful to talk with other parents and informed adults to gain their insights. Additional information can often solve problems before they get out of hand.

Another bit of homework that is necessary prior to the conference can be called "getting yourself together." First, make a list of things you want to remember. The list can include questions you want to ask, issues you want to discuss, and ideas and information you want to share with the teacher. The list will help you stay with the agenda and help you remember important thoughts. A second part of getting ready might include getting rid of emotional garbage. If a conference situation seems intimidating, practicing before a mirror can help. If I am anxious or angry, I rehearse in the car and try to remind myself to stay calm. Knowing that you are intellectually and emotionally ready for the meeting helps you reach mutual goals with the teacher.

Finally, before the conference occurs, check on the possibility of having the child in attendance. Including the child demonstrates to him or her that the home and school are a team that works together. It can also lessen anxiety for future conferences. Sometimes having the child present can help clarify a situation. The child and the teacher can share perceptions of events in the classroom, clarify the events, and help two divergent stories merge into one complete history of an event. The parent and child can clarify home events that relate to school success, providing another more complete picture for everyone. Finally, involving the child improves that child's self-esteem and gives him or her a sense of ownership in the educational process. The child may even have a unique and workable solution to problems. If the child cannot attend the conference, reassure him or her that you will discuss the conference after it is over.

The Conference Itself

Once the homework has been done and it has been decided if the child will attend, the conference itself may begin. Because your time and the teacher's time are important, the conference should start on time.

When following the agenda, be ready to give, as well as take, suggestions and information. If it is necessary to restate your agenda goals, do so. Now is the time to focus on concerns, issues, and solutions, not the time to cast blame on the child, the teacher, yourself, or any other person or system. As you make preparations, you may want to include a timetable as part of your plan to reach goals. In addition to learning more about your child, the parent-teacher conference can provide an opportunity to learn more about the teacher's curricular goals and school policy.

If the conference becomes stressful, remember to remain an adult. Be realistic and remember you are part of a team with mutual goals. Make sure you are ready to get the whole picture before you make decisions.

You may want to end the conference by summarizing with the teacher the plans, perceptions, and suggestions you shared during the conference. This will help establish direction for both of you. Just as the conference started on time, it should also end on time. You can always ask for another conference, if you feel you need more time.

Postconference Follow up

As mentioned earlier, if the child was not present at the conference, share your joint plans for his or her growth with the child afterward. Let your child see you and the school as a team working together. Remember that this is a sharing time, which requires listening to your child, as well as sharing information.

After sharing important information with your child, implement your parent-teacher-child plans. As plans are implemented, you may need to follow up with another conference with the teacher. If so, begin to get ready again.

It may seem that parent-teacher conferences are ongoing. That is the intent! Parents and teachers must look at conferences as necessary teamwork. When conferences are approached with an open mind, an even temper, and mutual goals, children become the winners!

There is little that cannot be remedied later; there is much that can be prevented from happening at all. —E. ERIKSON

CHAPTER TWELVE

"At-Risk" Youngsters in Public Education

ASA J. BROWN

Editor's Note: The partnership between home, school, and community, particularly with respect to shared policy making, is a dynamic one that characteristically consists of an ongoing series of topic-related accommodations. It is multifaceted, highly politicized, often heavily emotionally charged, but of tremendous importance to the success of our schools. The dialogue is often sufficiently tenuous so that every attempt should be made by the participating parties to reduce the amount of affective baggage that they bring to the encounter.

The matter of youngsters "at risk" in public schools is an important case in point. With its attendant issues of multiple cause (social and economic origins), questions of who is and who is not responsible for intervention, and cost (estimated as up to $21 billion dollars), the arena is fraught with potential for conflict. The current demography is rising, with estimates of one in three to one in five school-age youngsters so identified.

This chapter addresses the needs of at-risk students from a perspective of systemic curricular change rather than from one advocating the need for a proliferation of add-on compensatory programs based on subgroup membership.

Suggestions are made for ways to reduce the number of students at risk by sharpening attention to individual learning needs across grades K–12 for all pupils. It is hoped that such a focus will better serve the needs of the general student population including those posited as at risk and will provide a more positive base for home–school–community dialogue than would otherwise be possible within the more traditional view of those at risk in public education.

Certainly individuals and groups can be identified as "at risk" in any number of situations for any number of reasons both in and out of public education. Being "at risk" is not usually a static condition in anyone's life. For the most part it is situationally determined.

With respect to public education, being "at risk" simply means a prediction has been made by an adult or group of adults about the future well-being of a child or group of children based on the past experience of these adults in dealing with similar youngsters in similar learning situations. This usually relates to the probability of completing 12 grades of education. Because the standards of educational practice vary tremendously between classrooms, buildings, districts, and regions of the country, the utility of the label is often called into question. However fuzzy the classifications may be, they represent an attempt to alert educational professionals and the interested lay community about youngsters for whom schools have a special responsibility.

Such prognostications are made either on the basis of individual students demonstrating unusual academic or psychosocial problems, or the students may be members of some special group that historically has had untoward difficulty completing 12 grades of public education.

Factors Leading to Risk

Some students are thought to be at risk primarily on the basis of antecedent conditions—that is, factors not seen as primarily resulting from the schooling process. While there is increasing debate as to how cause and effect interact in such cases, there are, nonetheless, discrete sets of information available regarding educational practice as it relates to many groups including bilingual students, students from dysfunctional families, racial and cultural minority students, handicapped students, etc.

There seems to be no shortage of potential contributing factors. Druian and colleagues (1987) specify the following with respect to conditions that affect being at risk:

What conditions predict whether a student will be at risk? Researchers have found that it is possible to identify potential dropouts early—as early as elementary school, "We intervene too late in the course of a student's development, that certain parts of the profile of a dropout-prone student may be visible as early as the third grade." At the same time, there are a variety of conditions associated with being at risk.

1. Living in high-growth states
2. Living in unstable school districts

3. *Being a member of a low-income family*
4. *Having low academic skills (though not necessarily low intelligence)*
5. *Having parents who are not high school graduates*
6. *Speaking English as a second language*
7. *Having negative self-perceptions; being bored or alienated; having low self-esteem*
8. *Pursuing alternatives: males tend to seek paid work as an alternative; females may leave to have children or get married.*

When one aggregates the student numbers associated with the traditional at risk groupings, it is possible that as many as *one in four* school-age children is in some form of identifiable educational jeopardy, including the *46 million students* who received special education service during the 1989–90 school year. If one places no other value on this information, clearly schools can be much riskier places than many of us had previously thought.

The sheer magnitude of the numbers forces us to look at why so many of our children are in jeopardy. The static nature of much of the traditional public school curriculum is a major factor. Unique children, those presenting special challenges for individualization, are frequently the victims of a delivery system that is too often narrowly defined and rigidly presented. Many youngsters are thereby placed at risk by the schooling process itself.

Because it appears that public education may be simultaneously both a causative and remedial agent in this matter, the discussion that follows will not focus on strategies thought to be of benefit to the several traditional groups of students said to be at risk for public education. Instead, a series of suggestions aimed at increasing general curricular flexibility through attention on individualization will be presented. Such a focus is no panacea. There will continue to be certain groups of youngsters requiring specialized attention. If, however, this information is helpful in increasing the academic coping skills of a broader spectrum of the general school population than is now the case, we will have taken a major step toward addressing the issue of system-induced jeopardy.

Asa Hillard (1989) is most encouraging regarding the potential for growth in the at-risk population:

1. *The vast majority of at-risk children are fully capable of succeeding in the academic program of the public schools.*
2. *At-risk children do not need anything special by way of pedagogy. In the overwhelming majority of the cases, the at-risk children fail because an appropriate quality of regular instruction* is not made available to them.

3. *Even under circumstances where at-risk children have fallen behind in their academic work, when given appropriate regular pedagogy, they can catch up with their age peers and, under certain circumstances, may even do better than average for their age group.*

At Risk in Regular Education

On one hand, K–12 regular education is actively struggling with negative public perceptions regarding the overall literacy of students graduating from public schools in the United States. Among multiple other criticisms, there is special concern about the ability of graduates to contribute positively within a highly technological national work force that must compete in the international marketplace.

Notwithstanding the complex factors that have shaped our public schools over time, educators are busy reforming their current standards of practice. Many of these curricular changes are based on pedagogic concerns, but the reform efforts are in no small part a reflexive attempt to turn out a student product that will soften the public outcry. This more acceptable graduate appears to be one who is able to compete successfully in a more cognitively challenging curriculum than that perceived to be required in the past.

The dynamics at work in this action-reaction paradigm are worthy of and have received intense professional interest. Only one of these regular education reforms will be addressed here, however, as it demonstrates how the schools themselves — albeit with worthy intentions — contribute directly to the increasing number of children at risk in public education. Of particular interest is that piece of the regular education reform movement advocating a "return to basics" by making high school completion requirements more stringent. In many instances this means requiring more units of mathematics, science, foreign language, and English.

As graduation standards tighten, another pool of youngsters is created who are potentially at risk with respect to high school completion. These are the students who have been academically struggling at the bottom 10–15 percent of the regular school population before the imposition of more cognitively challenging requirements. These students certainly will require extra attention if they are to stay in school and graduate.

In this respect they resemble special education students. They do not, however, have the statutory protections and resources that their peers in special education do. They are simply another at-risk group placing yet another potential drain on school resources.

Special Education

Nationally, one in five professionals entering a school building on any given day in the United States will be there to provide some form of special education service. Over the past decade the associated costs have risen to a point where containment measures are being implemented across the country. One of the strategies used to reduce costs is to tighten the eligibility requirements for special education service.

Most of the regular education youngsters newly placed at risk for high school completion by the tightening of graduation standards will not be eligible for special education service. Given finite resources and an already overcrowded general education curriculum, it would seem important to search for some ways that curricular offerings might be positively influenced without the necessity for an infusion of outside money or introducing unnecessary major trauma to the delivery system.

Some critics point out that public schools are painfully slow to introduce systemic change. Others say that the opposite is true and that education tends to be too responsive to new ideas and that there is a reflexive incorporation of each new fad. There is probably some wisdom within each position. What is equally curious, however, is the question of which innovations are chosen over others for trial and which changes take root and which do not.

"Old Warhorses" of Curriculum Improvement

Perhaps we can learn a curriculum lesson from the way symphony conductors balance their concert programs. There is a term used by classical musicians to describe those master works of historically proven audience appeal and technical merit. They call these compositions "old warhorses."

When performances are formatted that include lesser-known or otherwise unproven pieces, musicians frequently balance the program by including one or more of the old warhorses. This not only serves as a palliative for audiences, but it also reinforces the new material within a contextual perspective of accepted tradition.

The program suggestions that follow represent a select group of old warhorses. All have been present in some form within public education for a long time and are of proven value. Many schools will have one or more in place now. Most will have at least vestiges of several. Each old warhorse chosen was picked from a larger warhorse menu on the basis of meeting each of five criteria: (1) Each can be incorporated into extant K–12 curricular offerings easily at little or no additional cost, (2) each is supported by a data base that demonstrates efficacy, (3) each impacts positively on the school experience of at-risk youngsters, (4) each is potentially more time-efficient than the current practices for which they may substitute, and (5) each melds into the curriculum at large, thereby offering potential benefit to the larger school population while avoiding the disruptions associated with pullout programs.

There is consensus in the literature regarding the importance of approaching this problem through the general education curriculum. McPartland and Slavis (1990) state:

> *Clearly, one of the most effective ways to reduce the number of children who will ultimately need remedial services is to provide the best possible classroom instruction in the first place. Therefore, in an overall strategy to serve at-risk students, introducing instructional methods with proven capacities to accelerate achievement — particularly among these students — is absolutely essential.*

Empowerment and Prioritizing the Existing Curriculum

Werner Von Braun, the rocket scientist, was once interviewed while working for the National Aeronautics and Space Administration regarding his thoughts about how science was approached in Germany, the Soviet Union, and the United States. He characterized American scientific thought as believing that "You can get a baby in one month by simply bringing together nine pregnant women."

Indeed there is a tendency, even within American education, to believe that problems can be solved simply by providing more resources. Recently, as the result of a sweeping study of curriculum in a large urban school system, the administrators were surprised to learn that those schools within the district with the lowest student achievement scores were also the schools receiving the most external resources. Classroom teachers were not surprised. A closer look revealed that the additional programs were simply added to an already crowded curricular menu, forcing staff to dilute their efforts across an impossible and often bewildering range of activity.

Sometimes more is not only ineffective; it is too much. To assume that "a good teacher will find time" is not a compliment; it is an affront. If good teaching is done by competent, disciplined, and caring professionals, forcing them to covertly prioritize an undeliverable curricular array portends serious disruption of their personal and professional effectiveness.

Within this perspective, the natural first step in the process of curricular reorganization is to match the list of possible tasks (new and old) with the teacher/administrator time demands associated with each and settle for what is realistically possible. The two key ingredients in reaching these determinations will be the opportunity for real participation in decision making by the classroom teacher and honest support by administration, especially at the building level. A major responsibility of this latter group will be to protect the classroom teachers from those who would load more into the schedule once it is fixed. The freedom for classroom teachers to have the time to do it right not only has to be fought for; it has to be constantly protected.

No discussion of empowerment would be complete without emphasizing the effect of parental involvement in formally and informally shaping the school life of the child. As parents take an increasingly active role in influencing school policy decisions, educators must work to ensure that parents have accurate information about what is happening in their schools and the major issues facing education.

It would seem that one of the most effective ways of doing this would be to involve parents across a spectrum of activity. Warner (1991) incorporates Joyce Epstein's five basic ingredients into the Indianapolis Program for Parental Involvement:

> *Developing parenting skills is the goal of the first component of Epstein's model. Parents are first and foremost supporters of their children; they provide food, clothing, shelter, and psychological support for their children as they grow up. Parents in Touch helps parents fulfill their parenting roles by providing information and ideas about the characteristics of and suggesting strategies for the development of a home environment that supports the learning behaviors of children at each grade level.*
>
> *The second component of Epstein's model and of the IPS parental involvement effort is communication. The staff words hard to design effective forms of communication that will reach all parents.*
>
> *The third component of the parental involvement model is the use of parent volunteers. IPS encourages parents to work as volunteers at the school or to attend and suport events and meetings.*
>
> *The fourth component of Epstein's model is encouraging children's learning activities at home. Parents in Touch provides ideas, materials, and training to parents through its own programs and through TIPS homework activities.*
>
> *The final component of the parental involvement model is encouraging parental participation in decision making across the district. The Parents in Touch staff supports this effort by recruiting parents and by helping to develop parent leadership.*
>
> *IPS believes it can better meet the academic and developmental needs of its students if substantive collaboration between parents, teachers, and administrators is increased. Parental involvement is viewed as an important component of the district's school improvement plan. If all children can learn, then all parents can help to make that happen.*

Maximizing Available Student Support

Serious consideration should be given to formalizing those practices shown to be effective in encouraging student learning and interest in staying in school. This is particularly true in situations where there are concentrations of at risk youngsters.

Two such practices warrant attention. The first involves associating groups of youngsters with their teachers across blocks of time longer than those usually allocated for a given grade. In practice, this most often means holding the same students and teachers together for a group of several school years. This may be done at one or two specific points in time. One is a block of kindergarten through grade three, or first grade through grade four. The second block involves middle or junior high school youngsters in some three-year combination involving grades six through nine.

Two of the benefits most frequently associated with this practice are quite appealing from the standpoint of increasing program flexibility: (1) Teachers are reported to be more willing to invest personally in their charges and directly address behavioral problems than when students are passed along at the end of an academic year, and (2) students develop deeper and more positive peer linkages in this system, particularly at the middle or junior high level. This is seen as an important ingredient in helping at-risk students maintain their interest in staying in school.

Shanker (1990) reports on a similar, but considerably more ambitious, plan at the Holweide Comprehensive School in Cologne, West Germany:

> *The results at Holweide are impressive. Most students come to the school already written off as lacking academic potential. Despite this, a disproportionately large number end up going to universities, which, in Germany, means passing a national examination that requires a high level of scholastic achievement.*
>
> *All of this is accomplished without the bureaucracy that characterizes American public schools. Holweide has only three administrators (a principal and two assistants), and all three continue to teach, as required by German law. In fact, the principal teaches six to eight periods a week and is a member of a teaching team. Though many elements of Holweide's structure are worth trying in some American schools, I'm not offering it as a panacea for our problems. What Holweide does represent, however, is a fundamentally different model of schooling. It is an example of the kind of rethinking we'll have to do if we are to develop schools that will reach the large numbers of youngsters who are failing in one way or another in the current system.*

The second practice involves associating small groups of children as interactive and interdependent working units within the classroom across time. Whether this is along the lines of the cooperative learning model or some local variation, the benefits of pursuing mutually beneficial goals are well documented. Slavin (1987) states, "There is now evidence that students working together toward a common goal can accomplish more than those students working independently."

In addition to positively affecting achievement, when used in combination with the tracking system described above, the peer support system is greatly strengthened by demonstrably placing the locus of responsibility for achievement and behavioral control more clearly in the collective hands of the learners. The teachers can then increasingly assume the more time-efficient and psychosocially healthy role of expediters.

Attention to Individualization in the Early Grades

Preschool educators have been particularly interested in at-risk children. The recently rediscovered Head Start program had its origins in an attempt to give assistance to youngsters from environments thought to be lacking in language stimulation. Somewhere in the rush to provide this stimulation, the essence appears to have become a bit cloudy. The concept of language stimulation is certainly one of the more popular of the old warhorses. It is time to restate the nature of the interaction involved for some of those practicing the craft, particularly in those programs supported by chapter funds where the actual one-on-one encounter is often done by paraprofessionals.

Calling the process *language stimulation* may have been somewhat unfortunate in that some practitioners believe that this means if adults provide a setting that immerses children in various forms of auditory stimulation, their language development will be enhanced. There needs to be a simple but very necessary reaffirmation of faith. The intent of the process is to create a situation in which the language product brought forward by *the child* is the focus. The prime enabling vehicle for this is the adult–child interaction.

Conceptually it is quite simple. The more such interactions there are, the more truly interactive they are, the more the language product of the child is respected, the more likely the desired result can be achieved.

We can do a great deal to advance the cause of this at-risk group by carefully revisiting the differences between language and stimulation with those that provide the direct service. Schaffer (1977) summarizes the feeling of child development researchers well when he remarks that the *amount* of stimulation is not nearly so critical as the *quality* and *style* of the encounter.

> *"The more the better" does not do justice to the facts. Take the notion that the slow intellectual development of underprivileged children is*

due to under stimulation (a premise at the root of Head Start). The
slightest acquaintance with the type of environment in which such
children are reared shows how far from the truth that is. Quite the con-
trary, these children appear to be subjected to a far greater *overall level*
of stimulation: rarely alone, surrounded by a great many adults and
endless TV—the total amount of stimulation impinging on them is likely
to be considerable. (pp. 57–58)

The issue of *learning styles* has piqued the interest of educators for the
last two decades. It is a notion that has both good face validity and a per-
suasive research base. It appears as a part of regular education practice less
frequently than one might expect. This appears to be caused, at least in part,
by the complex diagnostic and application procedures associated with its implementation in the classroom. There is little doubt that different children
acquire information in different ways. One rather simplistic but efficient
method of capitalizing on this knowledge without going through the weighty
process associated with pure learning style instruction is to simply gather those
youngsters of similar persuasion together from the several classrooms within
a given grade or grades and have them go to a certain teacher at a specified
time during the school day for their reading instruction.

After a few introductory weeks in their home classroom, elementary
teachers are usually able to identify which students are able to learn best
through which type of reading instruction. Some do better with phonics, some
with whole language, some with basal, and so on. Shanker (1989) states:

We need schools that reach out in different ways to different youngsters,
instead of having one system that says, "If you don't make it—if you
don't fit this mold—you're no good." We need to base our practice on
the understanding that different people learn in different ways and at
different rates and on the realization that school-learning has become
divorced from real-world learning.

If we group-instruct students using the system that seems most efficient for them, we will have substantially increased the potential for learning in a vital area. *This is especially true if the instructor sees this model*
as the most efficient way to teach reading. This type of recognition of individual differences is important in bringing about increased program
flexibility.

At Risk for School Entrance

If more focus on academic challenge at the secondary level increases
the potential at-risk pool, certainly some earlier practices cause children to

believe that school can be a risky place as well. *Kindergarten roundup and readiness screening* are cases in point. Kindergarten screening was initially conceived as a process through which teachers could learn more about their charges so that a dynamic curriculum might be shaped to meet the needs of the new arrivals. This process has somehow evolved over time in many settings to a stance opposite from the original intent: Students are now often tested to find out if they are developmentally "ready" to meet the demands of a static curriculum.

Notwithstanding the trauma for children and families associated with failing such a screening and the question of whether readiness can be accelerated by instruction, the instruments most frequently used in making the determinations are of questionable value in predicting school success. This issue has, of course, been raised time and time again in the literature. The practice of making entrance determinations based on readiness criteria is one of those school traditions that has mutated into a highly resistant strain of practice. There has been some surface change in the form of "prekindergarten" or "readiness" experiences. These are pallitatives only and do not answer the question of the static nature of the curriculum. The situation appears to be controlled to a considerable extent by a mindset that holds that children must be prepared earlier nowadays to meet an increasingly rigorous set of cognitive demands. Implicit in this position is the assumption that somehow students are developmentally ready for such experiences. Given the length of time that the controversy has been going on and the current state of the art, perhaps some less radical change than a complete return to the original intent might be more positively received.

Assuming for the sake of discussion that some combination of readiness criterion might predict early school success, *we still do not know much, if anything, about the learning potential of the new arrivals.* What we have gleaned by the screening is something about their maturational level and a bit about their previous experience. Except in obvious cases of serious handicap, the potential (or lack of it) for learning is not immediately apparent.

Perhaps the preschool screening process could consist of two sets of screens. The first screen would be made up of whatever readiness tests the district prefers. Students passing this portion of the evaluation would be automatically accepted for entrance. Those found wanting on the basis of the first evaluation, however, would then be invited to a one- or two-week simulation of the kindergarten experience. Their teachers could then investigate the potential of individual children to learn the necessary competencies quickly. Those youngsters demonstrating such facility would then join those passing through screen one and enter kindergarten directly, thereby reducing the number of children for whom the first introduction to school places them at risk both with respect to how they see themselves and how those adults responsible for their care see them. Mercer, Algoyzine, and

Mercer, et al. (1979) indicate the following with respect to the hazards attendant to early identification:

> *Disadvantages of early identification relate more to the effects of misdiagnosis than to the actual practice of attempting to identify children likely to experience school failure. Many of the instruments used in disability identification procedures are somewhat unreliable with certain groups of children (Divoky, 1974). Diagnosis of severe disabilities has traditionally been more efficient than that of mold or moderate problems. Alderich and Holliday (1971) demonstrated that cases of mild retardation were suspected over two years later than those of more severe retardation. When imprecise definitions and nonmedical or nonphysical symptoms are included as part of a "high risk" disability, physicians are reluctant to make diagnosis for fear of establishing inappropriate expectations in parents and other professionals who might deal with the children.*
>
> *Another problem related to misdiagnosis is that developmental/ maturational differences are most varied early in life. The preschool years are a period of rapid growth and development and large differences can be observed in the developmental rates exhibited by various children. Behavior which may seem inappropriate at a certain chronological age may be quickly outgrown depending upon the individual child's rate of development. Differential developmental patterns make it difficult to determine if a particular child is truly at risk or simply a child who needs more time to mature before becoming an efficient learner.*
>
> *Since measurement inadequacies and differential developmental problems make it difficult to accurately diagnose children at risk, the major disadvantage of early identification becomes evident. Many children who are not disabled receive a disability label and the detrimental effects of that label present a problem to the child and his/her family.*

Formal Operations

The concept of shifting from the unitary concrete information-processing techniques associated with conservation to seeing relationships and, among other things, becoming speculative is a Piagetian notion; it is one that has interested educators for decades. At this transitional point the child demonstrates flexibility in exploring alternatives, the capacity for abstract thinking, beginning hypothesis testing, and the consideration of alternative solutions in complex problem solving—no mean feat! Whether or not a child has this facility should be of pressing concern to teachers.

In terms of developmental time, it is roughly associated with early adolescence. There is, however, great variation. There are large numbers of children several years each side of the predicted onset that either demonstrate the facility very early or very late. In the interests of increased curricular flexibility, it might be interesting to examine the extent to which formal operations behavior is expected in the lessons of a local fourth-grade math series. It might be equally interesting to see, perhaps at random, how many students in a grade-nine classroom are really at the level of formal operations (proverb facility is a way to make a quick analysis). Such information is crucial with respect to how information is organized and presented by teachers and what product can be reasonably expected from students. An erroneous assumption on the part of the teacher could definitely induce risk for the learner.

A New Approach

There appears to be a warhorse in the making in the form of *social-skills training*. Behavior problems are frequently associated with children at risk. Educators advocating formal social-skills training as a bona fide curricular emphasis hold that many youngsters demonstrate behavior that is troubling to adults and some other children simply because they have never learned reasonable alternatives. It may then follow that school is the place to learn coping skills of this type as well as academic ones. Formal instruction in social skills certainly has real potential for risk reduction and should seriously be considered, even though the idea does not have quite enough history to quality for old warhorse status.

Social skill deficits are well documented among at-risk students. Because of learning disabilities (Epstein, Cullinan, and Lloyd 1986) these deficits appear early and can increase during adolescence to a degree of severity warranting clinical concern (McConaughy 1986).

Just as this presentation recommends consideration of certain curricular practices, several public school systems have attempted to codify a format for educating at-risk children incorporating the factors they felt most important. The North Carolina (where the rate is one in three) At-risk Children and Youth Task Force made the following recommendations in 1989:

Guarantee the appropriate educational and related services needed by at-risk children and youth.

The Task Force believes that all public school children and youth in North Carolina are entitled to have meaningful options upon completion of high school so that they can be productive workers and effective citizens. Children should be guaranteed discreet delivery of these services to avoid the unnecessary negative stigma often associated with risk factors.

Preschool programs for three- and four-year olds. *Most experts agree that prevention of problems through early intervention is more effective, has a greater impact, and is ultimately less expensive than later intervention. Research indicates that early efforts toward prevention result in fewer dropouts, fewer incarcerations, and lower rates of unemployment. Researchers also conservatively estimate that for every $1 spent on prevention, $7 can be saved in later services. The Task Force supports a developmentally appropriate preschool model which would include a wide range of settings and would be available universally to both disadvantaged and nondisadvantaged children. Such a model must adhere to educational and developmental standards established through the Department of Public Instruction and the Department of Human Resources relative to early childhood development, increasing the likelihood that these children will attain academic and social success upon entering and progressing through school.*

Early identification of all children and youth at risk of academic or social failure or unwanted outcomes. *While prevention is needed at the preschool level, changes (academic, social, health, and family) that negatively affect a child's life can occur at any time. Continuous awareness of a child's circumstances is necessary to ensure delivery of intervention at the earliest and most relevant point.*

Learning style assessment. *The Task Force endorses periodic assessment of children for adjustment of instructional techniques to accommodate changes in a child's learning style.*

Personal education plan. *A personal education plan, consistent with the learning style assessment and developed to meet a child's individual needs can ensure delivery of appropriate services.*

Alternative programs with individualized curricula. *Alternative programs allow a school to meet the different learning needs and styles of children. These programs must offer challenging and stimulating curricula appropriately taught in a setting conducive to a child's learning style.*

Summary

Children at risk in public education are too often described in terms that infer that they arrive with a fixed set of stereotypic problems, shaped by forces outside of school, with which the school is forced to struggle. Unfortunately, this may result in a mindset on the part of educators that holds that "This is really not our problem," thus compounding the difficulties of home–school–community collaboration.

This chapter was intended to develop the idea that while public education is indeed asked to assist in many situations that have their roots in extra-school experiences, the process of schooling itself can and does place many students at risk. Too many schools are finding that too many students cannot benefit from their available menu of learning options. We must spend more time trying to find ways to fit our curricula to the needs of our charges and less time offering compensatory programs that may help but tend to keep them alien and outside the real flow of the school experience.

They can because they think they can. – *VIRGIL*

CHAPTER THIRTEEN

The Education
of New Parents

BESS KYPROS

Editor's Note: One major objective of this book is to demonstrate how the family and the school are natural partners. It has been stated that parents are the primary teachers of their own children and that if they communicate to the school their interests and priorities, children's chances for success are enhanced.

However, to assume that effective parenting is instinctive to those able to produce a child is erroneous and potentially harmful. There are successful programs being sponsored through governmental and community agencies, health care, social services, and educational institutions committed to assisting parents and families develop skills in fulfilling their roles with children.

As more and more schools become involved in promoting and facilitating parental involvement, some are beginning to recognize that waiting until children enter kindergarten is often too late to encourage and empower parents. However, considering the fact that schools often stretch their personnel and resources to the maximum, can they really afford to become involved in teaching parents whose children are too young to be enrolled in school? With the public educational system already under fire for its involvement in education outside of the basic "three R" cuirriculum, how can it extend itself into yet another area? In short, should schools involve themselves in the education of parents of their future students? This chapter will attempt to answer these questions.

There is a strong historical precedent for the notion of parent education in the United States. That history and a review of current programs will be discussed in this section of the book. In examining the history, both distant and near, the author will explore the educational needs of new parents and the role that schools have in delivering parent education.

Historical Perspectives

The review of the history of parent education will include the sociological and theoretical aspects of parent education as it is traced from colonial times to the present. As the trends are examined, needs and interests of parents and society are identified.

American society's involvement in parent education can be traced from early colonial times to the present through a framework of interaction of the events, the social forces, and the ways in which people responded to them. Because early Americans came to the continent to escape religious persecution and to establish a colony "under God," moral and religious education was extremely important. The emphasis on moral and religious education yielded a focus on strict rules and obedience to God, community, and parents. Pastors, their wives, and other church officials offered education and support to parents to help them raise religious and moral citizens. Even state involvement in parent education had a religious mission. In Massachusetts, tithingmen were appointed to "oversee parents through direct intervention in the home" (Scholssman 1976, 400).

By the late 1800s the Puritan preformationist emphasis had been replaced with one of predeterminism. This belief system stated that man's nature and intelligence were predetermined and that intelligence and nature unfolded in stages. G. Stanley Hall, who refined the theories of Rousseau and Froebel, began a scientific study of child development. He accumulated data for his study from questionnaires filled out by parents who had observed their children.

Hall was considered the intellectual saint of the PTA, an organization concerned with extending its middle-class philosophy to the poor and the immigrant populations, which had moved to the cities to work in factors. The motive of the PTA was to "serve as moral and scientific missionaries to less fortunate women" (Scholssman 1976, 450). Thus, the goal of parent education changed from a religious mission, with morals and rules emphasis, to a sociological mission, with knowledge provided by Hall. The emphasis on obedience shifted to nurturing. During the Hall era the focus of study was on infants and young children.

The next wave of parent education reform shifted interest from infants and young children to adolescents. Hall and the PTA refocused on adolescents in 1904. In the early 1900s, new themes and experts arose. Parents in the 1920s were told to control the erotic impulses of their children. This renewal of rigidity continued into the 1930s, with firmness and regularity the themes of the Depression years.

In the next decade, another shift appeared. By 1940 children were viewed as harmless and were to be allowed the freedom to explore themselves and their environment. This change seemed to be influenced by the rise of Freud's emphasis on psychoanalytical thought, which cautioned parents about the harm in imposing too many restrictions on their children.

In the 1950s, Benjamin Spock, who also stressed an unrestricted environment, shared his medical opinions with the public. It was in the 1950s that Sputnik made its appearance, shaking American complacency. Parents were instructed to enrich the home learning environment and enhance education. Educational toys flooded the marketplace.

During the 1960s, dissatisfaction with traditionalism was expressed, as well as a demand for equal rights for all citizens. Bloom's research revealed that all children were capable of learning and that variability existed only in the amount of time needed for mastery. He also stressed the profound effect that the early years have on the development of intelligence. Piaget's findings that intelligence develops sequentially, as the young child interacts with the environment, motivated parents to directly affect their children's learning by enriching the child's experiences. The activism of the 1960s bred parents of the 1970s and 1980s, who were prepared to make and to act upon decisions of conscience (Pizzo 1983).

Parenthood of the 1990s has undergone tremendous changes due to economic, demographic, and sociological changes. Unprecedented stress is experienced by many families, whether due to being single, being a teenager, or being a family that finds it an economic necessity to have both parents in the work force. Empirical research, which formerly was reported in professional journals, now becomes known to the public through popular magazines or the press. The media presents the research of Yarrow (1979), Huntington (1979), Brazelton (1987), and Sigman and Parmelee (1979), who point out the magnificent learning abilities of infants and the importance of the infant years in the development of self-esteem. Parents are now encouraged to begin facilitating learning during the infant years. Research information provides motivation for some parents to become heavily involved with their babies. Yet, for those caught in the web of poverty and/or growing up themselves, such information adds to their already overtaxed survival coping mechanisms.

Added to the preceding stressors are two stress factors that are related to available, experienced, informal parental assistance. First, ours is a highly mobile society; therefore, many new parents find themselves living quite a distance from their own parents, who could have shared their parenting experiences with them. Second, as many women return to the work force, mothers are not available to offer information, resources, and support to their childbearing children

Current Parent Education Programs

Hospitals have come to the aid of new parents with skill training, information, and support services. Parent education in this setting has, for the most part, been delivered by pediatricians and nurses. Information and skill training occurs through lectures and demonstrations in hospitals or through home visits. The focus of this education has been to help parents adapt to their new roles. As they meet the physical and emotional needs of their new, very dependent family member, it is hoped that parents provide the newborn with optimum conditions for growth and development.

The schools have come to the aid of teenage parents since the 1970s. Many programs serving teens in local middle, senior, or alternative schools exist throughout the country. Their curricula include classes for completion of graduation requirements, parenting classes, and a variety of comprehensive services to this new family.

Since Burton White's work in the 1970s, several states have involved their schools in the education for new parents. White field tested his comprehensive educational support system (BEEP) for parents of very young children. His longitudinal study on early development, conducted through Harvard University Preschool Project, combined with other information on early growth and development, concluded that the young child is developmentally at risk in four areas between 8 and 36 months. These areas are language, curiosity, social skills and attachment, and sensory-motor intelligence (White et al. 1978). This research influenced the development of the Parents as First Teachers Project in Missouri.

Parent education continues to occur through several professions. Myriad parent education programs currently exist for parents of very young children. The National Family Resource Coalition, whose center is in Chicago, provides a roster in which many of the family-support programs mentioned in this section are listed. Kagan and Seitz (1986) categorized these programs with the following descriptors: (1) mainstream families, those which are intact and have no evidence of psychological or physical stress in mother or father; (2) nontraditional families, which are those who need additional supports for a long or short term because of the family structure, for example, foster families, adoptive families, blended families, and families of twins; and (3) high-risk families, which need intensive support because of biological, economic, or structural factors. Included in this latter category are families with premature infants, adults or children who are handicapped mentally or physically, depressed or mentally ill parents, or families who live below the poverty level. The next chapter subdivisions will briefly discuss sample programs for the three family categories.

Sample Programs for Mainstream Families

Services to mainstream families include parent education, information, and resource and referral. Even though mainstream families experience stress, they are free to concentrate on their parenting roles because they are not faced with constant problems that completely drain their energies. They participate in prenatal and infant parenting education. The New Parents as Teacher (NPAT) and the Minnesota Early Childhood Family Education Program (ECFC), two fine examples of programs for these families, will be examined in this section.

NPAT is based on White's research (1975) stating that families can informally make a greater impact on their children's educational development than the school can through its formal educational system. This program begins influencing the child's development soon after birth. The program consists of the following four components: (1) personal visits to the home or to the center by parent educators, who observe parent–child interactions and screen infants; (2) group meetings with a teacher and other parents who have children in the same age range; (3) screening of hearing, vision, and the development of language and social skills; and (4) a resource center equipped with toys, books, and films.

NPAT's evaluation supported the hypothesis that participating families had enhanced the social, intellectual, and language abilities of their children. Currently, 30 percent (53,000) of families in the 543 Missouri school districts receive funding of what is now called the Parent As Teachers (PAT) program. Parents in the program are empowered to be effective in their roles as designers, consultants, and controllers of their children's growth and development. Children benefit from the positive interactions with their parents and from the support services offered through the parent education (Vartuli and Winter 1989).

Three hundred forty school districts, which encompass 96 percent of the zero- to 4-year-old population, make use of the Minnesota ECFC program. The program began in 1974 as six pilot programs funded through the Minnesota Council on Quality Education. Today the legislature has made the program available to any school district with a Community Education Program.

The purpose of this program is "to strengthen families, to help parents provide for their children's learning and development, and to help young children develop to their full potential" (ECFC). Programs share common goals and characteristics, yet they are uniquely designed to meet the needs of the families in each community. The common goals are providing support, educational information and techniques, communication skills, and promoting positive attitudes throughout the school years for parents. Furthermore, the programs provide supplementary discovery and learning experiences for children. These goals are implemented by a quality staff, consisting of licensed parent educators and early childhood education teachers. Each local program is monitored by an advisory council, which is composed of professionals and parents, with parents forming the majority.

Benefits of the program are realized by children who continue to experience success in school. Parents feel better about their parenting role, as they experience more satisfaction. Parents gain skills and support by meeting and learning with other parents. Parents involved in the ECFC program usually continue being involved with their children, therefore benefiting the schools. The parental involvement has been shown to be cost-effective, saving the state remedial costs occurring during the school years. "The early investment increases the effectiveness and efficiency of the total investment already made in education by society" (ECFC). Evaluations such as this seem to indicate that schools certainly should be involved in the education of mainstream families.

Sample Programs for Nontraditional Families

Services for nontraditional families are similar to those offered to mainstream families. However, they differ in that their goals are aimed at the distinct descriptors found in these families—for example, for blended families or single-parent families or mothers of twins. Included in the programs offered by the ECFC in Minnesota are issues faced by nontraditional parents. If a local community has enough nontraditional families needing information and support, classes are formed that deal with the problems they face.

State departments of Social Service and private social service agencies also offer classes to foster parents and adoptive parents. These classes include such topics as: realistic expectations, setting up a healthy home environment, and licensing regulations. Agencies offer monthly support groups for these parents after their formal programs are completed.

Another program is the Stepfamily Association, founded by Emily and John Visher in 1979. Besides the Lincoln, Nebraska headquarters, there are currently 62 chapters throughout the country. Classes, which meet once a month, offer information and support. Discussions and speakers center around issues faced by stepfamilies. A $35 membership fee includes a copy of the Vishers' book *Making It as a Stepfamily*, as well as a subscription to a quarterly magazine.

The Southeast Community College in Lincoln, Nebraska uses the Vishers' book as a text in classes that the college offers for stepfamilies. Participants in the eight-week course are encouraged to join the local Stepfamily Association for continued support.

Current demographics indicate that single-parent and step families are common in today's society. Sixty percent of youngsters entering school today will spend some of their life living in a single-parent family before they graduate from high school. Should local schools involve themselves in offering classes and support to this large segment of our population? Minnesota's efforts seem noteworthy. Lincoln's Southeast Community College also sets an impressive precedent. Since so many children will be affected by the transition of moving from a nuclear to a single-parent family or stepfamily, and since we know that children's performance is affected by home situations, it would seem that schools need to be involved in this type of support.

Sample Programs for High-Risk Families

Myriad programs have been developed by many agencies and groups as a response to the very special needs of high-risk new families. Some of the programs that fit in the high-risk category are programs for low-income, black mothers of premature infants; programs for parents of mentally or physically handicapped children; programs for emotionally disturbed parents; programs for those who face problems with drug addiction in parents and in children; programs for poor, inner-city mothers expecting their first healthy baby; and programs for teenage parents.

A grim reality of the 1990s is the increase in number of unwed, adolescent parents. It is reported that teenage pregnancy in the United States ranks among the highest in the developed countries (Alan Guttmacher Institute 1981). Teenage pregnancy represents a crisis for the teenage mother. She and her baby will more than likely live in poverty. The mother is less likely to complete high school than her peers, increasing the likelihood of poverty. Her "syndrome of failure" (Klien 1975) will probably prevent her from developing self-confidence and a sense of personal identity. Both she and her child are likely to suffer. Her child is likely to have problems in academic and social growth. For these reasons, programs have been developed to help the teenage mother stay in school, continuing to work through her own psychosocial development and developing skills necessary to promote healthy development of her baby.

Merrill (1989) discussed several programs that provide these types of services for adolescent pregnant teens. She presented the need for comprehensive services, which include education in the classroom, early consistent prenatal care, postpartum services, and long-term counseling services. Merrill is involved in Teen-Aid, a Topeka School-Community Program, which is a comprehensive support program for teenage parents. The program encourages girls to complete their academic studies and provides counseling and education for parenting. In this public, alternative school setting, girls take required classes plus classes in nutrition, prenatal care, parenting, practical living skills, vocational skills, and physical education classes, which include LaMaze exercise and labor and delivery classes. Additionally, electives in home economics, business, math, and human relations are offered.

Nurses from the county health department meet with the girls to familiarize them with the hospital and the maternal and infant programs offered at the health department clinic. Counseling is provided through the community and school student-support services. Weekly group counseling discussions occur on such topics as parenting skills, sexuality and human relationships, teenage marriage, relationships with parents, and decision making about self and baby. Girls return to their home school after the pregnancy is completed.

Merrill stated that even though outcomes of the program were difficult to assess, self-evaluations by the students indicated that girls expressed an increased confidence level because they were able to care for themselves and their children. As students gain parenting information and skills, they are better able to understand and control themselves and their babies. The public school provides the most logical and natural place for this type of parent education to occur, because most girls complete their education and graduate or receive a general equivalency diploma.

Another at-risk family reveals itself in epidemic numbers in urban centers. That is the rise in the numbers of babies who are born to mothers who have taken drugs during their pregnancy. Dr. Barry Brazelton, speaking to a group of medical and educational professionals at the "Empowering Parents: A Day with T. Barry Brazelton, M.D." in Monroe, Michigan, stated that our nation is beginning to face a new phenomenon—the epidemic numbers of drug-addicted infants being born in large urban cities across our nation. He stated that 18 percent of the infants born at Boston's City Hospital are born drug-addicted.

In Detroit the number is 27 percent. A 1989 study conducted at Hutzel Hospital by Dr. Enrique Ostera, Jr. found that 52.5 percent of the 3,000 infants tested were born to mothers who had taken crack, THC, or heroin during their pregnancy. While all of these infants are not born addicted to drugs, they are all found by neonatalogists to have developmental disabilities.

Nationwide it is estimated that 375,000 infants are born each year to mothers who have taken cocaine. These infants are smaller, weigh less, and have smaller head circumferences than drug-free peers at birth. These descriptors are associated with infants with learning disabilities. At-risk behaviors exhibited by these drug-exposed infants include a difficulty maintaining a "quiet alert state," which allows them to acquaint themselves of their environment. Dan Griffith, a developmental psychologist participating in a study being conducted by the National Association for Perinatal Addiction

Research and Education, states that many of the children continue to be highly distractable by the age of 3 years. Language development problems, along with behavioral problems, put these children at risk for impaired learning.

In the sample programs the medical community provides care and speech and physical therapy as needed. Parent education occurs on an informal basis by apnea monitor manufacturers and by medical personnel. It would seem that they are the ones who could best give this type of early education, aid, and support. However, since Missouri and Minnesota's programs have found significant advantages for reaching mainstream families prior to birth of the first baby, it would seem that the parents who are at risk because of drug problems would greatly benefit from parenting education offered by the school system. As schools get ready to deal with the learning problems of drug-affected babies, all indications lead to the need for early parental education and involvement in the teaching of these children.

Conclusions

This chapter began with a question as to what role the school should play in the education of new parents. It has described the interaction of events and social forces within the American scene that have shaped philosophies, and policies that have affected and have been affected by people. Parents have been aided in the nurturing of their offspring by clergy, psychologists, educators, physicians, and politicians. The emphasis of this aid has reflected the goal of the American dream, as it was envisioned at the time. Currently, families and schools are being challenged to meet their responsibilities and roles in the facilitation of the development of competent and caring future citizens.

Research has indicated that children do better in school when parents and schools become partners in education. What happens in the living room affects what happens in the classroom. Can we risk allowing this early learning to happen by chance?

Two examples have been given of programs that planned for learning to begin during the last trimester of pregnancy. Missouri and Minnesota have researched their programs and have found them to be cost-effective. They can be replicated in other states, in other schools. Schools can work cooperatively with other community agencies to support and empower mainstream, nontraditional, and high-risk families as they fulfill their responsibility as the child's first and most significant teachers. Parents can be encouraged to help the child's very early beginning, and therefore shape the child's perception of self and the world.

Teachers can be instructed in the skills of pedagogy and androgogy so that they can effectively facilitate learning in both children and parents. The foundations for the development of caring and competency begin in the first five years of life, and schools can do much to help ensure these qualities, which may have much to do with the survival of the dreams and hopes of the people living at the dawning of a new century.

> *The child is not going to be somebody— The child is already somebody.*
> —*JOHN DEWEY*

CHAPTER FOURTEEN

Fostering Early Development

ELI SALTZ

Editor's Note: The Merrill Palmer Institute has a long and distinguished record in conducting research relating to the education of young children. Its director offers a practical set of ideas and activities for both parents and teachers that can be helpful in the emotional as well as intellectual development of young learners.

A number of the chapters in this book, especially those by parents, have talked about the aspirations we have for our children. This chapter presents some ideas on how some of these hopes can be realized. It is not enough to want the best for our kids. We need to understand better how we can help in our homes and classrooms. It is never too early to begin.

Giving Your Child a "Head Start"

It is easy to be glib about the importance of home and parents in the development of children, and about the importance of parental influences on their children's success in school and after. It is harder to spell out tangible, sensible activities that parents can engage in that will be relevant to their children's future. In this chapter, I shall outline some concrete types of approaches and activities that should, and can, occur in the home that will make a difference for children. First, however, let me give you some feeling for the particular approach of this chapter.

Do you believe that children should be given a "head start" before entering school? Much has been written about the importance of giving children an early advantage. In spirit, this is a very appropriate concept. Unfortunately, many parents (and some educators) appear to have misinterpreted the data coming from the Head Start projects, as well as related data based on research on young children. Certain popular educational TV programs, while on the whole very salutary in their effects on children, have perpetuated these misinterpretations.

Many parents have interpreted the head start notion to mean that there are specific "facts" that children should acquire before school that will ease their way once they enter the formal educational system. For many parents, these facts include the names of the letters of the alphabet, the names of the primary colors, number sequences ("Show Aunt Gert how you can count to 10, dear"), and so forth. One parent proudly informed me that her 4-year-old's preschool had learned to recite the Declaration of Independence in unison.

Evidence indicates that being taught facts in the early years is unrelated to later academic achievement. And yet, Head Start activities, as well as other types of "quality" preschool experiences, do make a difference later on.

How? The evidence indicates that they make a difference by socializing the children, by increasing the likelihood that these children will learn to get along with each other, will learn ways to cope with the frustrations of living with other children in a classroom, will learn to relate to adult authority figures (like teachers), and will learn to develop positive attitudes toward the school situation. In short, I am suggesting that much (though not necessarily all) of the critical acquisition involved in a "head start" is social and emotional in nature.

For most children the socialization provided by parents appears to be the critical factor in a child's ability to profit from an education. Certainly in terms of a broad social perspective, this is very clear. Let us take extreme cases, and look at two types of serious social problems that surface in adolescence; teen pregnancy in girls, and delinquency in boys. Across class and race, what is the single most critical predictor of both of these adolescent problems? Breakdown in family relations, poor communication patterns at home, family discord, simply not enjoying being at home. The second-best predictor of both teen pregnancy and delinquency is hatred of school. And interestingly enough, disrupted family relations and hatred of school tend to be highly related. Often the frustrations and problems in school reflect the frustrations and problems at home.

Suggestions for Promoting Success

What are the "rules" for raising children who are successful at schooling and who exhibit prosocial behavior? Let us examine some of the more important guidelines. The general rules that I shall discuss are all important, but some are easier to accomplish than others. Some of the most important are concerned with how we relate to the child as a person, and these are often the hardest to deal with since they often involve altering our typical patterns of interacting with our children. Let us postpone these to last, so that we can first have some successful experiences that motivate us to change. We shall start with some suggestions that are most concrete and easiest to implement.

Each of the issues discussed below will follow the same general pattern: a brief indication of the research evidence concerning the activity being suggested; an overview of the activity; and, finally, a "how-to" section.

At this point a cautionary note is in order. The how-to sections are not meant as strict rules of conduct—quite the contrary. These sections are meant to be aids in getting started, suggestions that may make the general idea behind an activity more concrete. Each of us will find his or her own way to accomplish the goals being described, and it would be terrible if we permitted some "expert" to freeze our spontaneous interactions into some artificial mold.

Read to Your Child

Research Evidence
The data from a number of studies is clear in showing that consistently reading to young children is strongly related to later school success for these children. This evidence is particularly strong for parental patterns of reading, but it has also been found for preschool teachers.

Overview
Reading aloud is an easy activity, and one that can be fun for both the child and the parents. Most parents believe that the most critical problem children have in reading is the sounding-out of letter patterns to determine the words on the page. Be assured, this is not the case! The most frequent, critical reason for failing to read well is *failing to read for meaning.*

How-To
Most young children love to sit on Mommy or Daddy's lap and have the parent read a children's story book. Pick a story that the child likes, a book full of pictures.

Hold the book so that the child can look at the page as you read it. Ask the child questions about the story as you read it. This should be an *interactive* experience. This will give the child an opportunity to participate and will help keep the child's attention. In addition, questions will stimulate the child to do a very, very important thing, something critical to good reading in later school experiences: It will encourage the child to *think* about what is being read. It will encourage the child to read for *meaning*.

For really young children (e.g., a 1-year-old who barely speaks) questions probably cannot be much more complex than asking the child to identify things and persons in the story. "Show Daddy the piggy." Or, pointing to the pig in the picture, "Tell Mommy, what's the name of this animal?"

For the 3- or 4-year-old, the questions can be more complex, involving anticipation of future events in a familiar story (and children often love to read the same story over and over, day after day). "What does the second little piggy use to build *his* house?" Ask the child what he thinks of the characters in the story. ("The wolf wants to eat the little piggies. Is that a nice wolf?") And don't be afraid to express your own opinions ("No, that's a bad wolf"). Finally, encourage the child to elaborate on the stories ("What other things could the little piggies have done to get away from the wolf?")

Anticipating future events in a story, giving opinions about the characters in the story, and elaborating on the story all engage the child in activities that require active participation and thinking, rather than just passive absorption of the passing scene

Imparting Curiosity and Active Engagement

At this point let us transcend the issue of reading, in and of itself, and touch on a larger, more comprehensive legacy that a parent can transmit. One of the most important things that a parent can do for a child is to impart curiosity and a willingness on the part of the child to explore the world to satisfy this curiosity. The type of active reading and stimulation that we have discussed in this section represents one way of encouraging an early start to such an active engagement between the child and his or her world.

We can contrast two metaphors for parent–child interactions (or teacher–student interactions, for that matter). One metaphor is that of "filling the child" with knowledge; the other is that of "challenging the child" to understand the environment. Clearly, what I have suggested as the parent's role in reading to a child is that of a challenger, a stimulator of the child's thought processes.

As you shall see, this general approach will guide much of what I have to suggest in this chapter.

Promote Communication

Research Evidence

One of the most critical predictors of later social adjustment for teens and young adults is the ease of parent–child communication. Extreme breakdown in such communication patterns is associated with delinquency in boys, teen pregnancy in girls.

Overview

"Talk to my baby?" a young mother asked me in amazement. "But why? He's too young to understand anything I say."

Infants begin to acquire the sounds and cadences of their native languages almost from birth. By the end of the first years of life, they often can have a surprisingly good understanding of what is said to them. However, this can occur only if people around them respond in a meaningful way to them.

Early communication interactions with the child are also very important for another reason. Such communication attempts are critical for the socialization of the child. Infants who are largely ignored soon learn to "tune out" the outside world and have difficulty developing close relationships with others. This could be a prelude to later feelings of isolation, disinterest in relating to adults, and an increased probability of school problems.

As the child grows older, it is important that channels of communication be kept open. Parents must be willing, indeed *eager,* to hear what their children are trying to tell them. This does not mean always agreeing with the children or giving them whatever they want—definitely not. Children typically try to explore the parameters of their world, and in doing so they push the limits of their parents' permissiveness. This is natural. And, for the good of the children, *there must be limits.* Extreme parental permissiveness does not produce a happy, satisfied child. Instead, it produces greater and greater demands on the parents and on the community at large. An absence of limits, strangely enough, often leads to surliness, anxiety, and dependent behavior.

Having said this about the dangers of an absence of limits, it is just as important that the child feel that the parents have reasons for the limits that exist. Later psychological adjustment is best for children whose parents attempt to explain the reasons for limits and who give the children alternative options from which to choose. Make your child feel responsible for decisions, and for their consequences, at an early age. Clearly, there are limits to what a young child can understand. But what is important is that the child feels that there are channels of communication.

How-To

Begin developing communications with your child early. Parents often learn very quickly how to communicate with their infants in what is sometimes referred to "Motherese." Each word is pronounced very distinctly, with particular emphasis on key words; sentences are slow; and there is a great deal of relevant pantomine. "Give Mommy the *bottle,*" is followed by touching the bottle or gently taking it from the child.

Reading to your young child, as described above, is an excellent way to start, if your child is a little older than infancy. As you get into the rhythm of reading, asking questions about what you have read and what will happen next, you will gradually develop a feeling for the way your child thinks and feels about the world, what makes your child anxious, and what pleases your child.

As the child grows a little older, it becomes possible to have real conversations. Learn to listen. Many parents, even those who feel that they are really loving and caring, often take for granted that their children perceive the world just as they perceive it; they do not try to find out how their children understand their own experiences.

Sometimes we can be very surprised to discover how children interpret the world. A teacher recently brought me a story told to her by a very bright 7-year-old boy, a student in her second-grade classroom, who described what was apparently, for him, a very disturbing Christmas visit to his grandparents who had retired to Florida. His grandparents, he stated, lived with other "retarded people." They took him to a "wrecked hall," but, if it had been wrecked "someone must have fixed it because it wasn't wrecked no more." The little boy was very intrigued by the guard at the entrance to the retirement community, whom he called a policeman in a dollhouse. The little boy wished that his grandparents would move back to their old home in Michigan so he could visit them more often, but concluded that they couldn't move back because "the policeman in the dollhouse won't let them." Clearly, the little boy and his parents had had completely different experiences visiting the child's grandparents.

What would it have taken for the parents to find out that what for them had been a pleasant vacation had been a somewhat frightening and puzzling experience for their son? Since the experience had been shared with him, they assumed that their understanding had also been shared. Clearly, they had not really talked to their son about the experiences they were sharing. This is not unusual.

Adults often talk to each other while ignoring their children who are silent audiences. At times, adults actually behave as though a child were not present, and will complain in the most amazing fashion about the child. The child's feelings of self-worth are often badly battered by such disloyalty. The most amazing aspect of this is that many such parents fiercely deny having engaged in such behavior. These parents are neither evil nor untruthful. They had become so engrossed in their own fears, anxieties, and hopes for the child that they became completely unconscious of the child's presence.

It is because children do not have an adult comprehension of what is going on around them that we must be careful what we say in their presence.

Most of us like to talk more than we like to listen. Adults talking to each other often engage in parallel speech, rather than interactive discussions. This is even more likely to happen when adults speak to children. Since we know better than they do (about almost any topic) we are likely to lecture to them for their own good. The problem is that we sometimes forget to do a reality check to determine if the little people are tuned in and have the slightest idea about the topic of conversation.

What can we do about this? The answer is simple. Listen to the children more. Ask questions and listen to the answers.

It is important to listen to your children. It is important to ask about *feelings*. Broad, nonspecific questions are likely to elicit very little. As most parents know, the typical answer to, "What did you do in school today?" is likely to be, "Nothing." That is often a conversation stopper. More specific inquiries about subjects or friends are better spurs to communication.

It is not necessary to always agree with your children as they grow up. But their ideas should be treated with respect, even if with disagreement. Parents sometimes interpret the most significant feature of intrafamilial communications to be the transmission of knowledge from parents to their children. This can lead to monologues, rather than discussion. Interestingly enough, the evidence suggests that to a great extent it is *not* the content of the conversation that is critical to the children's development; rather, it is the *form* of the conversation. For example, as was noted above, communication patterns in the family distinguish teens who are likely to experience premature sexual adventures from teens who are not likely to have such problems.

But what aspects of the communication patterns are most critical? Some parents are surprised to learn that the critical factor is not communication about sex. Indeed, in some of the families showing the best communication patterns and the least problems with teen sexuality, the teens respond, when asked if they have discussed sex with their parents, "Oh, no! I wouldn't talk to them about *that*."

Then what is the critical component of the communication patterns in these more socially adjusted families? It is that the parents do not attempt to dominate the communications. The parents may have firm opinions, and may express them, but not in the context of denying the children their opportunity to be heard.

By adolescence, children begin to seek independence, and their parents often feel they are losing influence with their teen-age offspring. Nothing could be further from the truth, if relations have been good up to this period. Research has found that most children internalize the values of their parents, without even realizing that they have done so. Because of this, the typical teen will choose friends whose values are very compatible with the values of the teen's parents.

In closing this section, it should be stressed that one of the factors that seems to most greatly distinguish families whose children succeed in school and who have relatively few problems at home is the high level of verbal communication in these families. Talk to your children. Listen to what they have to say in return. There will be more on the content of such interactions in later sections of this chapter.)

What about TV?

Research Evidence
The research evidence concerning the effects of large amounts of TV watching is very clear. For the most part, watching a great deal of TV is detrimental to children's cognitive and scholastic development. It is associated with poor reading and language skills. Over the past few decades, TV has absorbed more and more of children's time. During this period, there has been a steady decline in achievement scores for American children.

Overview
Can anything that children love so much be bad that for them? Unfortunately, the answer appears to be, "Yes."

Watching TV is essentially a passive activity. It is the antithesis of the types of activities that I encouraged in the previous section on reading. When children interact with adults, with other children, and with objects in the environment, we find an enhancement of the children's cognitive and social development, as well as an increase in their ability to develop a healthy curiosity about the world; the opportunity for this enhancement is sharply reduced when the television serves as a substitute for these interactions. Certain educational television programs encourage the child to interact with the program, and these have been found to lead to improvement in a number of cognitive abilities, including language development. These programs, however, are the exception.

How-To
Recently I had the opportunity to talk to a prominent physician who described his great difficulties early in elementary school, where he was considered "slow" by both his teachers and his fellow students. He had been a compulsive TV viewer, but fortunately his mother intervened and sharply limited the amount of television he could watch. In addition, she gave him the "assignment" of reading two books a week. Over the next year and a half there was gradual improvement in his school performance, he started to become genuinely interested in science as he read more and more, and eventually became a superior student.

It is not easy to curtail TV viewing. For one thing, the television often serves as a babysitter, permitting mother to do her housework, or just to relax. For another thing, television can very quickly take on addictive properties for the child. It can become a real battle to separate a child from the television set. But this is one of those situations in which parents must set limits. If possible, this should be done by negotiating with the child. The general rule: Less TV and more reading.

Fantasy Play

Research Evidence
Children who spontaneously engage in fantasy play tend to be advanced both in cognitive and in social-emotional development. Encouraging children to engage in fantasy play (e.g., enactment of fairy tales) has been found to facilitate both cognitive development and social development.

Overview
It is very interesting that many parents and even some teachers in our culture are wary of fantasy play in their children. Some parents are concerned that their children will not learn to cope with reality if they engage in fantasy play. For other parents, fantasy play has the connotation of mental instability. Yet, the research data are very consistent in indicating that these concerns are not warranted. Children with imaginary friends, for example, on the average tend to be well adjusted, social leaders, and more intellectually advanced than other children.

Young children are very tied to the stimuli of their environment and have problems when they must rely on inner resources. For example, most 4- and 5-year-old children have great difficulty resisting the temptation of touching an attractive, forbidden toy or refraining from taking a cookie that mother told them not to touch. However, after training to enact fairy tales, 4- and 5-year-olds are much better able to resist temptation.

Why does training a child to engage in fantasy play have such effects? There are probably several reasons. First, fantasy play appears to encourage the development of an inner life that can serve as a buffer between the child and the immediate, external stimuli of the world. Second, parents must learn that young children are very motoric in their thinking processes. They learn the meanings of many things in the processes of motorically interacting with these things. Consequently, it is not surprising that the most effective types of fantasy play are those that involve movement. Thus, being read fairy tales is not nearly as enhancing as enacting the fairy tales.

How-To
Parents can read stories to their children and can encourage the children to enact them. The parents can take roles in the enactment, or, if there are

several playmates together, can encourage them to enact the story. Fairy tales have proven much more enhancing for children than "playing store" or other types of play that require no more from the children than memory for some nondramatic event.

Don't expect the children to memorize the dialogues of the story. It is sufficient if they will recall the general story line. A good way to start is by reading the story to the children. Then ask, "Who wants to be Little Red Ridinghood? Who wants to be the wolf? Who wants to be Red Ridinghood's mother? How about grandmother? And who will be the hunter?" Once the children have decided on parts, start the action by cuing the characters. "What did Red Ridinghood's mother tell her when Red started out to visit her grandmother one day?" Then, after Mother has given her advice, ask Red Ridinghood, "What did Little Red Ridinghood do on her way to Granny's? Show me. Pretend this is the path through the woods." Then, "OK, Wolf, what did you do when you saw Little Red Ridinghood in the woods?"

If a child has forgotten the story, provide cues. For example, if the Wolf doesn't recall its lines, ask, "Did the Wolf ask Little Red Ridinghood where she was going? Yes? Well, show me how."

The next time the children enact the story, they will recall the story line much better and will require fewer cues. The next time? Yes, there will soon be a next time. As most parents well know, children love to repeat the same favorite stories over and over again. It's a way of gaining mastery over the environment. Do encourage the children to exchange roles in subsequent enactments, so that everyone has a chance to be good guys and bad guys.

It is both interesting and sad that many "academically oriented" preschool environments are very rigid and systematically discourage fantasy activity. Yet, in the end, such activities can prove much more important for a child's development than the acquisition of some supposed "basic" facts or skills.

Parental Nurturance

Research Evidence
Children reared by more nurturant parents tend to be better adjusted, popular, and socially adept than children reared by less nurturant parents.

Overview
What do we mean by *nurturant* parents? While the term has a technical definition in the research, we can safely characterize nurturance as having two dominant components. One involves physical affection: hugging, kissing, and in other ways showing physically that the parent loves the child. The second factor involves an environment of positive affect with regard to

the child and what the child is trying to accomplish. "That's good!" said with enthusiastic pleasure when the child accomplishes something that, for the child, is difficult. "Oh, that was really hard to do, wasn't it? But you can do it. Let's try again," said when the child does not succeed right away.

How-To

Remember, many things that are easy for you are not easy for a child. Encourage the child to try, but help the child save face in case of failure. It is amazing how an atmosphere of positive regard for the child and for the child's accomplishments can have a positive effect on the mood and spirit of the child.

Many parents grow impatient at a child's early incompetences, and parents take over and perform the task. This can be a mistake. Guidance can be helpful and may have a positive effect, but completely taking over in an attempt to provide a "model" for the child is often interpreted as failure by the child.

Much of this positive affect should be communicated by language. Many people are surprised, viewing videos of parent–child interactions, at how little positive affect many parents display in their interactions with their children. A stroll through any large shopping mall can be particularly heartbreaking. Typically, the children have been brought on the expedition because there is no convenient friend or relative with whom they can be left. Very young children may cry, and this frequently produces threats that are not comprehended by the children, often accompanied by slaps, which worsen the situation. Older children may run around and try to play, which again may lead to verbal abuse.

Both parents and children feel that they are the victims in these encounters. To the extent that such encounters characterize a sizable portion of the interactions between parents and their children, the children will certainly feel an absence of nurturance.

The best solution is to avoid these situations. Don't bring your child into a situation in which the child has no role and in order to adjust must, in effect, either tune out or become a pest. If there is no alternative and the child must be brought on the shopping trip, at least attempt to engage the child's attention in some way. Older children may be flattered by asking their opinions on what coat makes Mommy look nice. Younger ones just want some attention, and often an opportunity to run a little. You can handle this without a major fuss.

Verbal praise is very important. Language can be an important communicator of affect, and it is here that many parents seem strangely mute. Some parents actually state that they feel it will "spoil" their children to be praised. Such parents are more likely to say nothing, or to criticize even the most astonishing accomplishments of a young child. For the most part the effect of such lack of positive affect is to stunt effort by the child, who often feels inadequate and simply gives up.

This does not mean that you should flood a child with praise for every commonplace thing the child does. This cheapens the value of praise. but it is better to err on the side of too much praise than too little.

There Must Be Limits

Research Evidence

Extreme permissiveness has been found to produce anxious, yet demanding children. Evidence indicates that children feel more secure when they know what the limits are in situations, and the absence of limits often leads the children to push the boundaries, attempting to find limits. This may result in outrageous behavior.

Overview

Under what circumstances do parents fail to establish limits? There are several sets of conditions in which this is a frequent problem. One is the situation we frequently find these days in which both parents work outside the home. Some mothers become anxious about the fact that they spend so little time with their children, and they want the time that they spend together to be "quality time." Indeed, this desire is admirable and to be encouraged. However, many mothers often become concerned that the children will grow to love the care giver more than they love her. Under these conditions the parents may be reluctant to say or do anything that might displease the children, no matter how outrageous the children's conduct.

How To

Setting limits must be conducted in the same manner of open communications that we have already discussed. But the parents must accept the fact that limits are often, by their nature, arbitrary. And, yes, mother does deserve to have some time to talk to an old friend without 3-year-old Joey climbing all over her and demanding all her attention. It is not enough to try to ignore the chaos and act as though it were not happening. Even if Joey may not yet understand the cognitive meaning of what mother is saying, he will understand the loving yet firm affect with which she takes him to his room and finds some toys for him to play with while she is with her friend. "Mother loves you Joey, but at this time Mother wants to do something without you."

In short, setting limits is not a punitive affair. The beginnings of parent–child dialogue are often established at this juncture. But there should be limits. This applies to bedtime (when, where, and wearing what) as well as such things as watching TV, hitting other children (or hapless adult friends of the parents!), and sharing. Setting limits constitutes the beginnings of imparting parental values to the child and the development of conscience and of a moral code.

In short, parental love may be unbounded, but it must involve making demands on the child.

Fathers Are Important, Too

Research Evidence

Two statements are important to stress with regard to the role of fathers in child rearing. (1) Paternal nurturance has been found to be strongly related to positive intellectual and social-emotional development of children. (2) While fathers' interactions with their children are important for the children's development, fathers and mothers relate very differently to their children.

Often fathers feel almost irrelevant to the parenting experience. In terms of absolute time spent with the children, mothers are way ahead of their spouses. This is also true, in most families, as far as responsibilities for the children's care. Even when both parents work, it is the mother who makes the arrangements for child care, and in an emergency takes time off from the job (though this latter is less true than it once was, particularly when both parents have responsible positions). Despite this, research has clearly shown that the parenting time spent by the father can be very important in the child's development. Paternal nurturance has been proven to be an important factor in shaping the child.

Overview

It must be stressed that fathers are not merely male mothers when it comes to interacting with the children. Let us contrast the roles of mothers and fathers. Studies have shown that the maternal role is often a soothing and quieting one: For example, the mother's tone in speaking to her child is typically gentle and calming. The father's role, on the other hand, is often that of stimulating the child. The father is more vigorous, louder, and may "rough-house" with the child (yes, even with a girl). Both of these roles have proven to be critical to optimal development.

How To

The same general rules for nurturance, communication, and limit setting that were discussed above are relevant to both mothers and fathers. However, their styles are likely to be very different. Your instincts are often a good guide concerning how to act. Men appear to be more physical than women in their interactions with children, and this seems to be consistent with the behavior found in other primates. In other words, there is reason to believe that this difference is genetic. So be yourself. Fathers should no more force themselves to behave like mothers than mothers should try to behave like fathers.

The crucial thing is that the parent–child interaction (whether the parent is a mother or a father) should reflect love, nurturance, and communication. If it does, then the child has a fighting chance in the world.

Summary

The popular notion of giving children a "head start" at school success is often misinterpreted to mean filling young minds with "facts" and academic skills. Evidence shows that the critical factor in a child's ability to profit from formal education is the socialization provided by parents.

Specific socialization areas that research has shown to be especially salutory were discussed, along with concrete "how-to"s for parents. The suggested areas are reading to young children, promoting communication, discouraging TV watching, encouraging fantasy play, practicing parental nurturance, setting limits, and appreciating paternal involvement.

> *Parents teach their children by merely living with them in the family group. They are examples which children follow instinctively. They also teach directly by telling and showing, by praising when the children conform and punishing when they fail to measure up to the standards set by the family group. The family is first in time, and in many ways the most important teaching agency in any society.* —*S. E. FROST, JR.*

SECTION THREE

The University and Teacher Education

A call for reform is not the same as a plan of action. Suggesting that schools are not doing X but should do Y is a response, but is it enough? Clearly, the raising of awareness to the point of helping selected members of society recognize their ownership of the problem is key to the change process.

Section II of this book discusses some directions for schools in terms of many of society's concerns. The message is clear. Get schools involved by redefining their role as not only interested in the intellectual growth of students, but also as a major contributor to the total welfare of the learner. By better understanding the needs of the client, we better serve that client.

Chapter 15 considers the university as a natural change agent, developing and implementing innovative programs and shaping public opinion to improve the family-school connection. In Chapter 16, the university is considered as family itself, as well as an institution that must be concerned with its clients' family situations. Chapters 18–21 go into details of what the university can and should do in the important area of teacher education: take the lead in imparting the knowledge, skills, and especially attitudes that teachers need to function well in the home-school relationship. A course outline is even provided.

It becomes abundantly obvious that the university, as the agency most responsible for the education and training of professional educators, must be a leader in the reform movement. Is the university a change agent rather than a provider of already accepted information? Is the university a part of the community rather than an "ivory tower" located within a community, as many have suggested? Are teachers and administrators being adequately prepared within the hallowed halls of academic for the "real world?" The authors contributing to this section attempt a response. The reader is advised to consider these comments not as plans of action or the last word, but rather as the thoughts of colleagues in the battle.

CHAPTER FIFTEEN

The University as a Change Agent

BETTYE M. CALDWELL   JAMES H. YOUNG

Editor's Note: Although universities traditionally involve families less in the education of students than do early childhood, elementary, and secondary schools, they have an important role to play as a change agent in the development, testing, and dissemination of knowledge about the importance of school–family connections. In this article, two major functions of the university are discussed: the development and implementation of program innovations, and the shaping of public policy. Successful programs are cited that have exemplified the role of the university as a catalyst for effective social action in the area of family involvement. The provocative question of the university role in its *own* students' families is also examined.

Of all the components within the educational system, the university has been far less involved with families than any other. Young adults—not children—go to college, many of them "going away from home." Others who attend colleges in their home communities often move into apartments with friends and check in at home largely when tuition and rent are due and the stack of dirty laundry is no longer manageable. Involvement of their parents in decisions and activities is often the last thing the students want. Many parents feel the same way. And, to be honest, so do many college and university administrators and professors. "Parent Day" is sometimes just window dressing and an opportunity to generate alumni or public support. "It's time for the kids to make it on their own" is the unwritten credo justifying this separation of school and family at the university level.

This separation is so effective that it can actually be very difficult for concerned parents to learn much about what is happening in the lives of their children attending colleges and universities, much less participate in any meaningful way. Parents of students older than 18 are not automatically notified if their children are at risk of failure, are suspected of using drugs, have been arrested, or have stopped attending classes. Considering the legal aspects of the situation, these practices are entirely understandable. Most college students have either reached the age of majority at the time of enrollment or will reach it soon thereafter, at which time they can vote, enter into legal contracts such as rentals and purchases, obtain credit cards, obtain medical care without parental consent, join the armed services, and so on. Grades are customarily sent to the students, who then have the option of reporting them to or withholding them from their parents. Parents of university students do not have to sign report cards and send them back to school.

In view of this separation of school and home at the upper levels, one might question that the university has any role to play in acting as a change agent to foster more school–family collaboration. Yet, most powerful ideas that produce change in educational practices either originate at the university level or are augmented by the knowledge development and dissemination machinery that is an integral part of university life.

In the remainder of this chapter we shall explore various facets of the roles that universities (or, more technically, their personnel) can play in helping to generate support for an active partnership between schools and families. Obviously the university has a major role to play in the conduct of research that can strengthen the knowledge base upon which practices rest. However, we shall limit our discussion to two other critical roles the university can play in this arena. These are: (1) developing and implementing innovative approaches to education–family collaboration and (2) the shaping of public policy. In discussing each of these areas, we shall be selective rather than inclusive and present what are essentially case summaries of illustrative university efforts. It is hoped that in these summaries the important role played by the university as a catalyst for school–family collaboration at all levels will be apparent.

Development and Implementation of Programmatic Innovations

Forces that serve to keep the family out of the educational system are so effective that proof of the value of interaction is essential to the selling of the idea. Obviously, whatever proof we have, in the form of a knowledge base for action, is likely to have been generated in university-related research.

But generating new knowledge and applying it in extended service programs are two quite different tasks. In the application and implementation of innovative approaches to education, universities generally do not earn quite as high grades as they do in idea generation. In truth, university personnel have a reputation for generating new knowledge and then forgetting about it—letting research papers rest in peace on library shelves until some activist finds them and puts them to use. In fact, university professors are often caricatured as preferring not to dirty their hands with implementation. Although this view may be accurate in some instances, some academic personnel have played major roles in applying the knowledge that they and their colleagues have generated. In the field of education, attempts to help create model schools that expressed a particular philosophy based on research data or relevant psychological theory about how children learn and develop have been particularly noteworthy. Three examples that related to home–school involvement will be cited.

The Yale Model

One of the best attempts to infuse university-generated ideas into a public school system is the program developed by Dr. James P. Comer, a child psychiatrist with the Yale Child Study Center in New Haven, Connecticut. Dr. Comer and colleagues, who represented fields of psychology, social work, and special education, began working with the New Haven public schools in 1968, hoping to help create within the schools an ambiance more conducive to mental health and a favorable attitude toward schooling. Comer (1986) has described conditions in their first project school as follows: "By fourth grade the students were 19 months below grade level in reading and 18 months below grade level in mathematics. The school climate was characterized by apathy and conflict. Attendance was poor among students and staff members. There were frequent and serious behavior problems" (p. 445). The Yale model involved working collaboratively with teachers and administrators to develop for the school a new management procedure that included significant participation by parents. In their first project school the ranking on achievement tests in 1969 was 32nd out of 33 schools. By 1984, it had risen to third place in the New Haven rankings, with achievement scores that were seven months advanced for grade placement.

The Yale model has now spread to 10 other New Haven schools and to others outside the state, including Prince George's County, Maryland (Henderson and Hall 1990). Each of these schools has what is generally called a School Governance and Management Team (SGMT) consisting of the principal, teachers, parents, instructional aides, someone from the support staff, and a child development or mental health specialist. Together this group works out a master plan for its school in the areas of academic achievement, staff development, and school climate. Parents are mainly involved in working to improve the school climate. Title I funds have been used to employ parents to work as teacher assistants. Part of the program involves parent developmental activities similar to those provided the staff. Parents also participate in social events tied closely to the academic regimen.

In commenting on the highly favorable research findings emanating from their work, Comer (1986) is candid in admitting that the specific contribution of parental involvement cannot be separated from other aspects of the model. That is, the staff and the children had access to more mental health professionals, and there was greater site autonomy than usually characterizes a big city school district, as well as more parental involvement. However, parental participation was such an integral component of the model that there is no way to imagine that the results could have been achieved without it.

It is worth noting that in the New Haven project, Dr. Comer and his team did not expect a "quick fix" or abandon their efforts before enough time had elapsed to allow their efforts to bear fruit. The achievement test increases referred to above were noted 15 years after the project began. Enough time had elapsed to allow the new model to be fully assimilated. It is possible that only persons who have tried to introduce change in a public school system know how inordinately difficult it can be to put a new model into operation. One problem when university personnel attempt such change is that they sometimes get impatient. Furthermore, the typical grant machinery that funds most research projects contributes to this impatience; an investigator might be given a grant one year and be expected to produce dramatic changes the second and demonstrate effects in the third—at which time funding might terminate. Effective change that has the potential for making a real difference in the lives of children and families is rarely precipitous. It is unfortunate that so many good ideas are tested and discarded before enough time has elapsed to stabilize the desired change.

The University of Arkansas Kramer Project

About the same time that the Yale team began work in New Haven, a project with similar goals of involving parents in their children's education was begun in Little Rock, Arkansas (Caldwell 1972). As was true of the Yale project, the Kramer Project had goals broader than merely involving families; however, parental involvement and support were key components of the model. The project, located in a regular elementary school within the Little Rock School District, was called in some publications "the linked model." It attempted to link together a number of conceptual and operational facets of an "ideal" school for young children in hopes of creating a facility that could meet the developmental needs of low-income children. The different linkages highlighted in reports of the program were:

1. *Early childhood education and elementary education.* The school admitted children as young as 6 months and ran through the fifth grade. The major goal of the project was to provide early enrichment plus sustained support for learning during the elementary years.

2. *Education and day care.* The Kramer program recognized the increasing need for extended care for both preschool and elementary age children and advanced the position that quality care could be part of a regular public school. The school opened at 6:45 a.m. and closed at 6.15 p.m. and remained open during the summer.

3. *Parents and educators.* The Kramer philosophy acknowledged the primary role of parents in the lives of their children. Every attempt was made to involve parents in the daily program of the school and to support the families in their parenting and community roles.

4. *Researchers and teachers.* Based on the project director's feeling that some educational research had not been effective because of either covert or overt hostility toward researchers from teachers who were made to feel under the observational gun, a modest amount of role sharing was required of all personnel. All researchers were required to spend a few hours each week working directly with the children, and all teachers were required to participate in some of the research activities.

5. *A university and a public school district.* The project was jointly operated by the University of Arkansas (first the Fayetteville campus and subsequently the Little Rock campus) and the Little Rock School District, and its operations were guided by an Advisory Board consisting of representatives of both institutions plus community representatives and parents. Funding for different parts of the program came from both sources, and the project director held both a faculty appointment at the university and an appointment as principal of the project school.

For this chapter, the most relevant linkages are one, between the university and the public school administration and two, between parents and school personnel. The link between the university and the school district was never as comfortable as it should have been. In retrospect the mistakes were easy to identify. Administrative personnel in the school district vacillated as to how much autonomy Kramer personnel could have in such matters as hiring and transferring teachers, choosing reading programs, altering the daily schedule, and so forth; the Board of Education paid little attention to the project until its early childhood/day care program gained national attention. Some university personnel who expressed interest in participating in the research and program development were insensitive to concerns of the school district. In the Kramer Project the university failed to be an effective catalyst for major change at least in part because of insensitivity to the sometimes paralyzing problems with which public school personnel must frequently cope.

The linkage between the school and the family was clearly one of the most successful, albeit undocumented through formal evaluations, aspects of the program. All parental activities were coordinated through the Family Service Division of the school, which essentially encompassed a school social work division plus parenting education, cultural enrichment, and training in what is generally called empowerment. As in the Yale project, parents were encouraged to volunteer in their children's classrooms, and this not infrequently led to employment as teacher aides either at Kramer or in other local settings (such as Head Start). Many special "home work" projects (such as making audio tapes about their childhood experiences, joint television viewing), designed either by teachers or researchers or both, were carried out at the school.

Unfortunately, continued funding for Kramer became difficult if not impossible after only five years. From a research standpoint, everything that could go wrong did. The school selected as a control school was torn down to make way for a highway access road. A housing development in which some 60 of the school families lived was demolished and the residents relocated in housing no longer in the Kramer attendance zone. Mobility of the families in the project was so great that the early childhood–elementary continuity was rarely possible. In general the results showed cognitive gains on the part of children participating in the early childhood division but an attenuation of any advantages by roughly the third-grade level (Caldwell 1987).

The Kramer Project had a profound effect on attitudes toward each of its linkages that far exceeded what the statistical results showed. When the grant money expired, the Kramer parents fought harder than anyone for the continuation of the model. Perhaps to the university's shame, the parents lobbied harder to obtain local moneys to keep the project going than did anyone from the university, the School Board and delivered oral, including the project directors. Many of them wrote emotional testimonials of the extent to which Kramer had helped both them and their children. But at the same time there seemed no money available to keep the project alive in its entirety. However, the early childhood/day care component is still functioning as a Title XX day care program in another school to which the children were transferred after Kramer was closed. Furthermore, every public elementary school in Little Rock now offers extended day care (for which the parents pay a modest fee). And the model itself generated enough national and international attention that other communities are trying to develop similar programs. All such programs of which we are aware have heavy family involvement. However, they do not all have the level of university involvement that characterized Kramer. It is to be hoped that, in similar and superior future ventures, the value of the university–school linkage will not be overlooked.

The Baltimore School and Family Connection Project

A more contemporary example of the role of a university can be found in the jointly sponsored effort by the center for Research on Effective Schooling for Disadvantaged Students at the Johns Hopkins University and the Fund for Educational Excellence. These groups have established a large-scale project to support the Baltimore City Public Schools in part through more creative and extensive involvement of families in the education of their children. Currently the project involves five elementary and three middle schools.

The raw pragmatism that has fueled many efforts to improve the school–family connection is absent from the Hopkins/Baltimore project. Rather, a clear theoretical formulation stressing the overlap between school and family rather than a parallel but separate pattern of influence guides all project activities. Epstein (1990), the chief architect of both the theory and its implementation, stresses that families and schools are "a set of overlapping spheres of influence that alter the interactions of parents, teachers, students, and other members of the two institutions and affect student learning and development" (p. 100). She goes on to suggest that many students receive inconsistent messages from school and family and that these two vital influences often fail to combine forces in a meaningful way. Extending these ideas further, Epstein (1987) identifies community groups and peers as two additional spheres of influence on student development.

Table 15-1, adapted from Epstein (1990) and an undated newsletter describing the Baltimore project, illustrates the way in which school projects appropriate for different types of family involvement can be developed and implemented. This specification by Epstein of five specific types of parental involvement and the implications of each for appropriate school projects helps to avoid concentration on too narrow an approach to school–family connections. For many people the first category—basic obligations of parents—is the most important one. Also, they see it as the one that, if dealt with properly, would eliminate any need for other types of support activities. For others, the fifth type—involvement in governance and advocacy—is the only one that matters in that it represents parent empowerment. But, as is stressed by Epstein and buttressed by the theoretical underpinning of the project, all are important and must be included in any comprehensive school–family effort.

TABLE 15-1 • *Types of Parent Involvement and School Activity*

Type of Involvement	School Projects
1. Basic obligations of families— parenting conditions to support learning	Parenting workshops involving child development, discipline, guidance
2. Basic obligations of school— communications about policies	Memos, newsletters, report cards, conferences
3. Volunteers at school	Assisting teachers, administrators, helping children, being in audience for programs
4. Learning activities at home	Homework packets called TIPS (Teachers Involve Parents in School-work) that facilitate children's academic progress
5. School decision making	Parent empowerment, training in advocacy, serving on policy councils

The special contribution of a university to the goal of increasing family involvement in education can be seen in the caliber of research that is an integral part of the Baltimore/Hopkins project. Although the project is of such recent origin that some of the early results are not yet available in print, preliminary findings have been presented at professional meetings and summarized by Epstein (1990). On the basis of early evidence, it is possible to conclude that the development of this climate for cooperation between school and family does indeed lead to increased parental involvement in educational activities, to improved reading skills in elementary school, and to more positive and accepting attitudes toward parents on the part of teachers. The concern for rapport with personnel in the schools on the part of university personnel is impressive in the project—something not always observed by university-based researchers who work in schools. Results of the evaluations are always discussed first with personnel in the cooperating schools before any dissemination is made to other school personnel who might like to be involved and before any dissemination to the educational research public. Furthermore, ideas of the participating teachers, parents, and students are utilized in formulating future plans for the project. On the basis of public reports, this project earns as high a score on research citizenship as it does on relevance and scholarship.

Clearinghouses and Catalysts

Another function of the university in fostering school–family cooperation is the development of clearinghouses that serve as information centers for individuals and groups wishing to launch or improve programs.

The Harvard Family Research Project

The Harvard Family Research Project, directed by Heather Weiss (1988), is an excellent example of the clearinghouse function of a university. In operation since 1983, the Harvard project has provided information and technical assistance to many state and local groups concerned with parent support.

The philosophy of family support espoused by this group (see Seppanen and Weiss 1988) is one that recognizes that influence is bidirectional, that professionals learn as well as families, and that the alliances that must develop "are partnerships, or complex, multi-lateral relationships wherein parents, professionals and other parents exchange information and support" (p. 6). They would not accept as full-fledged representatives of such relationships the relatively superficial memos and communiques included in Type 2 involvement of Table 15.1 or even the provision of occasional speakers for parent groups. Only activities that facilitate sustained contact and support and lead to a sense of partnership would be accepted under their terms.

Personnel in this university-based project are vitally involved in school–family activities that take place outside the university walls. They monitor and record the history of project development in different cities and states and make that information available to agencies and individuals planning programs in different areas. In addition, they recommend evaluation strategies that can be used in program evaluations not likely to have the careful control generally maintained in small-scale university-based research. Personnel on the project staff are sought after and used as a resource by all groups concerned with school–family relations. The fact that they are with Harvard undoubtedly gives their information and their technical assistance the prestige that it might lack without this affiliation. The project personnel are catalysts for change, but the university acts as a social enzyme in generating a reaction.

The Missouri Parents As Teachers Program

A related catalytic function of the university as a change agent can be observed in the stimulation of direct action at the state and local level by work that was originally conducted on a smaller scale within the university environment. A good example of this process is the development of the Parents As Teachers program in Missouri directed by Mildred Winter. Originally patterned after the model developed by Burton White (both at Harvard and in a private organization he established), the program quickly became "Missourized" as the nature of the school outreach was adapted to local funding realities and perceived needs. The Parents As Teachers program is now statutorily mandated in all school districts as a service to all parents with children in the birth to 3 year age range.

In this project, parent educators work out of local schools, visiting parents every month to six weeks and offer additional group meetings that parents may attend. Considerable preservice training is offered to (largely) paraprofessional educators, and additional inservice training is required during the year. Funding derives from both state and local revenues. Some private foundations help during the piloting phase and with program evaluation. In addition to the educationally oriented home visits, periodic screening for physical, cognitive, and language problems is scheduled, and referrals are made to other agencies for needed services not provided directly within the project. Early evaluation data comparing 75 project families with similar controls demonstrated better intellectual and language development in the children and more knowledge of child development and better attitudes toward schooling in the parents (Pfannenstiel and Seltzer 1989). Currently a much more ambitious evaluation based on 2,500 families in 37 districts throughout Missouri is underway that will offer a more definitive test of the efficacy of the program.

In the operation of this project, close collaboration is maintained with the University of Missouri at St. Louis, where a National Training Center actually serves as the coordinating center. This center provides training for trainers who will work directly with the parent educators and who in turn work directly with the families. Also, a number of research and evaluation projects are conducted through the center, thereby contributing to the knowledge base for future program operation. In some respects this project has gone full circle in that the inspiration came from a university-based program and now, after almost unbelievable public support, the project has to some extent returned to the university for a more stable and permanent base of operation—but not for funding. Most of the operating funds for the project are appropriated directly by the state legislature. The remarkable growth of this school–family service during the past decade provides a reassuring example of university–lower school–state angency collaboration. It again demonstrates effectively how ideas initially generated within a university can be transformed into public policy when the proper climate for action exists in the larger community.

Shapers of Public Policy

University personnel have been major shapers of public policy that has supported and occasionally mandated parental involvement in educational activities for children. Two outstanding examples can be cited: Head Start and early intervention programs for the handicapped.

The Head Start Model

Perhaps Head Start illustrates the contribution of the university to national policy for children better than almost any other national program. Head Start is as close as America has ever come to putting together an intellectual elite to help design a federal initiative for children. Although they were not isolated in the desert, as was the case with top-notch physicists who developed the atomic bomb, the innovators were pulled together on a consultant basis from universities all over the country to pool ideas and principles that would undergird the program — which exploded between February and June of 1965 rather than emerging slowly as more typically occurs.

From this remarkable group of academicians (mainly pediatricians, psychologists, and educators), loosely pulled together on the basis of scholarly careers concerned with the effects of early experience on the subsequent development of children, came a quantum step in both concepts and practices concerned with home–school collaboration. They were men and women at the frontiers of knowledge in their academic specialties but who also were comfortable interacting with government officials, appointed and elected, liberal and conservative. After their truly revolutionary recommendations with respect to the role of parents in Head Start, the approach was never the same in any educational setting.

Head Start was designed to help children of poverty have enriching experiences that would compensate for what their home environments might not have provided as foundations for subsequent academic learning. The program was intended to be comprehensive, not exclusively educational, and to include major health, nutrition, and social service components. The program was part of the War on Poverty and was from the outset concerned with the whole family, even though children entering school in the fall constituted the main target group.

The group of academicians who wrote the blueprint for Head Start were all committed to an ecological orientation to child development and so to the necessity of targeting some of the intervention efforts toward the children's parents. Early discussions along those lines were slanted toward the provision of "parent education" within Head Start. However, it was soon recognized that this approach was more than a little patronizing (Richmond 1979) and was predicated on an assumption that what should be offered was one-way assistance, whereas a reciprocating mechanism of help and support was needed. In order to correct this pejorative attitude, the term "parental involvement" was substituted. This new term made clear that involvement of the parents in the entire spectrum of activities would be welcome—as volunteers, as paid staff, and as decision makers sitting and voting on advisory boards. The topping of this all-embracing concept came with the guideline that at least 51 percent of the members of the Head Start Advisory Boards in every community would be parents.

In programs dependent on federal funds, a regulation quickly becomes a mandate. And, following that mandate, parental involvement in early childhood programs would never be the same. For, though originally limited to Head Start, the concept was quickly disseminated to include other types of services by the academicians who had been instrumental in the development of the policy, the program operators, and the parents themselves.

Unquestionably this subtle shift in emphasis, in itself a significant departure from the approach to parents found in most segments of the child study or child guidance realm at that time, would have met resistance without support from the academic community. It called for a sharing of power and an attitude of humility on the part of the "experts" who would be running the programs—conditions not easily achieved in such ventures. But with prestigious faculty from some of the country's top universities—Yale, Harvard, Johns Hopkins, Vanderbilt/Peabody, Syracuse, Illinois, Cornell, and others endorsing the concept, mustering support from front-line workers was not difficult. It is our own conviction that the policy developed in Head Start provided the catalyst for the gradual adoption of a reciprocal and bidirectional approach to school–parent collaboration at all educational levels and in all settings.

In view of this fervent commitment to the necessity for involvement of parents in Head Start, it is unfortunate that the influence of the parents on program outcomes cannot be more unequivocally extracted from evaluation studies. In the Head Start Synthesis Project (U.S. Department of Health and Human Services 1985), based on an examination of some 210 research studies concerned with one or another of the outcome variables addressed by Head Start, it was not possible to extract the specific influence of parental involvement. Where there were benefits in academic, cognitive, and social functioning, as there tended to be on most measures for several years after program termination, these benefits were associated with early childhood education and parental involvement mixed together. Actually the analysis showed that children whose parents tended to be more involved in Head Start activities did show greater cognitive gains, but it was not possible to discern whether this was due to involvement per se or whether greater concern for the child's education led to both more parental involvement and more impressive cognitive gains. One aspect of parental involvement that was not equivocal in the analysis was that parents do indeed participate in such programs when made to feel welcome and wanted and that they value the experience both for their children and for themselves.

The Education of Handicapped Children Model

The other prime example of the influence of university personnel on public policies that foster school–family collaboration can be found in state and national programs for the education of handicapped children. Public Law 94-142 of 1975 — The Education of All Handicapped Children Act — mandated joint preparation by professionals and parents of an IEP (Individualized Educational Program) for each school-age child and provided a mechanism for parents to have a hearing if they disagree with what has been planned for their children. The more recent 99-457, which extends services downward into the early childhood years, actually mandates the development of an individualized family service plan that recognizes the family's strengths and weaknesses and essentially puts the family, not the child with a disability, at the center of the intervention efforts. For more than a decade, research aimed at improving the behavioral functioning of children with disabilities has stressed the importance of involving parents (see Lillie and Trohanis 1976; Turnbull and Turnbull 1978). Academicians have been among the most energetic and effective advocates for mandatory inclusion of this approach into all programs. School personnel did not exactly welcome this part of the law, but most districts have by now not only learned how to live with it but to appreciate its value. These laws are perhaps the first that have tackled the delicate issue of the extent to which parents have rights to help design and to critique educational services offered their children. It does not take a great deal of prescience to anticipate that similar guidelines for the rights of all parents in relation to the education of all children will become an everyday reality in the educational world of the future.

Implications for the Future

Historically, universities have made less of a commitment to the importance of involving the family in the education of students than have their predecessors — early childhood, elementary, and secondary schools. There are at least two reasons for this diminished concern. First, the students who populate university campuses are young adults who either have already achieved or will soon achieve legal majority and the legal right to be regarded as individuals and not merely as dependents of their parents. Second, the students who make it to the university level are generally an intellectual and social elite somewhat less likely to need academic supports than the unselected group of pupils who must climb all the lower rungs on the educational ladder. Clearly and unequivocally, the most important of these supports is that which the student's family must provide.

In this book, as well as in this chapter, the importance of linking schools and families is stressed. But in this chapter we have attempted to stress equally the importance of linking universities to social action networks that can give the new knowledge generated in universities the social relevance without which knowledge is meaningless. Universities do not have the resources to convert to the programmatic level all the ideas generated in university-based research. However, this does not exempt them from serving as a catalyst for the adoption, testing, and dissemination of worthwhile concepts and ideas.

Just as universities have an obligation to exert a role of moral leadership in the larger social community of which they are a part, so do they have the responsibility to act as a change agent for the development and dissemination of ideas that can ameliorate difficulties and facilitate the likelihood of academic success. In view of the evidence that family involvement is one of the most powerful predictors of a successful educational career for a child, this is clearly an area in which university leadership is needed. It is our hope that the examples of programs that facilitate school–family connections chronicled in this chapter, examples that have all been catalyzed by both the intellectual achievements and the commitment to social action characteristic of the modern university, have laid a firm foundation for expansion and institutionalization of such efforts in the future.

All education springs from some image of the future. If the image of the future held by society is inaccurate, its educational system will betray the young. —*ALVIN TOFFLER*

CHAPTER SIXTEEN

The University and Its Family

PEGGY GORDON ELLIOTT

Editor's Note: Not too many years ago, colleges and universities basically recruited 18- or 19-year-olds fresh out of high school. Typically, our undergraduates were young adults moving along the traditional road of grade 12 to freshman.

Today the scenario is much different. Just this past semester my Introduction to Education class seemed on a par with what I have been experiencing over the past few years. The average age of the student in this class was 28. Twenty percent of the students were married. Of this group, 35 percent had children. Eighty-five percent were employed full- or part-time to help pay for their education. The nature and needs of our clients have changed dramatically.

What is the role of the university in this changing population? This student is part of a family—and in many instances is the major breadwinner. One response is to suggest that universities continue to study the family to better understand the nature of our potential student body. Another response clearly identifies the university as a contributing member of the community and as such is a facilitator, nurturer, and supporter of its constituents.

Traditional Roles: As Families Change, So Too Must Universities

At 40-something Ron Jones found himself out of work, without skills, miserable and depressed. A single black male whose children married and moved away from home, the Gary, Indiana resident had structured his entire life around the steel mill job that supported his family for 25 years. Then came foreign competition, a nose-diving economy, and news that the U.S. steel industry was in big trouble. Company managers and employment outplacement experts told employees, "You must retrain." But Jones and thousands of his fellow workers didn't want to believe it.

"We thought those were some cold people," Jones recalls. "We wanted to feel sorry for ourselves because the Japanese took away our jobs." Eventually, however, Jones decided he was too young to be idle. He took out a loan, enrolled in classes at the university campus near his home, took a part-time job with the sheriff's department, and decided to study criminal justice. Today, with a degree and a new career, Jones says the university became his surrogate family for approximately five years, providing the encouragement and support mechanisms he needed to change his life. "It introduced me to another world," he says. "Now, I'm retooled for life. I could never go back to the job I had or to the person I used to be."

Jones's story is not an unusual one. In fact, most of us in higher education encounter similar success stories every day. The circumstances vary. The students are of different ages and come from many walks of life. Some are right out of high school, unsure about what they want to do and feeling their way toward the future. Others have been out of school for a while, are working, and have family responsibilities. For most of them the university, for a period of time, becomes such a significant part of their lives that, in a very real sense, it functions as an extended family.

In recent years there has been very little discussion and even less writing about the university and the family. To be sure, there have been discussions about the relationships of universities to communities, but even these most often centered on "town/gown" issues—campus parking spilling over onto nearby residential streets, student newspaper articles offending segments of the community, fraternity hazings stirring public controversy, etcetera.

Traditionally, the value of a university to a community has been measured in terms of cultural amenities, athletic entertainment, and economic benefits. If a campus fielded a winning football team, staged outstanding theatrical productions, provided numerous jobs for residents, and served as the conduit for large grants that poured dollars into the local economy, the university was viewed fairly favorably by its community. But times are changing. In the last half century, for example, the advent of arrangements such as North Carolina's Research Triangle,* with universities forging strong partnerships in support of business and industry, have caused the university–community connection to be more widely perceived as positive and mutually advantageous.

*Duke University, the University of North Carolina, Chapel Hill; and North Carolina State University.

If public schools are able to attract good teachers because there is a university nearby with a ready pool of well-prepared education graduates, the link between university and community is strengthened. If a new plant locates in the area because there are good schools and because its employees will have opportunities to upgrade their knowledge by attending classes at the local university, the bond becomes stronger yet. As universities reach out to serve the community (and the family) with campus child care, expanded course offerings, and flexible scheduling, the public views them in a new light and with increased appreciation.

Still, whether city leaders praise their local campuses as engines of economic and cultural enterprise, or whether they attempt to adopt taxes and laws designed to reduce the perceived nuisance qualities of campuses, few have given much thought to the university's relationship to the family.

Aside from the fact that students come from and are a part of some kind of a unit that we know as family, we might ask the question: What does the university have to do with the family? What has the university done to interest, involve, nurture, study, enhance, or assist families? What might have been done?

The most obvious response to the first question, and an accurate one, is that the university studies the family. Departments of sociology, psychology, home economics, economics, and a host of others have tried to figure out, among other things, what the family is, how it is structured, how it functions, and how well or how poorly it is doing measured against any one or all of a vast number of variables. In fact, as an area of inquiry, the family has provided the university with a rich data source for investigation and speculation. On occasion, such inquiry has brought forth some sound recommendations and even public policy assistance.

Much of the knowledge we have amassed about the family simply would be nonexistent were it not for university unquiry. We know, for example, that the number of single parents coming to the university is growing and that the majority of these are women. At Indiana University's Northwest campus in Gary, more than 63 percent of the students are women, approximately half of them 26 years or older (Indiana University Northwest, Fall 1990). That kind of knowledge should make a great deal of difference in how we structure the curriculum, schedule classes, and make arrangements for student programs.

Equally important, much family-directed public policy and law would be less knowledge-based than it is if accurate data had not been generated by the solid scholarship of university faculty. For example, when a family-leave bill went to the House Committee on Family and Children during the 1991 session of the Indiana General Assembly, significant information was presented by Linda Haas, an associate professor of sociology at the Indiana University-Purdue University campus in Indianapolis (*Indianapolis Star,*

1991). Haas told how her studies revealed that the bill would affect about two-thirds of the male employees in the state and half of the women. "Only 40 percent of American women have job security at childbirth through companies' disability policies. The remainder can be fired outright," said Haas, whose research has been used by Sweden and Australia in the establishment of family-leave policies.

To be sure, not all of the university's inquiry concerning the family is significant and of value, but much of it has been excellent and very useful. In addition, such study has demonstrated that the complexity of the family is real; that as its definitions change, so do its needs. In fact, the university's study of the family has been every bit as important, dramatic, and evolutionary as has the scientific scrutiny of squirming masses in Petri dishes or minute organisms visible only under microscope. University research has helped build a data base that allows us to spot trends, recognize patterns, and at least to hypothesize on ways of enhancing and reinforcing that which is positive for the family as well as ways of minimizing or eliminating those things that negatively impact the family. If we know that one million teenagers become pregnant every year and that half of those give birth (Alan Guttmacher Institute 1981), we can at least begin to understand how we must develop strategies to assist young people in handling family responsibilities and becoming fully prepared to participate in American society.

One of the most significant aspects of university study is research that has demonstrated profound shifts and changes occurring in the fundamental social institution we call family and in other societal structures related to the family. While these data have not halted slick print media or popular newscaster pronouncements about the family, they have made some modern myths easier to analyze and refute.

The burning question is why issues of family change are currently attracting so much attention in the academic world. After all, change is everywhere; it is pervasive at every level throughout our society. Yet, much of it has not aroused a great deal of curiosity among university scholars. An obvious, bottom-line answer to the question is that the university's clients come from and are members of families; thus, we must know about families if we are to understand what it is our clients need and demand. Just as most enterprises require clients, so, too, do universities. After all, funds are derived from client enrollment. Our clients are people, and people live in and come from the context of family.

One student, a 46-year-old mother of six on welfare, decided to enroll in college when her youngest child started kindergarten. Determined to do something positive for her family, she applied for federal, state, and institutional aid. When she received financial aid, however, her Food Stamp benefits dropped from about $250 a month to $148. It became more difficult to feed her family. She considered taking a part-time job, but that would have meant dropping to six hours of coursework rather than nine. Doing this would have made her ineligible for financial aid. Such information about families is the kind universities (and governmental agencies) need to know. Without it, clients cannot be properly served.

How does structural change—or any fundamental family change—affect the clients of the university? What impact does it have on their potential and on their enrollment? How does it affect their chances for success or failure? These questions go to the heart of any discussion of the university and the family.

An initial response is that radical and rapid change in family style and structure makes it far more difficult to generalize about *who* will attend college, *who* will select and make college attendance decisions, *when* the decisions will be made, *who* will pay for college, *where* the university should provide services and information, and *what* services and information need to be provided. The list could go on, but simply put, as the context in which people define themselves changes, the approach to and the support services for those people must change as well.

Necessary Roles: The Age of Assumption Is Over

Yesterday's assumptions and generalizations about families can no longer guide university decision making. Today, if a university is serious about adequate and appropriate service for itself, its faculty, and students, considerable detail about the family is a necessary part of the university's knowledge base.

The fluid demographics of today's family demand that even the most selective and traditional universities engage in ongoing examination of the family structure and style from which potential students and faculty members are recruited. While the specific information needed may be different for an Ivy League graduate school than it is for a rural community college, the context from which students or faculty members come and the primary affiliation with which they identify must be discovered. If half of the students enrolled as arts and sciences majors are married, self-supporting, and attending classes in the evening or on weekends, it makes little sense to schedule all of the foreign language or biology courses between 8 a.m. and 4 p.m. on weekdays. The age of assumption has ended, and operating on even the most general "guesstimates" can spell disaster in terms of meeting the needs of students or faculty.

Generally, the university gathers most of its data from student applicants, and any information pointing to a trend is taken seriously. Because of the nature of the university and its hiring practices, faculty diversity will tend to be determined in somewhat idiosyncratic ways, but the university does try to gather that information. Regrettably, some of the most prosaic data have been used to the best advantage. For example, it is highly unlikely that a university will continue to build single-sex dormitories if the majority of its students are married. On the other hand, when data indicate that the enrollment has shifted to include larger numbers of older adult learners, bilingual learners, at-risk learners (or a host of other kinds of learners), universities are slower to institute instructional and curricular changes, which may be even more important.

Consider the fact that most universities constructed their campuses, their curricula, and their student activities programming during the last half century around a majority enrollment that reflected 18- to 23-year-old full-time students living in university housing with substantial family financial support. Given the rapid change and fluidity in today's family, is it any wonder that universities are having difficulty as they scramble to learn what those changes are and what must be done if they are to meet the needs of their students?

We know that today at most campuses more than half of the students are part-time, over 23, and primarily self-supporting. These students *are* their family. They make the decision to come to college, and they will make the decision to stay or to leave. The family they grew up with is part of their past; they are attending college in the present. In many cases the university has the obligation of providing for these students the kinds of support that formerly came from the "historic family." Financial aid is probably the first of these supports that comes to mind. Federal, state, and private financial aid replaces the historic "help from home." Child care, personal counseling, support personnel, evening and weekend classes, mature social opportunities, career guidance, and even legal assistance are services that once were not extensively needed at the university because they were available to students who came from the context of the older family model. As the stability and support of that model diminishes, the university, in a sense, becomes a surrogate family, not only providing instruction but also offering services no longer available through the traditional family model.

Does the loss of the traditional monolithic family mean it is harder for people to obtain a university education? I would submit that it does not. In fact, it can be viably argued that the possibility for various types of caring units and the resulting institutional responses actually make it more possible for many. For well-intentioned and often good reasons, traditional family structures tended to be highly protective of the status quo. For example, female students frequently report that nobody at home felt they should go on to college. One young woman from an immigrant family was elated when she discovered that the university had offered her a scholarship. Her father had assumed her brothers would become doctors but insisted she should find a job because there was no money to support her dream of becoming a teacher. Besides, he argued, her role in life as a housewife and mother would not require that she have a university degree. On their own—as singles, with spouses, with significant others, as single parents, or in a host of other contexts—women are discovering the freedom to pursue their education goals.

What happens, then, in the scholarly area when "the family" is in the university and the study is of the family? At the very least, there is a readily available opportunity for increased inquiry—more primary research—that could produce a greater body of accurate and more useful data in a shorter length of time.

What happens in the human arena when father/son, mother/daughter, husband/wife are in school together? With limited research we can only generalize, but my own experience would suggest "wonderful things." Perhaps in no other human context can members of families become true peers. When father and daughter take the same calculus class or are given a group computer assignment, they are "together" as they have seldom, if ever, been. The same is true for husbands and wives. I remember well a couple who walked across the stage at the same commencement ceremony to pick up their bachelor's degrees. She is a counselor. He is a counselor working at a state correctional institution. Each talked about how proud they were of the other, and then they talked about how they had come back to school in part because they wanted their children to understand the importance of a college education.

When small children are dropped off at the campus day care center, they "go to college" with Mom and Dad, and they begin to develop their own sense of what education is in a way that has never occurred in earlier generations.* Where we have first-generation college-going parents with their children in university child care, we simultaneously educate the parents and set up college expectations as integral to the early mindset of the children, who then look toward college much as do children whose families have always gone to college. When students pay their own dollars for classes, they demand value. The class had better be good. The professor often has the pure pleasure of teaching students who want to learn badly enough to make sacrifices to do so.

Is there a campus downside when families in their infinite variety are a daily part of the university? Certainly there are some problems. Single parents attending the university often are overburdened with responsibility. It can take a long time to finish a degree or integrate the necessary knowledge base when competing and draining demands of parenting, breadwinning, and studying are present. Sober and painful reorientation is required during and after life traumas such as divorce, job loss, or illness. For the family

---

*Even during the returning G.I. post–World War II period, when families often lived on campus housing for married students, the children were "at home" with Mom.

attender who is his or her own family with no other context on which to rely, the strain can be even more debilitating. I am thinking of a young nursing student, a single mother who gave birth to a daughter during her senior year of high school, but came to the university the following fall determined to earn a degree. And I am reminded of a father of three, in his 30s, working two part-time jobs, who despite the struggle earned a coveted Truman Scholarship. For students like these, the journey is not easy.

All the human dilemmas that trouble the life of an individual become a part of the university context as the university becomes the extended family. It is true in a psychological sense as students in trauma or under strain interface with spouse, offspring, etcetera. It also is true in a physical sense as they draw upon the services of child care or participate in campus family outings and events. These are people whose context of living is being a student at the university, not the individuals we saw as students in earlier days.

Emerging Roles: Becoming All That We Can Be

The metaphor of family in the university culture is at least as old as Cardinal Newman's idea of the university, even though the cardinal probably never envisioned a campus child care center or three generations of one family receiving diplomas at the same commencement. He did, however, describe the university as "alma mater." This notion of the intellectual "mother" has been embraced in thought, celebrated in song, and literally become a tenet of faith of university people. Today we are seeing not only the original lofty ideal, but substantial evidence that for adults seeking advanced education the university also is expanding to be a nurturing, sustaining mother providing reinforcement and support services. Certainly, the university also assumes aspects of the traditional father figure in providing the material means for intellectual engagement through various types of financial aid. To extend the metaphor further, safe and consistent child care, story hours, and the like become the grandparenting we understood and experienced in the traditional family model.

As one looks at the multitude of changes in the basic family unit, it becomes evident that for better or worse those changes are necessitating responses in other social institutions, particularly in those that are a part of the preparation, induction, or social advancement processes. That those institutions will, like a coiled toy Stairclimbers, simple jiggle neatly into place to provide a smooth, congruent whole is wishful thinking. Universities, like other social institutions, will not become all that they need to be overnight or without discomfort. The process will likely resemble the snake swallowing the swine, with much gasping and choking as the change is accomplished.

The front page of virtually any newspaper on any given day offers testimony that this transitional discomfort is already taking place.

From the focus of the university, the fundamental change is twofold. One, the family is no longer the strong, monolithic structure we once knew. Two, people will need higher education throughout most of their lifetime, and, for the most part, they will come to the university for that education not in an individual context but in a family context. Oversimplified, a university that really meets educational needs must be prepared for extraordinary diversity in its students and must recognize that more than just one intellect arrives for registration. The young mother who leaves her baby with "Granny" arrives at registration with at least three intellects — hers, the child's, and the intellect of the grandmother, who may have just told her she has no business "going over there to that university."

While intellectual growth will, of necessity, remain an individual act, increasingly it will take place in a context that is not individual. Even those select students who come to the university in their late adolescence as individuals will likely return later in their lives in a family context. The U.S. Department of Education says that in 1987, the most recent year for which figures were available, 41 percent of all undergraduates were 25 years and older. The number of undergraduates over age 25 more than doubled between 1972 and 1987, from 2.5 million to 5.2 million, and a College Board study indicates that these students will be in the majority by the year 2000. The young scholar coming to the campus in his or her "last great springtime" is now in the minority and is likely to become increasingly rare.

Probably to their credit, universities do not tend to be "trendy" places. The notable changes they are undertaking to accommodate emerging family structures is in itself striking evidence that the change taking place is fundamental. Also to their credit, most universities do remember that dinosaurs became extinct because they could not adapt to a changing environment, and while a decade of argument and debate may be indulged in, ultimately the collective wisdom will react to the collective reality. The former is the academic equivalent of swallowing the swine, the latter the digestion.

There is ample evidence that progress is under way. Most universities recognize that financial aid needs to be calculated on how many have to be fed; that class schedules must reflect when students have to work; that libraries, computer centers, bookstores, and a host of other support systems must be open in evenings, on weekends, and at other convenient times for families. Today entire professional degrees are offered in the evening by some of the country's leading universities. Grandmothers edit school newspapers, grandfathers play intramural volleyball, day care participants go caroling on campus, and multigenerational study groups can be found huddled together in libraries and student centers. College advisors have to know about family issues and needs. Spouse and child counseling services are every bit as important as counseling for the adolescent who is searching for self or for a mate.

Leadership Roles: The New University

Work, age, children, and lack of singularity emerge as primary changes in the lives of students as they relate to the new university. It is interesting to speculate on what emergent designs could be developed if universities were to capitalize on these family changes, rather than merely accommodating them.

In the university there are promising indications of more openness than resistance to changes related to age and work. The executive M.B.A., summer business conferences for executives, and continuing education to meet the mandate in most professions are all familiar now at nearly all universities, frequently—and sometimes exclusively—located in the workplace rather than on campus. The need for continuing education without undue disruption of the family has been a driving force in changing the notion that the magic of education can be had, and held, in a specific time and place. It has generated a real understanding that universities are an intellectual delivery system that became place-bound but does not have to be. While libraries and laboratories generally are not mobile, electronic data transfer has addressed many of the challenges to the place-bound university. The day will come when the parent who is handling home and work responsibilities will be able to access information and review it without ever leaving home. Today the equipment and laboratories of the workplace are often superior to the best universities have to offer in health, science, and teacher education. So the linking up between campuses and businesses will be a logical and evolutionary process.

All of the foregoing indicates progress. It does not pretend that all the curricular and instructional data we have amassed about adult learning have been transported to the university or to the workplace. The phenomenon and importance of the older learner are generating an excellent and expanding body of knowledge known as *andragogy*. From this, one can certainly expect great strides will be made. As human bodies with proper maintenance begin to last a century (and more), human minds will require ongoing nurturing and maintenance as well.

Oddly, the university has not often coordinated as well with elementary and secondary schools as it has with the commercial workplace. Even in such mundane and logical matters as calendars, most universities have set their own timetables with little or no consideration of the calendars of area schools attended by the offspring of university students. Wouldn't it make sense that holidays and semester breaks of the university occur at the same time as those of area schools?

As a rule the opportunities for instruction in elementary and secondary schools have been limited to teacher education classes. While generating sufficient numbers in one place to justify instruction for all—both offspring and parents—may be an idealistic notion, the idea of bringing the educational enterprise together for all is one that warrants exploration. What parents might learn operating on a regular basis in the child's setting might offer the same potential universities have discovered in bringing children to the university or workplace setting of their parents.

The absence of a static, singular structure that can be defined as family may emerge as the most positive aspect of change. It certainly is one that the university should carefully study and advance, perhaps even celebrate. Even now some new constructions of family are faring pretty well. With adequate support systems to replace the old, many students may do just fine. The lack of singularity prevents the family from being used as an excuse for failure to achieve certain goals. Many people come from one-parent families; many of them are successes. Many people come from traditional families; many of them are doing well. What the lack of a monolithic structure provides is a responsibility to form an effective context, whatever that context may be. It may mean choosing to develop in an entirely different context from the traditional family model. What must be kept in mind is that the new family—and, consequently, the new university—has the possibility to be better. All social institutions can contribute to making that happen. Many universities are at least working to that end. The increasing enrollments and active participation of adults seem to indicate progress. While campus-based Brownie troops are still not as numerous as college intramural teams, they do exist. If all of this change sounds like a puzzling, complex, whirling vortex, it often is. Change is heady and frequently multidirectional.

Like the rest of society, the university struggles to discover what characteristics it must add, shed, or modify to meet the needs of those who come in splendid diversity and in changing context to its halls of learning. One thing is for certain—its role is likely to be increasingly complex. Indeed, in this age of technological and global reality, the university may well emerge as a vital extension of the nuclear family.

We must do more than identify major trends. Difficult as it may be, we must resist the temptation to be seduced by straight lines.
—ALVIN TOFFLER

CHAPTER SEVENTEEN

The Curriculum of Aspiring Teachers: Not a Question of Either/Or

DONNA EVANS   DAVID NELSON

Editor's Note: In our search for academic excellence, much has been said about the intellectual depth of our teachers. Many have concluded that teachers are inadequately prepared in subject matter content, thereby explaining low student test scores. Obviously, students cannot learn very much from instructors who themselves do not know very much. A call for more liberal arts in the preservice experiences of prospective teachers seems to be a solution to poor instruction.

Study after study indicates, however, that poor teaching is rarely attributable to poor content background. Incompetent teaching seems more to be a matter of poor organization, less than adequate management techniques, and little concern for the affective needs of students. More simply stated, some teachers are dull, unimaginative, and seemingly uninterested in the backgrounds, feelings, and needs of their students. However, they do know their history.

In a world growing in complexity, it is no longer acceptable to prepare teachers the way it has always been done. Far more is required to meld the cognitive needs of our clients with their other needs as learners. Business as usual will not suffice.

Beginning with *A Nation at Risk* published in 1983 by the National Commission on Excellence in Education and continuing through a dozen or more reports such as *Impaired Generation: Saving Urban Schools* published by the Carnegie Foundation in 1988, and *Tomorrow's Teachers,* a 1986 report of the Holmes Group, the alarm was sounded about the presumed causal relationship between the deficiencies of public education and the decline of the American economy and, by implication, the decline in quality of life for many Americans. This alarm was sounded certainly for those adults, children, and youth who have been and are being ill-served by the nation's public schools.

Throughout the twentieth century, there have been numerous efforts to reform American education—K–12 and higher education. Standards and criteria that guide such efforts, were, however, rarely based on research or reality. Public demands for immediate change and instant results were typically met with a resistance to invest the resources necessary to bring about meaningful change. As a substantive document, *A Nation at Risk* (1983), like a generation of succeeding reports and documents, leaves much to be desired. The recommendations are generally short-term or superficial. For example, one wonders, why, if educators are doing such a poor job with the time they have, simply requiring students to spend more time in school would help with the problem. Why do students who are reluctant at two o'clock suddenly become intrinsically motivated learners at four o'clock with the advent of the extended school day? Other reports recommended a longer school year. Simple advocacy—more time, more content, different organizational structure—is inadequate to address the difficult problems of educating children and youth. A school improvement plan *must* deal not only with the complex issue of the quality of instruction, teaching, and learning in a variety of school environments, but also the family background of children and youth must be considered.

Thus, what we have learned—but may not be ready to admit—is that however well intentioned school reform reports and programmatic policies have been, such reports are largely insufficient and usually ineffective in bringing about substantive improvement in the nation's 16,000 school systems. Further, the reform reports are often characterized by a simplistic response to complex, myriad issues of educating our youth, especially our urban minority youth.

Of particular concern is the policy suggestion that courses in pedagogy should be eliminated from teacher preparation programs, relying instead upon "alternative teacher certification plans" that enable college graduates who have majored in an academic subject to become teachers without the benefit of educational pedagogy. On the surface the public discourse is directed toward one or more educational concerns and corresponding proposals. The reformers claim that there must be more practical experience, more K–12 teacher involvement in teacher education, and higher "qualifications," which include higher admission standards, competence testing, and supervised internships. The reformers respond to the public perception of the problem as follows: Children and youth are not learning the basics, schools of education are not demanding enough, and clinical experiences and supervision models are too narrow. The criticisms of proposals for educational reform are heard with increasing frequency. Such criticisms are of special concern to professional teacher educators who are preparing teachers to work with children and youth in tomorrow's urban classrooms.

There is no convincing data to support the notion that the degree of knowledge of subject matter correlates with the knowledge and use of effective teaching strategies. In fact, the practice of eliminating and/or severely reducing the requirements for pedagogy for secondary school teachers has some history in universities with the result that "reports on high schools present a dismal account of high school teaching. Teaching consists chiefly of either dull lectures or fact-oriented workbook assignments. Most teachers exhibit no deep grasp of their subjects, nor any passion for them. Their pedagogy is as sadly lacking as their grasp on the material" (*Holmes Group* 1986, 15–16).

Part of the blame for this sad state of affairs must be shared by universities who prepare these teachers. Universities

> *strive to hire academic specialists who know their subjects well and do distinguish research. But few of these specialists know how to teach well, and many seem not to care. The undergraduate education that intending teachers receive is full of the same bad teaching that litters American high schools. . . .*
>
> *To eliminate the undergraduate education major would remedy none of this. In fact, it would probably worsen things. For most of the education majors in our universities are elementary teachers and most observers argue that pedagogy in elementary schools is better—more lively, imaginative, and considerate of students—than high schools. Cutting out the courses that help produce such teaching would do little good and the evidence from high schools suggests that it might well do some evil* (Holmes Group *1986, 16)*

Universities tend to be unreceptive to pedagogical expertise that is available to them through cooperation with colleagues from colleges of education, thus perpetuating poor teaching in the academy. "To cut down on courses in pedagogy for intending school teachers without improving pedagogy at the universities would be a horrible joke of educational reform" (*Holmes Group* 1986, 16).

It is important to note that most teacher education programs, both elementary and secondary, are structured so that students are admitted to the program at the end of their sophomore or the beginning of the junior year with academic majors from the liberal arts and sciences. As such, few university students actually "major" in elementary or secondary education.

Colleges of education are not, however, hapless victims in the swirling controversy. Teacher education curricula have undergone cosmetic change at many colleges and universities during the past decade, but little in the way of systematic change that addresses the needs of children and youth in this time and place. This is due in part to the low priority with which decision makers on many campuses view colleges of education, often resulting in a lack of support for funding, and in part to the faculty of colleges of education who should be the major change agents in the preparation of school personnel. University professors are, too often, resistant to intellectual change and academic risk taking.

Curriculum in colleges of education continue to be structured monolithically as if the K–12 school population is a single, homogenized unit of children or youth be they rural, suburban, urban, middle-class, poor, wealthy, white, Native American, Hispanic, black, or Asian. Little more than brief comment is given to the world in which children live today and the implications for future and current teachers. There is no question that the preparation of teachers for our nation's classrooms is an important and shared responsibility of the academic community and K–12 practitioners. Such preparation must include *both* a solid foundation in the knowledge base of the academic discipline *and* a firm grounding in teaching pedagogy by persons who are intelligent, committed, energetic, articulate, and enthusiastic. As critical as academic knowledge and pedagogical skills are, they are not enough, especially for those educators who choose the important and challenging task of educating our poor urban children and youth.

The Ecstasty and the Agony

One big city's newspaper headlines and articles reflect the potentials and the realities of urban schools through the decades:

> *First Graders Find Adventure First Day of School*
> —*DETROIT FREE PRESS, September 8, 1990*

> *The Books Open*
> *The Summer Ends*

> *. . . Despite the generally grim viewpoint on book learning among those who must do it, there were mostly smiles on the shining faces of the kids . . . even among the five-year-olds who were just starting kindergarten.* —*DETROIT FREE PRESS, September 9, 1990*

Most children begin school enthusiastically and happily, but somewhere along the way, usually in the early years, some children find schools not meeting their needs as young scholars or as persons to be respected and understood. We know that children, including poor minority children, who learn to read, write, calculate, and communicate in grade school usually go on to finish high school. Such persons usually lead responsible, productive, self-fulfilling, and rewarding lives. We as educators also know that there is a phenomenon called "the third-grade drop out syndrome." Educators who have taught young children know that unless children have a grasp of basic skills, have a positive self-concept, and have "environmental coping skills," it is quite likely they will begin to "flunk" their way to dropout.

Schools Should Halt Mass Invasions

Children would learn a good deal more in school if there weren't so many interruptions. . . .
                    —PAUL WOODRING, DETROIT FREE PRESS, September 11, 1990

Loafers Will Have to Move On
Deputy Sheriff To Clear Out the City Hall Corridor

The city hall corridors and steps are still a bum's paradise, as they have been for many years. . . .
     The county authorities never paid much attention to the matter until Thursday when Auditor Lou Hurt came in and found that somebody had taken a knife and slashed the rubber tire of this bicycle past all mending.—DETROIT FREE PRESS, August 18, 1900

Student Downfall—Lack of Study Skills Rob Many of Education
                              —DETROIT FREE PRESS, September 11, 1960

Youth Held in Slaying of Oldster
Victim Shot Down at Bus Stop
                              —DETROIT FREE PRESS, September 11, 1960

6 Buy Bad Drugs Then Fight to Live
                              —DETROIT FREE PRESS, September 3, 1970

Can We Afford to Let the Schools Down Again?
                              —DETROIT FREE PRESS, November 3, 1980

Free Bus Tickets Seek to Raise School Count

Detroit School officials will deliver free bus tickets to all of the district high schools today, hoping to increase the number of students who show up on Friday for the official enrollment count.
—*DETROIT FREE PRESS, September 27, 1990*

In significant respects the United States is a much different country than it was in the 1900s or even than it was several decades ago. The environment of children and their families has changed dramatically during the twentieth century. Nowhere is the change more dramatic than in urban areas. Urban issues are national issues since the future of our nation is tied directly to the fate of its cities, where a vast majority of its citizens live, work, and attend school. Our urban cities and metropolitan areas are in crisis—serious, desperate, heart-rending, and relentless crisis.

Few of us are unfamiliar with the statistics relating to the conditions of life in the United States for many families. Conditions such as the growing gap between the privileged and the poor result in 40 percent of the nation's children being classified as poor, often being raised by a single parent who is uneducated, unskilled, and untrained. A majority of persons living in poverty are minority; 90 percent of the increase of children in poverty are accounted for by children born to single black and Hispanic women, according to the Carnegie Report, *A Nation Prepared: Teachers for the 21st Century.*

Resulting from permanent lay-off decisions from the manufacturing sector of our cities, a newly formed class of poor families has emerged attendant with the symptoms of poverty, such as loss of financial security, loss of residence, extreme stress, and deterioration of self-esteem. For many "intact" families to retain intact and functioning, it is imperative that both parents work full-time, which results in problems of child care and nurturing.

The assaults on schools, children, and families continue with increased incidence of crime and drugs, rendering streets, neighborhoods, and in many cases, homes unsafe. Schools are unsafe in many urban areas. Children and teachers have been beaten, robbed, raped, and killed. The school day is over before it begins, often at 1:30 p.m., which is too short for serious teaching and learning and too long for some students for whom school is not a good place to attend or for those whose after-school jobs are an economic necessity.

The AIDS virus, which was unheard of 10 years ago, is now the most significant health problem confronting our nation. It has been estimated that the AIDS virus will touch every family in the country during the next decade. The suggestion has been made that AIDS education begin by third grade since children and youth are sexually active at an increasingly earlier age.

During 1987, 708 black youth between ages 14 and 29 were murdered in Chicago, nearly all of them by other black youth. Thirty-four percent of these victims were young black males, who make up only 3 percent of Chicago's population. This alarming statistic is not confined to Chicago but is repeated in most of the major urban areas of our country.

The preceding headlines, observations, and statistics give a snapshot of the world in which families struggle to survive with their children. These are some of the issues with which children come to our schools to be educated and socialized!

Reform efforts in education must not be attempted in isolation from the real world in which many of our children and families live—families driven by the needs that drive us all.

> *Humans not only need (1) to survive and reproduce, but also (2) to belong and love, (3) gain power, (4) to be free and (5) to have fun. All five needs are built into our genetic structure as instructions for how we must attempt to live our lives. All are equally important and must be reasonably satisfied if we are to fulfill our biological destiny. (Glasser 1986, 23)*

These human needs are no less for the poor, urban, and/or minority children and families who present themselves at the doors of our schools than for those of us who seek to provide the education so desperately needed to save our country. Teacher education curricula must include pedagogy that recognizes the urbanization of "Dick and Jane" and seeks to provide educators with the skills required to provide access and involvement for real families (in whatever form that family may be defined) of children and youth. Strategies that appropriately served social institutions in 1900 when a slashed bicycle tire was news will not serve today's families and children.

As important as it is for teachers to be well grounded in academic disciplines, those professionals who come to the classrooms of this country armed only with excellent subject matter credentials will find themselves sorely lacking in attempts to imbue cognitive skills, self-motivation, and life-long love of learning. In the absence of solid pedagogy that permits teachers to employ a variety of appropriate strategies for teaching children and youth, teaching will be a frustrating and generally unsuccessful activity. New goals for teacher preparation and professional development must be advanced.

Although current knowledge of teaching and learning has improved substantially in the last decade, we know relatively little about teacher education programs and about the values and norms reinforced therein. Lanier and Little (1986) discussed how limited resources, low status among university programs, and institutional politics have hindered the development of systematic knowledge about teacher education programs. Although demographic and survey data exist, there is very little information on what actually occurs in teacher education programs. There is every reason to believe that such programs vary widely from the dismal and disappointing to the significant and exciting. There is, however, agreement on one finding: Teacher preparation programs do not adequately prepare persons, majority or minority, to teach minority students in urban schools.

The National Council for the Accreditation of Teacher Education (NCATE) is a national agency that focuses on the demonstrated ability of a professional unit (college, school, or department of education) to meet rigorous national standards for the operation and support of high-quality programs for the preparation of teachers and other professional school personnel. Specifically, NCATE establishes standards and procedures to carry out the accreditation process. This mandate has specific criteria that delineate NCATE standards, which address five categories essential for program approval: (1) the knowledge bases, (2) relationship of the world of practice, (3) students, (4) faculty, and (5) governance and resources. Although these standards encompass desirable professional outcomes, they fail to address the needs of children and youth from diverse family situations.

The fulfillment of the American dream of quality and excellence is shared by many; however,

> *the seeds of failure for many children are sown early. Tomorrow's teachers will have responsibility for children who will not have an easy time of it. More will be raised by single parents. More will come from families strange to the mainstream culture. More will speak languages other than English. The biggest shadow falling over tomorrow's children will be the scourge of deep poverty. (Holmes Group 1990, 29)*

Indeed, tomorrow is here for many, if not most, children in our large urban areas. Tomorrow's teachers will have to understand the desperation of poverty, homelessness, alcoholism, child and spouse abuse, and hunger. To accomplish this, colleges/schools/departments of education must select candidates who are sensitive to the strengths and needs of urban children, provide curriculum and field-based experiences that reflect a changing society, and provide professional development for beginning and experienced teachers.

Selection, Retention and Recruitment of Minority Teachers

During the past two decades, minority students have gained limited access to predominantly white colleges and universities. During the past few years a concern with retaining minority students to the university and admitting minority candidates to teacher preparation programs has appeared in the academic literature.

When students of minority background enroll at a predominately white college or university, they are expected to adapt to the milieu of that environment. In fact, their capacity to adapt may significantly relate to their ability to achieve academically. But a question that is seldom addressed or incorporated into the success equation of minority students is: To what degree does their cultural and/or racial diversity impact their perception of this new environment? Such a question is difficult to answer when little attention has been given to the varied nature of cultural differences among multicultural populations. The impact of the current reform effort has left many educators doubting the survival of minority teachers, particularly black teachers.

The Carnegie Report, *A Nation Prepared: Teachers for the 21st Century* (1986) not only notes the changing demographics for the twenty-first century but also refers to "the acute need for minority teachers, and a declining supply of well educated applicants" (p. 32). Such a statement could lead many to believe that there are few blacks or other minorities competent enough to pass the growing number of established certification tests. This statement, if presented out of context, only feeds the belief held by many outside of teacher education that minority teachers are inferior.

Federal policies, legislative actions, and educational reform measures have greatly affected the supply of minority teachers. On the surface, it might appear that the effect is minimal; however, impact can be long-term, affecting generations of minority teachers. Changes in legislation, funding, and policy are a partial response to a national populace that realizes the future of this nation will depend on the education of today's teachers.

The Knowledge Base

Questions about the teaching knowledge base have become increasingly important to the profession, and particularly to teacher educators. The *knowledge base* refers to the entire repertoire of skills, information, and attitudes that teachers need to carry out their classroom responsibilities. Several attempts have been made to identify the range of knowledge teachers should have. For example, Shulman (1987) has suggested that if teacher education knowledge were to be organized in a course syllabus or textbook, the knowledge would be divided into four domains: (1) content knowledge, (2) general pedagogical knowledge, (3) curriculum knowledge, and (4) pedagogical content knowledge.

Organizations such as the American Association of Colleges for Teacher Education (AACTE), the National Association of State Directors of Teacher Education and Certification (NASDTEC), and NCATE have generated similar, but usually more specific, categories. These categories include such items as: familiarity with new technologies, detecting bias in subject matter, understanding the governance structure of schools, awareness of professional ethics and responsibilities, knowledge of statistics and research methods for improving practice, classroom management techniques, understanding classrooms and schools as social systems, and insight into cultural influences on learning. In this and other reports, however, the role of the family and the importance of environment are understated or totally ignored.

Although the knowledge base has been clarified by NCATE and other definitions, "how to" questions are rooted and presented in terms of contexts that have roots in social, historical, and situational perspective, rather than the framework of the family. Put another way, teaching must be examined in the context of the family, and the knowledge base should bring together the technical aspects of teaching within the context of the activity. As such, teachers should behave holistically—blend content area specialization with the basic needs of children and youth.

This goal suggests that the knowledge can be framed differently and there can be agreement on the knowledge base content but disagreement about the framework—the way the knowledge base is organized and presented— or the form(s) it takes, and on the relative importance of the sources. This may be addressed by a teacher education or professional development program that adopts a conceptual model that prepares teachers to work with culturally diverse students in unique family situations. The accomplishment of this objective will require new and innovative planning. One such program is a teacher education project located in Los Angeles, California. The program focuses on four levels of teacher development to facilitate reflective thinking about culturally diverse learners by promoting the following elements: (1) awareness, (2) knowledge, (3) acquisition and maintenance of skills, and (4) reflection (Burstein and Cabello 1989, 12).

Field Experiences

Historically, a major part of teacher preparation has been the student teaching experience. Although some teachers criticize education courses on the basis that the courses are too theoretical, that they are too repetitive, or that they are lacking in intellectual content, student teaching has continually been perceived as helpful, often being judged as the most important aspect of teacher preparation. Current NCATE standards not only support this idea; they extend the requirement to also "provide opportunities for education students to observe, plan, and practice in a variety of settings appropriate to the professional roles for which they are being prepared" (NCATE 1988).

During the past decade, schools of education have worked to develop an organizational structure, a curriculum and instructional mode, and a supervisory approach that foster the development of a reflective practitioner. The primary vehicle for accomplishing this task continues to be the "professional semester" or "student teaching semester." Many institutions have discovered the single classroom experience is inadequate and have adopted a four-phase model: (1) preeducation (prior to admission) exploratory field experience, (2) methods course field experience(s), (3) student teaching, and (4) induction. Most programs, however, continue to focus exclusively on the school and do not consider the environment of the family. One exception, however, is a model that focuses on the student's total environment. It is entitled the School-based Teacher Education Program (STEP) and is located at

Washington University in St. Louis, Missouri (Cohn and Gellman, 1988).

The curriculum of STEP, and of similar programs, is developmental in nature and has four essential elements. First, methods coursework and field-work are congruent. For example, students spend Monday through Thursday in the school, and Friday is devoted to more formal coursework on campus, where students receive methods instruction and participate in activities relevant to their own classroom teaching. Included in the program are instruction in and experience with extending the child's learning experience to include the family.

Second, there is a continuity of staffing. The same full-time faculty members who teach the methods courses do the field supervision. As methods instructors, they make assignments to be implemented in the classroom; as university supervisors, they observe and critique lessons; and as mentors, they assist parents as "home teachers." Additionally, university methods instructors prepare lessons, demonstrate various teaching techniques, and receive feedback from parents as well as students. In other words, university instructors model effective teaching practices to university students, K–12 students, and parents.

A third feature of this type of teacher preparation program is that students are clustered in schools in groups of 4 to 10. These cohort groups enable supervisors to maximize their time in schools and university students to interact with teachers and parents as well as to critique each other. Another component of this interaction is the formation of "quads"—university students, cooperating teacher(s), parents, and a university supervisor. Throughout the semester the quads meet to foster communication and to share perspectives on the teaching-learning process.

Fourth, a developmental approach for fostering inquiry in preservice teacher education is to require students to work in a variety of school *and* family situations. The ideal model requires preservice teaching experiences in rural, suburban, and urban schools as well as with students from a variety of family environments. More typically, resources are limited and field experiences are focused in one or two school environments. Regardless of setting, a successful clinical/field experience model provides all preservice teachers with classroom practice with minority children or youth.

The Holmes Report states:

> *Past efforts to teach understanding to students whose social or cultural background differed from that of school often faltered. Old assumptions need to be questioned. Established approaches to teaching may need scrapping—along with standard notions of assessment and instructional method. Teachers will need to be able to take time to reflect on what they are doing, how it is working, what might be more appropriate, and try out ways to reach and respond to students. (Holmes Group 1990, 35).*

As stated in the Holmes Report, this idea is a goal for the twenty-first century. In the future, education faculty might develop preservice sequences of courses, seminars, and practica that have as common threads the application of research and theory to the whole spectrum of diversity among students—race, culture, language, academic ability, gender, and physical ability. From university coursework and field-based experiences, teacher education students should understand diverse ways to consider subject matter specialization, teaching pedagogy, and learner needs from the perspective of student's family background.

Assistance to Beginning Teachers

Calls for reform of the teaching profession have come from many directions and have focused upon almost every aspect of teaching and teacher preparation. Demands for higher entry-level professional qualifications are coupled with suggestions for higher starting salaries and increased support. Although a great deal is understood relative to the concerns of beginning teachers, little is known of programs that effectively assist new staff members during the initial teaching experience. Only recently have public policy makers and administrators come to understand the importance of support for beginning teachers. Such programs are usually called *induction*.

Induction programs are frequently described as a means for improving the quality of beginning teachers. Teacher induction programs are generally considered to be of assistance to and be the assessment programs for beginning teachers, especially first-year teachers. While more stringent entrance standards and higher salaries are consistent with patterns found in other professions, assessment-oriented induction programs are common only in the teaching profession. Although induction programs are relatively new, it is important to identify the potential they have to support beginning teachers who work with various family situations.

Many induction programs include assistance in the following areas: printed materials on employment conditions and school regulations, orientation meetings and visits, seminars and training sessions on curriculum and effective teaching topics, observations by supervisors/peers/assessment teams, follow-up conferences with observers, consultations with experienced teachers, the assignment of an experienced teacher to be a "helping" or "buddy" teacher, opportunities to observe other teachers, released time or reduction in teaching load, group meetings of beginning teachers for emotional support, and the assignment of a beginning teacher to a teaching team (Huling-Austin 1986). How much of an induction program is "enough" for beginning urban teachers depends upon the goals of the program and the level of the support provided.

Program outcomes directly relate to the amount, types, and quality of experiences provided to beginning teachers through the program. Although induction programs vary significantly in scope, duration, and intensity, most have three basic objectives: (1) improvement of teaching performance, (2) increased retention, and (3) promotion of professional and personal well-being.

Given enough time and resources, almost every new teacher can develop into a capable professional who is able to assist children and parent(s) in a variety of family situations. Practically speaking however, most induction programs will not achieve such goals because of the excessive cost and tremendous investment in human resources. Most programs attempt to provide some support and assistance to nurture beginning teachers and encourage students from a variety of family situations.

Summary

In summary, the curriculum of aspiring teachers is not a question of *either* content knowledge *or* pedagogy. Rather, curricula of programs of teacher education must include both. These components must be coupled with sensitivity to an understanding of the environments, experiences, and strengths that children, especially urban children, bring to school.

Colleges and schools of education must be afforded resources as well as university and public support necessary to boldly reshape professional education programs.

Nothing is more important or more critical than our schools and the education of professionals for our schools. The very existence of our country is at stake!

> *Certainly possessing information has its importance but it strikes this writer that being able to use this in an intelligent manner is more important than pure memorization. I would hope that knowledge will produce learners who are valuing, feeling individuals capable of making decisions not only vital to themselves, but of value to others.*
>
> *—LEONARD KAPLAN*

CHAPTER EIGHTEEN

Parental Involvement Teacher Preparation: Challenges to Teacher Education

DAVID L. WILLIAMS, JR.

Editor's Note: It is difficult to speak of educational reform without specific reference to the role of the instructor. However reform is defined (it means so many things to so many people), it is clear that teachers must be prepared to function professionally. Their knowledge of content must be ensured as well as their knowledge of instructional strategies, pedagogy, and, most especially, students.

The volumes of words written about reform seem to center primarily on the public schools. One wonders how schools and colleges of education have by-passed the major brunt of the criticism.

The current preparation of teachers for today's as well as tomorrow's students and classrooms has become far more complex than most of us in teacher education even envisioned. Rapid social changes in our nation and the world result in a compelling demand for teachers with far more sophisticated knowledge, understanding, skills, and experiences. Responses to this demand cannot be left to change in the preparation of either prospective teachers or those already in service. Educators of teachers urgently need to exercise leadership in creating more practical and effective teacher preparation programs.

During the last few years, teacher education has been criticized for unimaginative approaches. These have resulted in traditional programs that produce too many new teachers who cannot handle the comprehensive learning and personal needs of today's students. Competing fiercely with the educational needs of these learners are those equally important social, family, health, economic, legal, mental, and child and day care needs. Added to this is the growing demand for action from constituents outside of education concerning school improvement and for systematic changes in educational process. As a result of these emerging circumstances, teacher educators face stern challenges in preparing teachers as effective "soldiers in the trenches" of education.

Education departments, schools, and colleges of education throughout the nation are being challenged to improve the preparation of teachers. Representatives from all segments of our society (including parents, political leaders, and the business community) have registered a wide range of concerns about the need for new kinds of teachers, more effective methods of teaching, an expansion of learning strategies as well as opportunities, and more success for those who are being taught, particularly students deemed at-risk. The Holmes Group (1990) indicates some of the broad concerns about teacher education are: (1) were not rigorous enough; (b) were not intertwined enough with liberal arts education, teaching and learning research, and school practice wisdom; (c) do not relate theoretical knowledge to personal, practical knowledge; (d) have insufficient provisions for systematic trial teaching followed by the appropriate critique for improving schools; (3) lack consensus about courses of study that draw on and integrate the disciplines and practical wisdom from expert practicing (or even retired) teachers; (f) continue to isolate university faculty from the realities of schools; and (g) lacked involvement with parents and representatives from the broader community as educational partners.

Although the above list is not all-inclusive, it does provide a basis for serious consideration in the development of concrete approaches and strategies for improving the preparation of both practicing and prospective teachers. Obviously, the concerns pose a unique set of challenges to teacher educators.

Background

Clearly, the improvement of teacher education at all levels will require closer examination and more significant movement toward change or reform. However, for purposes of this discussion, the emphasis will be on preparing elementary teachers for parental involvement in the education of children at home, at school, and within the larger community. The reason for focusing at this level of schooling is because it is where:

- Much of the parental involvement research has been conducted
- Many of the educational problems of students begin to surface
- Many of the major parental involvement efforts are concentrated
- Sustained parental involvement in their children's education could become long lasting
- Teachers and parents can solidify the critical kinds of partnerships necessary for ensuring student success in school and life
- Most parents can develop many of the essential skills needed to more successfully involve themselves in the educational process

There has been increasing emphasis on training teachers, particularly in the involvement of parents at the elementary school level (Sallworth 1982; Becker and Epstein 1982; Burns 1982; Williams and Stallworth 1983; Williams and Chavkin 1985; Joint Subcommittee on Parent Involvement 1986, 1989; Henderson, Marburger, and Ooms 1986; Epstein 1987, 1988; Education Commission of the States 1988; Sowers, Land, and Gowett 1980; Rich 1985; Cavazos 1989). In spite of these suggestions, most of our teacher education programs still lack the necessary steps to respond. However, some teacher educators have developed and implemented some basic as well as creative efforts for including parental involvement as part of the teacher preparation process (e.g., the University of California and the California State Department of Education Joint Subcommittee on Parent Involvement).

Across the nation there are a few efforts underway that emphasize the inclusion of parental involvement as part of elementary school teacher preparedness programs (e.g., Arkansas, California, Florida, Louisiana, and Texas). According to the late Dr. Ira J. Gordon, "Parent involvement in education can be traced as far back as Biblical times (e.g., 'Hear ye children the instruction of your parents, for this is good')." However, it appears that the beginnings of programs to prepare teachers for integrally involving parents as partners in their children's education cannot be traced to such an historic origin.

Typically, elementary school teacher education has provided both prospective and practicing teachers with parental involvement knowledge and skills that for the most part focused on informal discussions with parents or formal conferences with them at school. With the significant growth of parental involvement as part of federally sponsored early childhood and elementary school programs during the last 25 years, teacher educators, both preservice and inservice, have begun to incorporate parental involvement as part of teacher preparation. Much of this has occurred at the inservice level because schools and districts that received funding for such programs as Head Start,

Follow Through, Title I, and others had more immediate teacher staff development needs. Even with these growing needs, elementary education preservice (undergraduate) educators have reacted cautiously. The irony is that much of the early parental involvement inservice preparation was initially provided by professors who were specialists in elementary or early childhood education or human growth and development.

The 1980s saw a dramatic increase in the demands for school reform, school improvement, and school effectiveness. The U.S. Department of Education's 1983 report, *A Nation at Risk,* which was followed by a series of similar treatises, propelled this issue to the forefront. Each of these highlighted parental involvement as a key to future success in schools and education. But, as Williams and Stallworth (1980) found from a survey of teacher educators in the Southwest region, very few elementary education preparation programs require parental involvement courses for their teacher candidates.

The dearth of such preparation still appears to be widespread throughout the region and nation as well, despite clear recommendations for its inclusion from the aforementioned reports, from responses to them, and from discussions by parental involvement experts (PAR 1981; Stallworth and Williams 1982; McAfee 1983; Taylor and Dowling 1985; Ost 1988; Epstein 1989; Williams 1989). This continuing lack of training for teachers prompted the Southwest Educational Development Laboratory (SEDL) to undertake several initiatives to help address this problem at the professional preparation program level. Four of these efforts and their outcomes are briefly discussed below.

A Regional Conference

In 1983 the SEDL convened a conference of selected stakeholders from its region to obtain recommendations for the development of guidelines and strategies for preparing preservice and inservice elementary teachers for parental involvement. The participants represented parent organizations, state and local education agencies, teacher education institutions, parent and community advocate groups, and other education-related groups (e.g., state board of education). A variety of activities was conducted to allow ample opportunity for information sharing and individual and group interaction. The two-day conference produced recommendations from participants concerning the kinds of knowledge, attitudes, and skills that teachers need as part of their preparation for effectively involving parents in education. Examples of key recommendations for each of these areas are as follows:

1. *Knowledge*—that is, needs to know more about age appropriateness of and expectations for children, the curriculum for communicating best with parents, the difference between teaching and working with adults and

children, the importance of individualizing parental involvement, and the culture and environment of children and parents.

2. *Attitudes*—that is, needs a disposition that accepts responsibility for teaching and working with parents to become involved in education, accepts parents as partners in education, accepts and works with parents as unique individuals, respects parents' cultural and socioeconomic diversity, accepts that effective parental involvement requires extra time and effort, desires to communicate with parents in an understandable and comfortable manner, accepts ideas from parents and wants to work with parents in a variety of involvement roles.

3. *Skills*—that is, need to recognize differing levels of parental ability and motivation for effective involvement, individualizes involvement to fit needs of parents and children, communicates with a minimum of educational jargon, involves parents to benefit school and home learning success, assists parents and children in valuing parental involvement, demonstrates effective involvement approaches of strategies for and with parents, channels conflict into consensus among parents, children, teachers, and other school staff; explains goals and outcomes of classroom/school and how involvement will contribute to their accomplishment.

4. *Teacher training issues*—that is, must address such questions as: Is this an extra duty for prospective teachers? Is more coursework needed in an already crowded course of studies? Is existing teacher education faculty properly trained for this kind of instruction? Should this be required undergraduate preparation when state and local professional competencies do not require it? Is it best to provide training at the preservice or inservice level? And, how compatible is training with state, district, or school regulations, guidelines, programs, and projects?

The conferees' reports provided SEDL staff with very important insights, practically and theoretically, as a context for developing plans to produce a resource that could be used in preparing elementary teachers to involve parents more fully in education.

A Regional Survey

As mentioned earlier, SEDL conducted a six-year study of perceptions from key stakeholders in the Southwestern region (Arkansas, Louisiana, Mississippi, Oklahoma, New Mexico, and Texas). Those surveyed included elementary teacher education faculty, elementary school teachers, elementary school principals, parents with children attending elementary school, superintendents, school board presidents, and state departments of education staff responsible for elementary education programs. Their opinions were sought with respect to various aspects of parental involvement in education.

The discussion here focuses on findings from their opinions about training teachers for parental involvement. Each respondent group agreed overwhelmingly that teachers need to be trained for working with parents (see Table 18-1).

When teachers, principals, and teacher educators were asked if elementary education undergraduates should be required to take a course in working with parents, a clear majority agreed with this opinion statement (see Table 18-2). The percentage of principals who agreed was higher than that of teachers and teacher educators.

According to a majority of the teacher, principal, and teacher educator respondents, there was slightly stronger agreement, overall, with the statement about the need of an elective course on parental involvement for teacher training undergraduates (see Table 18-3).

TEACHER 18-1 • *Comparison of Agreement with Need for Parental Involvement Training for Teachers (N = 7176)*

	Parents	*Teachers*	*Principals*	*Supts.*	*School Bd.*	*SEA*	*Teacher*
Teachers need to be trained for working with parents.	72%	86.8%	92.1%	86.5%	80.1%	89.6%	81.0%

TABLE 18-2 • *Comparison of Agreement with Training as a Required Undergraduate Course (N = 2182)*

	Teachers (N = 881)	*Principals (N = 726)*	*Teacher Educators (N = 575)*
A course in working with parents should be required for undergraduates in elementary education.	73.4%	83.1%	83.8%

TABLE 18-3 • *Comparison of Agreement with Parental Involvement Training as an Elective Course (N = 2182)*

	Teachers (N = 881)	*Principals (N = 726)*	*Teacher Educators (N = 575)*
There needs to be an elective course about involving parents for undergraduates in teacher training.	75.5%	74.0%	88.5%

In spite of these indications, the results from respondents to SEDL's survey of teacher educators about their offerings on this topic were disturbing. Only 4 percent reportedly offered such a course; 15 percent specified they provided such instruction as a module or course section; 37 percent indicated they taught one class on the topic; and 28 percent reported that they only discussed the topic at some point (see Figure 18-1).

Other survey results found discrepancies between what principals reported as important kinds of undergraduate experiences prospective teachers should have and what teachers reportedly had during their undergraduate preparation. More than 90 percent of the principal respondents indicated that teachers should have experiences in (a) working with parent volunteers, (b) taking part in teacher-parent conferences, and (c) talking with inservice teachers about involving parents. Conversely, responses from teachers indicated that only 28 percent had worked with parent volunteers, 44 percent had taken part in parent-teacher conferences, and 48 percent had discussed how to involve parents with teachers from the field. These results contrast noticeably with findings about what actually has taken or is taking place in teacher education.

A Set of Training Guidelines and Strategies

Using the results from the survey as well as the conference, SEDL proposed and developed guidelines and strategies to train preservice and inservice

FIGURE 18-1 • *Survey of Undergraduate Training in parent Involvement**

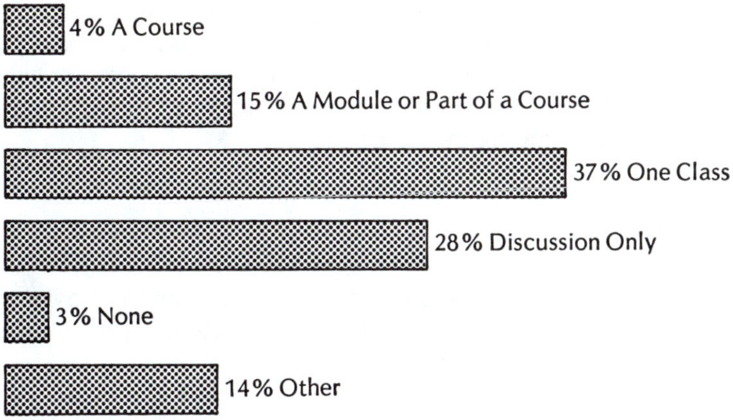

4% A Course

15% A Module or Part of a Course

37% One Class

28% Discussion Only

3% None

14% Other

*Number of Respondents = 575

elementary teachers for parental involvement. Input was obtained from teacher educators in the SEDL region and the nation. Experts critiqued and made recommendations for refining the document. The prototype set was produced and has been disseminated throughout the region and nation for application in developing teacher-parental involvement preparation activities as well as for further distribution to those interested in doing the same.

There are two major sections of the guidelines and strategies: (A) Training Teachers about Parental Involvement to Supporting Children's Learning and (B) Training Teachers about Parental Involvement in Shared Educational Decision Making. Each of these is subdivided into parts as shown in Figure 18-2.

As a result, these four SEDL efforts have provided useful information and important resources to assist in the preparation of elementary teachers for parental involvement. Alone, however, they cannot meet the unique challenges that teacher educators must or will face as they attempt to integrate parental involvement as part of elementary teachers' preservice (and inservice) learning experiences. Ammon (1990) notes that successful parental involvement requires not just more activities directed at or participated in by parents, but also includes developing and sustaining partnerships between parents and school staff that are based on mutual respect, trust, and understanding. An obvious void still exists in the training of teachers and administrators. Hence, there will be continuing difficulties in meeting the ever-increasing demands for wider parental involvement in students' education both at home and at school.

Challenges for Teacher Educators

Ironically, too few of the teacher education improvement demands directly call for teacher preparation institutions themselves to undertake this challenge, although clearly the responsibility falls squarely on their shoulders. Insights regarding what three of the major challenges are and some possible steps to take are presented in the following discussion.

Self-Development Challenges

In terms of their own dispositions and their preparation for providing parental involvement training, teacher educators themselves will face the greatest challenges. Among these are:

- How to develop, accept, articulate, and demonstrate the belief that parents are legitimate partners in education

FIGURE 18-2 • Format of Guidelines and Strategies

A. Training teachers about parent involvement in children's learning.

B. Training teachers about parent involvement in shared educational decision-making.

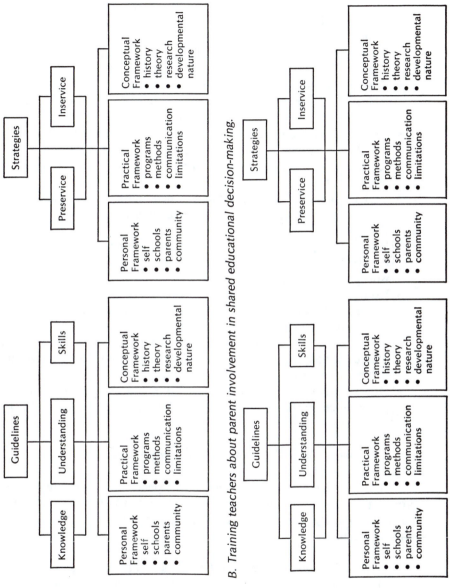

- How to become more familiar and well-versed with the parental involvement philosophical, theoretical, research, development, implementation, practice, and evaluation literature
- How to become more knowledgeable about various national, state, and local parental involvement program efforts or activities
- How to identify, locate, obtain, compile, and utilize and array of parental involvement materials, documents, resources, etcetera, for teacher training
- How to observe and participate in a variety of parental involvement activities at different levels of elementary schooling and in different socioeconomic, cultural, racial/ethnic, linguistic, and geographic settings
- How to internalize the tenet that teachers must work in partnership with parents to ensure the success of students at home, at school, and in life
- How to take part in parental involvement training activities as part of faculty professional growth and development (e.g., conferences, workshops, meetings, etc.)
- How to volunteer, advise, consult, and/or otherwise actively work with one or more local, state, district, regional, or national parental involvement program(s) for a sustained period of time
- How to conceptualize and make parental involvement an integral part of the elementary teacher preparation subject areas (e.g., reading, writing, computing, social studies, etc.)
- How to become proficient and instill in prospective teachers the importance of teaching and working with parents as well as students

Challenges within the Profession and with Colleagues

Another serious set of challenges to teacher educators are the environments (colleges/schools/departments of education) where they work and the various faculty with whom they work and interact. This involves such challenges as:

- How to develop a logical place(s) for incorporating parental involvement preparation into teacher education that enhances rather than intrudes upon the process
- How to inform and convince colleagues within the department/school/ college/university and across other related higher education fields about the value, need, and importance of parental involvement training
- How to facilitate the inclusion of parental involvement throughout the curriculum/coursework of elementary teacher instruction/training

- How to minimize or eliminate the attitudes, beliefs, and practices among many teacher educators that relegate parental involvement to being at best merely an attachment to mainstream teacher preparation experiences
- How to develop a cadre of parents and parental involvement experts to take part in the preparation of prospective elementary teachers
- How to make parental involvement training experiences part of the competencies that states and districts require for teacher certification and renewal
- How to establish a comprehensive materials resource base or collection of parental involvement documents and resources to supplement or complement teacher education curriculum and instruction in this area

Challenges for Teaching Candidates Successfully

The ultimate challenge for teacher educators is to ensure that their elementary teacher candidates are prepared to involve parents more fully in children's education at home and at school. The following might be considered good indications of this challenge being met:

- Increased opportunities and experiences for candidates that enable them to make parental involvement instruction applicable to their elementary teaching/learning efforts
- Increased methods for and development of skills in the implementation and assessment and refinement of home/classroom/school parental involvement efforts among elementary education teacher candidates
- Better candidates' skills in working with parents as partners in education and as adult learners
- Wider use of innovative ways to assess the parental involvement knowledge, understanding, and skill levels of elementary teacher candidates other than the traditional classroom or standardized tests
- Increased learning experiences for candidates that clearly connect college/university-based parental involvement theory with school/community-based reality
- Increased beliefs and actions by candidates demonstrating that parents and their full involvement are essential to school improvement and children's academic success
- Increased candidates' knowledge/skills in facilitating parental involvement in schools where there is teacher and/or principal resistance, where they are unaware of how to develop effective parental involvement programs or activities, and do not see parental involvement's relationship to students' academic success.

A Closing Thought

These examples of challenges to teacher educators who prepare elementary teaching candidates are designed to (1) stimulate deeper reflection among us about this topic area, (2) prod us into taking "one giant step toward more successfully educating these candidate teachers and one small step toward improving all schools and education;" (3) help bring the teacher preparation profession more in line with movements and practice in the field; and (4) provide a firmer basis for mounting more deliberate efforts that enjoin the collective resources of homes and schools in eliminating the barriers to learning success, school improvement, and effective education. If these challenges can be considered as potential "batteries" for the "innumerable points of light" needed to enhance the overall preparation of elementary teachers rather than as bones of contention in the continuing controversy about parental involvement in education, then teacher educators can help reestablish the profession as a leader in developing the kinds of productive citizens that our nation and the world need, now as well as in the future.

> *The family is, as far as we know, the toughest institution we have. It is, in fact, the institution to which we owe our humanity. We know of no other way of making human beings except by bringing them up in a family.* —M. MEAD

CHAPTER NINETEEN

Needed: A New Knowledge Base in Teacher Education

W. ROBERT HOUSTON   ELIZABETH HOUSTON

Editor's Note: A certain professor had a habit of audio-taping his lectures and having a student assistant play them in class. In this way the professor did not have to appear in class, permitting him to pursue more important issues. The story goes that one day he did appear in class and to his surprise found 25 tape recorders in the room but no students. The story may be funny, but it does make a significant point. We teach people content; not the other way around.

Generalized Statistics and Particularized Reality

"Maria!" Ms. Barker's sharp command broke into Maria's drowsy state. "Where is your homework? We discussed yesterday the consequences of your refusal to do your homework." Maria lowered her head and bit her trembling lip. How could she tell Ms. Barker that every day after school and until her mother returns from work about 9 p.m., Maria, a fifth-grader in Indiana, cares for her two sisters, aged 6 years and 8 months. Maria fixes dinner, cleans the house, and puts the baby to bed. Her teenage sister, Patricia, used to care for her younger sisters, cook, and clean house, but she has refused to do it any longer, and the responsibility of managing the household has fallen on Maria. Patricia has lost interest in school, is failing, and is suspected of using drugs and hanging out with a boy five years older than she.

Maria and her sisters are part of the statistics gathered by government agencies and university researchers, that widely quoted, reflect the changing lifestyles and family cultures that characterize America.

- Between 1960 and 1987, the number of families headed by females with children under 18 tripled (U.S. Bureau of the Census 1988)
- A single parent heads one-fourth of all households; of these, 8 out of 10 work full- or part-time. Black families are particularly likely to consist of a single parent. Both parents work in two-thirds of the families with two parents (Metropolitan Life Survey 1987).
- Living in a female-headed family increased the odds of dropping out of school by more than 122 percent among whites and by 30 to 55 percent among blacks and Hispanics (Berlin and Sum 1988).
- In 1985, 20 percent of all children, 54 percent of children in female-headed families, and 78 percent of black children in female-headed families lived in poverty (Edelman 1987).

But generalized statistics are meaningless if you are the teacher for such children. These are real children, with specific needs, desires, hurts, and aspirations. Statistics synthesize the generalized conditions in our nation about families and family life, but the classroom teacher must be concerned with particular families and specific instances with real students.

Students bring to school the genetic markings of their biological parents, physical characteristics that can be traced back over generations. Students also bring the psychological and cultural markings of their sociological family, and these are just as real as physical family characteristics but often unrecognized by teachers. Students' dreams, aspirations, needs, and problems, often unknown except by inference, are influenced by powerful forces that shape their achievement and motivation, their energy, and their future. These forces, with a primary basis in biological and sociological family orientations, continue changing at an amazing and increasingly rapid rate in America. "Norman Rockwell's tranquil family scenes lose out to evening news dramatizations about child abuse, youth gangs, teenage crime and pregnancy, and battered teachers" (Watstaff and Gallagher 1990, 102).

Paucity of Concern for Families in Teacher Education

Teacher education programs must emphasize the influence of families on students and their implications for instruction. Multicultural education is required in many states, and a course in cultural foundations is required in almost all teacher education programs. It is disconcerting, then, that the family in this social context is seldom considered. Prospective teachers are not being adequately prepared to deal with an important part of students' lives. Inservice education too often focuses specifically on elements of classroom practice, yet during their first year, beginning teachers become increasingly concerned about and sensitive to the influence of homes and family life on their students.

Two recent studies demonstrated the importance of such knowledge and skills for both prospective and practicing teachers. Fuller (1969) demonstrated that teachers' concerns are first about self, then self as a teacher, and finally about students and the impact of instruction. More than 250 first-year teachers were subjects in a year-long study of teacher induction and the influence of mentors (Houston, Marshall, and McDavid 1990a, 1990b). The study found that after two months in the classroom, first-year teachers considered parents a *minor* problem, ranking *ninth* of 14 problem areas. But six months later their perception was quite different; parent problems were ranked *fifth* of 14 areas. This shift in their concerns may be related to the broadening horizons of first-year teachers as they develop their skills and extend their knowledge of teaching.

In the second study, 42 elementary teachers were queried about their teacher preparation program a year after completing it. "Parents were particularly challenging and frustrating to these beginning teachers. Virtually every one of them mentioned concerns about parents. They mentioned uncooperative parents, uninterested parents, uninvolved parents, unhappy parents, noncompliant parents, untruthful parents, and lack of parental support" (Houston and Williamson 1990, 6). Relations with parents was considered a major missing dimension of their preservice programs. Communication with families and conferencing skills were inadequately covered, if at all (Houston and Williamson 1990). One teacher pointed out that in her teacher preparation program, parent-conferences were not even mentioned; and several recommended that at least there should be simulated parent-conferences so prospective teachers would know what to expect.

Preparing prospective teachers to be knowledgeable about parent-conferences is too low an expectation for effective teacher preparation programs. The influence of the family on the child is too great to ignore. Simply having the skills to conduct parent conferences does not go beyond technical competence to tap the essence of professional preparation. The psycho/sociological influence of the family is commanding and powerful. It deserves to be placed in its proper perspective in the study of culture and society in education as well as the techniques of parent-conferences. General principles with specific examples to make the principles real may be effective for preservice preparation; however, this needs to be greatly expanded and made more context-specific for the practicing teacher.

When teachers were asked to rank seven possible causes of students having difficulty in school, "children who are left on their own after school" ranked highest—higher than poverty in the home, single-parent families, and families where both parents work full-time. Forty-one percent of parents indicated that their children are alone between the end of school and 5:30 p.m. More likely to be on their own were junior and senior high school students, black children, and children of parents working full-time. This large and growing number of children and youth are referred to as "latch key" children because of the house keys they wear on their necks. However, "this problem is *not* confined to certain groups of families; it exists at *all* economic levels of society and in *all* geographical locations throughout the country" (Metropolitan Life 1987, 61).

Teacher Priorities and Families

Research has shown that teachers are consistent when identifying the major reward of teaching—that is, seeing the results of their efforts. Houston and Williamson (1990) found that it is in the growth of students that teachers find reward. For two-thirds of beginning teachers, this change was in *academic progress* ("Seeing students suddenly understand; exciting!" "Having the achievement test scores of my students as high as experienced teachers"). For some, reward took on *affective connotations,* ("A child in my class came to me to tell me about her father who had been sexually abusing her for five years. We reported it and he is out of the house and she is getting counseling"). A survey of 374 prospective teachers concluded that people choose teaching as a career for altruistic reasons; teaching is important to society and prospective teachers believe they can make a difference in the lives of their students (Hollis and Houston 1990).

Teachers generally support the concept of parental interaction but expect such contacts to be on their own turf—the school. Teachers generally are reluctant to go to homes, particularly unannounced, in apartment complex or in strange parts of town. Two factors affect this reluctance. First, teachers work long hours under tremendous emotional stress. The time they have to devote to encouraging parental support and participation is limited. Teachers work on the average 49 hours per week, spend approximately 10 hours per week on noncompensated school-related activities, and have, on the average, 32 minutes to eat lunch. Almost half of the nation's teachers are required to eat lunch with their students (National Education Association 1987).

Second, teachers are older; in 1986, the median age was 41, with 15 years of experience (28 percent had over 20 years of experience). This contrasts sharply with 1971 when the median age of teachers was 35, with only 8 years of experience (National Education Association 1985–86). Older adults are less likely to enter into new and potentially challenging situations; further, they are more likely to have competing demands during nonschool time from their own families and community responsibilities.

Preservice Teacher Preparation

Teacher preparation programs need to prepare teachers more adequately for dealing with the realities of America today rather than the generalized and dated perceptions of family life in Norman Rockwell's placid pictures. One dimension that needs to be more effectively considered is the trauma of divorce, or single parents barely surviving, with little physical and psychological energy for their children after working all day. Another is the trauma of child abuse. Teachers today are liable if they do not report cases of child abuse, yet the signs of such problems are seldom included in either preservice or inservice education programs. Mental and emotional abuse is as much a problem as physical abuse.

The following areas were not so important in Norman Rockwell's era, but are vital for teachers today:

- Physical and emotional abuse of children
- Violence on TV and in crowded urban areas that appears to be the norm rather than the exception
- Substance abuse, its ready access to the young, and the attractiveness with which it is portrayed by dealers and peers
- Single parent homes, often with their lack of supervision, exhausted parent, and shortage of adequate income
- Projection of favored lifestyles on American television that conflict with the realities of most families
- Increasing mobility of people, leading to decreased roots in an area
- Scattering of relatives and decrease of the influence of the extended family, whether from biological relatives or cultural leaders as found in communities
- Decreased lack of commitment among minorities to education as the path to a better future
- Diminished respect for authority of the primary institutions that characterized America a generation ago—church, school, and home, and the authority figures represented in these primary institutions

These cultural factors have little to do with the technical competence of teaching reading, knowing algebra, or asking higher-order questions. While teacher education programs are focused primarily on competence, it is cultural factors that finally lead to teacher exhaustion, discouragement, and early retirement. This is not to disparage the development of professional knowledge and skills in future teachers; they are *necessary but not sufficient* for the modern school that is set in a world different from the one in which most university professors, school administrators, and teachers were children.

Continued Preparation as a Teacher

Inservice teacher education programs need to be set in a broad-based context, because the context differs from city to suburb to rural area, from school to school, and from individual family to family. Principles of instruction and practices of effective teaching must be modified to meet these varying societal contexts. Only with such broad-based preparation will teaching become the profession it strives to be with teacher education as the basis for lifetime professional development.

Teacher Initiatives with Respect to Families

The following admonitions by effective practicing teachers provide not only good advice for novice teachers, but also an indication of the substance needed in inservice teacher education programs. Staff development programs need to help teachers demonstrate the following, especially in their content areas.

Be consistent. Inconsistent behavior by teachers is a problem for children; for example, laugh at an action one day and punish it the next, grade strictly at one time and not another, or change the schedule of events and classes often or erratically. For example, 15-year-old Sandra and her mother have lived with Joe for six months. Sometimes when Sandra comes home, Joe is lovely to her, courteous and caring; at other times, particularly when he has been drinking, he slaps her around and calls her foul names. Sandra does not know what to expect at home; she needs stability in her life. School may be the only stability she has.

Give structure to students' lives. Harold's parents both work; he is a latch-key child. They leave for work before he leaves for school. He comes home to an empty apartment and fends for himself until after 6:00 p.m. For three hours, he can watch TV, be with the older boys, bully the younger ones, be his own person. When his parents get home, they are tired from a hard day of work but still must fix supper (often from a can or frozen TV dinner), get Harold to bed, and fall exhausted into bed themselves. They have little emotional energy for Harold, and it takes emotional energy and time to provide the kind of direction and structure he needs.

Hold high expectations for students. Should knowledge of students' home lives mean lower expectations of them? Evidence from a seminal study, *Pygmalion in the Classroom* (Rosenthal and Jacobson 1968), suggested that when teachers expect high levels of achievement from individual students, those students achieve at higher levels. Research on effective teachers indicates that students tend to live up to expectations, however high or low they might be (Brophy and Evertson 1981; Weinstein 1985). To excuse students from homework because of their home conditions is a disservice to them; it robs them of the education they need and deserve.

Make the family integral to students' learning. This is easier said than done, given the conditions considered in this chapter. Yet, parents need to know how important they are in their child's success, to feel welcomed at school, and to have specific ideas about how they can help their children. Many parents do not have the time to devote to projects or programs at their child's school, yet they all want a good education for their children.

Parents can help their children in a number of ways. Parents can listen to reading by primary grade children, call the teacher when they have questions about school or have information they believe would help make education more effective, provide a quiet place for study, encourage their children to complete their homework, ensure that they go to bed at a reasonable hour, send them to school regularly and punctually, spend some time each day reading with or to them, and attend school functions. Parents of teenagers can be interested in school activities and athletic events in which their children are involved, support their children with controlled independence, and express pride in accomplishments even when their children give that "Oh Mom!" look and disavow all knowledge of their existence to their peers. For some parents this may not be possible, but the ideas provide direction. Teachers need to be aware of problems their requests of parents may present and be creative in collaboration with parents in finding solutions.

According to the Metropolitan Life Survey (1987), both parents and teachers endorse a role for parents that includes volunteer work, supportive activities, and promotional efforts. However, parents, but not teachers, believe that parents should help determine school policies and decide on the curriculum of the school.

Be positive. Consider parents as allies, not enemies; be positive about them and their children. Communicate good things about their children, and as early in the year as possible. Teachers should remember that each child is the most precious possession that the parents have, contrary to the public display they might make when the actions of a child or youth embarrass them. Unfortunately, 55 percent of parents and 23 percent of teachers indicate that their school only contacts parents when there is a problem with their children (Metropolitan Life 1987).

Be empathic. Joan taught the bilingual class last year and was a good teacher; she had all the technical skills of teaching and made top scores on classroom observations because she was able to demonstrate the skills of effective teaching. This year, Kate was assigned to teach the bilingual class when Joan resigned. Kate too was good, but different as a teacher. She established a time during the day when any child could come to her desk for a private conversation. She listened, really listened, to her children. They told her about their families, their dreams, their needs. They shared their secrets; she delighted in their triumphs and hugged them often. She constantly bragged about her class—in public. She believed in them and told them so. What happened? The students in her class blossomed! Their attendance went up; their achievement skyrocketed; their self-confidence with academic subjects and English dramatically increased. Individual teachers have different personalities and ways of teaching; there is no single best way to teach, and effective teachers have learned to use their strengths to best advantage.

John teaches biology in a senior high school. If you walk down the corridor between class periods or after school, you will recognize him by the knot of students surrounding him. He teaches biology, but he also teaches students. He knows them not only by name, but by their needs and problems; and he never laughs at their sad tales of lost love. He knows many of their families and understands how family influence affects his students.

Sarah has her students keep a journal that is read only by the teacher. Even second-graders can write one-sentence entries each day. Sometimes Sarah has them complete sentences like, "When I feel sad, I _____"; When I feel angry, I _____"; or I like my best friend because _____."

Enhance communication with parents. Some teachers send home a folder each week containing work and notes for parents. Others make it a habit to call parents about the positive accomplishments of their children; the telephone is excellent for improving communications with many families, and dinner usually a good time to find people at home for a short call. Seventy-six percent of parents rated teachers as readily available and responsive when they called; however, only 54 percent of teachers rated parents positively, with those in inner-city schools and in districts with below-average wealth rating them even lower (Metropolitan Life 1987).

Be flexible and realistic in expectations of parents. The mismatch of teacher and parent schedules affects their availability for conferences. One-third of parents prefer to meet in the evening, but only 9 percent of teachers find that time convenient (Metropolitan Life 1987). Parents working full-time are most likely to prefer evening meetings. Parents whose jobs are lower on the job scale often fear losing their jobs if they miss work because of school conferences or ill children. Because they are usually hourly employees, they are paid only for time on the job.

The demography of the American family has profound implications for relations between the home and the school. The substantial proportion of single parents and the large proportion of working parents can affect the time available for parents to be with their children and to work with the school. They can render some of the traditional forms of home–school contact difficult or impossible to schedule. They can create the need for mutual adjustments by teachers and parents, and the necessity for new programs or measures to strengthen home–school links (Metropolitan Life 1987).

Make school less intimidating and more open. The chasm that divides many schools and their teachers from families, particularly parents, is the lack of initiative on the part of either. Parents are as reluctant to contact the school as teachers are to call them. Fifty-five percent of both parents and teachers indicated they were uneasy or reluctant about approaching the other (Metropolitan Life Survey 1987).

Parents who are active in school affairs, meet regularly with teachers, and attend parent-teacher organizations are proactive in the relationship. But, for many parents, school is not an accessible place to go. Maria's mother doesn't go to school, probably because she works long hours at an hourly rate and is unsure her boss will let her off. She is also reluctant to go to school because experiences with school have seldom been positive and she is embarrassed to be the mother of her children.

Maria's mother has feelings that are typical for many parents. For others, a language barrier prevents their seeking contact with teachers. Schools are intimidating for them when the spoken words are understandable only through an interpreter. If school-age children must interpret for their parents, the balance of family power shifts, causing other problems. Language isolates non–English-speaking parents from the American community. This isolation is often exacerbated by the lack of an extended family support system. The extended family in their native community not only provided the major social system, but helped children develop, cared for them when mother was ill or working, and gave the family psychological support.

State Initiatives

Educators and policy makers have discovered again that parent–school relationships have a positive effect on student achievement (Jennings 1990), and a rash of legislation and new programs promise to improve this partnership. Of the 47 states responding to a survey of legislation and regulations promoting school–home partnerships, only 20 had enacted legislation, and most of this simply encouraged districts to reach out to parents. Four states (Massachusetts, Missouri, Oregon, and South Carolina) mandated that districts involve parents in the education of their children (Jennings 1990). Six states had guidelines for parental involvement, and 21 had neither legislation nor guidelines (Jennings 1990). Some schools have begun to reach out to parents with activities such as "sponsoring parenting workshops, creating parent centers, visiting students' homes, developing contracts that detail the obligations of parents and teachers, and enhancing communication between home and school" (Jennings 1990).

About two-thirds of the states have implemented staff development activities for school district personnel to enhance family–school relations (Jennings 1990). Sixty percent of parents and 41 percent of teachers favor such programs (Metropolitan Life 1987). When implemented, school-based inservice should focus specifically on the local community and its family mores, not on general principles of cultural change.

Several school districts have implemented exemplary home–school partnership programs. Indianapolis has hundreds of parents working in schools, a "Dial-a-Teacher" phone line operated by two teachers to answer parents' questions, a "Homework Hotline" call-in television program, parenting seminars on topics such as preparing children for tests and home discipline, and luncheons and social events to make parents feel more comfortable at school (*Education Week,* August 1, 1990).

According to a study by the Carnegie Council on Adolescent Development (1990),

> *Families are the most important support system in the lives of adolescents, and young people report that their parents are the people they turn to first for moral guidance. Yet parents are frequently unavailable to them, physically and psychologically. Very little is known about the diversity and efficacy of efforts aimed at reengaging families in the education and health of American youth or at informing and supporting families with adolescents. In contrast to the early childhood years, there are few networks or associations of family support groups for this age group. (p. 3)*

Many of the programs previously described apply equally to secondary as well as elementary schools. However, because of the developmental stage of teenagers and their desire to be independent of parents, such cooperative programs are more difficult to implement in middle and secondary schools. Parents often must be involved and visible, even when their children refuse to recognize publicly their existence. For non–English-speaking parents, involvement is even more difficult and more vital, for they often are forced to rely on their children to communicate with the school. Secondary schools should have programs for parents that are tailored to the specific needs of the community. In neighborhoods of non–English-speaking adults, this includes English classes; for others, courses for adults might include woodworking or crafts classes, history or chemistry, vocational classes, computer use, and recreation or physical fitness. The purpose is not only to extend the adult's education, but also to draw parents and community members to the school during evening hours. During such times, someone should be on duty who can talk with them about school and their children. Secondary schools are complex organizations, and parents can contribute in a number of ways. Opportunities for such contributions should be open and the school receptive to their assistance.

Conclusion

The education of teachers is one of the most vital aspects in improving the education of America's youth and is integral to the future of the nation itself. But such education of prospective and practicing teachers cannot be based on yesterday's realities for tomorrow's schools. Within an evolving societal context, the family is changing rapidly—becoming more diverse and more tied to economic and social necessities. Schools and universities, along with their faculties and educational programs, are more effective when they relate to the new reality.

Basic knowledge of family structures and values should be included in teacher education programs. In addition, teacher education programs should (1) develop in prospective teachers those skills necessary for working with parents, (2) provide experiences in schools with parents, (3) require sociological studies of school communities, and (4) emphasize the importance of families in student achievement. Technical competence alone in teachers is inadequate for the twenty-first century; customizing instructional strategies for specific cultural groups and events, and particularly by considering the influence of the family, is vital to the profession of teaching.

The three grand essentials to happiness in this life are something to do, someone to love, and something to hope for. —*IMMANUEL KANT*

CHAPTER TWENTY

Teacher Education: Linking Universities, Schools, and Families for the Twenty-First Century

FRANCIS KOCHAN   BARBARA K. MULLINS

Editor's Note: As society changes, so must educators as they view family life and structure. Courses in family styles and cultural diversity, as well as society's influences on the lives of children, must be a part of the university curriculum.

Educational reform has been at the forefront of attempts to solve the economic and social problems of our society over the last two decades. Teachers are a prime element in educational reform, as evidenced in reports from the Carnegie Task Force and the Holmes Group. These reports stress the need to focus upon the quality of teachers and their teaching environments (Lewis 1986). They have called for the elimination of undergraduate programs of education and the development of professional schools that would make student teaching a more meaningful experience. These reports also stressed making teaching more professional through differentiated staffing and career opportunities and a more stimulating and self-directed working environment (Keppel 1986). These reforms, with their emphasis upon structure and form, seem to ignore a fundamental component for success that should be addressed when preparing preservice teachers and assisting teachers currently in the field. That component is children and the environment in which they live.

Children and Their Environment

Our society is involved in rapid and pervasive change. Our lives and the lives of our children are marked not by traditions and stability as in the past, but by a temporariness that has resulted in feelings of impermanence and insecurity (Toffler 1970). Our social and cultural structures have broken down, and the impact upon our society, our children, and our schools is profound. Schools are being called upon to change in fundamental ways in order to meet the needs of children and the society in this troubled age. Teachers entering the field and those already there must have an in-depth understanding of the factors involved in this change and be equipped to use the available resources to strengthen themselves, their students, and their school.

Although our culture has been and will continue to be involved in myriad changes, one constant remains. The child's first teacher is the family. It is the fundamental structure through which every child is initially molded. In the past the family had many support systems to assist it. But those systems—the extended family, close-knit neighborhoods and communities, religious institutions, and a national value system—are no longer available for many families. Teachers must be aware of the state of the family, the impact of the social structure upon the family and the child, and how to build relationships that will mutually support the needs of the child, the school, and the society.

The State of the Family

Paul Nelson, professor at Florida State University, asked his undergraduate education majors to work in groups and create murals of the family. Invariably they drew mom, dad, two children, and a dog, all with white skin and all with appropriate smiles upon their faces. This picture matches what most of us think of as the typical family. Yet, today, only 7 percent of American families fit the pattern known as the traditional family—mother staying at home, father in the workplace, family secure and intact (Kirst 1989).

The structure of families now includes many more forms than the traditional one drawn by Nelson's students. Single parents, blended families that include stepparents, and adults other than biological parents, such as grandparents, aunts, or uncles, may take the responsibility for raising children.

Communities are no longer homogeneous groups of families. Geographic mobility and the influx of immigrants to our country are other factors that have contributed to the change in families. Diverse ethnic and cultural groups are found across our nation. It is estimated that by the year 2000 over 50 percent of our nation's school-age children will represent minorities (Kirst 1989). These children bring significantly different traditions, values, and beliefs to school than do children from the cultural mainstream.

Wax and Wax (1971) identify two traditions. The traditions of the school are termed "great traditions" and the traditions of the home and family are termed "little traditions". They suggest that school is, to a large extent, an effort to substitute one kind of tradition or knowledge for another within the mind of the child. For example, a child is expected to look a teacher directly in the eye when speaking or being spoken to. In some Native American cultures, children show respect by lowering their eyes and looking down. Frequently this is interpreted by teachers as shame or dishonesty. Prior experience is of little value to these children when their established ways of communicating and making sense of the world are deemed unacceptable in the classroom. Misunderstandings such as these can be a source of academic difficulty for children from minority families (Heath 1983; Philips 1983).

Individual competition is highly valued in America. In some folk communities, individuals may excel only when their excellence enhances the position of their peers. Hence, when called upon in class to recite, a child, adhering to family traditions, will not respond because reciting the correct answer would set the child apart and above fellow students. Thus, children are forced into a position of having to choose between little traditions of the family and great traditions of the school. When faced with a conflict between home and school, children often respond by withdrawing, resisting, or fleeing from the school environment. Ethnic characteristics are a part of the basic identity of many individuals. When forced to deny their ethnic cultures, children are rejecting an important part of themselves and their families.

The structural and cultural diversity in families means that we can no longer assume our students have similar backgrounds and experiences. Our teacher education programs, in order to be effective, need to recognize the diversity of families from which children come (Ascher 1988; Atkin and Bastiani 1988; Cohen and Cohen 1986; Henderson 1982; Lightfoot 1975; Philips 1983; Rich, Mattox, and VanDien 1979). Yet, if it is unreasonable to expect teachers to know about each and every culture and family form, what is it that teachers need to know?

What Teachers Need to Know

In order to work with the family, teachers need knowledge, skills, and attitudes that will enable them to be effective with students and parents. They will need these in the area of family lifestyles and their effects upon attitudes and self-esteem, communication to permit them to relate effectively with students and parents, and stress management to allow them to cope with the pressures of teaching. Preservice and inservice teacher training programs can accommodate these components to better prepare teachers for their role in partnerships with families. Teachers who are familiar with the relationships between different social worlds and ways of life will be better able to understand and relate to their students.

Rich (1987) has identified two priorities for change in teacher education. First, teachers and administrators need training to deal with today's families, and, second, teachers must gain an appreciation of the constraints of various family forms. A familiarity with the family from which the student comes is the first step in identifying ways in which differing family styles and cultural diversity of pupils can be meaningfully represented in the curriculum in teaching/learning strategies and examinations. Recognizing and respecting differences in families will lead to better, more honest communication between teachers and families.

Teachers must recognize that nearly all parents want their children to succeed. Research has found that parents from all kinds of backgrounds are far more interested in their children's education than many teachers and administrators believe. However, parents have very different ideas about their own role as educators and the purpose of schools. (Stallworth and Williams 1982). Some parents believe the job of educating children should be left to the teacher. Others want to be actively involved in the school organization. Still others believe their role should be to help their children at home.

Teachers need special knowledge, attitudes, skills, and strategies to communicate effectively with families. They must respect parents' attitudes, knowledge, and skills. Moreover, teachers should strive to develop a non-elitist attitude. They must become aware of the impact of societal structure upon children and gain an understanding of how to help children cope in a world of constant change.

Once teachers gain a sense of the diversity of their students' family backgrounds and understand the need to create partnerships with parents, they need to acquire communication techniques and strategies to work effectively with parents. With respect for parents and families and knowledge of several communication techniques, teachers will gain confidence when the occasion arises to communicate with the family at home. There is no single communication technique that is preferred by adult family members. A range of techniques such as letters, phone calls, home visits, and family conferences will result in information reaching more families and families feeling that the teacher is accessible.

Teachers are expected to be well versed in a variety of skills. Demands upon educators continue to increase. Along with these demands, teachers frequently experience a corresponding rise in the level of stress within themselves as well as within their students. When teachers come to know and understand their students, as proposed in partnership efforts, communication between teachers, students, and families will improve, which should ease the stress. Teachers who know their students well will be able to recognize those students who need help early and be able to refer students to the appropriate agency for assistance.

Knowledge of how to manage stressful situations will aid teachers in their partnership roles. Teacher training institutions can cooperate with other community agencies, such as hospitals, that have expertise in stress management education. Together they can develop approriate training programs and materials for teachers.

Both preservice and inservice teacher education can raise awareness among teachers about families. In addition, positive attitudes and high self-esteem, communication skills, and stress management techniques are skills that will serve teachers well as they work with families. It is in the colleges where future teachers prepare to work with students of our culturally diverse population that these skills must be learned.

The Role of the University

The university, the institution that sets the pattern for teacher preparation and provides the theoretical and research knowledge base for teaching and learning, must take a leadership role in connecting training, theory, and research with the world of parenting, teaching, and learning. This will require boldness, restructuring, and rethinking not only the teacher education curriculum but also ways in which the teacher, the schools, the parents, and the community interact and relate with and to the university. Universities must recognize their role in responding to society as it is and to the changing structure of the family, the school, and the community. It can be a pivotal force in forging new partnerships and in equipping teachers to deal with the realities of today's classroom and the needs of the children and families.

Deans of colleges of education must recognize that teacher education reform initiatives cannot be separated from the society or the children being served. They must recognize the interdependency of our educational and community institutions and reach out to strengthen those bonds in a proactive manner. Colleges of education must begin by examining themselves to discover the extent to which they understand the need to change, and the willingness to do so. Barriers must be examined and ways for reducing them identified.

One of the most important things universities can do is to equip teachers to understand families, tap into this resource, and use it to the fullest extent. Initially this can be accomplished by adding units of study to courses already in place. Adding home visits to teacher internship programs and including parents and teachers as speakers in undergraduate and graduate classes are ways in which initial curricular changes can be easily made. Courses in family styles, cultural diversity, the impact of society on children and schools, forming parent partnerships, communication skills, dealing with stress, and similar areas can be added after study and collaboration.

Teacher education institutions cannot sit on the sidelines and operate in a vacuum when dealing with the education and reeducation of teachers. They must become prime movers in creating collaborative relationships to meet the needs of the school, the teachers, the children, and the society. Parents, teachers, university students, university personnel from other colleges such as sociology and psychology, as well as community members should be invited to join the teacher education staff to study the teacher education curriculum and program and help determine what should be addressed and how teachers can be better prepared to deal with families. Ways in which university resources can be used in teacher and parent training should also be explored.

Traditionally, universities are institutions that work independently and competitively. They must begin to work collaboratively and cooperatively with a broadened constituency that includes not just teachers and professional educators but also the families of the communities where our children, the future of our country, are nurtured and educated. The problems of our families and society today demand that people and institutions work together.

Universities can set the example for change through cooperation. Universities have a responsibility to the community that must be expanded to include not only training those who will work in those communities and creating knowledge that can be used to educate our children, but also uniting the parties involved into a powerful and important educational force that will ensure that teachers and children will succeed. There are a number of barriers that must be recognized and overcome to accomplish this change.

Barriers to Change

A conference was held at Florida State University in May 1989 to study issues involved in family–school partnerships. It included classroom teachers, teacher educators, administrators, school board members, business representatives, and parents who met to discuss the concerns of building family–school–community partnerships. These experts identified several problems that make it difficult to achieve such partnerships.

Many teacher educators in colleges and universities have not been in a school classroom for years. They are not familiar with the school environment for which they are preparing their own students. In addition, parents, teachers, administrators, and teacher educators alike often perceive schools as the source of knowledge. Teachers are not prepared to detect, nor deal with, differences that might exist between the family and the school. Teacher educators expressed concern that they were not adequately informed about families to address these concerns in their classes.

While the awareness of the need to build relationships with families is growing, both administrators and teacher educators argue that the curricula are already overloaded and it is impossible to add additional requirements. Many believe that the knowledge, skills, and attitudes for working with parents flow naturally from the teaching experience. Yet, teachers in classrooms are frequently just as uncomfortable dealing with families as are the teacher educators who trained them.

Teachers who are not trained during the course of their college preparation to work with families may have to rely on inservice training once they are employed in a school. However, inservice programs have been limited by lack of time, money, and coordination. Frequently, the programs focus on teaching or discipline techniques. Working with parents does not have the appeal of day-to-day responsibilities (McAfee 1987).

Conclusion

In the search to reform teacher education, it is important to take a comprehensive view. The success of students, of teachers, of schools, of our country is becoming increasingly dependent upon our mutual ability to think, plan, and work together (Scherer 1972). We must form collaborative partnerships focused upon pooling our knowledge and resources to create teacher education programs. We must equip teachers with knowledge, skills, and attitudes to join forces with parents and the community to meet student needs. This will require that we put community interest above self-interest, restructure our thoughts and our institutions, and accept the expertise of others as part of a true knowledge base for change.

Universities, schools, parents, and the community must become part of a single process of making teacher education responsive to the changing society. It is up to the universities to take a leadership role in forging this collaborative effort. If they do not accept the challenge, we shall fail to achieve the kind of quality education our children so richly deserve. If they do not take action, we see little hope for those who come after us. Nor do we believe that those entering the teaching field nor those already in it will have the knowledge, the skills, the attitudes, the fortitude to be successful at educating our children and preparing them to create a better world tomorrow.

Schools must be a place where students are not afraid of taking cognitive risks, not afraid to ask questions and not afraid of not pleasing the teacher. – JOHN HOLT

CHAPTER TWENTY-ONE

Parent Education in Home, School, and Society: A Course Description

LEONARD KAPLAN

Editor's Note: One cluster of studies, which has become known as the "effective schools" research, has examined the processes, interactions, and practices that are found in effective schools. In general, the key characteristics of schools in which children perform well are strong instructional leadership, focus on basic skills, orderly school climate, high expectations of students, and frequent monitoring of parental participation. Other researchers have been investigating family processes—expectations, beliefs, attitudes, and communication patterns—to identify those that occur in families where children do well in school.

A promising area of inquiry has examined the relationship between families and schools: to look at the pattern of communication, contact, and mutual support between school personnel and parents and to discover how they influence each other. The primary purpose of what has been termed the "family–school interactions" affect children's learning and school success. The assumption here is that the efforts of schools and families are linked, that they can either support and reinforce each other or they can compete and undermine each other. A course based on that assumption has proven popular with—and, one would hope, valuable to—teacher education students.

A few years ago, in response to a survey of recent graduates, a course was developed for the graduate program for majors in early childhood and elementary education. It was apparent that teachers and administrators in these fields were feeling the need to know more about the home–school relationship. The undergraduate preparational program did include some discussion of parent-teacher conferencing, but these discussions were infrequent and primarily left for the student teaching phase. The assumption was that student teachers would experience these conferences firsthand and would be able to ask the supervising teacher specific questions. Since the supervising teacher had little or no preparation in this area, it was apparent that firsthand experience was the sole criterion for how much or how little was discussed. It was also clear that the attitude of the teacher and principal as to how parents can be significant providers of input and/or help to the school was important to whether this relationship was perceived as positive or negative.

To the credit of the field-based staff, many saw that they were not meeting the needs of many children in today's families because they lacked the understanding of the structural and emotional changes that are occurring to members of these family units. It is evident that the pressures of poverty, work, cultural and socioeconomic issues are inhibiting the family's involvement in the school environment of the child. It is equally evident that schools are most inconsistent in their willingness and ability to reach out to the family. The faculties in the preservice preparation of both elementary and secondary teachers or administrators do not yet require their students to take any course in this area.

Course Description

In any event, the course was developed and is available. (It has become one of the most popular courses in the program.) The general objectives for the semester are:

1. Students will develop an understanding of the relationship that exists between society's needs and the general principles of schools and schooling.
2. Students will develop an understanding of the relationships that exist between school practice and research findings in the family–school interaction process.
3. Students will identify major contributions of leading family–school theorists.
4. Students will demonstrate how curriculum is developed around family interests and concerns.
5. Students will demonstrate familiarity with urban family issues including, but not limited to, demographics, economics, race, ethnicity, politics, and future trends.

6. Students will understand the dynamics of how family relationships affect the school climate and the general behavior of those who attend. Students will further recognize that behavior generated in school affects family cohesion.
7. Students will identify and analyze various successful home–school programs and understand the reasons for their success.
8. Students will examine adult learning theories.
9. Students will understand the legal rights and responsibilities of parents and educators in the home–school relationship.
10. Students will demonstrate an understanding of the knowledge base underlying the nature of the American family.
11. Students will analyze curriculum materials specifically developed for home utilization for content validity.

Topics for Discussion

1. The Nature of Parental Education
   (Instruction Learning Objective I.L.O.: Students will demonstrate familiarity with effective home–school partnerships, past and present.)

   a. Overview of the American Family
   b. Demographics
   c. Stages of Family Development
   d. Dysfunctional Families
   e. The Parental Education Movement
   f. Parental Education in the Schools

2. Theoretical Frameworks
   (I.L.O.: Students will demonstrate familiarity with themes of parental education that foster successful practice.)

   a. Understanding Children's Behavior
   b. Research in Family Education
   c. Designing Parent Effectiveness Programs
   d. Evaluating Parental Education Programs

3. Subject Matter—The Knowledge Base
   (I.L.O.: Students will analyze the relationship of subject matter to process.)

   a. Selecting Appropriate Content
   b. The Relationship of Content to the Problems and Possibilities of an Urban Society
   c. Needs of Special Children
   d. The Adult Learner

4. School
(I.L.O.: Students will develop an understanding of what schools can do to enhance parent/child interaction).

    a. The School as a Socializing Agent
    b. Parent–School Interaction
    c. Conferencing
    d. The Accessible Teacher
    e. Teachers as Instructors of Adults
    f. Administrators and Other Ancillary Personnel
    g. The Parent as Teacher
    h. Working with Aides
    i. Homework
    j. Classroom Organization
    k. Parent Groups
    l. Schools of the Future
    m. Teacher Education

Class Requirements

1. Class attendance and participation
2. Written examination
3. A unit of instruction developed for parents to be taught in both home and school
4. A prospectus or plan of action for a school wishing to implement an effective home–school program.

Text: Education and The Family

This course is taught over a semester or approximately 15 weeks. Each week, material discussed is organized in such a manner as to elicit student involvement. One of the more popular activities is to have small-group presentations around one of the topics. Each group is held responsible for leading the discussion and supplying supplementary materials useful for the particular topic.

Speakers have been utilized as they are available. These outside sources have come from the health profession, schools, social agencies, government agencies, parent groups, and anywhere else expertise can be located.

The selection of the instructor for the course is of paramount importance. In addition to the normal criteria of scholarship, wit, and charm, that individual must understand the natural relationship that exists between home and school and be fully supportive of the concept. Someone who lectures right from the text is wrong for this experience. There is a large body of content to be covered and uncovered. Until this course of study is important enough to move out of a methods class, it must be taught by someone on a mission who can attract students ready to internalize and carry forth the message. Of course, this type of instructor should be available for all classes. However, until more people involved in the teacher preparation program are convinced that parents are indeed the primary instructors of their children, these type of classes will not be institutionalized. There is much work to be done.

Conclusion

A promising area of inquiry has examined the relationship between families and schools: to look at the pattern of communication, contact, and mutual support between school personnel and parents and to discover how they influence each other. The primary purpose of what has been termed the "family–school interaction" research is to assess how family–school interactions affect children's learning and school success. The assumption here is that the efforts of schools and families are linked, that they can either support and reinforce each other or they compete and undermine each other.

> *Education is an active process. It involves the active efforts of the learner himself. In general, the learner learns only those things which he does. If the school situations deal with matters of interest to the learner he will actively participate in them and thus learn to deal effectively with these situations. –RALPH TYLER*

SECTION FOUR

Response to the Prologue

Education is everyone's business. Few topics are discussed as openly and as passionately. Hardly a day goes by that an article in the paper, a new commission report, a political statement, or some other public response to the inequities of our school systems does not appear. Just the sheer weight of these comments is staggering.

The remarks of the parents presented in the Prologue represent a cross-section of views from some important people. Having responses to these colleagues from some major leaders—the developer of New Partner-ships/Megaskills and the presidents of the UAW, the National PTA, and the NEA—suggest that the parents are worthy of response and also gives evidence that our children clearly are this nation's major resource.

CHAPTER TWENTY-TWO

Mega Skills and New Partnerships for Student Achievement

DOROTHY RICH
in collaboration with
JAMES VAN DIEN

Editor's Note: The word *reform* is one of the most overused words in our vocabulary. Reform can range from what may happen after a revolution to a program change of the slightest magnitude. Discussion regarding education reform is common today. We seem to have generated as many reports as there are agencies and committees to prepare them.

It is clear that any change in our present method of educating children will be too slow for many. The demographics of poor achievement, dropouts, etcetera, described throughout this manuscript indicate that change is not only necessary; it is mandatory.

If change is to be meaningful, all concerned must work together. Schools cannot shoulder all of the responsibility of the change process. New coalitions must be established.

Children spend most of their time and get most of their education outside of school, yet the focus of most educational reform today has primarily concentrated on what happens at school. In contrast, the focus of the Home and School Institute's reform initiative concentrates on what happens at home, what parents can do to teach their children and to support their children's progress in school.

In 1989 the Home and School Institute was invited to take on a new challenge—to reach out beyond the home and the school to involve community organizations in helping families help their children learn. A three-year demonstration project entitled New Partnerships for Student Achievement (NPSA) was begun with funding from the MacArthur Foundation.

Question: How Did You Get Started?

New Partnerships, a large-scale program with large vision, really began as a small-scale program with large vision in 1964 in Arlington, Virginia. That's when the concept of the family role in children's education was translated for the first time by Dorothy Rich into classes for parents called Success for Children Begins at Home. That's when the home learning "recipe" was first developed and found to be remarkably effective.

To extend the impact of this effort to reach many more parents, teacher training programs begun in the early 1970s were entitled *School and Parent-Community Involvement.* These were followed by research projects in bilingual and in special education to document the impact of this school–home partnership model.

Throughout the 1970s and the 1980s, the Home and School Institute moved to widen the community circle to meet family educational needs. New Partnerships was the next logical step—to involve organizations and unions in sharing educational responsibilities with teachers and families for the education of the community's children.

New Partnerships was designed to demonstrate that a variety of community organizations with little or no previous experience with parental involvement in education, could work with families to enhance the educational role of parents. Five very different kinds of organizations—The Association for Library Service to Children of the American Library Association, The American Red Cross, The American Postal Workers Union, The National Association of Colored Women's Clubs, and Parents Without Partners—were initially selected for the program.

These organizations in turn selected demonstration sites where local chapters recruited families and worked with them using parental involvement programs and materials developed by the Home and School Institute. Sites ranged from Tampa, Florida to Denver, Colorado, from Tuscaloosa, Alabama to Chicago, Illinois. The families were extraordinarily diverse, from Hispanic migrants to middle-class library users, from teen parents to senior citizens. The American Postal Workers Union and Parents Without Partners, broad-based membership organizations, worked with families recruited from their local chapter memberships. The other three are service organizations and worked with families from local communities.

The ultimate goal of the program was to enable these organizations to institutionalize parental involvement in education as an ongoing service initiative of their organization. This goal has been achieved. How this happened is described in this chapter.

Because New Partnerships provides a plan for involving community organizations in the education reform movement, its working offers a useful blueprint, a map of what worked, and why.

Over 4,000 parents directly participated in the demonstration program. On the basis of documented reports from the organizations, tens of thousands of additional families also became more aware of the importance of the family in the educational process. The project has served as a rich laboratory for learning about community organizations, volunteerism, and parental involvement.

An intensive basic intervention model of approximately 10 weeks (sending home learning "recipes") was employed to ensure impact upon the participating families. In the first year, 176 families with 226 children participated in the program at the five demonstration sites. In the second year, each organization added a replication site, for a total of 10 local sites serving 401 families. Additional ways of serving families were also developed in Year II. These included a special early childhood activities program for younger children, reinforcement activities for participating families, and "MegaSkills" workshops for parents. This component, which proved to be the most replicable aspect of the program, is described later in the chapter.

The primary focus of the initial year was to make the project operational and to determine whether community organizations could effect outreach to families and work with them to enhance their educational role. In the second year, attention was given to the demonstration of impact. The participating families were interviewed in a pre- and post design to determine whether the program met expectations and how it affected attitudes and behaviors of participating parents and children. The Year II data confirmed the viability of the intervention as a parental involvement model. Among the major findings are:

- 75 percent of the families completed the voluntary participation program.
- 85 percent of the parents and 94 percent of the children reported that the program was a success for them.
- 54 percent reported better parent–child interaction.
- Parents and children also reported positive changes in such areas as school work, academic skills, and life/coping skills.

By the end of Year II, the effectiveness of the model both as a way for community organizations to involve families in education and as an intervention with positive outcomes for parents and children had been demonstrated. The Institute, invited three new organizations, which had expressed interest in the project and the work of the Institute, to become affiliate members of NPSA in the final year. These organizations were the Department of Defense Dependent Schools (DODDS), Extension 4-H, and the National Coalition of Title I/Chapter I parents.

Each of these organizations has special interest in working with families. The DODDS provides education to the children of members of the armed forces overseas and on military bases in the United States. Parental involvement and reinforcement of the family's educational role are especially important since these families are frequently transferred or may be separated while one parent is on special active duty. The National Coalition of Title I/ Chapter I Parents serves as an advisory council to ensure that parents are represented and actively involved in Chapter I programs. The Extension 4-H has a rich tradition and wide variety of activities for children and youth at various ages but less experience in reaching out to the families of 4-H Club members.

While these organizations comprised a wide range of organizational structure, operating style, resources, and levels of funding, all had one thing in common: They were national. However, the real point of contact with families for the delivery of program services is the grassroots, local chapter level. Local chapters enjoy considerable autonomy of operation, particularly in selecting and adopting activities for local implementation. Expansion and institutionalization of the program involved a great deal of internal promotion by the national organizations to create awareness and interest in the program and to recruit volunteers at the local chapter level.

Each organization was asked to develop and implement an institutionalization plan, selecting and adapting those New Partnerships program components that they could continue after the demonstration was completed.

Continuing the 10-week basic program was an option but not required, for it was recognized that shorter program interventions that would reach a larger number of families might better meet the needs and capabilities of some organizations.

The remainder of this chapter outlines findings from New Partnerships along with recommendations for taking advantage of these findings.

Key Findings

Four key insights and understandings evolved out of the project: the involvement of community organizations, volunteer commitment, parental involvement, and the MegaSkills workshops.

Involving Community Organizations to Foster Parental Involvement

Community organizations do have the capacity to reach out to and work with parents to enhance the educational role of the family. All of the five original participating organizations "stayed the course" over the three years, and the program was able to attract new affiliate organizations in its final year. Moreover, all of the core organizations succeeded to some degree in institutionalizing the program.

Schools have traditionally assumed the entire responsibility for parental involvement, usually as the "something extra" tacked on to already full agendas and job descriptions. Parental involvement has always been a seriously underfunded area of school activity, and today's shrinking budgets and expanding enrollments mean even fewer dollars for new and additional initiatives. New Partnerships demonstrates that schools do not have to carry the full burden. Community organizations represent a resource for reaching out to parents, a resource that schools need to learn how to tap.

Organizations with a large membership base of families who can directly benefit from NPSA services are apt to have more success since they can promote the program internally and recruit parents from their own memberships. Two other factors that contribute strongly to organizational success are: (1) the degree of commitment at the top and the ability to relate the program to the central mission of the organization and (2) the extent to which the organization networks with other organizations, agencies, and schools at the local community service-delivery level.

Volunteer Commitment

The delivery of NPSA programs to families rests ultimately on the strength of the volunteer effort at the local site level. Promoting the program, recruiting families, conducting program activities, and providing coordination and follow-up are time-consuming, labor-intensive activities. To reach out and work effectively with families, organizations need both a broad volunteer base at the local level and programs that distribute the work and the rewards among a number of volunteers.

Volunteers need roles that provide a high degree of inner satisfaction. While external recognition and rewards are important and should not be neglected, volunteering by its very nature depends largely on the intrinsic rewards and personal fulfillment derived from the service ethic.

Parental Involvement

In Year III, to increase the capacity of the organizations to deliver NPSA programs at the local level, HSI scheduled a series of *MegaSkills Leadership Training Institutes* across the country. Each organization was invited to send up to five volunteers to receive training in conducting MegaSkills Parent Workshops. This is the NPSA program component that the organizations were most interested in adopting.

MegaSkills Parent Workshops are a series of eight workshops designed to train parents how to develop their children's MegaSkills.® MegaSkills, formulated for the New Partnerships program, are the superbasics, the inner engines of learning, that make it possible for children and adults to learn basic skills and more. They are the values, attitudes, and behavior, more important today than ever before, that determine individual achievement. These superbasics, drawn from school report cards and job performance evaluations, are confidence, motivation, effort, responsibility, initiative, perseverance, caring, teamwork, common sense, and problem solving. They are our "never-ending report card."

Each workshop is built around one or more of the 10 identified MegaSkills and includes activities for the parent to do at home with the child. The at-home activities help to develop MegaSkills as well as reinforce study habits and basic skills learning.

In 1989 to mid-1990 the following data on the workshops was reported:

Voluntary Participation in Workshops
321 workshops have been conducted with an enrollment of 4,542 parents in 25 states.

Program Impact
72 percent of parents in pre- and post-surveys have reported positive changes in children's school performance. Changes most frequently mentioned: children more interested in school, have better attitudes, accept more responsibility for doing homework, enjoy school more, like reading better.

Parents reported working 39+ minutes per week per child with their children as a result of this program. This figure is double the amount of family time documented in the study *Time Allocation in American Households* (1981).

Program Feedback
99.8 percent of the parents said they enjoyed participating in the workshops. 98.3 percent said they learned new information. 99.7 percent said they will try to use what they have learned. Evidence from these reports indicates that parents, children, and teachers see positive effects from these

programs even after a short period of time. Children say parents spend more time with them. Teachers report more involvement with parents and better behavior of children in school. Plus — and this is a big plus — children report watching less television. They have something more valuable to do.

The MegaSkills Impact

School personnel have lamented for decades that parents are no longer available to attend meetings and workshops, citing the large increase in dual-career and single-parent families with mothers working outside the home. The success of the MegaSkills Parent Workshop Program challenges this conventional wisdom and raises intriguing questions as to the optimal form parental involvement should take. Parents clearly wanted and indicated they derived benefit from the sharing and support received through contact with other parents. The appeal to parents of the MegaSkills Parent Workshop Program appears to rest on the following attributes:

- MegaSkills focus on family process variables that almost all families are able to modify and control, rather than on academic skills building, where some parents feel inadequate to help their children.
- The workshops build upon parents' strengths and needs; they are perceived as addressing the parents' own agenda of concerns, not just the agenda of the schools.
- The workshop format is built around discussion, role playing, and modeling. Parents are asked to reflect upon both their own upbringing and how they are bringing up their children. This provides an immediate experience base to which everyone can relate and share and helps to explain the universal appeal of the program across the socioeconomic spectrum.
- The workshop leadership role is facilitative and peer-oriented rather than didactic. This encourages parents to "open up" and helps to bridge educational and cultural barriers within the group. Parents gain the support of other parents.
- The workshops can be conducted effectively by ordinary folks, non-professionals as well as professionals.
- The program provides concrete follow-up through skill-building activities that parents can take home and do with their children.
- Parents can derive benefit from a manageable number of meetings. The MetaSkills workshops are more than a one-shot activity but do not require the kind of extended participation that, in volunteer programs, almost invariably entails a high dropout rate.

- The program is heuristic. The understandings and life/coping skills developed can continue to be applied and transferred after direct participation in the program ends.

The success of the MegaSkills Workshop Program is attributable not only to its appeal to parents but also to the degree to which it provides volunteers with a very visible and personally rewarding leadership role. Whereas the duties of basic program coordination is largely administrative, requiring a great deal of paperwork and record keeping, the MetaSkills Parent Workshop Program places the volunteer leader in a very direct and strong personal relationship with parents, providing immediate feedback and recognition of the leadership role.

In retrospect, one of the limitations of the NPSA basic programs that hindered widespread replication was that they placed too heavy a burden on one person, the local coordinator, while the other volunteer roles needed for program implementation remained less fully defined and developed. The MegaSkills program can easily be expanded to reach more families by training additional volunteers to provide the parenting workshops.

Question: Where Is This Program Now?

The goal of New Partnerships was to "institutionalize" these efforts into the service portfolios of these diverse organizations. This is the ultimate accolade that can be paid to any program.

Based on this criterion, New Partnerships is a major success. Every participating organization is now training leaders for the MegaSkills Workshops Program. For example, Parents Without Partners (PWP) offers the MegaSkills program to members at its local regional and national conferences. The by-laws of PWP have been altered to reflect this new educational initiative. The American Postal Workers Union is not only continuing New Partnerships within its own union but also reaching out with information and materials about the program to other unions nationally.

It is a credit to these groups that not only have they participated in a research demonstration, but now they are the demonstrators and the beacons for other organizations throughout the nation.

Expanding New Partnerships: Implications for Schools and Businesses

The New Partnerships/MegaSkills model is a program that can be used by businesses in support of education. An example is *Learning Is Homegrown* sponsored by the First Tennessee Bank in Memphis, Tennessee.

Learning Is Homegrown

The Home and School Institute provided training, programs, and materials for this Memphis initiative, developed in large part from New Partnerships. The First Tennessee program (1989–1990) was a response to goals of the Memphis schools to prevent dropouts and to have third-graders performing on grade level in reading and math by 1991. The bank worked with the Parenting Coalition, a network of local organizations to support these goals. These organizations—civic associations, church groups, PTAs and the other school-based organizations, Women Clubs, etcetera—provided the corps of volunteers trained to give MegaSkills workshops for parents.

The First Tennessee Bank provided the seed money for the training and materials as well as overall coordination for the project. The *Memphis Commercial Appeal,* the leading local newspaper, ran home-learning activities in its columns for 40 consecutive days at the outset of the program to provide direct outreach to parents and to stimulate awareness of and interest in the workshop program. The Parenting Coalition and other community organizations in turn scheduled the workshops, arranged for logistical support, and conducted the program. The school system endorsed the program, helped the Parenting Coalition to promote it and recruit parents, and made its facilities available for giving the workshops. A major local food chain provided door prizes as incentives for workshop participation. The Rotary Club raised money for lunches and refreshments at workshop sessions.

The College of Education of Memphis State University agreed to conduct an evaluation of the project. The volunteer workshop leaders were very enthusiastic and recommended program continuation. In its first year the workshop program reached at least 950 families. Workshop leaders estimate that at least half of these families attended several workshops in the series. Program feedback from parents, as reported by the volunteer workshop leaders, was uniformly positive.

The Memphis initiative provides a strong demonstration of how community organizations working in a concerted, coordinated effort can help a school system expand its outreach to parents and involve them in activities that enhance their educational role and reinforce the work of the schools.

The Memphis program illustrates a key principle demonstrated throughout the NPSA program: The capacity of community organizations to reach out and work with parents is considerably strengthened when they network and cooperate with other community organizations and agencies. This networking not only serves to promote the program and recruit families but also helps to enlarge the scope and recognition of volunteer service. Almost all the organizations in one way or another reached back to the schools in the local communities being served. Working with schools served not only to promote the program and recruit parents but also helped to legitimize the program in parents' eyes as valid, significant parental involvement. Working with other community-based organizations and enlisting the support of the local media also increased the organizations' capacity for outreach.

The Learning City® Approach

Drawing upon the NPSA experience base and as an outgrowth of the project, the Home and School Institute has developed the Learning City® plan as a comprehensive community-based approach for building support and involvement with the schools. Learning City creates a network of special partners, representing local government, business, community organizations and agencies, and the volunteer sector, who work in a concerted, coordinated effort with the schools fostering parental involvement and support for education. While families with school-age children are the special focus of attention, Learning City starts with the premise that education is everybody's business and that everyone can play a supportive role. It creates complementary, mutually reinforcing roles for different kinds of organizations, capable of reaching citizens in all walks of life: volunteer opportunities for senior citizen organizations; home learning activities appropriate for distribution to customers in banks, supermarkets, gas stations, and the like; opportunities for businesses to provide in-kind goods and services; mentoring opportunities for local chapters of professional organizations, etcetera.

Broad-based, comprehensive community involvement is especially important since many parts of the country are now experiencing the demographic phenomena of both a "baby boomlet" requiring expansion of school services after many years of declining enrollment and a "graying" of the population so that larger segments of the community than ever before have no direct stake or contact with the schools.

The Learning City design adapts and utilizes many of the elements developed for the NPSA programs: home learning activities, MegaSkills workshops, MegaSkills leadership training, training and guidance for coordinators and other volunteers, local awareness media campaigns, strategies for program promotion and recruitment, evaluation techniques, and feedback forms. Conducting a community needs assessment is the initial step in the Learning City process so the community can both identify needs and problems and build upon strengths and programs already in place.

On the one hand, Learning City provides program infrastructure for the immediate, direct, hands-on involvement of many different kinds of community groups and organizations; on the other, its networking, cooperative approach builds the capacity of the community to deal effectively with educational issues and problems. As its name suggests, Learning City represents a new strategy, based on New Partnerships, to translate into reality the

the vision of an entire community working together to support and improve education.

The Message and the Legacy of the New Partnerships

- The same basic program worked in the same basic way with diverse populations in very different parts of the country. Conventional wisdom, especially in education, has emphasized different local programs for local needs.
- Parents across socioeconomic lines appear to need support from other parents perhaps more than ever before and are willing to come to meetings and to invest serious time in learning how to help themselves and how to work with their children.
- Today parents and teachers need broad-based help in working with children. Even young children no longer live in the small world bounded by the living room and the classroom. They live in a large world confronting the chaos and dangers of AIDS, drugs, violence. With so much coming at them so fast, so soon, it takes a collaborative effort to keep children productively focused and educationally involved.
- Today's children need new kinds of basic skills. The literacy problem today is not that our children don't learn how to read. Recent research on Chapter I programs indicates that most children do learn the basics of reading and math in the early grades. What happens is that many children do not keep on reading and wanting to learn more.
- If ever there was a need for literacy, it's today. But what is needed is not just traditional literacy—but a literacy for learning in the century ahead.

The comments from people involved in the program echo the "message" of New Partnerships:

What People Are Saying about the New Partnerships/MegaSkills Curriculum

- *From Brooklyn:* After doing the first activity with her daughter a parent called: "I just had to tell you. I didn't really believe doing these activities would make much difference. The other day my neighbor walked in and saw us doing an activity, laughing and talking together like she had never seen. That was different! But the big surprise was the next morning. It was not the chip on the shoulder daughter I'm used to who came into the kitchen, but someone who gave me a friendly good morning and some nice talk. It's wonderful, and we're going to continue."

- *From Geneva, NY:* A 15-year-old became the "parent" when his mother was unable to do the activities with her 9-year-old son. When asked why he became involved, the teenager said, "I wanted to do this for my brother!"

- *From Washington, DC:* A father called to say that his family would not be able to participate because his wife had not done the activities and wasn't finding time. "What about you?" asked the coordinator. The father was hesitant. But a few weeks later he called; "I started the activities with my child; now we are all doing them together. We didn't realize how much fun it would be."

- *From Chicago:* A mother told how excited she is about the changes in her relationship with her 9-year-old daughter as a result of the program. "I have become more observant about what's going on with her. We look at things together. And I'm helping her take on more responsibility. Before, I didn't give her the chance. When we cook I say: You do it, try it for yourself. I never did this before."

- "Our kids are watching the news on TV before I get home," reports one mother. "At dinner, they tell me what's going on. They're more interested in national events since we've done the program activities. They no longer see TV just as entertainment."

- *From Tampa:* Migrant families were targeted for program services by the American Red Cross. At the year-end awards, more than 100 parents, children, volunteers, and aides took part. The children made all the table decorations. Parents said: "This is the most wonderful thing we have ever seen!"

- *From Dahlgren, VA:* I'm seeing that my parenting skills match other parents, GADS! I'm doing something right!"

- It's not so much that I learned new information but that I've learned better what to apply, what I know and feel and think—even for myself not just my child."

For more information:

The Home and School Institute
Special Projects
1201 16th St. N.W.
Washington, DC 20036
PH: 202-466-3633

At the desk where I sit, I have learned one great truth—the answer for all national problems. The answer for all the problems of the world comes down to a single word. That word is "education."
                                                    —LYNDON BAINES JOHNSON

CHAPTER TWENTY-THREE

Labor and the Schools: Forging a Working Relationship

OWEN F. BIEBER

Editor's Note: The economy of the country is a topic always of interest. How much we bring home in our paychecks and what these dollars will purchase plays heavily in how we live our lives. The love of money may be the "root of all evil," but it is safe to say that living "the good life" is something each of us wants for ourselves and for our families.

The organized labor movement is sometimes accused of being only concerned with economic issues for its membership at the expense of larger issues, issues that affect the overall welfare of society. Certainly the president of one of the most important trade unions in the world is in a unique position to comment on how unions in general and the UAW specifically are committed to improving the overall life of its members and their families and by doing so making a dramatic difference in the continued development of our society. Labor is involved. This chapter is a progress report.

Preparing teachers for their role in the classroom ranks as one of the most important functions in American life. It is a special privilege for me as a trade unionist to have this opportunity to contribute to so vital a process. It is an opportunity, unfortunately, that trade unionists rarely get.

In recent years, business leaders and government officials have been shocked to discover what the labor movement has known for a long time: The U.S. education system has been let down by the political leadership of this country. Since teachers are the target readership of this volume, it is not necessary to recount in detail the dismal education statistics of the Reagan-Bush years. It suffices to say that U.S. spending on pre-primary, primary, and secondary education (K–12) as a percentage of gross domestic product ranks among the lowest of any industrialized nation. The chart in Figure 23-1, (Rasell and Mishel 1990), based on a recent report of the Economic Policy Institute, gives details.

While there has been growing lip-service about the need for educational reform, to date, resources and actions have lagged far behind. Despite his soothing rhetoric about wanting to be the "Education President," George Bush is heir to a Republican administration that has continued to cut billions of dollars out of programs to educate Americans over the past 10 years.

It is the children of working people and especially of poor people who have been shortchanged the most. As the recent widely acclaimed report, *America's Choice: High Skills or Low Wages* (Commission on the Skills of

FIGURE 23-1 • *Eduction Spending (K–12) as a Percent of Gross Domestic Product**

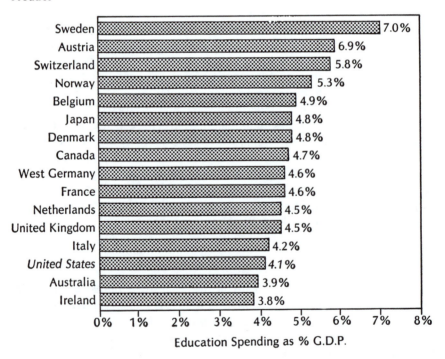

Education Spending as % G.D.P.

Source: Economic Policy Institute.

*Adjusted for differences in enrollment between countries.

the American Workforce 1990) makes clear, the United States has the world's best universities but neglects shamefully the education of youths who are not college bound. For these millions of young people, we manage the transition from school to work less successfully than perhaps any other industrial nation, gravely damaging their life chances in the process and condemning many to a career of unemployment or low-wage drudgery. The contrast with our toughest international competitors such as Germany and Japan, who place high priority on educating the noncollege bound, could not be more stark.

For poor youngsters the situation is even worse. Reduced federal expenditures for public education, diminished funding for compensatory programs, and the declining local tax base of the poorest districts have led to a deterioration of the essential infrastructure in most inner-city schools. The gulf between per-pupil spending in the richest and poorest districts is the widest it has been in 20 years.

The emphasis on tougher tests and higher standards for graduation while cutting funds for early education programs has worsened the position of children from low-income families. Tougher tests at graduation, without enhanced and solid educational programs in the previous 12 years, function only as a punitive attack on those we have shortchanged over time.

"Excellence" has become a catch word for inequality and a cynical attempt to rationalize injustice by identifying a few impressive schools and creating our dual system of education—a dual system that perpetuates economic segregation must be considered as serious and be fought with the same fervor as racial segregation.

Labor's Role in the Schools

A healthy democracy and a strong economy demand a well-educated, informed citizenry. International competition and changing technology require an educated work force that has had access to quality public schools.

In building a quality education system, the role of organized labor is essential. Most students learn little or nothing about organized labor and its contributions to the development of this country. They do not understand that labor is a rich part of our heritage and a significant dynamic institution within our society. Of even greater importance is how organized labor will affect their future—what they choose to do in life, where they work, and the conditions of that employment. Unless young people understand more about organized labor and its function in society, their future role as citizen-voters and workers will be diminished and the community will be weakened. Current curricula in elementary and secondary schools pay scant attention to the trade union movement and its contributions to workers and American society.

It is vitally important, for example, for young people to know that the quality of life and the standard of living is better for *all* of society when unions are strong than when they are not. This fact is illustrated by comparing some states that have laws restricting the strength of unions (so-called "right-to-work" laws) with other states that do not have such laws. Wages and per-capita personal income are higher while unemployment rates and workplace fatalities are lower in the 29 states that allow unions to engage in free collective bargaining than they are in the 21 states that restrict unions by means of such laws. Furthermore, right-to-work states rely far more heavily on regressive sales taxes that hit hardest on those with lowest incomes than do the free collective bargaining states.

International comparisons convey a similar point. As Table 23-1 shows, in countries where unions are strong, unemployment is lower, income is distributed more fairly across the total population, and government spending on social programs is higher than in countries where unions are weak. Yet how many of our youngsters are being taught these important facts?

Meanwhile, there is a growing danger that our school children will be even more influenced than in the past by the private business world's view

TABLE 23-1 • Unions and Economic Policy

	Countries with Strong Union Influence*	Countries with Moderate Union Influence†	Countries with Small Union Influence‡
Average un- employment 1973–1986	4.4	6.0	7.1
Share of income received by the richest 20% of population 1985	38	40	41
Government social expenditure as percent of gross domestic product 1985	29.5	23.6	22.1

Source: OECD, World Bank.

*Countries with strong union influence: Sweden, Norway, Austria, Denmark, Belgium, and Finland.

†Countries with moderate union influence: Netherlands, West Germany, Britain, Ireland, Australia, and Switzerland.

‡Countries with small union influence: Italy, Canada, United States, Japan, France, and Spain.

of society. As revenues decline, more school districts are turning to private corporations for school curriculum materials. Because of their origins, such materials can reflect, even subtly, an anti-labor viewpoint. Trade unionists must, therefore, work to guard against that danger in two ways—by supporting adequate public funding so that schools can produce or obtain their own curriculum materials untainted by business propaganda and by providing alternatives, like the UAW's "Labor Bookshelf," to the public schools so that students will have access to another point of view.

Because we know that good schools depend on good teachers, we support fair compensation and democratic rights for public school employees. Teachers, like other workers, should be guaranteed the right to collectively bargain and, when necessary, the right to strike.

Breaking New Ground

Beyond assisting educators in teaching young people about the history and role of unions, the labor movement is a valuable and largely untapped resource for developing and enriching school curricula at all levels. The following highlights some of the best programs the labor movement has to offer to educators.

When many teachers think of bringing the labor movement into the classroom, all too often they want to tack labor onto an existing project. Usually it is up to the social studies teacher to do a labor history unit. In reality, the labor movement is a far broader resource for innovative curriculum development. The experience of the labor movement around the world is one of the richest human experiences available for drawing lessons for the classroom.

Integrating labor issues into the classroom is best achieved through partnerships. Trade unions have a responsibility to make themselves a part of the educational process, and educators need to be open to the role of unions and labor issues. This partnership requires effort on both sides. Not every union local will be an effective participant in educational projects. Nor is every educator receptive to partnership with labor in the classroom.

We know from experience that partnership between educators and labor can be difficult to establish and maintain. Our union recently engaged in an existing renewal of our vision called the Commission on the Future of the UAW. In meetings with rank and file members and local union leaders around the country, we heard time and again from trade unionists who had offered to talk with students in local classrooms but were denied the opportunity by school administrators. It is disheartening when labor is denied even this minimal role in the schools. The kind of partnership that is needed goes well beyond occasional show-and-tell by union members.

Some "Best Practice" Examples

Although it is undeniable that some unions will not be as responsive as they could be to opportunities from educators, it is also true that the labor movement offers outstanding examples of innovative commitments to education. There was a time when teachers who were interested in integrating labor into their teaching would have had trouble finding materials or people to help. Those days are long gone. The following examples are just a few of the many cases of positive, mutually beneficial engagements between the labor movement and educators.

The American Postal Workers Union

The Postal Workers are engaged in a pathbreaking effort through the Home and School Institute in Washington, DC (see Chapter 22). Their effort is a unique parent effectiveness training system focusing on critical learning skills for children. Working parents are taught "recipes" they can use to improve the learning abilities of their children. The effort was first tried in Denver and is now being replicated in Atlanta. In this effort the union acts as a conduit for service delivery, linking the home, workplace, and school.

The International Brotherhood of Teamsters

For three summers from 1986 to 1988 the Teamsters sponsored two-week summer curriculum development scholarships for prekindergarten through high school teachers. Each of those summers the Teamsters paid for tuition, room, board, and books for about 125 teachers to receive three accredited graduate school credits each. The programs were held at Cornell, Wisconsin and Berkeley, California, and all a teacher had to do to attend was write to the Teamsters for information. The courses were not, incidentally, specifically about the Teamsters. They were general courses about teaching labor studies.

New York State AFL-CIO

Paul Cole, Secretary-Treasurer of the New York State AFL-CIO, is also an American Federation of Teachers member. Under Cole's direction, New York State recently sponsored the publication of *The Working Teenager,* a reader and workbook dealing with issues around child labor. The document and curriculum guides were a response to abuses of teenage labor in the state. The document was assembled by the Labor Legacy Committee, which has also worked on a seventh- and eighth-grade unit on the history of child labor around the world. Unions around the state are also sponsoring Adopt-A-School programs.

The George Meany Memorial Archives

The AFL-CIO Archives' publication *Labor's Heritage* is one of the finest labor history publications available. It is well written and filled with beautiful photographs. Stuart Kaufman, editor of *Labor's Heritage,* recently began publication of two curriculum guides per year to accompany particular articles from the magazine. Each guide is produced with input from teacher consultants. The guides take different forms and target specific age groups.

The AFL-CIO Department of Education

The AFL-CIO booklet "Labor in the Schools: How to Do It!" gives extensive references for books, films, and curriculum development. The booklet also provides sample lesson plans. Their publication "How Schools Are Teaching about Labor" is a collection of guidelines and lesson plans. The Education Department has also provided "Labor in the Schools" workshops in several states and the District of Columbia.

The UAW

The UAW has an extensive history of successfully bargaining for training and educational assistance for our members. Our approach to elementary and secondary education involves two levels of engagement. At one level, through our Community Action Program (CAP), we try to have a positive influence on education policy, to broaden access and distribute educational funding more equitably. At a second level, closer to the grassroots, we sponsor Adopt-A-School programs, speakers' bureaus, and a free "Labor Bookshelf" assortment of books for school libraries. The UAW has initiated a high school labor studies program to provide both students and teachers more information about the world of work. The program stresses labor's role in the struggle for economic and social justice and explores workers' obligations in the workplace. A number of high schools include this program in their curriculum.

Through the UAW's Adopt-A-School program, the Labor Bookshelf program, and "This Union Cause" program, local unions and CAP Councils can provide schools with an array of educational materials. These resources — which include speakers, films, video cassette tapes, and books — help students develop an understanding of the role and purpose of unions.

The UAW also has a remarkable Family Education Center at Black Lake, Michigan. The Center opened in 1970 to fulfill the mandate of Walter Reuther: "We have to find a way to get the workers and the family together so we cannot only educate the worker to leadership, but raise the level of understanding of the spouse and give youngsters some understanding of the spouse and give youngsters some understanding about what the labor movement is all about."

Today the Center is the site of an array of UAW educational programs for thousands of UAW members, their spouses, and their children. In addition, the Walter and May Reuther Memorial Fund has made scholarships available to college students, high school teachers, and college and university instructors and administrators, so they can participate in two-week scholarship programs.

Drawing Connections: Labor in the Classroom

These fine examples of labor movement activity around education share some common themes. First, the programs always encourage *debate* in the classroom. They are not intended to indoctrinate students or present some sort of union "line." The labor movement is presented "warts and all," and students draw their own conclusions.

Second, it is clear that the best links between the labor movement and education are links that go beyond including a history unit in a social studies class. The best links make deep connections and are inspired by sustained cooperation.

Cooperation is a daily part of the trade union experience. The labor movement is, first and foremost, a movement based on the concept of solidarity: shared experience, working together. This fundamental basis for labor's struggle represents a valuable moral contribution to the classroom: team work and cooperation. The core values of the labor movement and the basis for excellence in the classroom are strikingly similar. Labor studies drive home the unavoidable lesson that cooperation among workers is the key to their prosperity—a valuable image for today's youth who are so often fighting among themselves.

Partnership should mean more than simply building rapport between individual teachers and particular trade unions. Figure 23-2 gives a sense of the complexity of the linkages. Teachers and parents form a partnership for education directly and through parent-teacher organizations of various kinds. Teachers and trade unions interact in curriculum development and, quite directly, when teachers have union representation. These partnerships almost always exist, but they are rarely developed into strong working relationships.

Trade unions can play a key role in forging partnerships out of mere connections. Trade unions are part of the fabric of democracy. They provide a source for mediating disputes, resolving conflict, and giving a voice to millions of people who might not otherwise be heard. Trade union members with children in school are simultaneously workers, union members, and taxpayers. Their experience as union members and their contract with so many education-related institutions make them particularly able participants in partnerships for education.

FIGURE 23-2 • *Partnerships for Education*

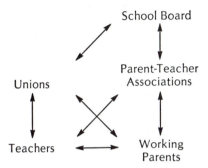

The trade union experience facilitates partnerships in a broader way as well. The UAW has a special view, shared by some other unions, of the role of trade unions in the lives of working people. When the UAW built its Black Lake educational facility in northern Michigan, our union was making a clear statement that trade union business does not end when the whistle blows on a worker's shift. Trade unions at their best are an integral part of workers' lives. Thus, the UAW has a Community Services Program that works, in part, with children. We represent current members, and we have extensive programs for retirees. In other words, we believe trade unionism needs to be a social movement, a source of inspiration throughout the life of a worker and his or her children. Again, the relationship is a partnership, like the relationship between parents and schools. The emphasis is not only on providing services, but also on working together to develop programs. This broader perspective means that union members grow accustomed to making connections between their home life and their workplace. They also learn to be effective participants in group efforts. Such perspectives make them excellent partners in the education process.

This chapter began with a challenge to educators to link the labor movement to the curriculum at all levels. This may have sounded unrealistic to many readers. But the information in Table 23-2 should provide some food for thought. The examples listed were the result of some brief brainstorming. These examples should not be seen as extra work. Today's teachers have enough to do already! The process being described, infusing labor into the education process, can actually be less work than the usual "tack-labor-on-somewhere" strategy of curriculum development. Building linkages between classroom subjects and the labor movement needs to become an ongoing and continual part of the teaching routine.

TABLE 23-2 • *Linking the Labor Movement to Curricula*

Subject	Projects	Insights
Art	Murals WPA projects	The social basis of art Biographies of artists
Language Arts or English	Vocabulary building Labor-oriented novels Current event essays	Language and reading as exciting, relevant pursuits
Social Studies	World of work Labor history Labor studies	Labor movement as a living experience. History is everyday life, not just famous people
Foreign Languages	Comparative labor studies Vocabulary	Illustrates the different cultural experiences of work
Music	Protest songs Labor songs	History of music as a force in people's lives. Link between lyrics and social setting
Shop Classes or Industrial Arts	Visits by skilled trades workers and engineers	Link coursework and experience of actual jobs. Stress importance of training
Math	Contract costing Economics	Applications of math

Toward the Future

Recent evidence suggests that the United States is in real danger of having a permanent two-tiered educational system. The graph in Figure 23-3 shows how different the educational prospects are for children depending on the economic status of their parents. In the graph, "socioeconomic status" is determined by parental education, family income, father's occupation, and household characteristics in 1980.

This alarming polarization of educational outcomes has been getting worse. The fraction of high school seniors who had achieved a bachelor's degree six years after high school fell for all socioeconomic groups between 1978 and 1986, but the rate fell faster for lower socioeconomic groups.

Children of poor and working parents are being denied the opportunities that they need to make economic progress. Over time, the bias against these children, and their lack of awareness of the importance of organized labor combine to stratify society. Trade unions are a critical source of economic

FIGURE 23-3 • *Highest Educational Attainment of 1980 High School Seniors, 1986*

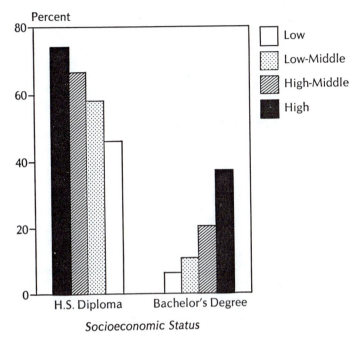

Source: U.S. Department of Education.

progress for students who do not go on to college. young people need to know about them in order to make informed choices during their working lives.

The 1980s were difficult both for American workers and for schools. It is a hopeful development that the business community is waking up to the decline of the U.S. education system, but their voice should not be the only one that is heard. As we develop new educational programs and institutions, it is crucial that the labor movement be a full partner in change. Today's labor movement is better equipped than ever before to be a partner in the challenge of linking the school and the workplace. Few institutions in our society have a greater stake in the need for better schools or greater untapped resources in the energy and talent of our members that can be harnessed to help achieve this vital goal.

> *The future is not an endless road we are condemned to follow.*
> *It is a fan-shaped array of alternative possibilities.*
> *It is essential to remember that we create the future. —HAROLD SHANE*

CHAPTER TWENTY-FOUR

The Importance of Parental Involvement

ANN LYNCH

Editor's Note: Parents are not the enemy. They care; they are concerned. It is the responsibility of the school to aggressively seek their cooperation, support, and commitment. Educators must not assume that parents will support any effort of the school. Teachers are adult educators and parent advocates as much as they are the intellectual mentors of our youth.

Education is far too important to be left solely to professional educators. It is imperative that educators provide the framework for parental participation in the educational process so that more parents can avail themselves of this opportunity. The attitude that education should be the responsibility of professional educators is being replaced with the recognition that professionals can be more effective when supported by informed parents.

To promote positive parental involvement in education, educators must remove existing barriers, which can be easily overlooked but tend to keep parents away. Some educators may unknowingly be sabotaging their own efforts. For example, many schools post signs at their doors: "All visitors must register in the office." Although this serves to protect students and staff from intruders, some parents may view this as an "unwelcome" sign. A simple change of language can set a more positive tone for parents, such as "Welcome to our school. Please register in the office." Always try to maintain an open-door policy with parents.

Educators should also encourage and support the organization of parent groups such as the PTA and invite parent volunteers into the classroom participation in other school activities. One way of doing this is to offer many school activities that involve students, parents, and educators together, such as reading enrichment programs, sports events, and recognition ceremonies to honor student achievement. Evaluate what you offer now; then talk to students, parents, and the PTA for suggestions about new activities and improving current ones.

Consider also the needs of illiterate or non–English-speaking parents. Their children are among those most at risk of failing in school. Give extra attention to reaching and involving these parents. If they are not responding to correspondence (not showing up at parent-teacher conferences or returning phone calls), find out why. Some parents may be intimidated because they had bad school experiences or are themselves dropouts.

Let parents know that it is helpful to be involved 20 minutes a day if that is all the time they have to give to their child. Parents should be encouraged to read to their children during this time or help them with homework. Ask parents to look over and sign and date homework assignments.

Always continue to seek ways to strengthen and promote the parent-child–teacher relationship. When evaluating students, include comments that help the students and parents better understand the evaluation. Communicate often and openly with parents by requesting conferences or taking time to telephone parents to update them on their children's progress. Also, remind parents that it is okay for them to call you, and let them know the best time to call. To accommodate working parents, try scheduling conferences and meetings during after-work hours.

It is important for schools to provide a wide variety of ways to involve parents in activities with their children. Teachers should always have examples of children's work to show parents when they visit. Send notes home when a student has done something special—parents love to receive good news. Parental involvement may be increased by sending home special exercises to be completed by the students with the help of their parents. Also, be sure to listen to both students and parents, and take the time to get to know each child.

It is important for parents and educators to work together to build each child's self-esteem. A child with a high IQ but low self-esteem may do poorly in school, while a child with average intelligence but high self-esteem may excel.

Involve working parents by asking them to assist in organizing a schoolwide career day, or by arranging a field trip to their workplace (if appropriate), or by inviting them into the classroom to talk about their career.

To facilitate further parental involvement, try setting up at least one session for parents in which an overview of classes and school goals is presented. Consider having the students present for the meeting. Outline expectations and responsibilities: yours, the parents', and the students'. Each might then sign an agreement to adhere to what has been discussed. Ask parents what their family goals are for their children. There's a good probability those goals are the same as your goals for the children. Be prepared to answer how goals are being met by the class and school curriculum. Send home a monthly calendar of plans and goals for each school day or week and overviews of topics to be studied, accompanied by a one-page newsletter indicating how parents might complement the lessons at home.

The National PTA applauds educators' ongoing efforts and hopes that together we can all lead our children to a brighter future. Remember that parents and teachers need each other and children and youth need both—more today than ever before.

A child miseducated is a child lost. —*JOHN F. KENNEDY*

CHAPTER TWENTY-FIVE

Health, Education, Welfare: America's Families and America's Priorities

KEITH GEIGER

Editor's Note: The organizations striving to generate a culture of cooperation between parents and teachers—and to break down the walls of mistrust
and misunderstanding that too often separate them—stand on the cutting edge
of the education reform movement. These organizations include the National
PTA, the National Community Education Association, the National Committee
for Citizens inEducation, the Home-School Institute, the National Coalition
for Parental Involvement in Education, and the National Education Association.

The common thread that unites these organizations is their recognition
of the reservoir of goodwill and good sense that flourishes at the grassroots
level of American society. These organizations demonstrate—in word and
deed—their belief in democracy in America. They give meaning to the phrase
parental empowerment. And they give substance to the most fundamental
and the most forgotten message of the 1983 *A Nation at Risk* report—the
message that "our schools can rise no higher than the communities that support them."

Families under Siege

The evidence is now both abundant and incontrovertible: Closer ties between
home and school, between parents and educators, translate into improved
attendance, higher academic achievement, and accelerated social adaptation.

What this means, in more pragmatic terms, is less apathy, less violence, less despair, fewer drugs, fewer pregnancies, fewer dropouts. It means more learning. It means better education.

The agenda for parental involvement reflects the insight that the real forces for educational excellence do not reside in district offices or state houses or even the White House. No, the real forces for substantive change are found in our local communities, in America's families, in the visions of so-called ordinary men and women who display extraordinary devotion to their children—and to the America of tomorrow.

These are the first teachers of the children who later enter our classrooms. These are our most valuable allies.

Today, these allies are under siege. America's families are under siege. And we must come to their aid. For if we, America's educators, are to be effective advocates for children, we must first be effective advocates for parents. We must march to the forefront of the pro-family movement. We must reclaim this territory from all those whose restrictive definition of the term *family* is derived from watching reruns of "Ozzie and Harriet" and "Leave It to Beaver."

Our mission is to reach out to all those who are the care givers for America's children. The single parent, the noncustodial parent, the adoptive parent, the separated or divorced parent, the homeless parent—these people, too, must become full members of a new and dynamic network of collaboration between families and schools.

We must also recognize that the potential inherent in this comprehensive network of collaboration will never be fully realized until we reverse the social and economic policies that today brutalize far too many families. It falls to us to rekindle the understanding that family life is sacred. At every level of American society, we must insist on policies that demonstrate an abiding respect for America's families. And that means we must take our case to corporate America—and to America's government.

America's Families and Corporate Priorities

Corporate America now embraces without reservation the tenet that America's success or failure in the global marketplace depends above all else on success or failure in the local schoolhouse. As this understanding has taken hold, America's businesses have become determined to do their part to help us meet the challenges facing our schools. The CEOs of America's most powerful corporations can now be counted among teachers' most vocal allies. And this support goes beyond words: Business is now in the business of helping schools.

Is this new attitude making a difference? No doubt about it. Does this pro-education consensus need further refinement? That's equally beyond doubt. For it is not at all clear that corporate America yet understands that a pro-education agenda demands a pro-family agenda.

Former Primerica CEO William Woodside made this point, at least indirectly, more than four years ago. Woodside noted that business–school partnerships—adopt-a-school programs, for example—had made a positive difference. But, he added, they have not made enough of a difference—and probably never will. Woodside then expressed his conviction that corporations need to shift their focus to the political arena.

"Many of us," said Woodside, "have vigorously supported school-business partnerships. But have we been as vigorous in opposing public policy decisions we knew would harm schools? Have we backed our words with deeds that could help generate the broader political and public policy support our schools so desperately need?"

There's the pivotal question. Our business leaders, I submit, ought to give that question more thought.

This is not to suggest that corporate America should abandon the principle of self-interest. But it is to insist that businesses need to rethink the issue of precisely what, in the long run, best serves their self-interest.

- Is it not in the self-interest of the corporate community to be our active allies when we seek shared decision-making arrangements that unite parents and educators in common cause?
- Is it not in the self-interest of corporate America to adopt policies—flex time, for example—that facilitate parental involvement in the education of their children?
- Is it not in the self-interest of corporate America to stand with parents and with educators when we petition Congress to reauthorize the Vocational Education Act, the Education for All Handicapped Children Act, and the new child care bills now pending in the U.S. House and Senate?
- Finally, should not corporate America have been the most active lobbyist for passage of the Family and Medical Leave Act that President Bush vetoed last year? This was the chance for corporate America to support schools by supporting families. This was a chance missed.

My point is this: We cannot expect the parental involvement that is essential to improved education unless and until employers demonstrate real and meaningful respect for parenting—and for parents. If corporate America expects today's children to take their places as tomorrow's productive workers, that respect must be translated into policies that reflect appreciation for the unprecedented challenges confronting today's families.

America's Families, America's Economy, and the Principle of Self-Interest Rightly Understood

It was Alexis de Toqueville, writing in 1832, who commended Americans, particularly our entrepreneurs, for their mastery of "the principle of self-interest rightly understood."

Today's entrepreneurs need to regain this mastery—then pass it on. And they're ideally positioned to do exactly that. They have the clout. They have the influence. Perhaps only they can make the case—and make it stick—that the family is not only the foundation of our democracy, but the foundation of our economy.

What a remarkable contribution to the life of our republic this would be. For in the long run, the United States may face no greater challenge than the challenge of ending the inequities that are making a shambles of American family life.

We cannot continue to ask parents to choose between caring for their children and caring for their job security. That either/or quandary guarantees a guilt trip no one deserves to take. Anyone who has ever raised a child knows that parenting may begin, but in no way ends, with putting bread on the table. But today, too often, this is exactly where it ends. And in that there is a terrible sadness. The mother or father who misses Susie's performance as a tree in the school play or who isn't there at the exact moment when a word of encouragement or maybe a hug could mean so much soon learns how easily such actions break the heart.

Sylvia Ann Hewlett makes this point in more analytical terms. In *When the Bough Breaks: The Cost of Neglecting Our Children,* Hewlett exposes the social dynamic eating away at the core of American family life. Hewlett's argument is not complex. The bottom line, she says, is this: In the scramble that has single mothers working two or even three jobs, that has mothers and fathers in traditional families spending longer and longer days at the workplace, the absentee parent has become the norm. The time parents spend with their children is dwindling. In fact, over the past quarter century, the total contact time between parents and children has dropped by a stunning 40 percent.

Hewlett says that, under current economic policies and especially current tax policies, the rich get richer, the poor get poorer, the middle class gets trapped in a frantic effort to make ends meet, and our children get left alone. Hewlett hammers this point home:

> *Faster and faster they go, harder and harder they push, but like hamsters on a wheel, America's working families are stuck at the bottom. Clobbered on two fronts, they must work twice as hard to stay even. On*

the income side, wages have gone down while taxes have risen. On the
expenditure side, living costs have soared. . . . This squeeze on families
bodes ill for children. . . . Perhaps the resource in shortest supply to
families is time.

These are not the words of a left-wing ideologue. William R. Mattox
Jr., writing in the deeply conservative *Heritage Foundation Policy Review,*
echoes Hewlett's concerns. Like Hewlett, Mattox assails our current tax structure. His central argument: Only when we give families more control of their
income will we give them more control of their time. And that's essential,
argues Mattox, because the lack of time parents have to spend with their
children is a "deficit that is at least as serious as the budget deficit."

Combine these analyzes, and the conclusion that emerges is America's
fiscal policies are destroying the American family. It's that simple. And it's
that tragic.

Of course, the people who defend these fiscal policies (who support,
most notably, the Social Security tax increases that fall so heavily on low-
to middle-income families) are the same people who wrap themselves in the
cloak of pro-family rhetoric. They should be ashamed of themselves. Because
the fact is that our current fiscal priorities pulverize America's families. And
they hit hardest where it hurts most.

This fact ought to create grave concern throughout the business world.
And corporate America, if it should choose to exercise "the principle of self-
interest rightly understood," will start spending less energy demanding lower
capital gains taxes and more energy demanding both higher tax exemptions
for children and expansion of the Young Child Tax Credit.

Common sense and long-term economic sense demand freeing families
from the covert assault they are now enduring. That's why, at this year's NEA
regional conferences, I'll be encouraging our Association leaders to increase
our involvement in the pro-family movement. More specifically, I'll ask our
13,000 local NEA affiliates to demand that corporations and businesses in
their communities design a family-friendly workplace that gives parents the
gift of time. In addition,I'll appeal to each and every one of our two million
NEA members to petition their elected representatives for federal legislation
granting tax breaks—not to the richest corporations, but to the most
enlightened corporations, to corporations that offer flex time, part-time work
with benefits, job sharing, parental leave, and home-based employment opportunities to working parents.

The family under siege deserves relief. NEA intends to be a key player
in seeing that this relief is codified in corporate policies and in state and federal
mandates. And we invite every member of the education community to join
us in this pro-family, pro-education campaign.

America's Families and Federal Priorities

The shift in corporate policies that will free families to be families may count for little—perhaps for nothing—unless accompanied by an equally dramatic shift in federal policies.

Where to begin? Fairness would seem to dictate beginning with the goals to which the federal government itself has pledged its allegiance.

Among the pledges that our government has made most solemnly and most publicly are those announced following last year's Education Summit. At the conclusion of that much publicized event, President Bush announced six national education goals. And he reserved the top spot for the goal of ensuring that by the year 2000, all children will arrive at school physically, emotionally, and intellectually ready to learn. This was a promise to America's educators. But even more fundamentally, it was a promise to America's families.

Since the day that promise was made, a year has now passed. How much fidelity have we seen to this promise? Not much. What White House actions reflect serious commitment to making good on this promise? Almost none. How many children will enter school for the first time next fall with their potential already maimed beyond repair? Too many.

What is now clear is that the President and the governors who joined him at the Education Summit failed to realize that the goal of student readiness could be met only by instituting a system of comprehensive, universal national health care.

That's no small oversight.

What is now clear is that the goal of student readiness will remain an illusion until America's health care system becomes a system America's families can count on. Right now, this system brutalizes families. America's health care system is in critical condition. The symptoms are everywhere. And the symptoms are devastating America's families.

- Each year, one million families seek medical care only to be told— after a "wallet biopsy"—that they do not qualify for treatment.
- Each year, 75,000 women receive prenatal care for the first time at the moment they enter the delivery room.
- Each year, 40,000 babies die before reaching their first birthday.
- Each year, a half million children under the age of 3 go unimmunized against the most common childhood diseases.
- Medicaid, the federal and state program that covers medical expenses for the indigent, now serves only 38 percent of the poor. As many as 37 million Americans now have no health insurance at all.
- The U.S. infant mortality rate is higher than Singapore's. The life expectancy of U.S. citizens is lower than the life expectancy of Cubans.

This cannot continue. We no longer have a health care delivery system; we have a health care rationing system. And the best rations are reserved for the rich. Health care has become a luxury item. And the cost of this luxury is borne by families struggling to afford necessities.

All of this tells us that the decade of the 1980s—that decade when federal leaders exploited pro-family values—is still with us.

At the outset of the 1980s, we listened to a president who told us it was morning in America. Then we elected a President who spoke of a thousand points of light. And all the while, the darkness enveloping America's families grew darker.

More and more of our children live in this darkness. They are trapped in a cycle of deprivation. They are deprived of hope because they are deprived of an education. They are deprived of an education because they are deprived of the health care that would make them more physically, emotionally, and intellectually ready to learn.

What will become of them? To answer this question, we need only look at today's adolescents. They were toddlers when the federal policies that ripped the so-called safety net to shreds first took shape. The condition of the teens who grew up in the '80s is profiled in the 1990 *Code Blue* report of the National Commission on Adolescent Health.

The *Code Blue* document details an adolescent health crisis spinning out of control. It paints a vivid picture of teenagers caught in a spiral of declining academic achievement, declining physical health, and declining emotional stability. Every sentence in the National Commission report tells us that the time has come for America's policy makers to get serious about the goal of student readiness for learning. Right now, our health care system is making a mockery of that goal. It's making a farce of the 1990 education summit. It's making victims of our children. And it's depriving families of hope.

The adolescent health care crisis reflects our national health crisis. It points to the inadequacy of prenatal health care and early childhood health care. In sum, it constitutes an indictment of federal policies that deny 12 million American youth access to comprehensive medical insurance coverage.

Dr. Birt Harvey, former president of the American Academy of Pediatrics, hits the critical point: "In other countries, children are considered a national resources. . . . Support is given to children and families in the form of paid parental leave, child care, and—most importantly—comprehensive health care benefits." Not so in America, adds Harvey. Not so in the America of the 1980–90s. Harvey describes America's child health care system as "unplanned, disorganized, and fragmented."

This is one part—perhaps the cruelest part—of the 1980s legacy that lives on in the federal priorities of 1991. It is time to erase that legacy. It is time for a kinder, gentler America. And the place to begin is with a mammoth overhaul of health care—and health care financing. The place to begin is with a guarantee, to every American, that the right to the highest-quality health care is a right that will not be abridged or denied. It is time to give America's families freedom from the nightmare of illness that goes untreated and from health insurance premiums that break the family bank.

Conclusion

The cause of improved education demands parental empowerment. It demands parental involvement. America's families must become equal partners in the education reform movement—and first-class citizens within the education community.

As we strive to meet this imperative, we find there are mountains in our way. This chapter has focused on those mountains. It has focused on the obstacles to a meaningful and comprehensive family–school alliance. But those obstacles are not immovable. And the responsibility of the educational community is to start moving the mountains.

Samuel Sava, executive director of the National Association of Elementary School Principals, goes to the heart of the matter: "It's not better teachers, or texts, or curricula that our children need most. It's better childhoods."

America's families are doing their part to meet this need. They are besieged. But they are not beaten.

America's educators owe these families an enormous debt of gratitude. We can repay that debt only by battling on their behalf.

Our responsibility is clear. Let us not dodge that responsibility. Let us not "leave it to George." Let us instead say, in words that President John F. Kennedy used during an earlier time of national crisis, "We do not shrink from this responsibility—we welcome it."

> *Children learn for the same reason that birds fly. They are learning machines. If your child is having problems in school, the question you should ask yourself is:* What's turning off this learning machine?
> *—EDWARD ZIGLER*

Epilogue

Concluding a project as large and, it is hoped, as important as this one brings conflicting feelings. There is the feeling of relief, a job completed. Anyone who has worked on a major project understands the feeling of "getting the monkey off your back." There is also the concern that the work will be accepted by those you respect as a worthy contribution to the field.

More importantly the question arises; was anything accomplished? Will this manuscript, in total or in part, provoke comment enough to move people to action? This effort of the Association of Teacher Educators will have meaning if it encourages teacher education institutions to offer opportunities for their students to become better prepared to assist their learners and the families of these learners.

This work will be useful if it helps parents, parent groups, and community organizations realize their full potential in the educational process. We want this effort to provide some incentive for teachers and administrators to do more than is presently being done. We will have some impact if our government, at all levels, facilitates the improved relationship between home and school.

We ask a great deal of a manuscript. Why not!

What lies behind us and what lies before us are tiny matters compared to what lies within us. —*AUTHOR UNKNOWN*

Bibliography

Abelson, R. (1979). Differences between belief systems and knowledge systems. *Cognitive Science, 3,* 355–366.

AFL-CIO Department of Education. *Labor in the schools; How to do it!* Washington, DC: AFL-CIO.

AFL-CIO Department of Education (1988). *How schools are teaching about labor.* Washington, DC: AFL-CIO.

AFL-CIO. (1990, January). *Economic comparisons between open shop states and free collective bargaining states.* Washington, DC: AFL-CIO.

American Federation of Teachers. *Working in America Series.* Posters, 11 Dupont Circle N.W., Wshington, DC 20036: AFT.

Ahorns, C. (1989). *Divorced families.* New York: Norton.

Ainsworth, M. D. S. (1967). *Infancy in Uganda: Infant care and growth of attachment.* Baltimore, MD: Johns Hopkins University press.

Ainsworth, M. D. S., & Bell, S. M. (1969). Some contemporary patterns of mother-infant interaction in the feeding situation. In A. Ambrose (Ed.), *Stimulation in early infancy* New York: Academic Press.

Ainsworth, M. D. S., Bell, S. M., & Stayton, D. J. (1971). Individual differences in strange-situation behavior of one-year olds. In H. R. Shaffer (Ed.), *The origins of human social relations* London: Academic Press.

Ainsworth, M. D. S., Blehar, M., Walther, E., & Wall, S. (1978). *Patterns of attachment.* Hillsdale, NJ: Erlbaum.

Alan Guttmacher Institute (1981). Teenage pregnancy: *The problem that hasn't gone away.* New York: Alan Guttmacher Institute.

Allington, R. L. (1977). If they don't get to reach much, how they ever gonna get good? *Journal of Reading, 21,* 57–61.

Amble, B. R. (1967). Teacher evaluations of student behavior and school dropouts. *Journal of Educational Research, 60,* 53–58.

Ammon, M. S. (1990). *UC project on teacher preparation for parent involvement — Report 1.* Berkeley, CA: University of California.

Apple, M. W. (1982). *Education and power.* Boston: Routledge & Kegan Paul.

Apple, M. W. (1986). *Teachers and texts: A political economy of class and gender relations in education.* New York: Methuen.

Arbeiter, S. (1987). Black enrollments: The case of the missing students. *Change: The magazine of higher learning, 19*(3), 14–19.

Arend, R., Gove, F., & Sroufe, L. A. (1979). Continuity of individual adaptation from infancy to kindergarten: A predictive study of ego-resiliency and curiosity in preschoolers. *Child Development, 50,* 950–959.

Aronowitz, S., & Giroux, H. (1985). *Education under siege.* South Hadley, MA: Bergin & Garvey.

Ascher, C. (1988). Improving the school-home connection for poor and minority urban students. *The Urban Review, 20*(2), 109–123.

Asher, S. R., & Wheeler, V. A. (1985). Children's loneliness: A comparison of rejected and neglected peer status. *Journal of Consulting and Clinical Psychology, 53,* 500–505.

Asher, S. R., & Coie, J. D. (Eds.). (1990). *Peer rejection in childhood.* Cambridge, MA: Cambridge University Press.

Association for Supervision and Curriculum Development. (1962). *Perceiving, behaving, becoming: A new focus for education.* Washington, DC: Association of Supervision and Curriculum Development.

Atkin, J., & Bastiani, J. (1988). *Listening to parents.* London: Croom Helm.

Auerbach, E. R. (1989). Toward a social-contextual approach to family literacy. *Harvard Educational Review, 59*(2), 165–182.

Baig, K. (1976). *Home training of parents and their trainable mentally retarded children.* Unpublished doctoral dissertation, Toronto: University of Toronto.

Blaine, D. (1988). *Handicapped children in developing countries: Assessment, curriculum, and instruction.* Edmonton, Alberta: Vector, University of Alberta Printing Services.

Bandura, A., & Walters, R. H. (1959). *Adolescent aggression.* New York: Ronald.

Bandura, A. (1977). *Social learning theory.* Englewood Cliffs, NJ: Prentice-Hall.

Barnes, D. (1976). *From communication to curriculum.* New York: Penguin.

Baron, R. M., & Gsanz, R. L. (1972). Effects of locus of control and types of feedback on the task performance of lower-class black children. *Journal of Personality and Social Psychology, 21,* 124–130.

Baron, R. M., Cowan, G., Ganz, R. L., & McDonald, M. (1974). Interaction of locus of control and type of performance feedback. Considerations of external validity. *Journal of Personality and Social Psychology, 30,* 285–292.

Barr, R. C. (1974). Instructional pace differences and their effect on reading acquisition. *Reading Research Quarterly, 9,* 526–554.

Barringer, F. (1990, August 19). What is youth coming to? *The New York Times,* 1E, 5E.

Bauch, P. A. (1988). Is parent involvement different in private schools? *Educational Horizons, 66,* 78–82.

Baumrind, D. (1971). Current patterns of parental authority. *Developmental Psychology Monographs,* 4.

Baumrind, D. (1973). The development of instructional competence through socialization. In A. D. Pick (Ed.), *Minnesota symposia on child psychology: Vol. 7.* Minneapolis, MN: University of Minnesota.

Baumrind, R. (1988). *Familial antecedents of social competence in middle childhood.* Unpublished manuscript.

Beauchamp, G. A. (1984). *Curriculum theory* (4th ed.). Itasca, IL: Peacock.

Becker, W. C. (1964). Consequences of different kinds of parental discipline. In M. L. Hoffman & L. W. Hoffman (Eds.), *Review of child development research, Vol. 1.* New York: Russell Sage Foundation.

Becker, W. C., Peterson, D. R., Hellmer, L. A., Shoemaker, D. J., & Quay, H. C. (1959). Factors in parental behavior and personality as related to problem behavior in children. *Journal of Consulting Psychology, 23,* 107–118.

Bell, M., & Morsink, C. (1986). Quality and equity in the preparation of black teachers. *Journal of Teacher Education, 17*(2), 16–19.

Bennett, K. P., & LeCompte, M. S. (1990). *How schools work: A sociological analysis of education.* New York: Longman.

Berger, E. H. (1981). *Parents as partners in education*. St. Louis, MO: Mosby.

Berger, E. (1987). *Parents as partners in education*. Columbus, OH: Merrill.

Berlin, G., & Sum A. (1988). *Toward a more perfect union: Basic skills, poor families, and our economic future*. Occasional paper no. 3, Ford Foundation Project on Social Welfare and the American Future, Ford Foundation.

Berliner, D. C., & Rosenshine, B. V. (1977). The acquisition of knowledge in the classroom. In R. Shapiro & W. Montague (Eds.), *Schooling and the acquisition of knowledge*. Hillsdale, NJ: Erlbaum.

Berliner, D. C. (1979). *The beginning teacher evaluation study: Research to inform policy. The Generator, 9*, 7–8.

Berliner, D., & Cassanova, U. (1985, October). Is parent involvement worth the effort? *Instructor, 95*(3), 20–21.

Berninger, J. M., & Rodriquez, R. C. (1989, April). The principal as a catalyst in parent involvement. *Momentum, 20*(2), 32–34.

Bernstein, B. (1970). Education cannot compensate for society. *New Society, 387*, 344–347.

Bernstein, B. (1972). A critique of the concept of "compensatory education." In V. J. Cazden & D. Hymes (Eds.), *Functions of language in the classroom*. New York: Teachers College Press.

Bernstein, R. J. (1976). *The restructuring of social and political theory*. Philadelphia: University of Pennsylvania Press.

Betsey, C. L., Holister Jr., R. G., & Papageorgiou, M. (1985). *Youth employment and training programs: The YEDPA years*. Washington, DC: National Academy Press.

Bhatia, T. K. (1984). Literacy in monolingual societies. In R. B. Kaplan et al. (Eds.), *Annual Review of Applied Linguistics* (pp. 23–38). Rowley, MA: Newbury House.

Bliss, B. (1986). Literacy and the limited English population: A national perspective. In C. Simich-Dudgeon (Ed.), *Proceedings of the symposium on issues of parent involvement and literacy* (pp. 17–24).

Bloom, B. S. (1972). Innocence in education. *School Review, 80*, 1–20.

Bloom, B. S. (1976). *Human characteristics and school learning*. New York: McGraw-Hill.

Bogenschneider, K., Small, S., & Riley, D. (1990). *An ecological risk-focused approach for addressing youth-at-risk issues*. Chevy Chase, MD: National 4-H Center.

Borke, H. (1971). Interpersonal perceptions of young children: Egocentrism or empathy. *Developmental Psychology, 5*, 263–269.

Borke, H. (1973). The development of empathy in Chinese and American children between three and six years of age: A cross-cultural study. *Developmental Psychology, 9*, 102–108.

Bower, G. H. (1981). Mood and memory. *American Psychologist, 36*, 129–148.

Brandt, R. (1989). On parents and schools: A conversation with Joyce Epstein. *Educational Leadership, 47*, 24–27.

Brazelton, T. B. (1987, March). How to raise your child's self esteem. *Family Circle*, 37–42.

Brazelton, T. B. (1990, May). "Touchpoints for anticipatory guidance." A presentation at the Empowering parents: A day with T. Berry Brazelton, M. D. Conference, Monroe, MI:

Bronfenbrenner, U., & Weiss, H. (1983). *Beyond policies without people: An ecological perspective on child and family policy*. New York: Cambridge University Press.

Brookover, W., Beady, C., Flood, P., Schweitzer, J., & Wisenbaker, J. (1979). *School social systems and student achievement: Schools can make a difference.* New York: Praeger.

Brophy, J. E., & Good, T. L. (1970). Teachers' communication of differential expectations for children's classroom performance: Some behavioral data. *Journal of Educational Psychology, 61,* 365–374.

Brophy, J. E., & Good, T. L. (1976). Teacher behavior and student achievement. In M. C. Wittrock (Ed.), *Handbook of Research on Teaching,* (3rd ed.). New York: Macmillan.

Brophy, J. E., & Evertson, C. M. (1981). *Student characteristics and teaching.* New York: Longman.

Broudy, H. S. (1966). Needed: A unifying theory of education. In R. E. Leeper (Ed.), *Curriculum change: Direction and process.* Washington, DC: Association for Supervision and Curriculum Development.

Brown, B. B. (1968). *The experimental mind in education.* New York: Harper & Row.

Brown v. Board of Education of Topeka, KA. Court case, 349, U.S. 294, 75 S. Ct. 753.

Brown, L. H. (1988). *Dropping out: From prediction to prevention—A four-year study of dropout rates in rural school districts.* New Orleans, LA: Annual Meeting of the American Educational Research Association.

Brown, L., Sjhiraga, B., York, J., Zanella, K., & Rogan, P. (1984). *Ecological inventory strategies for students with severe handicaps.* Madison, WI: University of Wisconsin–Madison Metropolitan School District.

Brown, R. (1986). State responsibility for at-risk youth. *Metropolitan Education, 2,* 5–12.

Bruner, J. S. (1963). Needed: A theory of instruction. *Educational Leadership, 20,* 523–532.

Burleson, B. (1985, April). *Communicative correlates of peer acceptance in childhood.* Paper presented at the biennial meeting of the Society for Research in Child Development, Toronto.

Burnett, J. (1970). Culture of the school: A construct for research and explanation. *Council on Anthropology and Education Newsletter, 1,* 4–13.

Burns, G. (1982). *The study of parental involvement in four federal education programs.* Washington, DC: U.S. Department of Education, Office of Planning, Budget and Evaluation.

Burnstein, N., & Cabello, B. (1989). Preparing Teachers to work with culturally diverse students: A teacher education model. *Journal of Teacher Education, 20*(5), 9–17.

Burtoff, M. (1985). *Haitian Creole literacy evaluation study.* Washington, DC: Center for Applied Linguistics.

Business and Higher Education Forum. (1990). *Three realities: Minority life in the U.S.* Washington, DC: Business and Higher Education Forum.

Bussis, A. M., Chittenden, F., & Amarel, M. (1976). *Beyond surface curriculum.* Boulder, CO: Westview.

Byrne, E. A., & Cunningham, C. C. (1985). The effects of mentally retarded children on families—A conceptual review. *Journal of Child psychology & Psychiatry, 26*(65), 847–864.

Calabrese, R. L. (1990). The public school: A source of alienation for minority parents. *Journal of Negro Education, 59,* 39–49.

Calassi, J. P., Frierson, H. T., & Sharer, R. (1981). Behavior of high, moderate, and low test anxious students during an actual test situation. *Journal of Consulting and Clinical Psychology, 49,* 51–62.

Caldwell, B. M. (1972). *Kramer School—Something for everyone.* Worthington, OH: Charles A. Jones Co.

Caldwell, B. M. (1987). Staying ahead: The challenge of the third grade slump. *Principal, 66,* 10–14.

Caminiti, S. (1990, Spring). A bigger role for parents. *Fortune, 121,* 25–32.

Capuzzi, D., & Cross, D. R. (1989). *Youth at risk: A resource for counselors, teachers and parents.* Alexandria, VA: American Association for Counseling and Development.

Cardoso, J. (1987). *Citizen and principal influences on the implementation of Massachusetts' Chapter 188 school improvement councils.* Dissertation Abstracts International, 47(3916-A).

Carnegie Task Force on Teaching as a Profession. (1986). *A Nation Prepared: Teachers for the 21st Century.* Princeton, NJ: The Carnegie Foundation.

Carnegie Task Force on Teaching as a Profession. (1988). *An Imperiled Generation: Saving Urban Schools.* Princeton, NJ: The Carnegie Foundation.

Carnegie Commission on Adolescent Development. (1990). Adolescence: Path to a productive life or a diminished future. *Carnegie Quarterly, 25*(1,2), 1–3.

Carnevle, A., Garner, L., & Meltzer, A. (1988). *Workplace basics: The skills employers want.* Alexandria, VA: American Society for Training and Development.

Carter, T. P., & Segura, R. D. (1979). *Mexican Americans in school: A decade of change.* New York: College Entrance Examination Board.

Carter, R. T., Jones-Wilson, F. C., & Arnez, N. L. (1989). Demographic characteristics of greater Washington, D.C. Black parents who choose non-public schooling for their young. *Journal of Negro Education, 58,* 39–49.

Caruso, A. M. (1990). *The perceived impact of computerizing a parent outreach program.* Unpublished masters thesis, University of Toronto.

Castell, S., & Luke, A. (1983). Defining "literacy" in North America schools: Social and historical consequences. *Journal of Curriculum Studies, 15*(4), 373–389.

Catterall, J. S. (1986). Dropping out of school: The dollar impact on society. *Education, 4*(1), 8–13.

Cavazos, L. (1989). *A report to the president—educating our children: Parents and schools together.* Washington, DC: U.S. Department of Education.

Cazden, C. B. (1986). Classroom discourse. In M. E. Wittrock (Ed.), *Handbook of research on teaching* (3rd ed.). New York: Macmillan.

Center for the Study of Social Policy. (1989). *Lawrence's new futures initiative: Progress and remaining challenges.* Washington, DC: The Center for the Study of Social Policy.

Cervantes, L. (1969). *The dropout: Causes and cures.* Ann Arbor, MI: University of Michigan Press.

Chance, j. E. (1972). Academic correlates and material antecedents of children's belief in external or internal control of reinforcement. In J. B. Rotter, J. E. Chance, & E. Phares (Eds.), Applications of a *social learning theory of personality.* Toronto: Holt Rinehart.

Children's Defense Fund. (1990). *Children 1990: A report card, briefing book, and action primer.* Washington, DC: Children's Defense Fund.

Chubb, J. E., & Moe, T. M. (1988). *What price democracy: Politics, markets, and American schools.* Washington, DC: Brookings Institution.

Chubb, J., & Moe, T. (1990). Politics, markets, and American schools. Washington, DC: Brookings Institution.

Cicourel, A. V., Jennings, S. H. M., Jennings, K. H., Leiter, K. C. W., MacKay, R., Mehan H., & Roth, D. R. (1974). *Language use and school performance.* New York: Academic Press.

Ciner, S. J. (1990). Crisis of confidence: Public confidence in the schools of the nation's capital in the twentieth century. *Urban Education, 25,* 119–136.

Clark, M. M. (1976). *Young fluent readers.* London: Heinemann Educational Books.

Clark, M. M. (1982). Literacy at home and at school: Insights from young fluent readers. In A., Goelman, A. Oberg, & F. Smith R. (Eds.), *Awakening to literacy* (pp. 122–130). London: Heinemann Educational Books.

Clarke-Stewart, K. (1973). Interactions with mothers and their young children: Characteristics and consequences. Monograph of the *Society for Research in Child Development, 38,* 153.

Clifford, G. J. (1984). Buch und lesen: Historical perspectives on literacy and schooling. *Review of Eduational Research, 54*(4), 472–500.

Cohn, M., & Gellman, V. (1988). Supervision: A Developmental approach for fostering inquiry in preservice teacher education. *Journal of Teacher Education, 19*(2), 2–8.

Coie, J. D. (1990). Toward a theory of peer rejection. In R. S. Asher & J. D. Coie (Eds.), *Peer rejection in childhood.* Cambridge, MA: Cambridge University Press.

Coie, J. D., & Dodge, K. A. (1983). Continuities and changes in children's social status: A five-year longitudinal study. *Merrill-Palmer Quarterly, 29,* 261–281.

Coie, J. D., & Kupersmidt, J. B. (1983). A behavioral analysis of emerging social status in boys' groups. *Child Development, 54,* 1400–1416.

Coie, J. D., & Koeppl, G. K. (1990). Adapting intervention to the problems of aggressive and disruptive rejected children. In R. S. Asher & J. D. Coie (Eds.), *Peer rejection in childhood.* Cambridge, MA: Cambridge University Press.

Cole, P. (1989). *The working teenager.* Albany, NY: AFL-CIO.

Coleman, J. S., & Hoffer, T. (1982). *Public and private high schools: The impact of communities.* New York: Basic Books.

Coleman, J. S. (1985). Schools and the communities they serve. *Phi Delta Kappan, 66,* 527–532.

Coleman, J. S. (1987). Families and schools. *Educational Researcher, 16*(6), 32–38.

Collins, R. (1979). *The credential society: An historical sociology of education and stratification.* New York: Academic Press.

Collins, G. (1987). Day care for infants: Debate turns to long-term effects. *The New York Times.* B9.

Combs, A. W. (1959). *Individual behaviors.* New York: Harper.

Comer, J. P. (1984). Home school relationships as they affect the academic successes of children. *Education and Urban Society, 16*(3), 323–337.

Comer, J. (1986). Parent participation in the schools. *Phi Delta Kappan, 67,* 442–446.

Commission on the Future of the UAW. (1989). *A strong union in a changing world: Report of the Commission on the Future of the UAW.* Detroit, MI: UAW.

Commission on the Skills of the American Workforce. (1990, June). *America's choice: High skills or low wages.* Rochester, NY: National Center on Education and the Economy.

Coontz, S. (1988). *The social origins of private life: A history of American families 1600–1900.* New York: Routledge, Chapman & Hall.

Coontz, S. (1989a). *America's families: Rhetoric and reality.* Olympia, WA: The Evergreen State College.

Coontz, S. (1989b, June 11). Families: Myth and reality. *Seattle P.I., A Hearst Newspaper,* D4.

Craft, M., Raynor, J., & Cohen, L. (1980). Linking home and school—a *new review.* London: Harper & Row.

Crandall, V. C., & Lacey, B. W. (1972). Children's perception of I-E control in intellectual-academic situations and their embedded figures test performance. *Child Development, 43,* 1123–1134.

Crawford, J. (1989). *Bilingual education: History, politics, theory, and practice.* Trenton, NJ: Crane.

Crnic, K. A., Friedrich, W. N., & Greenberg, M. T. (1983). Adaptation of families with mentally retarded children: A model of stress, coping and family ecology. *American Journal of Mental Deficiency, 88*(2), 125–138.

Cruickshank, D. (1981). What we know about teachers' problems. *Educational Leadership, 38,* 401–405.

Cummings, E. M. (1987). Coping with background anger in early childhood. *Child Development, 58,* 976–984.

Cummings, E. M., & Cummings, J. S. (1988). A process-oriented approach to children's coping with adults' angry behavior. *Developmental Review, 8,* 296–321.

Cummings, E. M., Ianotti, R. J., & Zahn-Waxler, C. (1985). The influence of conflict between adults and on the emotions and aggression of young children. *Developmental Psychology, 21,* 495–507.

Cummings, E. M., Zahn-Waxler, C., & Radke-Yarrow, M. (1981). Young children's responses to expressions of anger and affection by others in the family. *Child Development, 52,* 1273–1282.

Cummings, E. M., Zahn-Waxler, C., & Radke-Yarrow, M. (1984). Developmental changes in children's reactions to anger in the home. *Journal of Personality, 35,* 547–561.

Cummins, J. (1981). The role of primary language development in promoting educational success for language minority students. In California State Department of Education, Office of Bilingual Education (Ed.), *Schooling and language minority students: A theoretical framework* (pp. 3–49). Los Angeles, CA: Evaluation, Dissemination and Assessment Center, CSULA.

Cummins, J. (1984a). Wanted: A theoretical framework for relating language proficiency to academic achievement among bilingual students. In C. Rivera (Ed.), *Language proficiency and academic achievement* (pp. 2–19). Avon, England: Multilingual Matters.

Cummins, J. (1984b). Language proficiency and academic achievement revisited: A response. In C. Rivera (Ed.), *Language proficiency and academic achievement* (pp. 71–76). Avon, England: Multilingual Matters.

Cummins, J. (1985). *Bilingualism and special education: Issues in assessment and pedagogy.* San Diego, CA: College-Hill Press.

Cummins, J., & Swain, M. (1986). *Bilingualism in education.* New York: Longman.

David, R., & Garber, M. (1989, June). *Implementing a Parent Outreach Program for parents of developmentally delayed children in India.* Montrea: VIIth World Congress of Comparative Education.

Davies, D. (1976). *Schools where parents make a difference.* Boston: Institute for Responsive Education.

Davies, D. (1981). Citizen participation in decision making in the schools. In D. Davies (Ed.), *Communities and their schools* (pp. 83–119). New York: McGraw-Hill.

Davies, D., Stanton, J., Clasy, M., Zerchykov, R., & Powers, B. (1977). *Sharing the power? A report on the status of school councils in the 1970's.* Boston: Institute for Responsive Education.

Davis, W. L., & Phares, E. J. (1967). Internal-external control as a determinant of information-seeking in a social influence situation. *Journal of Personality, 35,* 547–561 deCharms, R. (1976). *Enhancing motivation change in the classroom.* New York: Irvington.

Demos, J. (1979). Changes in the American family: Fiction and reality. In V. Tufte & B. Myerhoff (Eds.), *Changing images of the family* (pp. 43–60). New Haven, CT: Yale University.

Demos, J. (1986). *Past, present, and personal: The family and life course in American history.* New York: Oxford Press.

Denham, D., & Lieberman, A. (1980). *Time to learn.* Washington, DC: National Institute of Education.

Detroit Free Press. (1900, 1960, 1970, 1980, 1990). 321 W. Lafayette Street, Detroit, MI 48226.

Dewey, J. (1902). *The school and society.* Chicago: University of Chicago Press.

Diamond, S. A. (1985). *Helping children of divorce.* New York: Schocken Books.

Diner, J. S. (1990). Crisis of confidence: Public confidence in the schools of the nation's capital in the twentieth century. *Urban Education, 25,* 112–137.

Dodge, K. A., & Feldman, E. (1990). Issues in social cognition and sociometric status. In S. R. Asher & J. D. Coie (Eds.), *Peer rejection in childhood.* Cambridge, MA: Cambridge University Press.

Dreeben, R. (1984). First grade reading groups: Their formation and change. In P. L. Peterson, L. C. Wilkinson, & M. Halinen (Eds.), *The social context of instruction: Group organization and group process.* New York: Academic Press.

Drickson, F. (1984). School literacy, reasoning, and civility: An anthropologist's perspective. *Review of Educational Research, 54*(4), 525–546.

Druian, G., et al. (1987). *School improvement research series: Research you can use.* Portland, OR: Northwest Regional Educational Laboratory.

Earls, F. (1986). A developmental perspective on psychosocial stress in childhood. In M. W. Yogman & T. B. Brazelton (Eds.), *In support of families.* Cambridge, MA: Harvard University Press.

Early Childhood Family Education. 992 Capitol Square Building, 550 Cedar Street, St. Paul, MN, 55101: Minnesota Department of Education.

Ecksel, I. B. (1990). *An interdisciplinary approach to enhancing learning: Implications of a program for teaching skills for emotional facility.* Unpublished doctoral dissertation, Wayne State University, Detroit, MI.

Ecksel, I. B., Cobb, F., & Stettner, L. J. (1990). *The influence of role perception in the socialization of emotion.* Unpublished manuscript, Wayne State University, Detroit, MI.

Ecksel, I. B., Kaplan, L., & Stettner, L. J. (1990a). *Emotion socialization in schools: What are we really teaching?* A paper presented to the National Conference on Troubled Adolescents. Stout. WI: University of Wisconsin.

Ecksel, I. B., Kaplan, L., & Stettner, L. J. (1990b). *Affect, cognition, technology: A recipe for enhancing learning.* Toronto, Canada: Joint E.C.O.O. & I.E.T.E. Conference.

Edeburn, C. E., & Landry, R. G. (1976). Teacher self-concept and student self-concept in grades three, four, and five. *Journal of Educational Research, 69,* 372–375.

Edelman, M. W. (1987). *Families in peril: An agenda for social change.* Cambridge, MA: Harvard University Press.

Edmonds, R. (1979). Effective school for the urban poor. *Educational Leadership, 37,* 15–18.

Edmonds, R. (1982). Programs of school improvement: An overview. *Educational Leadership, 40*(3), 4–11.

Education Commission of the States. (1988). *Drawing in the family: Family Involvement in the schools.* Denver, CO: Education Commission of the States.

Eisenberg, N. & Strayer, J. (1987). *Empathy and its development.* Cambridge: Cambridge University Press.

Eisenberg, N., & Mussen, P. H. (1989). *The roots of prosocial behavior in children.* Cambridge, MA: Cambridge University Press.

Elazar, D. J. (1984). *American federalism: A view from the states.* (3rd ed.). New York: Harper & Row.

Elkind, D. (1981). *The hurried child.* Reading, MA: Addison-Wesley.

Elmore, R. (1987). Reform and the culture of authority in schools. *Educational Administration Quarterly, 23,* 60–78.

Emmer, E. T., Evertson, C. M., Sanford, J. P., Clements, B. S., & Worsham, M. E. (1989). *Classroom management for secondary teachers.* Englewood Cliffs, NJ: Prentice-Hall.

Endelman, M. W. (1987). *Families in peril: An agenda for social change.* Cambridge, MA: Harvard University Press.

Epstein, J. L., & Becker, H. J. (1982). *Teacher reported practices of parent involvement: Problems and possibilities.* Baltimore, MD: Johns Hopkins University Press.

Epstein, G. (1984). School policy and parent involvement: Research results. *Educational Horizons, 62*(2), 70–72.

Epstein, J. L. (1987a). Parent involvement: What research says to administrators. *Educational Horizons, 19*(2), 119–136.

Epstein, J. L. (1987b). Toward a theory of family-school connections: Teacher practices and parent involvement. In K. Hurrelmann, F. Kaufmann, & F. Losel (Eds.), *Social intervention: Potential and constraints.* New York/Berlin: Aldine de Gruyter.

Epstein, J. L. (1988). How do we improve programs for parent involvement? *Educational Horizons, 66,* 58–59.

Epstein, J. L. (1989). *The home-school connection: Implications for teacher education.* Berkeley, CA: University of California.

Epstein, J. L. (1990). *School and family connections: Theory, research, and implications for integrating sociologies of education and family.* New York: Haworth Press.

Epstein, M., Cullinan, D., & Lloyd, J. (1986). *Behavior disorders of children and adolescents.* Englewood Cliffs, NJ: Prentice-Hall.

Eron, L. D. (1982). Parent-child interaction, television violence, and aggression of children. *American Psychologist, 37,* 197–211.

Evertson, C. M., & Emmer, E. T. (1982). Effective classroom management at the beginning of the school year in junior high classes. *Journal of Educational Psychology, 74,* 485–498.

Evertson, C. M., Emmer, E. T., Clements, B. S., Sanford, J. P., & Worsham, M. E. (1989). *Classroom management for elementary teachers.* Englewood Cliffs, NJ: Prentice-Hall.

Featherstone, J. (1987). Organizing classes by ability. *Harvard Education Letter, 3,* 1–9.

Feinman-Nemser, S., & Buchmann, M. (1985). Pitfalls of experience in teacher preparation. *Teachers College Record, 87,* 53–65.

Fernandez, G. (1984). *Parents' influence on school policy and practice: A narrative of the Philadelphia Parents Union for Public Schools, 1980–82.* Dissertation Abstracts International, 45(1577-A-1578).

Field, T. M., Widmayer, S. M., Stringer, S., & Ignatoff, E. (1980). Linking formal and informal support systems. In B. H. Gottlief (Ed.), *Social networks and social support* (pp. 259–75). Beverly Hills, CA: Sage.

Fisher, J., & Roberts, S. (1983). The effect of the mentally retarded child on his siblings. *Education, 103*(4), 399–401.

Fishman, J. A. (1966). *Language loyalty in the United States: The maintenance and perpetuation of non-English mother tongues by American ethnic and religious groups.* Berlin: Mouton.

Fishman, J. A. (1980a). Language maintenance. In S. T. Thernstrom et al. (Eds.), *Harvard encyclopedia of American ethnic groups* (pp. 629–638). Cambridge, England: Cambridge University Press.

Fishman, J. A. (1980b). Ethnocultural dimensions in the acquisition and retention of biliteracy. *Basic Writing, 3*(1), 48–61.

Footlick, J. K. (1990, Winter/Spring). What happened to the family? (Special Issue). *Newsweek,* 15–20.

Fordham, S., & Ogbu, J. V. (1986). Black students' school success: Coping with the burden of "acting white." *Urban Review, 18,* 183.

Foster, K. (1984). Parent advisory councils. *Principal, 63,* 26–31.

Freire, P. (1970). *Pedagogy of the oppressed.* New York: Herder & Herder.

Fuller, F. F. (1969). Concerns of teachers: A developmental conceptualization. *American Educational Research Journal, 6*(2), 207–226.

Furstenberg, F. (1976). The social consequences of teenage parenthood. *Family Planning Perspectives, 81,* 48–164.

Gage, N. L., & Berliner, D. C. (1989). *Nurturing the critical, practical and artistic thinking of teachers. 71*(3).

Galassi, J. P., Frierson, H. T., & Sharer, R. (1981). Behavior of high, moderate, and low test anxious students during an actual test situation. *Journal for Consulting and Clinical Psychology, 49,* 51–62.

Gallup, A., & Clark, D. (1987). The 19th annual Gallup poll of the public's attitudes toward the public school. *Phi Delta Kappan, 69,* 17–30.

Garber, M., & Perry, M. (1983). Training paraprofessional outreach workers for families of developmentally delayed children. *Special Education in Canada, 58*(1), 22–26.

Garber, M., Pass, L. & Perry, M. (1985). Parents helping parents through a community outreach program for mentally handicapped children. *Canadian Journal of Special Education, 1*(1), 83–91.

Garber, M., Perry, M., & Stanley, L. (1987, April). The reactions of a group of teachers to working with paraprofessionals in an outreach program for families of developmentally delayed children. *Teacher Education, 30,* 60–73.

Garber, M., Lindsay, P., & Perry, M. (1988). Computerizing a family outreach program. *Canadian Journal of Special Education, 4*(2), 181–188.

Gee, J. P. (1986). Orality and literacy: From the savage mind to ways with words. *TESOL Quarterly, 20*(4), 719–746.

Gilligan, S. G., & Bower, G. H. (1984). *Cognitive consequences of emotional arousal.* Cambridge, MA: Cambridge University Press.

Giroux, H. (1988). *Teachers as intellectuals: Toward a critical pedagogy of learning.* South Hadley, MA: Bergin & Garvey.

Gittell, M. (1977). Critique for citizen participation in education. *Journal of Education, 59,* 7–22.

Glasser, W. (1986). *Control theory in the classroom.* New York: Harper & Row.

Gnepp, J. (1983). Children's social sensitivity: Inferring emotions from conflict cues. *Developmental Psychology, 19,* 805–814.

Goldberg, M. F. (1990). Portrait of James P. Comer. *Educational Leadership, 48,* 40–42.

Goldstein, S., & Turnbull, A. P. (1982). Strategies to increase parent participation in IEP conferences. *Exceptional Children, Special Education and Pediatrics: A New Relationship, 48,* 360–361.

Goodlad, J. I. (1984). *A place called school.* New York: McGraw-Hill.

Goodman, K., & Goodman, Y. (1976). *Learning to read it natural.* Pittsburgh, PA: Conference on Theory and Practice of Beginning Reading Instruction.

Gordon, I. J., & Associates (Eds.). (1969). *Reaching the child through parent education: The Florida approach.* Gainesville, FL: Institute for the development of human resources, College of Education, University of Florida.

Gordon, I. J. (1970). *Parent involvement in compensatory education.* Urbana, IL: University of Illinois Press.

Gore, D., & Rotter, J. B. (1963). A personality correlate of social action. *Journal of Personality, 31,* 58–64.

Gough, P. B., & Hillinger, M. L. (1980). Learning to read: An unnatural act. *Bulletin of the Orton Society, 30.*

Graff, H. J. (1979). *The literacy myth: Literacy and social structure in the 19th century city.* New York: Academic Press.

Grant, L. (1984). Black females "place" in desegregated classrooms. *Sociology of Education, 57,* 98–110.

Grant, L., & Rothenberg, J. (1986). The social enhancement of ability differences: Teacher-student interactions in first and second grade reading groups. *Elementary School Journal, 87,* 29–50.

Greene, K. R. (1990). School board members' responsiveness to constituents. *Urban Education, 24,* 363–375.

Gursky, D. (1990, June/July). A plan that works. *Teacher Magazine, 1*(9), 46–54.

Hakuta, K. (1986). *Mirror of language: The debate on bilingualism.* New York: Basic Books.

Hamby, J. V. (1988). *Report of survey concerning programs to train teachers about dropouts operating in colleges and schools of education in state universities and land grant colleges.* Unpublished manuscript, Clemson University, National Dropout Prevention Center.

Hamby, J. V. (1990). *Successful components of programs for at-risk students and dropouts.* Unpublished manuscript, Clemson University, National Dropout Prevention Center.

Harding, E., & Riley, P. (1986). *The bilingual family: A handbook for parents.* New York: Cambridge University Press.

Harris, L. (1990). *The metropolitan survey of the American teacher 1989.* New York: Metropolitan Life.

Harter, S. (1983). Developmental perspectives on the self system. In P. H. Mussen (Ed.), *Handbook of child psychology, Vol. IV: Socialization, personality, and social development.* New York: Wiley.

Hausman, B. (1989). Parents as teachers: The right fit for Missouri. *Educational Horizons, 67*(1), 35–39.

Heath, S. B. (1983). *Ways with Words.* New York: Cambridge University Press.

Heath, S. B. (1988). *What no bedtime story means: Narrative skills at home and at school.* Yarmouth, MA: Intercultural Press, 162–184.

Henderson, R. (1989). *Teacher relations with minority students and their families.* (ERIC Document Service No. 249 213).

Henderson, A., Marburger, C., & Ooms, T. (1986). *Beyond the bake sale.* Columbus, MD: National Committee for Citizens in Education.

Henderson, J. (1988). A curriculum response to the knowledge base reform movement. *Journal of Teacher Education, 19*(5), 13–18.

Henderson, A., & Hall, S. H. (1990). Restructuring schools through parent involvement. *Network for Public Schools, 15,* 1–8.

Henry, W. A. (1990, April 9). Beyond the melting pot. *Time.* 28, 30.

Hettena, C., & Ballif, B. (1981). Effect of mood on learning. *Journal of Educational Psychology, 73,* 505-508.

Hill, T. (1982). Self-respect reconsidered. In O. Green (Ed.), *Respect for persons: Tulane studies in philosophy* (pp. 129-137). New Orleans, LA: Tulane University.

Hill, D. (1990, June/July). A theory of success and failure. *Teacher Magazine, 1*(9), 40-45.

Hilliard, A. G. (1989). *Public school support for successful instructional practices for at-risk students* (ED 313464).

Hodgkinson, H. (1985). *All one system.* Washington, DC: Institute of Educational Leadership.

Hoffer, T., & Coleman, J. (1990). Changing families and communities: Implications for schools. In B. Mitchell & L. Cunningham (Eds.), *Educational leadership and changing contexts of families, communities and schools.* Chicago: National Society for the Study of Education.

Hoffman, M. L. (1963). Child-rearing practices and moral development: Generalizations for empirical research. *Child Development, 34,* 295-318.

Hogan, D. (1985). *Class and reform: School and society in Chicago, 1880-1930.* Philadelphia: University of Pennsylvania Press.

Holdaway, D. (1979). *The foundations of literacy.* Sydney: Ashton Scholastic.

Hollandsworth, J., Glazeski, R., Kirkland, K., Jones, G., & VanNorman, L. (1979). An analysis of the nature and effects of test anxiety: Cognitive, behavioral, and physiological components. *Cognitive Therapy and Research, 3,* 165-180.

Hollis, L. Y., & Houston, W. R. (1990). Recruiting mature adults as teachers. *Teacher Education and Practice, 6*(2).

Holmes Group. (1986). *Tomorrow's teachers.* East Lansing, MI: The Holmes Group.

Holmes Group (1990). *Tomorrow's schools—Principles for the design of professional development schools.* East Lansing, MI: The Holmes Group.

Houston, W. R., & Williamson, J. L. (1990). *Perceptions of their preparation by 42 Texas elementary school teachers compared with their responses as student teachers.* Houston, TX: Texas Association of Colleges for Teacher Education.

Houston, W. R., Marshall, F., & McDavid, T. (1990a). *Perceptions of first-year teachers of the assistance provided by experienced support teachers* (Study 90-92). Houston, TX: University of Houston.

Houston, W. R., Marshall, F., & McDavid, T. (1990b). *Perceptions of first-year teachers of the assistance provided by experienced support teachers at the end of the year* (Study 90-92). Houston, TX: University of Houston.

Howe, H., & Edelman, M. W. (Chairpersons) (1985). *Barriers to excellence: Our children at risk.* Boston: National Coalition of Advocates for Students.

Howe, K., & Eisenhart, M. (1990). Standards for qualitative (and quantitative) research: A prolegomenon. *Educational Researcher, 19*(4).

A huge gain in the poverty war. (1990, October 31). *The New York Times,* A18.

Huguenin, K., Zerchykov, R., & Davies, D. (1979). *Narrowing the gap between intent and practice: A report to policymakers on community organizations and school decision making.* Boston: Institute for Responsive Education.

Humphrey, J. H., & Humphrey, J. N. (1981). *Reducing stress in children through creative relaxation.* Springfield, IL: Thomas.

Hunter, C., & Harman, D. (1979). *Adult literacy in the United States.* New York: McGraw-Hill.

Huntington, D. S. (1979). Supportive programs for infants and parents. In J. D. Osofsky (Ed.), *Handbook of infant development* (pp. 837-51). New York: Wiley.

Hymel, S., & Franke, S. (1985). Children's peer relations: Assessing self-perceptions. In B. Schneider, K. H., Rubin, & J. E. Ledingham (Eds.), *Children's peer relations: Issues in assessment and intervention.* New York: Springer-Verlag.

Illich, I. (1979). Vernacular values and education. *Teacher's College Record, 81*(1), 31–75.

Indianapolis project keeps parents "in touch" with children's schools. (1990, August 1). *Education Week,* 25.

The Indianapolis Star, January 17, 1991.

Impink-Hernandez, M. V. (1985, June). *Literacy and minority language families.* Memo.

Izard, C. E. (1984). Emotion-cognition relationships and human development. In C. E. Izard, J. Kagan, & R. B. Zajonc (Eds.), *Emotions, cognition, and behavior.* Cambridge, MA: Cambridge University Press.

Izard, C. E., Nagler, S., Randall, D., & Fox, J. (1965). The effects of affective picture stimuli on learning, perception and the affective values of previously neutral symbols. In S. S. Tomkins & C. E. Izard (Eds.), *Affect, cognition, and personality.* New York: Springer-Verlag.

Izard, C. E., Wehmer, G. M., Livsey, W., & Jennings, J. R. (1965). Affect, awareness, and performance. In S. S. Tomkins & C. E. Izard (Eds.), *Affect, cognition, and personality.* New York: Springer-Verlag.

Jackson, B. L., & Cooper, B. S. (1989). Parent choice and empowerment: New roles for parents. *Urban Education, 24,* 263–286.

Jahoda, M. (1953). The meaning of psychological health. *Social Casework, 34,* 349–354.

Jahoda, M. (1958). *Current concepts of positive mental health.* New York: Basic Books.

Jencks, C., Smith, M., Acland, H., Bane, M. J., Cohen, D., Gintis, H., Heynes, B., and Michelson, S. (1972). Inequality: A reassessment of the effect of family and schooling in America. New York: Basic Books.

Jenkins, P. W. (1981). Building parent participation in urban schools. *Principal, 61*(2), 20–23.

Jennings, W. (1989). How to organize successful parent advisory committees. *Educational Leadership, 47,* 42–45.

Jennings, L. (1990, August 1). Parents as partners: Reaching out to families to help students learn. *Eduction Week. 23*(4), 26–32.

Johnston, J. (1990). J. (1990). *The new American family and the school.* Columbus, OH: National Middle School Association.

Joint Subcommittee on Parental Involvement. (1986). *Joint Statement committing the Colleges of Education and the State Department of Education to require the incorporation of parent involvement content in teacher education program throughout the University of California System.* University of California and California State Department of Education.

Joint Subcommittee on Parental Involvement. (1989, April 21–22). First University of California Conference on Teacher Preparation for Enhancing Teacher Preparation for Enhancing Parent Involvement. University of California and California State Department of Education.

Julian, G. (1985). *A multidimensional analysis of power and participation in politics and education.* Dissertation Abstracts International, 46(784-A).

Kagan S. (1986). *Cooperative learning and sociocultural factors in schooling,* Los Angeles: Evaluation, Dissemination and Assessment Center, California State University.

Kagan S. L., & Seitz, V. (1988). Family support programs for new parents. In G. Y. Michaels & W. A. Goldberg (Eds.), *The transition to parenthood: Current theory and research* (pp. 311–314). New York: Cambridge University Press.

Kahneman, D. (1973). *Attention and effort.* Englewood Cliffs, NJ: Prentice-Hall.

Kalter, N. (1990). *Growing up with divorce: Helping your child avoid immediate and later emotional problems.* New York: Free Press.

Kang'ethe W., & Garber, M. (1989, June). *Teaching parents of developmentally delayed children in Kenya using a computer assisted Canadian Outreach Program.* Montreal: VIIth World Congress of Comparative Education.

Kapel, D. E., & Pink, W. T. (1978). The schoolboard: Participatory democracy revisited. *Urban Review, 10,* 20–34.

Kaplan, L. (1978). *Developing objectives in the affective domain.* San Diego, CA: Collegiate Press.

Kaplan, L. (1986). *Asking the next question.* Bloomington, IN: College Town Press.

Kaplan, L., Stettner, L. J., Ecksel, I. B. (1990). *Enhancing human learning through the integration of affect and technology.* A paper presented at the Seventh International Conference on Technology and Education. Brussels, Belgium.

Katz, M. B. (1971). *Class, bureaucracy, and schools.* New York: Praeger.

Kaufman, P., & Frase, M. J. (1990). *Dropout rates in the United States: 1989.* Washington, DC: National Center for Educational Statistics.

Kausch Studios (Producers) & McCarthy, A. R. (Director). (1988). *Children in my dreams. Must the dragon win?* Videotape. Grosse Pointe Woods, MI: Center for the Advancement of the Family.

Kelly, G. P., Nihlen, A. S. (1982). Schooling and the reproduction of patriarchy: Unequal workloads, unequal rewards. In M. W. Apple (Ed.), *Cultural and economic reproduction in education: Essays on class, ideology, and the state.* London: Routledge & Kegan Paul.

Keppel, F. (1986). A field guide to the land of teachers. *Phi Delta Kappan, 68*(1), 18–23.

Kiresuk, T., & Sherman, R. (1986). Goal attainment scaling: A method for evaluating comprehensive community mental health programs. *Community Mental Health Journal, 4,* 443–453.

Kirst, M. (1989). *Conditions of children.* Berkeley, CA: Policy Analysis for California Education (PACE).

Kirst, M., & McLaughlin, M. (1990). Rethinking policy for children: Implications for educational administration. In B. Mitchell & Cunningham, L. (Eds.), *Educational leadership and changing contexts of families, communities and schools* (p. 86). Chicago: National Society for the Study of Education.

Klien, L. (1975). Models of comprehensive service—Regular school-based. *Journal of School Health, 45,* 271–273.

Knapp, M., & Miller, G. (Eds.), (1985). *Handbook of interpersonal communication.* Beverly Hills, CA: Sage.

Kohn, A. (1986). *No contest: The case against competition.* Boston: Houghton-Mifflin.

Kozol, J. (1985). *Illiterate America.* Garden City, NY: Anchor Press.

Krashen, S., & Binder, D. (1988). *On course: Bilingual education's success in California.* Sacramento, CA: California Association for Bilingual Education.

Krasnow, J. (1990). *Building parent-teacher partnerships: Prospects from the perspective of the Schools Reaching Out Project.* Boston: Institute for Responsive Education.

Krathwhol, D. R., Bloom, B. S., Masia, B. B. (1964). *Taxonomy of educational objectives. Handbook II: Affective domain.* New York: McKay.

Kresnak, J. (1990, September 13). Court orders more investigation of boy's home. *Detroit Free press,* 1A.

Kunisawa, B. (1988). *A nation in crisis: The dropout dilemma.* National Educational Association, 6(6), 61–65.

Kupersmidt, J. B., Coie, J. D., & Dodge, K. A. (1990). The role of poor peer relationships in the development of disorder. Im S. R. Asher & J. D. Coie (Eds.), *Peer rejection in childhood.* Cambridge, MA: Cambridge University Press.

Labor's Heritage. The George Meany Memorial Archives. 1000 New Hampshire Ave., Silver Spring, MD 20903.

Labov, W. (1972). *Language in the inner city: Studies in the black English vernacular.* Philadelphia: University of Pennsylvania Press.

Ladd, G., & Mize, J. (1983). A cognitive-social learning model of social skill training. *Psychological Review, 90,* 127–157.

LaFrance, M. (1985). The school of hard knocks: Nonverbal sexism in the classroom. *Theory into Practice, 24,* 40–44.

Lamm, R. D. (1986). Can parents be partners? *Phi Delta Kappan, 68,* 4, 211–213.

Landa, L. N. (1976). *Instructional regulation and control: Cybernetics, algorithmization, and heuristics in education.* Englewood Cliffs, NJ: Educational Technology Publications.

Lanier, J., & Little, J. (1986). Research on teacher education. In M. Wittrock (Ed.), *Handbook of research on teaching.* New York: Macmillan.

Lareau, A. (1987). Social class differences in family-school relationships: The importance of cultural capital. *Socioogy of Education, 60,* 73–85.

Lareau, A. (1989). Home advantage: *Social class and parental intervention in elementary education.* London: Falmer Press.

LeBlanc, P. (1990). *Massachusetts school improvement councils and the local political culture.* Unpublished doctoral dissertation, Boston University.

Lee, P. C., & Gropper, N. B. (1974). Sex-role culture and educational practice. *Harvard Educational Review, 44,* 369–409.

Lee, P. C., Statuto, C., & Vedar-Voivodas, G. (1983). Elementary school children's perceptions of their actual and ideal school experiences: A developmental study. *Journal of Educational Psychology, 75,* 838–847.

Lee, F. R. (1990). Trying times for guidance counselors. *The New York Times,* B1.

Lefcourt, H. M., Hogg, E., Struthers, S., & Holmes, C. (1975). Causal attributions as a function of locus of control, initial confidence, and performance outcomes. *Journal of Personality and Social Psychology, 32,* 391–397.

Lefcourt, H. M., Miller, R. S., Ware, E. E., & Sherk, D. (1981). Locus of control as a modifier of the relationship between stressors and moods. *Journal of Personality and Social Psychology, 41,* 357–369.

Lefkowitz, M., Eron, L., Walder, L., & Huesmann, L. (1977). *Growing up to be violent: A longitudinal study of the development of aggression.* New York: Pergamon.

Leibowitz, A. H. (1971). *Educational policy and political acceptance: The imposition of English as the language of instruction in American schools.* Washington, DC: Center for Applied Linguistics.

Leichter, H. J. (1982). Families as environments for literacy. In A. A. Goelman Oberg & F. Smith (Eds.), *Awakening to literacy.* Portsmouth, NH: Heinemann Educational Books.

Leitch, M. L., & Tangri, S. S. (1988). Barriers to home-school collaboration. *Educational Horizons, 66,* 70–74.

Leichter, H. (1979). *Families and communities as educators.* New York: Teachers College Press.

Lemann, N. (1986). The origins of the underclass. *The Atlantic,* 31–68.

Levin, H. (1985). *The educationally disadvantaged: A national crisis.* Philadelphia: Youth Initiatives Projects: Public/Private Ventures.

Levine, K. (1982). Functional literacy: Fond illusions and false economies. *Harvard Educational Review, 52*(3), 249–267.

Lewis, A. (1986). A growing consensus outside of education. *Phi Delta Kappan, 68*(1), 3–4.

Lickona, T. (1988). How parents and schools can work together. *Educational Leadership, 45*(8), 36–38.

Lightfoot, S. (1978). *Worlds apart: Relationships between families and schools.* New York: Basic Books.

Lightfoot, S. L. (1981). Exploring family-school relationships: A prelude to curricular designs and strategies. In R. L. Sinclair (Ed.), *A two-way street: Home-school cooperation in curriculum decision making.* Institute for Responsive Education.

Lillie, D. L., & Trohanis, P. L. (1976). *Teaching parents to teach.* New York: Walker.

Lindle, J. C. (1989). What do parents want from principals and teachers? *Educational Leadership, 47,* 12–14.

Lovelock, J. (1984). Elements. In N. Myers (Ed.), *Gaia: An atlas of planet management.* Garden City, NY: Anchor Books, Anchor Press/Doubleday.

Lynch, A. (1990). Break barriers between home and school. *School Administrator, 47*(6), 40.

Maccoby, E., and Zellner, M. (1970). *Experiments in primary education: Aspects of Project Follow Through.* New York: Harcourt Brace Jovanovich.

Maccoby, E., & Martin, J. (1983). Socialization in the context of the family: Parent-child interaction. In E. M. Hetherington (Ed.), *Handbook of child psychology: Volume 4. Socialization, personality, and social development.* New York: Wiley.

Macías, R. F. (1979). Choice of language as a human right: Public policy implications. In R. F. Padilla (Ed.), *Ethnoperspectives in bilingual education research: Bilingual education and public policy in the United States* (pp. 39–57). Ypsilanti, MI: Eastern Michigan University.

Macías, R. F. (1988). *Latino illiteracy in the United States.* Claremont, CA: Tomas Rivera Center.

MacPhail-Wilcox, B., Forbes, R., & Parramore, B. (1990). Project design: Reforming structure and process. *Educational Leadership, 47*(7), 22–25.

Main, M., & Weston, D. (1981). The quality of the toddler's relationship to mother and to father: Related to conflict behavior and the readiness to establish new relationships. *Child Development, 52,* 1265–1277.

Main, M., & George, C. (1985). Responses of abused and disadvantaged toddlers to distress in agemates: A study in the day care setting. *Developmental Psychology, 21,* 407–412.

Malen, B., Ogawa, R. T. (1990). Community involvement: Parents, teachers and administrators working together. In S. B. Bacharach (Ed.), *Educational reform: Making sense of it all* (pp. 103–119). Boston: Allyn Bacon.

Malendez, W. A. (1990). *Native language instruction: An approach to combat illiteracy among language minority communities.* Sacramento, CA: California Literacy Task Force.

Marburger, C. L. (1990). The school site level: Involving parents in reform. In S. B. Bacharach (Ed.), *Educational reform: Making sense of it all* (pp. 82–91). Boston: Allyn and Bacon.

Marriott, M. (1990). Great expectations hobble black superintendents. *The New York Times,* B5.

McAfee, O. (1987). Improving home-school relations: Implications for staff development. *Education and Urban Society, 19*(2), 185–189.

McConaughy, S. (1985). Using the Child Behavior Checklist and related instruments in school-based assessment of children. *School Psychology Review, 14*(4), 479–494.

McDermott, R. P., Gospodinoff, K., & Aron, J. (1978). Criteria for an ethnographically adequate description of concerted activities and their contexts. *Semiotica, 24,* 3–14.

McLaughlin, M. W., & Shields, P. M. (1987). Involving low-income parents in the schools: A role for policy. *Phi Delta Kappan, 69,* 156–160.

McPartland, J. M., & Slavis, R. E. (1990). *Increasing achievemnent of at-risk students at each grade leve.* Washington, DC: Office of Educational Research and Improvement.

Meighan, R. (1989). The parents and the schools—Alternative role definitions. *Educational Review, 14,* 105–112.

Melvin, J. (1982). *Parent involvement in education projects: Final interim report.* Austin, TX: Southwest Educational Development Learning.

Mercer, C. D., Algoyzine, B., & Trifiletti, J. (1979, Spring). Early identification—An analysis of the research. *Learning Disability Quarterly, 2*(2), 176.

Merino, B. J. (1990). The effectiveness of a model bilingual program: A longitudinal analysis. *CPC Brief* (A Publication of the California Policy Seminar), *2*(3), 1–5.

Merrill, M. A. (1989). Teenage pregnancy and parenthood education. In M. J. Fine (Ed.), *The second handbook on parent education* (pp. 173–193). San Diego, CA: Harcourt Brace Jovanovich.

Metropolitan Life Survey. (1987). *The American teacher, 1987: Strengthening link between home and school.* New York: Louis Harris and Associates.

Michalson, L., & Lewis, M. (1985). What do children know about emotions and when do they know it? In M. & C. S. Lewis (Eds.), *The socialization of emotions.* New York: Plenum.

Milgram, N. A., & Milgram, R. M. (1975). Dimensions of locus of control in children. *Psychological Reports, 37,* 523–538.

Miller, G. (1976). *Explorations in interpersonal communications.* Beverly Hills, CA: Sage.

Miller, P., & Sperry, L. L. (1987). The socialization of anger and aggression. *Merrill-Palmer Quarterly, 33,* 1–31.

Mitchell, B. (1990). Children, youth and educational leadership. In B. Mitchell & L. Cunningham (Eds.), *Educational leadership and changing contexts of families, communities and schools.* Chicago: National Society for the Study of Education.

Mize, J., & Ladd, G. W. (1990). Toward the development of successful social skills training for preschool children. In S. R. Asher & J. D. Coie (Eds.), *Peer rejection in childhood.* Cambridge, MA: Cambridge University Press.

Moen, P. (1990, August). *Career ladder bars women from high powered fields.* Ithaca, NY: Cornell University.

Moles, O. C. (1987). Who wants parent involvement? Interests, skills, and opportunities among parents and educators. *Education and Urban Society, 19,* 137–146.

Montemayor, A. (1988). *New voices: Immigrant studies in U.S. public schools.* Boston: National Coalition of Advocate for Students.

Morrow, L. M. (1983). Home and school correlates of early interest in literature. *Journal of Educational Research, 76,* 221–230.

Morrow, L. M. (1989). *Literacy development in the early years: Helping children read and write.* Englewood Cliffs, NJ: Prentice-Hall.

Mueller, J. H. (1979). Anxiety and encoding processes in memory. *Personality and Social Psychology Bulletin, 5,* 288–294.

Mussen, P., & Eisenberg-Berg, N. (1977). *Caring, sharing, and helping: The roots of prosocial behavior in children.* San Francisco: Freeman.

National Alliance of Black School Administrators. (1984). *Saving the African American child.* Washington, DC: NABSE.

Naisbitt, J., & Aburdene, P. (1990). *Ten new directions for the 1990's: Megatrends 2000.* New York: Morrow.

National Commission on Excellence in Education. (1983). *A Nation at risk.* Washington, DC: U.S. Government Printing Office.

National Council for the Accreditation of Teacher Education. (1990). *NCATE standards, procedures, and policies for accreditation of professional educational units.* Washington, DC: NCATE.

National Council on Family Relations. (1990). *Presidential report, 2001: Preparing families for the future.* Mineapolis, MN: National Council on Family Relations.

National Education Association (1972). *The American public school teacher, 1970–1971.* Washington, DC: NEA.

National Education Association. (1985–86). *Status of the American public school teacher.* Washington, DC: NEA.

National Institute of Education. (1978). *Violent schools—safe schools: The safe school study report to Congress.* Washington, DC: Department of Health, Education and Welfare, U.S. Government Printing Office.

National School Boards Association. (1989, March). *An equal chance: Educating at-risk children to succeed: recommendations for school board action.* Alexandria, VA: NSBA.

New York State AFL-CIO. (1989). *The working teenager.* Albany, NY: New York State AFL-CIO.

Nicolau, S., & Ramos, C. L. (1990). *Together is better: Building strong relationships between schools and Hispanic parents.* Washington, DC: Hispanic Policy Development Project, Inc.

Nihira, K., Foster, R., Shellhass, M., & Leland, H. (1974). *AAMD Adaptive Behaviors Scale.* Washington, DC: American Association on Mental Deficiency.

Nordheimer, J. (1990, October 18). Stepfathers: The shoes rarely fit. *The New York Times,* B1, B6.

North Carolina State Department of Public Instruction. (1989). *Ready or not . . . They're here.* Raleigh, NC: North Carolina State Department of Public Instruction, At-Risk Children and Youth Task Force.

Norwicki, S., & Walker, C. (1974). The role of generalized and specific expectancies in determining academic achievement. *Journal of Social Psychology, 94,* 275–280.

Nottleman, E. D., & Hill, K. T. (1977). Test anxiety and off-task behavior in evaluative situations. *Child Development, 48,* 225–231.

O'Neill, D. M., & Sepielli, P. (1985). *Education in the United States: 1940–1983.* Washington, DC: U.S. Department of Commerce, Bureau of the Census.

Obgu, J. (1981). School ethnography: A multilevel approach. *Anthropology and Education Quarterly, 12*(1), 3–20.

Obrzut, A., Nelson, R. B., & Cummings, J. (1987, August). *School dropout vs. high school graduates: A discriminant analysis.* New York: 95th Annual Convention of American Psychological Association.

Office of Bilingual Education. (1989). *California demographics.* Sacramento, CA: California State Department of Education.

Ofnstein, A. C. (1983). Redefining parent and community involvement. *Journal of Research and Development in Education, 16*(4), 37–45.

Oldham, N. B., & Oldham, A. D. (1979). *Making friends for your schools.* Waterford, CT: Croft Leadership Action Folio.

Olson, D. R. (1977). From utterance to text: The bias of language in speech and writing. *Harvard Educational Review, 47,* 257–281.

Olson, D. R. (1982). See! Jumping! Some oral language antecedents of literacy. In A. Goelman, A. Oberg, & F. Smith (Eds.), *Awakening to literacy* (pp. 185–192). Portsmouth, NH: Heinemann.

Olson, L. (1990, August). Prescriptions for a revolution. *Teacher Magazine, 1*(8), 46–52.

Orlosky, D. (Ed.). (1988). *Society, schools, and teacher preparation.* Washington, DC: ERIC Clearinghouse on Teacher Education.

Ornstein, A. C. (1983). Redefining parent and community involvement. *Journal of Research and Development in Education, 16*(4), 37–45.

Ost, D. (1988). Teacher-parent interactions: An effective school-community environment. *The Education Forum, 52*(2), 166–176.

Oyemade, U. J., Washington, V., & Gullo, D. F. (1989). The relationship between Head Start parental involvement and the economic and social self-sufficiency of Head Start families. *Journal of Negro Education, 58,* 5–15.

Parelius, A. P., & Parelius, R. J. (1978). *The sociology of education.* Englewood Cliffs, NJ: Prentice-Hall.

Parker, J. G., & Asher, S. R. (1987). Peer relations and later personal adjustment: Are low-accepted children at risk? *Psychological Bulletin, 102,* 357–389.

Pastor, D. L. (1981). The quality of mother-infant attachment and its relationship to toddlers' initial sociability with peers. *Developmental Psychology, 17,* 357–389.

Peck, N., Law, A., & Mills, R. C. (1989). *Dropout prevention: What we have learned.* Ann Arbor, MI: The University of Michigan, ERIC Counseling and Personnel Services Clearinghouse.

Petit, D. (1980). *Opening up schools.* New York: Penguin Books.

Pfannenstiel, J. C., & Seltzer, D. A. (1989). New parents as teachers: Evaluation of an early parent education program. *Family Childhood Research Quarterly, 4,* 1–18.

Phares, E. J. (1976). *Locus of control in personality.* Morristown, NJ: General Learning Press.

Phi Delta Kappa. (1981, December). *Practical Applications of Research (PAR).* Phi Delta Kappa's Center on Evaluation, Development and Research Newsletter.

Philips, S. (1983). *The invisible culture.* New York: Longman.

Piaget, J. (1963). *The origins of intelligence.* New York: Norton.

Pizzo, P. (1983). *Parent to parent.* Boston: Beacon Press.

Postal Workers. Home and School Institute. 1201 16th Street N.W., Washington, DC 20036: Special Projects Office.

Profile. (1990, April). *Teacher Magazine,* 38–39.

Pyskowski, I. (1990). The decline in public confidence in education: Can education influence change? *Education, 110,* 304–312.

Quality Education for Minorities Project. (1990). *Education that works: An action plan for the education of minorities.* Cambridge, MA: Massachusetts Institute of Technology.

Rachman, S. J. (1979). The concept of required helpfulness. *Behavior Research and Therapy, 17,* 1–6.

Radke-Yarrow, M., Zahn-Waxler, C., & Chapman, M. (1983). Prosocial dispositions and behavior. In E. M. Hetherington (Ed.), *Manual of child psychology, vol. 4. Socialization, personality and social development.* New York: Wiley.

Radke-Yarrow, M., & Zahn-Waxler, C. (1984). Roots, motives, and patterns in children's prosocial behavior. In E. Staub, D. Bar-Tal, J. Karylowski, & J. Reykowski (Eds.), *The development and maintenance of prosocial behavior.* New York: Plenum.

Rajecki, D. W., Ickes, W., & Tanford, S. (1981). Locus of control and reactions to strangers. *Personality and Social Psychology Bulletin, 7,* 282–289.

Ranard, D. A. (1989). Family literacy: Trends and practices. *America: Perspectives on Refugee Resettlement, 7,* 1–7.

Rasell, E., & Mishel, L. (1990). *Shortchanging Education.* Washington, DC: Economic Policy Institute.

Rasinski, T. V., & Fredericks, A. D. (1989). Working with parents: Dimensions of parent involvement. *The Reading Teacher, 43,* 180–182.

Ratner, H. H., & Stettner, L. J. (1991). Thinking and feeling: Putting Humpty Dumpty together again. *Merrill-Palmer Quarterly, 37.*

Rawson, C. (1977). *The effect of a paraprofessional outreach program on the behavior of parents and their respective trainable mentally retarded children.* Unpublished master's thesis, Toronto: University of Toronto.

Reigeluth, C. M., & Stein, F. S. (1983). The elaboration theory of instruction. In C. M. Reigeluth (Ed.), *Instructional-design theories and models: An overview of their current status.* Hillsdale, NJ: Erlbaum.

Resneck, D. P., & Resneck, L. B. (1977). The nature of literacy: An historical exploration. *Harvard Educational Review, 47*(3), 370–385.

Resnick, L. (1987). Learning in school and out. *Educational Researcher, 16.*

Rich, D. (1985). *The forgotten factor in school success—The family.* Washington, DC: Home School Institute.

Rich, D. (1987a). *Schools and families: Issues and actions.* Washington, DC: National Education Association.

Rich, D. (1987b). *Teachers and parents: An adult-to-adult approach.* Washington, DC: National Education Association.

Rich, D., Mattox, B., & VanDien, J. (1979). Building on family strengths: the "nondeficit" involvement model for teaming home and school. *Educational Leadership.*

Richmond, J. B. (1979). The early administrators. In E. Zigler & J. Valentine (Eds.), *Project Head Start: A legacy of the War on Poverty* (pp. 120–128). New York: Free Press.

Roach, P. B., Bell, D., & Salmeri, E. R. (1989–1990). The home-school link: New dimensions in the middle school preservice curriculum. *Action in Teacher Education, 9*(4), 14–17.

Robson, B. (1982). Hmong literacy, formal education, and their effects on performance in an ESL class. In B. T. Downing & D. P. Olney (Eds.), *The Hmong in the West* (pp. 201–225). Minneapolis, MN: Center for Urban and Regional Affairs, University of Minnesota.

Rosenthal, R., & Jacobson, L. (1968). *Pygmalion in the classroom: Teacher expectation and pupils' intellectual development.* New York: Holt, Rinehart & Winston.

Rutter, M. (1979). Protective factors in children's responses to stress and disadvantage. In M. W. Kent & J. E. Rolf (Eds.), *Primary prevention of psychopathology: Social competence in children* (pp. 49–74). Hanover, NH: University Press of New England.

Salisbury, R. (1980). *Citizen participation in the public schools.* Lexington, MA: Lexington Books.

Salvin, R. (1987, November). Cooperative learning and the cooperative school. *Educational Leadership, 44,* 7–13.

Sameroff, A., & Seifer, R. (1983). Familial risk and child competence. *Child Development, 54,* 1254–1268.

Saphier, J., Bigda-Peyton, T., & Pierson, G. (1989). *How to make decisions that stay made.* Alexandria, VA: Association for Supervision and Curriculum Development.

Sarason, S. B. (1971). *The culture of the school and the problem of change.* Boston: Allyn and Bacon.

Saxe, R. W. (1975). *School community interaction.* Berkeley, CA: McCutchan.

Scandura, J. M. (1977). *Problem solving: A structural/process approach with instructional implications.* New York: Academic Press.

Scandura, J. M. (1980). Theoretical foundations of instruction: A systems alternative to cognitive psychology. *Journal of Structural Learning, 6,* 247–394.

Scarr-Salapatek, S. K., & Williams, M. L. (1973). The effects of early stimulation on low-birth weight infants. *Child Development, 44,* 94–101.

Schaffer, R. (1977). *Mothering.* Cambridge, MA: Harvard University Press.

Scherer, J. (1971). *Contemporary community: Sociological illusions or reality?* London: Tavistock.

Schieffelin, B., & Cochran-Smith, M. (1982). Learning to read culturally: Literacy before schooling. In A. Goelman, A. Oberg, & A. Smith (Eds.), *Awakening to literacy* (pp. 3–23). Portsmouth, NH: Heinemann Educational Books.

Schneider, J., & Chasnoff, I. (1987, July). Cocaine abuse during pregnancy: Its effects on infant motor development—A clinical perspective. *Topics in Acute Care and Trauma Rehabilitation,* 59–69.

Scholssman, S. S. (1976). Before home start: Notes toward a history of parent education in America, 1897–1929. *Harvard Educational Review, 47*(3), 436–467.

Schorr, L., & Schorr, D. (1988). *Within our reach.* New York: Doubleday.

Schwartz, G. (1975). Individual differences in cognition: Some relationships between personality and memory. *Journal of Research in Personality, 9,* 217–225.

Scollon, R., & Scollon, S. (1981). *Narrative, literacy and face in interethnic communication.* Norwood, NJ: Ablex.

Scribner, S. (1984). Literacy in three metaphors. *American Journal of Education, 93*(1), 6–21.

Seefeldt, C. (1985). Parent involvement: Support or stress. *Childhood Education, 62*(2), 98–102.

Seeley, D. S. (1981). *Education through partnership: Mediating structures and education.* Cambridge, MA: Ballinger.

Seeley, D. S. (1984). Educational Partnership and the dilemmas of school reform. *Education and Society, 7*(2), 21–38.

Seeley, D. S. (1989). A new paradigm for parent involvement. *Educational Leadership, 47*(2), 24–27.

Seidman, E. (1988). *Handbook of social interventions.* Beverly Hills: Sage.

Seppanen, R. S., & Weiss, H. B. (1988). *Parent involvement and education: State initiated family support and education.* Cambridge, MA: Harvard University, Harvard Family Research Project.

Shanker, A. (Ocober 28 1989). *Remarks of Albert Shanker, President, American Federation of Teachers.* New York: Educational Testing Service Conference.

Shanker, A. (1990, January). The end of the traditional model of schooling – And a proposal for using incentives to restructure our public schools. *Phi Delta Kappan, 71*(5), 344–357.

Shantz, C. U. (1975). The development of social cognition. In E. M. Hetherington (Ed.), *Review of child development research.* Chicago: University of Chicago Press.

Shapiro, S. (1989). New directions for the sociology of education: Reconstructing the public discourse in education. *Education and Society, 7*(2), 21–38.

Shavelson, R. J., & Stern, P. (1981). Research on teachers' pedagogical thoughts, judgements, decisions, and behavior. *Review of Educational Research, 51,* 455–498.

Shulman, L. (1987). Knowledge and teaching: Foundations of a new reform. *Harvard Educational Review, 57*(1), 1–22.

Sigman, M., & Parmelee, A. H. (1979). Longitudinal evaluation of the preterm infant. In T. M. Field, S. Sostek, S. Goldberg, & H. Shuman (Eds.), *Infants born at risk* (pp. 193–219). New York: Spectrum.

Simich-Dudgeon, C. (Ed.). (1986). *Proceedings of the symposium on issues of parent involvement and literacy.* Washington, DC: Trinity College.

Simon, P. (1988). *The tongue tied American.* New York: Continuum.

Simonds, M. P., & Simonds, J. F. (1981). Relationship of maternal parenting behaviors to preschool children's temperament. *Child Psychiatry and Human Development, 12,* 19–31.

Slaughter, D. T., & Johnson, D. J. (Eds.). (1988). *Visible now: Blacks in private schools.* New York: Greenwood Press.

Slavin, R. E. (1983). *Cooperative learning.* New York: Longman.

Smith, W. F., & Andrews, R. L. (1989). *Instructional leadership: How principals make a difference.* Alexandria, VA: Association for Supervision and Curriculum Development.

Smith, W. F. (1989). *School-based management: Metaphor for motivation.* Olympia, WA: Association of Washington School Principals.

Sobol, M. P., & Earn, B. M. (1985). What causes mean: An analysis of children's interpretation of the causes of social experience. *Journal of Social and Personal Relationships, 2,* 137–149.

Sowers, J., Land, C., & Gowett, J. (1980). *Parent involvement in the schools: A state of the art report.* Newton, MA: Education Development Center.

Stallings, J. A. (1980). Allocated academic learning time revisited, or beyond time on task. *Educational Researcher, 9,* 11–16.

Stallworth, J. (1982). *Parent involvement at the elementary school level: A survey of teachers – executive summary.* Austin, TX: Southwest Educational Development Laboratory.

Stallworth, J. T., & Williams Jr., D. L., (1981, April). *Parent involvement training in elementary teacher preparation.* Los Angeles: American Research Association.

Stallworth, J., & Williams, D. (1982). *Executive summary of the final report: A survey of parents regarding parent involvement in schools.* Austin, TX: Southwest Educational Development Laboratory.

Stannard, D. E. (1979). Changes in the American family: Fiction and reality. In V. Tufte & B. Myerhoff (Eds.), *Changing images of the family* (pp. 83–96). New Haven, CT: Yale University.

Stewart, J. (1986). *Bridges not walls.* New York: Random House.

Stipek, D. J., & Weisz, J. R. (1981). Perceived personal control and academic achievement. *Review of Educational Research, 51,* 101–137.

Street, B. V. (1984). *Literacy in theory and practice.* Cambridge, England: Cambridge University Press.

Swap, S. (1987). *Enhancing parent involvement in schools.* New York: Teachers College Press.

Swap, S. M. (1990). *Parent involvement and success for all children: What we know now.* Boston: Institute for Responsive Education.

Tallerico, M. (1989). The dynamics of superintendent–school board relationships. *Urban Education, 24,* 215–232.

Taylor, c., & Dowling, E. (1985). Working with family and school systems: A model for training. In E. Dowling & E. Osborne (Eds.), *The family and school: A joint system approach to problems with children.* Boston: Routledge & Kegan.

Taylor, D. (1983). *Family literacy.* London: Heinemann Educational Books.

Taylor, D., & Dorsey-Gaines, C. (1988). Growing up literate. Portsmouth, NJ: Heinemann.

Teale, W. (1978). Positive environments for learning to read: What studies of early readers tell us. *Language Arts, 59,* 922–932.

Teale, W. H. (1982). Reading to young children: Its significance for literacy development. In H. Goelman, A. Oberg, & F. Smith (Eds.), *Awakening to literacy* (pp. 110–121). Portsmouth, NH: Heinemann Educational Books.

Teltsch, K. (1990). In Detroit, a drug recovery center that welcomes the pregnant addict. *The New York Times,* A14.

Tetrault, M. K. (1986). The journey from male-defined to gender-balanced education. *Theory into Practice, 25,* 227–234.

Texas Dropout Prevention Clearinghouse. (1989). *Parent and community involvement.* Austin, TX: Texas Education Agency.

Theobald, R. (1987). *Rapids of change: Social entrepreneurships in turbulent times.* Knowledge Systems.

Theobald, R. (1990, Nov. 1). Personal communication.

Thurtell, J. (1990, November 8). Two sixth graders suspended for carrying loaded gun. *Detroit Free Press,* 1–2B.

Timar, T. (1989). The politics of school restructuring. *Phi Delta Kappan, 71,* 265–275.

Tobier, E. (1984). The changing face of poverty: *Trends in New York City's population in poverty, 1960–d1990.* New York: Community Service Society.

Toffler, A. (1970). *Future shock.* New York: Random House.

Toffler, A. (1980). *The third wave.* New York: Morrow.

Toffler, A. (1990). *Power shift: Knowledge, wealth, and violence at the edge of the 21st century.* New York: Bantam Books.

Trueba, H. T. (1988). English literacy acquisitions: From cultural trauma to learning disabilities. *Linguistics and Education, 2*(1), 125–152.

Tufte, A., & Myerhoff, B. (1979). *Changing images of the family.* New Haven, CT: Yale University.

Turnbull, A. P., & Turnbull, H. R. (1978). *Parents speak out.* Columbus, OH: Merrill.

Twilling, L., & Bock, N. (1989). Team up for school-sponsored parent support relationships. *Perspectives for Teachers of the Hearing Impaired, 7*(5), 2–6.

Tyack, D., & Hansot, E. (1981). Conflict and consensus in American public education. *Daedalus, 110,* 1–25.

Tyler, R. W. (1978). How schools utilize educational research and development. In R. Glaser (Ed.), *Research and development and school change.* Hillsdale, NJ: Erlbaum.

UAW Education Department. 8000 East Jefferson Ave., Detroit, MI 48214.

U.S. Bureau of Census. (1987). *Who's minding the kids?* Washington, DC: U.S. Government Printing Office.

U.S. Bureau of census. (1988a). *Family summit chart book*. Washington, DC: U.S. Department of Commerce.

U.S. Bureau of Census. (1988b). *Household and family characteristics*. Washington, DC: U.S. Bureau of Census.

U.S. Bureau of Census. (1989a). *Fertility of American women: June 1988*. Washington, DC: U.S. Government Printing Office.

U.S. Bureau of Census. (1989b). *Households, families, marital status, and living arrangements: March 1989*. Washington, DC: U.S. Government Printing Office.

U.S. Bureau of Census. (1989c). *Marital status and living arrangements*. Washington, DC: U.S. Government Printing Office.

U.S. Bureau of Census. (1989d, November). *Singleness in America*. Washington, DC: U.S. Government Printing Office.

U.S. Bureau of Census. (1989e, August). *Stepchildren and their families*. Washington, DC: U.S. Government Printing Office.

U.S. Bureau of Census. (1990a). *Child support and alimony: 1987*. Washington, DC: U.S. Government Printing Office.

U.S. Bureau of Census. (1990b). *Money income and poverty status in the United States*. Washington, DC: U.S. Government Printing Office.

U.S. Department of Education. (1988). *Digest of Higher Education Statistics: 1988*. Washington, DC: U.S. Government Printing Office.

U.S. Department of Health and Human Services. (1985). *Executive summary: The impact of Head Start on children, families and communities: Head Start Synthesis Project*. Washington, DC: CSR, Inc.

Valli, L., & Tom, A. (1988). How adequate are the knowledge base frameworks in teacher education. *Journal of Teacher Education, 19*(5), 5–13.

Vargas, A. (1986). *Illiteracy in the Hispanic community*. Washington, DC: National Council of La Raza.

Vargas, A. (1988). *Literacy in the Hispanic community*. Washington, DC: National Council of La Raza.

Vartuli, S., & Winter, N. (1989). Parents as first teachers. In M. J. Fine (Ed.), *The second handbook of parent education* (pp. 99–117). San Diego, CA: Harcourt Brace Jovanovich.

Viadero, D. (1990, September 5). Study of drug-exposed infants finds problems in learning as late as 3. *Education Week, 15*.

Vinovskis, M. A. (1987). Family and schooling in colonial and nineteenth-century America. *Journal of Family History, 12*(d1-3), 19–37.

Visher, E. B., & Visher, J. S. (1988). *Old loyalties, new ties: Therapeutic strategies with stepfamilies*. New York: Bruner/Mazel.

Vosk, b., Forehand, R., Parker, J. B., & Rickard, K. (1982). A multimethod comparison of popular and unpopular children. *Developmental Psychology, 18*, 571–575.

W.T. Grant Commission on Work, Family and Citizenship. (1988). *The forgotten half: Pathways to success for America's youth and young families*. Washington, DC: Grant Commission.

Wadeson, R. (1978). *Evaluation of a home training program using behaviour modification techniques and paraprofessional help*. Unpublished master's thesis. Toronto: University of Toronto.

Wagstaff, L., & Gallagher, K. (1990). Schools, families and communities: Idealized images and new realities. In B. Mitchell & L. Cunningham (Eds.), *Educational leadership and changing contexts—Families, communities and schools.* Chicago: National Society for the Study of Education.

Walberg, H. J. (1984). Families as partners in educational productivity. *Phi Delta Kappan, 65*(6), 397–400.

Walberg H., Schiller, D., & Haertel, G. (1979). The quiet revolution in educational research. *Phi Delta Kappan, 61,* 179–183.

Waller, K. (1932). *The sociology of teaching.* New York: Wiley.

Warner, I. (1991, January). Parents in touch: District leadership for parent involvement. *Phi Delta Kappan, 72*(5).

Warren, R. (1978). *The community in America.* Chicago: Rand McNally.

Walters, E., Wippman, J., & Sroufe, L. A. (1979). Attachment, positive affect, and competence in the peer group: Two studies in construct validition. *Child Development, 50,* 821–829.

Wax, M., & Wax, R. (1971). Great tradition, little tradition and formal education. In M. Wax, Diamond, & Gearing (Eds.), *Anthropological perspectives on education.* New York: Basic Books.

Weber, J. M., & Klinger, K. (1990). *The dropout prediction scale: User's guide.* Columbus, OH: Ohio State University, Center on Education and Training for Employment.

Weinberg, M. (1977). *A chance to learn: A history of race and education in the United States.* Cambridge, England: Cambridge University press.

Weiner, B., Frieze, I., Kukla, A., Reed, L., Rest, S., & Rosenbaum, R. (1971). *Perceiving the causes of success and failure.* Morristown, NJ: General Learning Press.

Weinstein, R. S. (1985). Student mediation of classroom expectancy effects. In J. B. Dusek (Ed.), *Teacher expectancies.* Hillsdale, NJ: Erlbaum.

Weiss, M. (1988). *The clustering of America.* New York: Harper & Row.

Weiss, H. B., Hausman, B., & Seppanen, P. (1988). *Pioneering states: Innovative family support and education programs: Connecticut, Kentucky, Maryland, Minnesota, Missouri.* Cambridge, MA: Harvard University, Harvard Family Research Project.

Wells, G. (1986). *The meaning makers: Children learning language and using language to learn.* Portsmouth, NH: Heinemann.

Wells, S., Bechard, S., & Hamby, J. V. (1989, July). *How to identify at-risk students.* Clemson, SD: Clemson University, The National Dropout Prevention Center.

Wells, S. E. (1990). *At-risk youth: Identification, programs, and recommendations.* Englewood, CO: Teacher Ideas Press.

Wenger, S. (1985). *Prepared statement before the select committee on children, youth, and families. House of Representatives.* Washington, DC: U.S. Government Printing Office.

West, D. J., & Farrington, D. P. (1973). *Who becomes delinquent?* London: Heinemann.

West, D. J., & Farrington, D. P. (1977). *The delinquent way of life.* London: Heinemann.

White, B. L., Kan, B. T., Attanucci, J., & Shapiro, B. B. (1978). *Experience and environment: Major influences on the development of the young child.* Englewood Cliffs, NJ: Prentice-Hall.

Wiley, T. G. (1986). The significance of language and cross-cultural barriers for the Euro-American elderly. In C. Hayes (Ed.), *The Euro-American elderly: A guide for practice* (pp. 37–50). New York: Springer.

Wiley, T. G. (1988). *Literacy, biliteracy, and educational achievement among the Mexican origin population in the United States.* Doctoral dissertation. University of Southern California.

Williams Jr., D. L. (1989, April 22). *Attitudes toward parent involvement and implications for teacher education.* Berkeley, CA: University of California.

Williams Jr., D. L., & Chavkin, N. F. (1989). Essential Elements of strong parent involvement programs. *Educational leadership, 47*(2), 18–20.

Williams, D. L., & Stallworth, J. T. (1980). Parent involvement in education: A survey of teacher educators. Austin, TX: Southwest Educational Development Laboratory.

Williams, D. L., & Stallworth, J. T. (1983). *Parent involvement and elementary school teacher training.* Austin, TX: Southwest Educational Development Laboratory.

Williams Jr., D. L., & Chavkin, N. (1985). *Teacher/parent partnerships: Guidelines and strategies for training parent improvement skills.* Austin, TX: Southwest Educational Development Laboratory.

Williams, M. (1989). *Neighborhood organizing for urban school reform.* New York: Teachers College Press.

Willis, H. D. (1986). *Students at risk: A review of conditions.* Elmhurst, IL: North Central Regional Educational Laboratory.

Wilson, C. (1985). *Parent participation and parental perceptions of openness and excellence in the Eureka Public Schools.* Dissertation Abstracts International, 43(1401-A).

Wilson, W. (1987). *The truly disadvantaged: The inner city, the underclass and public policy.* Chicago: University of Chicago Press.

Wine, J. (1971). Text anxiety and direction of attention. *Psychological Bulletin, 76,* 92–104.

Wirt, F. M., & Kirst, M. W. (1982). *The politics of education: Schools in conflict.* Berkeley, CA: McCutchan.

Wolf, J. S., & Stephens, T. S. (1989). Parent/teacher conferences: Finding common ground. *Educational Leadership, 47,* 228–237.

Yarrow, L. J. (1979). Historical perspectives and future directions in infant development. In J. D. Osofsky (Ed.), *Handbook of infant development* (pp. 897–917). New York: Wiley.

Zahn-Waxler, C., Radke-Yarrow, M., & Kilng, R. A. (1979). Child rearing and children's prosocial initiations toward victims of distress. *Child Development, 50,* 319–330.

Zahn-Waxler, C., & Radke-Yarrow, M. (1982). The development of altruism: Alternative research strategies. In N. Eisenberg (Ed.), *The development of prosocial behavior.* New York: Academic Press.

Zatz, S., & Chassin, L. (1983). Cognitions of text-anxious children. *Journal of Counseling and Clinical Psychology, 51,* 526–534.

Zeigler, L. H., Jennings, M. K., & Peak, W. G. (1974). *Governing American schools: Political interaction in local school districts.* North Scituate, MA: Duxbury.

Zeller, R. H. (1966). *Lowering the odds on student dropouts.* New York: Prentice-Hall.

Zerchykov, R. (1984). *School boards and the communities they represent: An inventory of the research.* Boston: Institute for Responsive Education.

Index

Academic progress, as teaching reward, 258
Adaptive Behaviors Checklist, 50–51
Administrators, as force for change in schools, 127–128
Adolescents
  at-risk, treatment continuum for, 56, 58
  behavioral problems of, 54–55
  developmental influences, 57
Adult illiteracy, 70
Affective connotations, as teaching reward, 258
AFL-CIO Department of Education, 299
AIDS education, 235
Alternate teacher certification plans, 231–232
American Association of Colleges for Teacher Education (AACTE), 238
American Postal Workers Union, 298
Andragogy, 228
At-risk students
  contributing factors, 164–167
  curriculum improvement, 167–175
  definition of, 163–164
  parental involvement and, 129–130
  potential for growth, 165–166
  in regular education, 166
  schooling and, 176–177
  social-skills training and, 175–176
  special education, 167
Autonomous model of literacy, 71

Baby Boom, 7
Baltimore School and Family Connection Project, 211–212
Bilingual education
  literacy and, 81–83
  theoretical foundations, 82–83
Biliteracy, significance of, 77
Blacks
  murders among, 235
  poverty rates, 21
Brown v. Topeka decision, 104
Business corporations, self-interest, 309

Business leaders, as force for change in schools, 128–129

Carnegie Council on Adolescent Development, 264
Carnegie Report, 238
Child-adult interaction, socialization and, 89–90
Child Care and Development Block Grant, 24
Child care arrangements, 20–21
Child-centered model, of parental involvement, 106–107
Child-peer relations, 91–92
Child support, 17
Citizen participation
  enhancement of, 137–138
  parent-school interaction and, 133
  suggestions for success, 138–139
Citizens' advisory committees, 104
Classroom Activity Centers, 66
Classroom culture, 86–88
Classroom environment, socialization and, 92–93
Code Blue report, 313
Collaboration model, of parental involvement, 107
Collective participation, 133–134
Colleges. *See* Universities
Comer, Dr. James P., 207–208
Communication
  promotion between parent and child, 191–195
  skills, in parent-teacher interactions, 151–152
  techniques for teachers, 269
Community
  collaborative partnerships, 272
  composition of schools and, 134–135
  context, solutions, 37–38
  definition of, 28
  diversity of population, 267–268
  in Learning City plan, 290–291
  relationship with universities, 220
  schools in, 30–31

sense of, building in inner-city students, 33–34
Community Action Programs (CAP), 299
Community organizations, in fostering parental involvement, 285
Competition, individual, 268
Computers, in Parent Outreach Program, 47, 52
Continuum-of-treatment approach, for dropout problem, 56, 58
Coping, by family of developmentally delayed children, 44
Corporate priorities, families and, 308–309
Crime, urban, 235
Culture
    of home, conflict with school culture, 97
    influences on school participation, 134–135
Curriculum
    college, 232–233
    existing, empowerment and prioritizing of, 168–169
    field experiences, 239–241
    knowledge, pedagogy and, 242
    proven programs, 167–175
    relevance, 33–34

Decisional participation model, of parental involvement, 107–108
Decision making level, of parental involvement hierarchy, 124
Demographic indicators, 29
Developmentally delayed children
    families of, 42–45
    Parent Outreach Program and, 41–42
Dial-a-Teacher phone line, 264
Distress, states of, 6
Dropouts
    adolescent behavior and, 54–55
    causes of, 55–56
    ecological approach to prevention, 56–57
    economic hardships and, 25
    family factors, 68
    incidence of, 54
    potential, identification of, 164–165
    school-family connection and, 57–58
    solutions, correlates of, 55–56
    third-grade drop out syndrome, 234

Ecology, family of developmentally delayed child and, 44–45
Economic policy, unions and, 296
Economic status, organized child care facility usage and, 20

Education, in inner cities, research goals for, 37–38
Educational attainment, age at first marriage and, 10–11
Educational interventions, 27–28
Educational reform
    definition of, 243
    human needs and, 236
    meaningful change and, 281
    organizations of, 307
    in twentieth century, 231
Educational status, child support amounts, 17
Education in inner cities, research goals for, 32–33
Education of All Handicapped Children Act (Public Law 94-142 of 1975), 104, 217
Education of Handicapped Children Model, 217
Education spending, as percent of gross domestic product, 294
Effective schools research
    course description, 274–276
    nature of, 273
Elementary and Secondary Education Act, 104
Elementary, teachers, preparation for parental involvement in education, 244–246
Emotional abuse, 259
Empathy, in parent-teacher interactions, 149–150
Employment systems, 31–32
Engagement level, of parental involvement hierarchy, 122–123
Environment, children and, 267
Epstein, Joyce, 169, 211–212
Ethnic minorities, negative impact of schooling, 72–73
Ethnic minority population, 7
Expanded advocacy/activism projects, 110

Families
    assumptions of, university decision-making and, 223–226
    changes in, 101, 267–268
        culture of, 256
        nature of, 310–311
        university population changes and, 219–223
    conditions in, home-school collaboration and, 59–60
    corporate priorities and, 300–309
    with developmentally delayed children, 42–45
    earnings, squeeze on, 23

Families *(Continued)*
  of educated parents, literacy development in, 77–78
  federal priorities and, 312–314
  graphic overviews, 5–24
  household composition, 13–14
  as integral part of students' learning, 261
  interaction with public school system, historical background, 102–105
  knowledge of, universities and, 221
  literacy development of child and, 70
  population composition and growth, 7–13
  schools and, 3–4
  traditional pattern, 267
  in university culture, 226
Family literacy
  models of, reconceptualization, 83–84
  neglected aspects of, 84–85
  programs, low appeal of, 83
Family-school interactions, 273
Family-school partnerships, barriers to change, 271–272
Family size, households and, 15
Fantasy play, 196–197
Fathers, importance of, 200–201
Fertility rates, 12–13
Financial aid, student, 222–224, 227
First Tennessee program, 289
Fiscal policies, 311
Florida Parent Educator Model, 45–47, 52

Gaia hypothesis, 44
Gordon, Ira J., 45–48, 53
Great traditions, 268
Gross domestic product, education spending and, 294

Hall, G. Stanley, 179
Harvard Family Research Project, 213
Harvey, Dr. Birt, 313
Head Start model, 24, 215–217
Health care system, 312–313
Health-Social Service System, 32–33
Hewlett, Sylvia Ann, 310–311
Hispanics
  birth rates, 7
  fertility rates, 12–13
  poverty rates, 21
Holmes Report, 240–241
  Home and School Institute
    address of, 292
    home learning activities, 63–64
    parental involvement programs and materials, 281, 282, 289

Home learning activities, 63–64
Home-school collaboration. *See* Parent-school partnership
Homework Hotline, 264
Home Workshops, 66
Household composition, 13–14
Households, maintained by women, poverty rates in, 16–18
Human development, ecological approach, 29

Illiteracy
  in language minorities, 76
  vs. low second language proficiency, 76–77
  vs. non-English literacy, 75–76
Indianapolis Program for Parental Involvement, 169
Individualistic political culture, enhancement of participation, 138
Individual participation, 133
Induction programs, 241–242
Inner-city schools
  community context for, 35–37
  teacher education for, 38–40
Inservice education, 257, 268–270
Instruction theories, 97
Instrumental participation, 108
Infant-mother attachment, 90
Intelligence, of child, parental involvement and, 60
Intensive Training Institute, 65–66

Knowledge
  in parent-teacher interactions, 150–151
  for teacher preparation, 246–247
Knowledge base, 238–239

Labor force participation, by women, age at first marriage and, 10, 11
Labor movement
  commitment to education, 298
  integrating issues into classroom, 297
  linking to curricula, 302
  linking to curriculum, 300–302
  role in schools, 295–297
Language minorities
  literacy development among, 79
  literacy/illiteracy of, 76
  negative impact of schooling, 72–73
Language of literacy, as instrument of social control, 81–82
Latch key children, 258
Law, family-directed, 221–222
Learners, parents as, 64–65
Learning, recommendations for, 94–99
Learning by doing, 33–34
Learning City plan, 290–291

Learning style assessment, 176
Learning theory, linking to educational
    practice, 94
Limits, setting for children, 199–200
Linked model, 208–211
Literacy
    acquisition and, 71–72
    bilingual education and, 81–83
    definition of, 71
    demographic diversity and, 75–77
    development
        in families of educated parents,
            77–78
        in language-minority immigrants,
            79
        natural vs. unnatural, 71–72
        in nonliterate environment, 78
        schools and, 72–74
        social practices and, 72–74
    elitist view of, 73
    family models, reconceptualization of,
        83–84
    focus on, broadening of, 69–74
    instruction for, 74
    as instrument of social control, 81–82
    in language minorities, 76
    non-English, vs. illiteracy, 75–76
    policy and program implications, 83–85
    programs, recommendations for new
        directions, 84–85
    significance of biliteracy, 77
    societal expectations, 70–71
Little traditions, 268

Mainstreaming process, 81
Marriage
    age at first marriage, 9–12
    postponement of, 11–12
Mattox, William R., 311
Media, local, community outreach and,
    289–290
MegaSkills Leadership Training Institutes,
    286
MegaSkills Parents Workshops, 283
    program feedback, 286–287
    program impact, 286
    voluntary participation in, 286
Mental abuse, 259
Merrill Palmer Institute, 188
Minority teachers, selection, retention and
    recruitment of, 237–238
Missouri Parents as Teachers Program,
    213–214
Monolingualism, 75–76
Moralistic culture, enhancement of par-
    ticipation, 139
Motherese, 192
Multilingualism, 75–76

National Association of School Ad-
    ministrators, 109
National Association of State Directors of
    Teacher Education and Certifica-
    tion (NASDTEC), 239
National Coalition of Advocates for
    Students, 134
National Council for the Accreditation of
    Teacher Education (NCATE),
    237–239
National Education Association (NEA),
    103, 109, 311
National School Boards Association, 109
A Nation at Risk, 104–105, 231
*A Nation Prepared: Teachers for the 21st
    Century,* 238
New Futures Initiative, 36
New Partnerships for Student Achieve-
    ment (NPSA)
    current status, 288
    development of, 282–284
    expanding, implications for schools and
        businesses, 288–291
    growth of, 282–284
    key findings, 284–288
    legacy of, 291–292
    message of, 291–292
Nonfamily household, 14
Nonmainstream families
    family literacy promotion and, 84
    home/school mismatch of language, 80
North Carolina Research Triangle, 220
Nurturant parents, 197–199

One-parent families, 15
Organizational dynamics, 110
Oversight Collaborative, 36

Paraprofessionals, in Parent Outreach
    Program, 46, 49
Parent(s)
    collaborative partnerships, 272
    as consumers of information from
        school, 65
    as force for change in schools, 125–126
    fostering early development, head start,
        188–189
    as learners, 64–65
    in married-couple families, 19
    new, education of, 178–187
    non-English-speaking, 305
    participation in educational decision
        making, 100
    as partners in school activities, 64
    promotion of communication with
        child, 191–195
    reading to children, 190–191
    relationship with teacher, 142–143

Parents *(Continued)*
  socialization and, 87
  societal expectations of literacy and, 71
  in stepfamilies, 19
  as teachers, 63–64
  views of school, 155–156
Parent activist model, 108–109
Parental empowerment, 307, 314
Parental interaction, teacher support for, 258
Parental involvement
  at-risk students and, 129–130
  collaboration model, 107
  community organizations and, 285
  decisional participation model, 107–108
  as educational process, 119–120
  forces of change, 125–129
  hierarchy, 120–124
  models
    child-centered, 106–107
    taxonomy of, 105–109
  NSPA program and, 286
  at organizational level, 100–101
  parents profile form, 131
  plan of action form, 131
  promotion of, 304–306
  in public schools, 114–115
  with public schools
    conceptual orientations, 102
    underlying assumptions, 101–102
  in school decision making, PTA and, 112
  on School Planning and Management Team, 33
  school recruitment of, 62–63
  student achievement and, 59
  teacher training and, 244–246
  teacher training for, 247–249
  types of
    perceived significance of, 113
    school activities and, 211–212
  at university level, 205–206
  use of term, 216
Parental nurturance, 197–199
Parental participation
  forms of, 133–134
  vs. parental involvement, 132–133
Parent-Child Program, 66
Parent Cooperative Preschool
  Laboratories, 66
Parent education
  current programs, 181–187
  historical perspectives, 179–180
Parent Educator Model, Parent Outreach
  Program and, 45–48
Parent groups/organizations, encourage-
  ment and support of, 304–305
Parenting Coalition, 289

Parenting education, 110
Parenting style, socialization of child and, 90
Parent involvement organizations,
  dyamics of selection, 109–114
Parent involvement programs, 65–67
Parent Outreach Program (POP)
  description of, 41–42, 66
  ecological objectives, 45
  evaluation of, 48
  implementation in Third-World coun-
    tries, 50–52
  Parent Educator Model and, 45–48
  program description, 49–50
Parents As Teachers Program, 67, 214
Parent-school partnership
  at-risk students and, 129–130
  barriers, 60–61
  effective parent involvement practices,
    61–65
  inherent conflicts, 109
  involvement vs. participation, 132–133
  school leadership role, 59–61
  Yale model and, 207–208
Parents Without Partners (PWP), 288
Parent-Teacher Association (PTA)
  dynamics of, 109–110
  educational concerns, 113–114
  founding of, 103
  G. Stanley Hall and, 179
  profile, 110–113
  support value of, 120
  types of parental involvement, per-
    ceived significance of, 113
Parent-teacher conferences
  contexts of, 141–143
  interactions between parent and
    teacher, 147–153
  nature of conference itself, 161–162
  parental view of schools and, 155–156
  parent's perspective, 158–162
  positive results through teachable
    moments, 143–147
  postconference follow up, 162
  potential outcomes, 141
  preparation for, 149, 151, 160–161
  purpose and nature of, parent's
    perspective, 159–160
  scenarios of, 144–147
  significant topics, 153
Parent-teacher interactions
  empathy in, 149–150
  goals, 147
  knowledge in, 150–151
  respect and, 148–149
Peer rejection, 91–92
Permissiveness, 199–200
Personal education plan, 176

Personal relationships, range of, 151–152
Politics, school participation and,
    135–137
Population composition and growth,
    American families and, 7–13
Positive affect, nurturance and,
    198–199
Poverty
    drop out rates and, 25
    dysfunctional families and, 59–60
    in families, 21–24
    minorities and, 235
    rates, in women maintained
        households, 16–18
Premarital childbearing women, 12–13
Preschool programs, 176
Preservice education
    course description, 274–277
    for Parents as Teachers program, 214
    for teacher preparation, 259–260
    teacher training programs, 268–270
Primary language instruction, 83
Problem solving, 93–94
Professional semester, 239
Project Regroup, 67
Prosocial behavior, 95
Public Law 94-142 of 1975 (Education of
    All Handicapped Children Act),
    104, 217
Public policy
    family-directed, 221–222
    shapers of, 215–217
Public school system
    interaction with family, historical back-
        ground, 102–105
    in nineteenth century, 103
    in twentieth century, 103–105
    Yale model and, 207–208

Race, educational access and, 32
Reading, to children, 190–191
Reform, 281
Regional conference, 246–247
Regional survey, 247–249
Resilience, 93
Rich, Dorothy, 282
Right-to-work laws, 296

Schismogenesis, 74
School(s)
    academic functions of, 88
    activities of, parents as partners, 64
    civic functions of, 88
    collaborative partnerships, 272
    in communities, 30–31
    community context for, 35–37
    connection with family, dropout prob-
        lem and, 57–58

dependency on community, 136
education of parents, of future
    students, 178
failure in, 73–74
forces of change, 125–129
labor role, 295–297
as leader in home-school collaboration,
    59–61
literacy development and, 72–74
making less intimidating and more
    open, 263
match/mismatch with home, literacy
    development and, 79–81
parental views of, 155–156
participation in, 134–140. See also
    Citizen participation; Parent
    participation
    politics and,d 135–137
personal functions of, 88
as problem, 36–37
proposals for change, 35–38
recruitment of parental involvement,
    62–63
responsibility to help parents, 142
socialization and, 86–87
as solution, 35–36
status-ascribing function, 73
success, promotion of, 189–201
traditions of, 268
vocational functions of, 88
School and Parent-Community Involve-
    ment, 282
School-based Teacher Education Program
    (STEP), 239–240
School climate, 33
School-family partnership, university role
    in, 206–218
School Governance and Management
    Team (SGMT), 207–208
School-parent relationship, 156–157
School personnel, state PTA officials
    and, 111
School systems, 33–34
Second language, low proficiency, confu-
    sion with illiteracy, 76–77
Singleness, in America, 13
Single-parent families, parent-child time,
    60
Single parents, problems as students,
    225–226
Site-based management, 34
Skills, for teacher preparation, 247
Socialization
    beliefs and practices in, 90–91
    environment and, 92–93
    parents and, 87
    process of, 89–93
    schools and, 86–87

Social practices, literacy development and, 72–74
Social-skills training, for at-risk youngsters, 175–176
Socioeconomic status
  educational access and, 32
  educational attainment and, 302–303
  home-school collaboration and, 60
  literacy and, 81
Spock, Benjamin, 180
Stannard, 5
State initiatives, for teacher education programs, 263–265
Status, schooling and, 73
Stepfamilies, 18–20
Stress, on family of developmentally delayed children, 43
Student(s)
  at-risk. *See* At-risk students
  causes of difficulty in school, 257–258
  consistency of teacher and, 260
  expectations for, 260–261
  low-track, 96
  negative interactions with teacher, 93
  promotion of communication with parent, 191–195
  self-concept, teacher self-concept and, 96
  structure in life of, 260
  success or failure of, 98
Student teaching, 239, 266
Success for Children Begins at Home classes, 282
Support
  for mothers of mentally handicapped children, 43
  in parental involvement hierarchy, 122

Tasks, in Parent Outreach Program, 49
Teachable moments strategy, 143–144, 156–157
Teacher(s)
  beginning, assistance for, 241–242
  communication techniques to deal with parents, 269
  continued preparation of, 260
  educational reform and, 266
  education for inner-city schools, 38–40
  empathy of, 261–262
  encountering parents with different views, 153–154
  enhancement of communication with parents, 262
  expectations of parents, 262–263
  as force for change in schools, 126–127
  initiatives with respect to family, 260–263
  intellectual depth of, 230

knowledge and skills of prospective and practicing teachers, 257
knowledge needs of, 268–270
minority, 237–238
negative interactions with student, 93
parents as, 63–64
partnership with unions, 297
positive attitude toward parents, 261
providing parents with appropriate help, 144–147
relationship with parent, 142–143
reluctance to students homes, 258
rewards for, identification of, 258
self-concept, student self-concept and, 96
student failure and, 61
training guidelines and strategies, 249–251
Teacher education
  curricula, 236
  parental involvement and, 67–68
  paucity of concern for families, 256–260
  restructuring of, 68
Teacher education programs
  concerns, 244
  field experiences, 239–241
  improvement of, 244
  knowledge of family structures/values and, 265
  NCATE standards, 237
  parental conference knowledge and, 257
  state initiatives, 263–265
  structure of, 232–233
  values and norms, 236
Teacher educators challenges
  with colleagues, 252–253
  within profession, 252–253
  for self-development, 250, 252
  for teaching candidates successfully, 253
Teacher preparation programs, 97–98
Teachers
  elementary, preparation for parental involvement in education, 244–246
Teacher training issues, 247
Teacher training programs
  inservice education, 257, 268–270
Television watching, 195–196
Theobald, Robert, 25–26
Theoretic construct, 29–30
Third-grade drop out syndrome, 234
Traditionalistic culture, enhancement of participation, 139
Transitional relationship, 151
Transmedical, 32

UAW, 299–300, 301

Unions
  in classroom, 300
  economic policy and, 296
  as economic source for non-college
     bound students, 302–303
  quality of life for members and, 293
United States government, education
     goals, 312
Universities
  calendars of, 228–229
  catalytic function as change agent,
     213–214
  as change agent in development, 205
  collaborative partnerships, 272
  curriculum changes, 270–271
  curriculum of, 232–233
  development of informational clear-
     inghouses, 213–214
  enrollment, family assumptions and,
     223–226
  family-oriented services, 227–228
  implications for future, 217–218
  leadership roles, 228–229
  role in teacher education, 270–271
  shapers of public policy, 215–217
  student diversity, 227

  student population, 219
  teacher preparation, 232–233
University of Arkansas Kramer Project,
     208–211
University of Missouri, Parents As
     Teachers program, 214
Urban decline, 32
Urban ecological approach, 28–30

Volunteer commitment, NSPA program
     and, 285
Voucher plans, 133

Weekly Evaluation Report Document, 51
Weiss, Heather, 213
Winter, Mildred, 214
Women
  age at first marriage, 9–12
  educational goals of, 224–225
  households maintained by, 14–16
  maintained households, poverty rates
     in, 16–18
Woodside, William, 309

Yale model, 207–208
Young Child Tax Credit, 311